# SUPERBIKES

# SUPERBIKES

## THE WORLD'S GREATEST STREET RACERS

### GENERAL EDITOR: ALAN DOWDS

CHARTWELL
BOOKS, INC.

This edition published by

**CHARTWELL BOOKS, INC.**

A Division of

**BOOK SALES, INC.**

114 Northfield Avenue
Edison, New Jersey 08837

ISBN 0-7858-1878-2

Editorial and design by:
Amber Books Ltd
Bradley's Close
74–77 White Lion Street
London N1 9PF
www.amberbooks.co.uk

Project Editor: Michael Spilling
Design: EQ Media


CREDITS
Photographs © Art-Tech/Summertime Books Ltd
Except pages 6–11, 152–153, 224–225 and 264–265,
courtesy of Alan Dowds


Some of the material in this book has previously appeared
in the partwork set *Essential Superbike*.


Printed in Singapore

# CONTENTS

# Introduction

It is difficult to establish exactly when the term 'superbike' was first coined in relation to a motorcycle. It was certainly used by excited journalists in the late 1960s, when firms such as Honda began to release new, high-performance machines like the CB750 to replace the humdrum, utilitarian models on offer. And it had entered common currency by the late 1970s, when the premier production-based racing class was the legendary AMA Superbike championship, contested by such illustrious names as Eddy Lawson and Kenny Roberts.

Wherever it was used though, the term was reserved for the most high-performance machinery available: cutting edge bikes, with high power outputs, dynamic handling and exciting chassis performance. The term retains that distinction today – the modern superbike is an incredible piece of machinery, with every technological sinew straining in the pursuit of ever-greater performance.

Motorcycling itself finds its roots much earlier. The first generally accepted powered two wheeler was produced by Gottlieb Daimler in 1885, using a single cylinder four-stroke internal combustion engine. This pioneer development machine produced one horsepower at 600rpm: hardly a superbike, but definitely a start.

By the middle of the twentieth century, the motorcycle market was massive, fuelled by the post-war boom years and a growing demand for personal transport. Before the advent of cheap mass-produced cars such as those produced by American giants Ford and British company Austin, a motorcycle (often fitted with a huge sidecar) was the only private transport option available for the majority of working people. In Britain, for example, up until the late 1960s, the UK motorcycle industry was dominant,

*Opposite: Yamaha's 600 Supersport model had a full revamp for 2003, with a 123bhp fuel-injected engine, new frame and featherweight 162kg (434lbs) mass. But it was outperformed by Honda's 2003 model CBR600RR and Kawasaki's ZX-636R.*

producing huge numbers of relatively low-tech motorbikes. It was a rather complacent industry though, and was low on both investment and innovation – fatal mistakes considering the advances being made by the Japanese manufacturers.

The current 'Big Four' Japanese manufacturers – Honda, Yamaha, Suzuki and Kawasaki – had fought their way back from the rubble of post-war Japan, and were making big improvements in their products. Many Western firms underestimated the threat from the Japanese, judging them by their early utilitarian products and refusing to believe they posed any real competition.

## Japanese innovation

The writing appeared on the wall in 1969, in the form of the Honda CB750. Its air-cooled, 736cc (44ci) SOHC four-cylinder engine produced a then-incredible 66bhp, while the chassis boasted an exotic hydraulic disc brake and sporty suspension. The styling was amazing too, rounded off by an audacious four-into-four chromed exhaust system, chromed mudguards and a coachlined fuel tank. The CB750's performance was devastating compared with the machinery of the time, especially mainstream models from Triumph, Norton and Harley-Davidson. The rest of the 1970s produced a succession of such blows to the UK bike industry, as it responded too little, too late to turn the rising tide of improved Japanese bikes.

And what a tide. It was not just Honda's CB750 which out-performed British and American machinery: the four big Japanese firms produced huge numbers of wildly different models, all aiming at the lucrative European and American markets, all with different technologies. For several years, it looked as if large-capacity piston-ported two-stroke engines would fulfill the performance end of the market, and both Kawasaki and Suzuki produced various machines in this class. Kawasaki's range of air-

*Above: The successor to the legendary 998, the 2003 Ducati 999 matches a classic 90° V-twin engine and steel tube frame with advanced electronics, radical design and top chassis components.*

cooled triples were available in capacities ranging from 250cc to 750cc, all of them providing awesome straightline performance in ill-handling, unreliable packages. Machines like the 750cc (45ci) H2 typified the breed, and scared a generation of bikers with its wayward chassis, massive thirst for fuel and random unreliability. Suzuki's machines were less focused, but models like the GT750 provided strong performance from a two-stroke powerplant.

Japanese manufacturers dabbled with other engine configurations, including ill-fated machines such as Suzuki's RE5, with a rotary Wankel-type engine, and Honda's CX650 Turbo, a turbocharged V-twin. Other unusual layouts were more successful: Honda's inline-six CBX1000 and Kawasaki's Z1300 six were strong performers, well deserving of the 'superbike' moniker. But in the background, the inline-four cylinder four-stroke layout pioneered by the CB750 was growing in acceptance. Kawasaki's 900cc (54ci) Z1 and Suzuki's GS1000 developed the breed throughout the 1970s, and when the 1980s broke, the world of performance motorcycles really belonged to this layout. Indeed, for a time these bikes – and their smaller capacity siblings – were often referred to (rather disparagingly) as 'UJM' – Universal Japanese Motorcycles.

## A new generation

It was 1984 when the next leap forward in superbiking took place. Kawasaki unveiled a truly next-generation machine in the form of its GPZ900R Ninja. This incredibly advanced machine featured a 16-valve cylinder head and liquid cooling, together with advanced chassis technologies such as monoshock rear suspension with an aluminium swingarm, anti-dive brakes and full plastic bodywork. Its performance was light years ahead of the opposition, and it took the top three places at that year's Isle of Man TT races. The Ninja's compact, efficient engine made 100bhp, permitting a top speed of around 240km/h (150mph), and in a first for the Japanese, the chassis could easily deal with all that power. Many previous superbikes from Japan had focused on sheer horsepower, while weak frames and poor running gear caused handling and stability problems. But in the GPZ900R, Kawasaki had developed a holistic machine with all-round performance.

Throughout the 1980s, Japanese dominance continued, Kawasaki largely inventing the hugely important 600cc (36ci) sportsbike class with its 1985 GPZ600R, before Yamaha's FZR1000R took the performance crown from the GPZ900R in 1988. But towards the end of the decade, European firms began to increase in importance. Germany's BMW had always been a steady niche manufacturer, producing well-built, if rather staid, roadsters based on the 'R' series flat-twin, air-cooled 'Boxer' engine which traced its roots back to WWII. But in 1983 the Bavarian firm launched its first four-cylinder motorcycle, the fuel-injected eight-valve K100. The 'K' series has continued since, developing into the K1200LT luxury tourer and other grand tourer models.

## European challengers

Further south, in Italy, the motorcycle industry has always been filled with passion, and the Bologna firm of Ducati is no exception. The eighties were dark times for the company though, as it lurched from one financial crisis to another. But the seeds of its revival as a serious superbike firm were sown in 1986, when Massimo Bordi built the four-valve, water-cooled desmodromic V-twin engine he'd designed at college. This 748cc (45ci) engine powered a racer in that year's Bol D'Or endurance race, and retired in

*Left: Released in 2003, Buell's XB12R Firebolt/Lightning is a radical model – it holds fuel inside its aluminium frame and is powered by an air-cooled fuel-injected 45° V-twin engine. This long-stroke 1,203cc (74ci) version has strong, torquey performance and sharp handling.*

seventh place with engine failure. Nevertheless, the basic design was developed, first as an 851cc (51ci) design, then 888cc (54ci), and then 916cc (55ci). It was this final capacity which powered Massimo Tamburini's legendary Ducati 916, one of the most evocative modern motorcycle designs ever seen, when launched in 1993. Bordi's engine in its various forms was to dominate World Superbike racing throughout most of the 1990s and, indeed, into the twentyfirst century. Meanwhile, in Noale, a small firm called Aprilia was improving its range of small-capacity machines, ready for an attempt on the superbike world in the mid 1990s.

In England too, a sleeping giant was awakening. Housing magnate John Bloor had purchased the Triumph name when the old Meriden-based firm closed down in 1983, and he spent the remainder of the 1980s preparing to relaunch the once-famous marque. The old firm had failed because it did not (or could not) update its products to compete with mainly Japanese competition. Bloor's new Triumph company solved this problem by building a range of bikes largely based on then-current Japanese design principles. When the first range of new Triumphs was unveiled at the Cologne show in 1990, their water-cooled, four-valves-per-cylinder, DOHC engines would have been unremarkable in any of the Japanese models on show. In order to get a wide range of machinery into production quickly, the Hinckley-based firm used a modular design, producing three and four cylinder engines in a range of capacities, from 750cc (45ci), to 1,200cc (73ci) without massive investment in research and tooling.

## Japanese dominance

Of course, the Japanese firms had not stood still, and 1992 saw the next generation of superbikes appear, fittingly from Honda. The CBR900RR FireBlade was a litre-class sportsbike like no other, the design aim being to make it as small as a 600 machine, with lightweight and super-dynamic handling matched with the massive performance of a 893cc (55ci) 16-valve engine. The year before, Honda had unveiled its NR750, an oval-pistoned rolling exhibition

*Above: The revised 2003 model of the Triumph Daytona 600 solved some of the performance problems of the firm's TT600, with more advanced fuel injection and more power. It retains the TT's fine handling, matched to new, more radical styling.*

*Right: Italian firm MV claims awesome performance from the one litre version of its gorgeous F4 1000. The radial-valve inline-four engine produces nearly 180bhp, in an exotic, Italian superbike chassis.*

of the firm's engineering prowess, laden with carbon fibre, titanium and cutting edge technology. In comparison with the NR750, the CBR900RR was much less technically impressive, but this was a pragmatic superbike.

Designed by Honda's maverick designer, Tadao Baba, the FireBlade's central concept of minimal weight and 'total control' was unlike anything produced before. Although its engine was less powerful than Yamaha's FZR1000 EXUP or Kawasaki's ZZ-R1100, its 122bhp was incredibly potent considering the sylph-like mass – at 185kg (405lbs) the CBR was 24kg (64lbs) lighter than the Yamaha, 43kg (115lbs) less than the Kawasaki. This high power-to-weight ratio did not only affect acceleration, it also gave much finer handling, more akin to a 600cc (36ci) sportsbike than a lumbering heavyweight sportsbike. The FireBlade stunned the opposition, and the lack of any

serious competitor machine for five years suggests no-one saw it coming. Yamaha made the best stab at taking on the FireBlade's dominance in 1996 with its Thunderace, but it wasn't until late 1997 that Honda's dominance was toppled, by another Yamaha.

The YZF-R1 used the principles of small size, low-weight and large-capacity power pioneered by the FireBlade, and took it to another level. New engine and chassis design techniques dropped dry weight down to 177kg (474lbs), 3kg (8lbs) less than the Honda, while a next-generation 20-valve inline-four 998cc (61ci) engine made a full-bore 150bhp, topping the Blade's output by 20bhp. The R1 also used new suspension design to improve usability; long-travel front forks kept the front wheel on the ground under harder acceleration, and an extra-long rear swingarm improved rear tyre traction.

However, by the late 1990s, other firms were beginning to catch up, though, and Yamaha didn't have things its own way for long. Suzuki launched its GSX-R1000 in 2001, taking over the ultimate performance crown, and massively improved models from Honda and Kawasaki intensified the competition. The R1 just nosed ahead in 2002 with an updated fuel injected engine and improved chassis, only for a revised GSX-R1000 to retake its crown in 2003.

By this time though, all the litre-class superbikes from Japan had achieved an incredibly high level of performance, and picking a winner between them became increasingly difficult. The 2004 model year saw Yamaha, Honda, Suzuki and Kawasaki all producing flagship sportsters with dry weights, engine power outputs and

*Left: Launched in 2003, the 172bhp, 179kg (480lbs) Honda CBR1000RR used design principles from Honda's RC211V MotoGP bike. The result was a potent, yet controllable and fine-handling superbike.*

*Below: Yamaha's 2003 update on the FSZ600 Fazer roadster produced a more advanced bike, with an aluminium frame and fuel injection. Its engine is based on the 2003 YZF-R6 unit.*

chassis complexity which could have competed in GP and WSB races barely a decade previously.

Kawasaki's 2004 ZX-10R produced a claimed 182bhp, in a chassis weighing just 170kg (455lbs), and the 2004 R1 and CBR1000RR Fireblade were both in the same ballpark, leaving many observers wondering how much more performance could be produced in a roadbike package. At a less rarified level of performance, the rest of the motorcycle world was also benefitting from advanced design and materials too.

The 600cc (44ci) supersports class became increasingly important through the 1990s, offering a cheaper, less intense performance solution that suited many riders better than the unlimited class. Bikes like Honda's CBR600 and Kawasaki's ZX-6R married great day-to-day practicality with super track performance, while Suzuki's GSX-R600 and Yamaha's R6 offered more track-biased ability. All these models provided excellent performance: their 100bhp engines giving top speeds over 250km/h (160mph), with chassis packages to match.

## The Tourers

The more sedate world of touring bikes moved on at a slower pace than sports models, but improvements in refinement and equipment continued apace. Honda's Gold Wing began in the mid 1970s as a sports model with no fairing, but developed through the 1980s and 1990s until by 2000 it was a luxury tourer without parallel, incorporating advanced sound systems, computerized suspension, huge protective bodywork and a smooth, elegant flat-six 1,832cc (111ci) powerplant. More practical tourers such as Yamaha's FJR1300 and Honda's ST1100 Pan European offered almost as much comfort in a more usable, smaller package.

Fans of fast, sporty touring were also well served in the 1990s. Honda's VFR800 practically invented the class, then dominated it, with the 2003 version including a sophisticated variable valve system, ABS and fuel injection. BMW's R1100S offered strong competition, as did Aprilia's Futura and Ducati's ST4S, but the VFR was a hard act to beat when a rider had to cover 1200km

(800 miles) – with a passenger – in a day, then enjoy sports riding on twisty mountain roads the next day.

Not all superbikes offer amazing performance though: some are built as much for show as for go. Honda's amazing F6C Valkyrie put a GL1500 Gold Wing engine in a chrome-clad custom cruiser chassis, making an audacious machine with blistering straightline performance. BMW's R1200C, made famous in the James Bond movie *Tomorrow Never Dies*, further expanded the boundaries of cruiser design, while Harley-Davidson's 2001 V-Rod rewrote the rulebook for American customized machines, with a radical hot-rod design and strong engine performance.

*Above: The Aprilia RSV Nera is a special edition version of Aprilia's 2003 RSV Mille. It boasts carbon-fibre bodywork and a range of track accessories. Its punchy 60° V-twin engine, radial brake calipers and Ohlins suspension make it one of the best circuit machines around.*

In this book, we have brought together some of the most important superbikes of the last few decades, examined the technologies used in their designs, and the performance they achieve. Most importantly though, we have tried to convey the riding fun and emotions these most extreme machines can give – amongst the most exhilarating vehicular experiences on offer today.

# aprilia **RS125**

*Single floating 320mm (12.6in) disc and four-piston caliper hauls the RS125 up at an impressive rate. Feel and feedback is good too.*

**Front forks**
The 40mm (1.8in) upside front forks offer fine handling, especially on the race track.

**Aluminium swingarm**
To match the aluminium frame, Aprilia developed an exotic aluminium swingarm, with a braced section on the right, and a 'gull-arm' curved section on the left. This curved section allows the exhaust to be tucked out of the way, improving ground clearance.

**Exhaust**
The RS125 benefits from a large, well-designed expansion chamber-type exhaust with a separate silencer. The shape of the chamber reflects pulses in the exhaust gas flow to improve the power delivery.

**Rear brake**
The 220mm (8.7in) single disc is grabbed by a single caliper which uses a pair of 32mm (1.25in) diameter pistons.

## RS125

**The RS125 will do** *around 160km/h (100mph), handles beautifully, is very reliable and attracts stares like you would not believe. Small, but perfectly formed, Aprilia's RS125 is a pocket-sized superbike, with all the styling and performance equipment of its bigger brothers, and superb handling.*

*The frame looks like it belongs on something bigger. The beam is made from aluminium and uses thin walls and additional bracing to ensure it is both light and ultra-strong.*

**Fuel tank**
Has a capacity of 14l (3.7gals), which includes a handy reserve of 3.5l (0.9gals).

**Clutch**
Utilizes the typical multi-plate in an oil bath arrangement and withstands surprising abuse. Hard use can cause the plates to slip, but leaving the engine to cool down usually restores full strength.

**Silencer**
Looks every inch the grand prix design and packs a bark as hefty as the bike's bite. On a crisp winter's day, it can be heard for miles but remains fully road legal too.

**Engine**
The single-cylinder two-stroke is liquid-cooled, has a square 54 x 54,5mm bore and stroke, a compression ratio of 12.5:1, and a 124.8cc (7.6ci) displacement. The cylinder's bore is coated with Gilnisil to extend its life.

# aprilia RS250

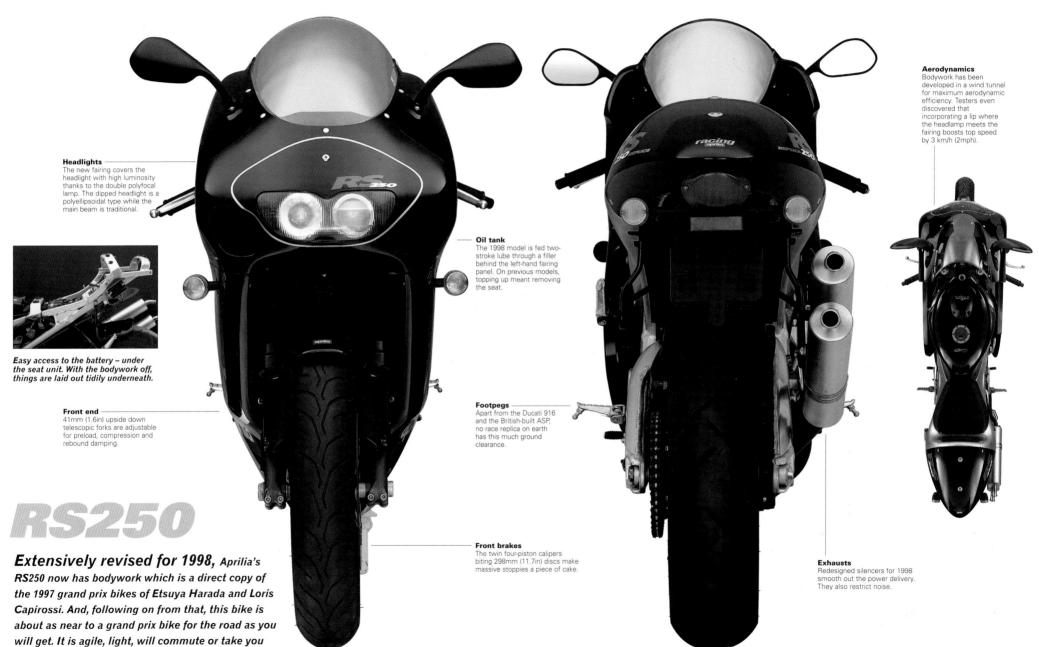

**Aerodynamics**
Bodywork has been developed in a wind tunnel for maximum aerodynamic efficiency. Testers even discovered that incorporating a lip where the headlamp meets the fairing boosts top speed by 3 km/h (2mph).

**Headlights**
The new fairing covers the headlight with high luminosity thanks to the double polyfocal lamp. The dipped headlight is a polyellipsoidal type while the main beam is traditional.

*Easy access to the battery – under the seat unit. With the bodywork off, things are laid out tidily underneath.*

**Front end**
41mm (1.6in) upside down telescopic forks are adjustable for preload, compression and rebound damping.

**Oil tank**
The 1998 model is fed two-stroke lube through a filler behind the left-hand fairing panel. On previous models, topping up meant removing the seat.

**Footpegs**
Apart from the Ducati 916 and the British-built ASP, no race replica on earth has this much ground clearance.

**Front brakes**
The twin four-piston calipers biting 298mm (11.7in) discs make massive stoppies a piece of cake.

**Exhausts**
Redesigned silencers for 1998 smooth out the power delivery. They also restrict noise.

# RS250

**Extensively revised for 1998,** Aprilia's RS250 now has bodywork which is a direct copy of the 1997 grand prix bikes of Etsuya Harada and Loris Capirossi. And, following on from that, this bike is about as near to a grand prix bike for the road as you will get. It is agile, light, will commute or take you touring, and is still a bit of a demon.

The new tail unit is another aid to aerodynamics while containing a roomy compartment under the saddle, which can hold the pillion saddle if the rider wants to use it on the track or just wants to keep it a 'solo' bike.

*Aprilia have used a mix of aluminium and magnesium a lot on the RS250 – and it works well on the swingarm.*

**The centre of gravity has been shifted lower and further forward for 1998 to improve handling. The chassis is, of course, made of aluminium and magnesium alloy.**

**Integration**
The mirrors and hand shields have been integrated well into the bodywork, with turbulence almost eliminated.

**Fuel tank**
A 1.6l (4.3gal) capacity is essential for a bike that guzzles petrol.

**Front tyre**
The width of the front rim has been increased from 76mm (3in) to 88mm (3.5in) and the front tyre from 110/70 to 120/60. The radial tubeless tyre is a good choice for road holding and performance.

**Manic motor**
The six speed, V-twin engine gives the bike a top speed of 209km/h (130mph) while displacing only 249cc (15ci). It claims 186kW (72 bhp) – or 215kW (289 bhp) per litrre (61ci).

**Rear suspension**
Boge monoshock is adjustable for preload, ride height, and compression and rebound damping.

# Specifications

*The Aprilia **RS250** is well-known in the racing world as one of the most successful 250cc machines. And the 1998 road version, with its new bodywork, follows that racing tradition faithfully. The engine is a 90° V-shaped twin cylinder with liquid cooling, the chassis is shaped from aluminium and magnesium alloy and its digital instrumentation keeps everything under control. Aprilia's pride in the RS250 seems fully justified.*

**Seat height:** 790mm

**Width:** 710mm (28.0in)

**Trail:** 102mm (4.0in)

**Wheelbase:** 1365mm (53.7in)

## ENGINE

| | |
|---|---|
| Type | 2-stroke |
| Layout | 90° V-twin |
| Total displacement | 249cc (15ci) |
| Bore | 56mm (2.2in) |
| Stroke | 50.6mm (1.9in) |
| Compression ratio | 13.2:1 |
| Fuel system | 2 x 34mm (1.3in) Mikuni TM SS flatslides |
| Ignition | digital electronic |
| Cooling | liquid |
| Maximum power | 40kW (54.90 bhp) @ 9612 rpm |
| Maximum torque | 4.1kg-m (29.67lb-ft) @ 9612 rpm |

## TRANSMISSION

| | |
|---|---|
| Primary drive | straight-cut gear |
| Clutch | wet multiplate |
| Gearbox | 6-speed |
| Final drive | sealed O-ring chain |

## WEIGHTS & CAPACITIES

| | |
|---|---|
| Tank capacity | 19.5l (5.2gals) |
| Dry weight | 140kg (309lb) |
| Weight distribution | |
| — front | not available |
| — rear | not available |
| Wheelbase | 1365mm (53.7in) |
| Overall length | 1980mm (78.0in) |
| Overall width | 710mm (28.0in) |
| Overall height | 1090mm (42.9in) |
| Seat height | 790mm (31.1in) |

## CYCLE PARTS

| | |
|---|---|
| Frame | aluminium and magnesium alloy twin spar |
| Rake/trail | 25°/102mm (4in) |
| Front suspension | 41mm (1.6in) Showa upside-down telescopic forks |
| Travel | 120mm (4.7in) |
| Adjustment | preload, compression and rebound damping |
| Rear suspension | Sachs-Boge monoshock |
| Travel | 130mm (5.1in) |
| Adjustment | preload, ride height, compression and rebound damping |
| Tyres | |
| — make | Dunlop |
| — front | 120/60 x ZR17 |
| — rear | 150/60 x ZR17 |
| Brakes | |
| — make | Brembo |
| — front | 2 x 298mm (11.7in) steel semi-floating discs, opposed four-piston calipers |
| — rear | 220mm (8.6in) steel disc, opposed two-piston caliper |

## TORQUE

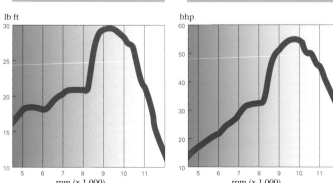

lb ft / rpm (x 1,000)

## POWER

bhp / rpm (x 1,000)

**Independent test measurements (above) differ from the manufacturer's claimed maximum power and maximum torque figures.**

# aprilia PEGASO 650

The fuel tank holds 22l (5.8 gals), including a 5l (1.3gal) reserve.

**Clutch**
Wet, multiplate design with easy operation at the handlebars.

**Front brake**
Single two-piston floating caliper, 300m (11.8in) disc. Pistons use different diameters (30 and 32mm/ 1.2 and 1.3in).

**Gearbox**
A five-speed gear box drives the 130-section rear tyre through a chain drive.

**Exhausts**
Twin underseat silencers give a sleek tail unit design.

**Rear Suspension**
Monoshock with 165mm (6.5in) travel.

# PEGASO 650

**The Pegaso is Aprilia's entry** *into the popular middleweight trail-styled bike category. While its offroad capabilities are limited, the bike is a great all-rounder and its styling make it suitable for street and backroad action. It is fun, cheap and rider-friendly.*

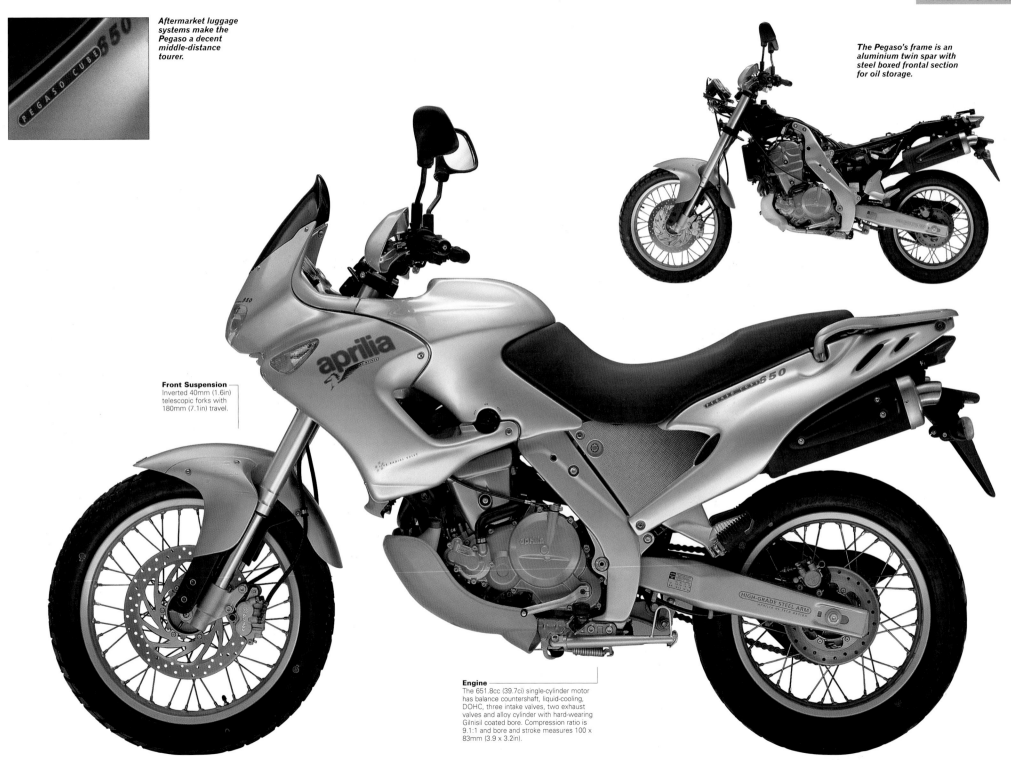

*Aftermarket luggage systems make the Pegaso a decent middle-distance tourer.*

*The Pegaso's frame is an aluminium twin spar with steel boxed frontal section for oil storage.*

**Front Suspension**
Inverted 40mm (1.6in) telescopic forks with 180mm (7.1in) travel.

**Engine**
The 651.8cc (39.7ci) single-cylinder motor has balance countershaft, liquid-cooling, DOHC, three intake valves, two exhaust valves and alloy cylinder with hard-wearing Gilnisil coated bore. Compression ratio is 9.1:1 and bore and stroke measures 100 x 83mm (3.9 x 3.2in).

# aprilia **RSV Mille**

*Aprilia has opted for dry sump rather than wet sump lubrication, enabling a more rigid and compact engine.*

*Twin 320mm (12.6in) discs are gripped by pads controlled by opposed four-piston Brembo calipers. Although lacking in initial bite, the calipers, with pad-operating pistons varying in size from 30 to 34mm (1.4–1.5in), actually have tremendous overall stopping power, as witnessed during our telemetry-monitored performance testing.*

**Ignition**
Generated digital-electronically at source, the electrical charge passes to each combustion chamber through two spark plugs per cylinder, ensuring a near-totally clean burn.

**Clutch**
The extreme engine braking forces inherent in a large capacity twin can, under deceleration and down-gearchange, cause the rear wheel to lock up. So Aprilia designed a servo clutch to 'slip' when the forces are high, eradicating the potential problem. It works by fitting an air chamber, which is fed by the bike's intake ducts, alongside the internal clutch assembly. Deceleration creates a drop in air pressure in the chamber, in turn reducing the load on the clutch springs, allowing the plates to 'slip'.

**Fuel system**
The electronic fuel injection system, with 51mm (2.0in) throttle bodies, was the subject of last-minute factory tweaks to ensure it delivered its charge cleanly but not too suddenly. The result is well-balanced and akin to a sorted carburetted bike.

**Forks**
Inverted 43mm (1.7in) Showa forks are adjustable for preload, plus compression and rebound damping and have 120mm (4.7in) of travel.

**Rear brake**
A 220mm (8.7in) disc is gripped by pads controlled by a single opposed two-piston Brembo caliper with 30mm (1.2in) pistons.

**Rear suspension**
The rear monoshock is adjustable for preload, ride height, plus compression and rebound damping. It has a maximum stroke of 50mm (1.97in) and, combined with the aluminium alloy swingarm, allows wheel travel of up to 135mm (5.3in).

# RSV MILLE

*Aprilia's RSV Mille* was awaited eagerly for quite a considerable time. But the Italian firm had the right idea – it wanted it to be perfect before releasing what is its first superbike. And it certainly has not disappointed. A top speed of 268km/h (166.5 mph), powerful brakes and a chassis that is stable but also nimble on track and road mean this is a bike to be reckoned with.

**Tyres**
The front is a standard 120/70 x ZR17, the rear a large 190/50 x ZR17.

Aprilia wanted to keep it light and so designed a 2-into-1 system that is both smaller and less weighty than typical 2-into-2 systems. Performance is not strangulated, though; it still manages an internal volume of over 9l (2.4 gals). It is made of durable stainless steel.

The aluminium alloy twin spar chassis was the first part Aprilia designed, bearing heavily on its grand prix expertise. The firm absolutely refused to compromise the design, forcing engineers to build the engine and all subsequent parts around the frame instead of vice versa.

**Fuel tank**
Holds a useful 20l (5.3galls) but is not intrusive.

**Underseat storage**
There is enough room (just) for an optional anti-theft U-lock.

**Headlamps**
The triple light design makes the RSV's front end immediately distinguishable. The shape is partly a result of extensive wind tunnel aerodynamics testing.

**Engine**
Bucks the trend of 90° V-twins by opting for a 60° layout instead. In a no-compromise move to perfect the bike's chassis, geometry and handling, Aprilia's engineers found that a motor of typical design simply would not fit in the resulting engine bay space – and radically went with their own design instead.

**Wheels**
The aluminium alloy Brembo rims are 89mm (3.5in) wide front and 152mm (6in) rear. They sport a five spoke design.

# aprilia **RSV Mille**

# Specifications

**It is hard to imagine** the Mille is Aprilia's first large capacity road-going sports machine. It is so good from the crate that even hardened cynics have been amazed. The secret to its formidable handling properties comes from the fact that the chassis was the first component to be developed – and everything else has subsequently been designed to complement it. Aprilia saw no point in releasing a blisteringly powerful machine if it did not handle as well as it possibly could. The final package proves their point.

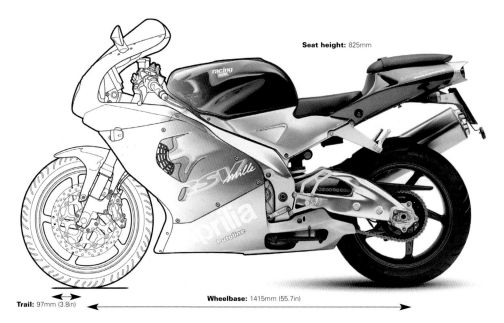

Seat height: 825mm

Width: 725mm (28.5in)

Trail: 97mm (3.8in)

Wheelbase: 1415mm (55.7in)

## ENGINE

| | |
|---|---|
| **Type** | 4-stroke |
| **Layout** | DOHC 60° V-twin |
| **Total displacement** | 997.62cc (24.2ci) |
| **Bore** | 97mm (3.8in) |
| **Stroke** | 67.5mm (2.7in) |
| **Compression ratio** | 11.4:1 |
| **Valves** | 4 per cylinder |
| **Fuel system** | fuel injection, 51mm (2.0in) throttle bodies |
| **Ignition** | electronic digital, twin spark |
| **Cooling** | liquid, double radiator |
| **Maximum power** | 83.5kW (112 bhp) @ 9250 rpm |
| **Maximum torque** | 9.9kg-m ((72 lb-ft) @ 7250 rpm |

## TORQUE

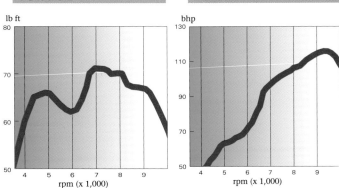

## POWER

Independent test measurements (above) differ from the manufacturer's claimed maximum power and maximum torque figures.

## TRANSMISSION

| | |
|---|---|
| **Primary drive** | gear |
| **Clutch** | wet multiplate, servo-assisted |
| **Gearbox** | 6-speed |
| **Final drive** | chain |

## WEIGHTS & CAPACITIES

| | |
|---|---|
| **Tank capacity** | 20l (5.3gals) |
| **Dry weight** | 189kg (415.8lb) |
| **Weight distribution** | |
| — front | 49.2 % |
| — rear | 50.8 % |
| **Wheelbase** | 1415mm (55.7in) |
| **Overall length** | 2070mm (81.5in) |
| **Overall width** | 725mm (28.5in) |
| **Overall height** | 1180mm (46.5in) |
| **Seat height** | 825mm (32.5in) |

## CYCLE PARTS

| | |
|---|---|
| **Frame** | aluminium alloy twin spar |
| **Rake/trail** | 24.5°/ 97mm |
| **Front suspension** | inverted 43mm (1.7in) Showa telescopic forks |
| **Travel** | 120mm (4.7in) |
| **Adjustment** | spring preload, plus compression and rebound damping |
| **Rear suspension** | monoshock with 50mm (2in) stroke |
| **Travel** | 135mm (5.3in) |
| **Adjustment** | ride height, spring preload, plus compression and rebound damping |
| **Tyres** | |
| — make | Michelin Hi-Sports |
| — front | 120/70 x ZR17 |
| — rear | 190/50 x ZR17 |
| **Brakes** | |
| — make | Brembo |
| — front | twin 320mm (12.6in) steel floating discs, opposed 4-piston calipers with 34mm (1.33in) and 30mm (1.2in) pistons |
| — rear | single 220mm (8.66in) fixed steel disc, 2-piston caliper |

# aprilia **SL1000 FALCO**

**Pillion seat**
The pillion seat looks a little precarious once you remove the cowl and see the position of the pegs and the thinness of the seat padding.

**Rear Suspension**
The rear Sachs shock is only adjustable for preload and rebound and is a hydraulic unit. It fastens up to a progressive link with APS and at the back end of the swingarm gives 130mm (5.1in) of travel.

**Front suspension**
The Showa upside-down forks are fully adjustable, with 120mm (4.7in) of travel and a 43mm (1.7in) girth. They allow for excellent feedback even on stock settings and do a great job of absorbing those nasty holes in the road.

**Saddle**
If you like your weekend tourers wide and comfortable, this will disappoint. It may not be like sitting on a razorblade, but a 480km (300mile) round trip would be your limit.

 **SL1000 FALCO**

*The Aprilia Falco was first launched in 1999 as a more middle-of-the-road machine for those of us unwilling to ride an out-and-out race bike. The half fairing says it all: this machine is caught between two worlds, those of the race machine and the weekend tourer. The amazing thing seems to be that it succeeds, where other hi-breds have failed miserably, the Honda VFR being the exception.*

*Nicely laid out clocks and easy to read. The clocks and switchgear do not show much of the Italian design flair but they do work very well.*

**Engine**
A 60° V-twin powers the SL1000 Falco, borrowed from its big brother the RSV Mille. It has been completely re-worked to give slightly less power but more torque. Do not be fooled by this engine: it is radically different from the RSV Mille unit and a lot of thought has gone into it.

**Colours**
Colours available are a weird orangey colour and a grey – not very inspiring. But this is meant to be a more respectable version of the RSV Mille, so it did not need the red and black race paint of its Aprilia forbears.

**Swingarm**
The swing arm has race style 'bobbins' at the back for easy lifting and removal of tyres, and is a nice reminder of the bikes heritage.

**Brakes**
The front brakes are excellent and only need the lightest of touches to bring the Falco back to earth. The Gold Brembo callipers have a radical design using different sized pistons to apply pad pressure to the optimum spot.

**Fairing** The fairing is a three quarter job, leaving much of the frame exposed. From the front, the ram air intakes and stylish triple headlight say 'get out of my way'; from the back, it says 'please signal before overtaking'!

# Specifications

*Aprilia's multi-talented Falco* is viewed by some as the poorer cousin of the top-of-the-range Mille. But the SL1000 is very much its own bike, and as the spec shows, the word 'economy' does not figure at all: you get a bike with an engine that is a direct descendent of the Mille coupled with wonderful styling – just check out the exposed double alloy frame – and top-class handling. A joy all the way!

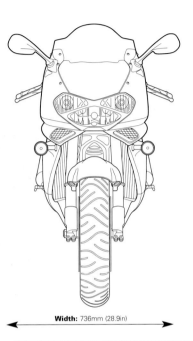

Width: 736mm (28.9in)

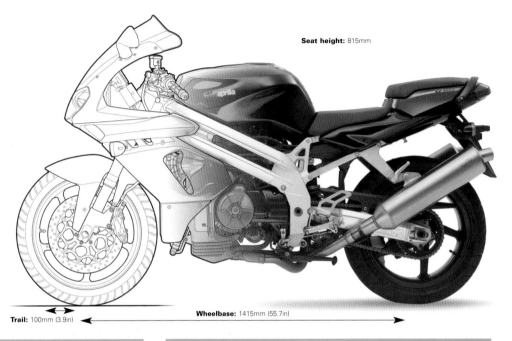

Seat height: 815mm

Trail: 100mm (3.9in)

Wheelbase: 1415mm (55.7in)

## ENGINE

| | |
|---|---|
| Type | 4-stroke |
| Layout | 60° V-twin |
| Total displacement | 997 cc (60.8ci) |
| Bore | 97mm (3.8in) |
| Stroke | 67.5mm (2.7in) |
| Compression ratio | 10.8:1 |
| Valves | 4 valves per cylinder |
| Fuel system | indirect multi-point injection |
| Ignition | digital |
| Cooling | liquid |
| Maximum power | 79kW (105.7 bhp) @ 9100 rpm |
| Maximum torque | 9.2kg-m (67 lb-ft) @ 7000 rpm |

## TRANSMISSION

| | |
|---|---|
| Primary drive | gear |
| Clutch | multiple discs in oil bath |
| Gearbox | 6 speed |
| Final drive | chain |

## WEIGHTS & CAPACITIES

| | |
|---|---|
| Tank capacity | 21l (5.5gals) |
| Dry weight | 190kg (419lb) |
| Weight distribution | |
| — front | 49% |
| — rear | 51% |
| Wheelbase | 1415mm (55.7in) |
| Overall length | 2050mm (80.7in) |
| Overall width | 736mm (28.9in) |
| Overall height | 1210mm (4.8in) |
| Seat height | 815mm (3.2in) |

## CYCLE PARTS

| | |
|---|---|
| Frame | Aluminium and magnesium alloy double twin beam |
| Rake/trail | 24.5°/100mm (3.9in) |
| Front suspension | 43mm upside-down Showa fork |
| Travel | 120mm (4.7in) |
| Adjustment | rebound, compression and preload |
| Rear suspension | Sachs hydraulic shock-absorber |
| Travel | 130mm (5.1in) |
| Adjustment | extension and preload |
| Tyres | |
| — make | N/A |
| — front | 120/70 ZR17 |
| — rear | 180/55 ZR17 |
| Brakes | |
| — make | N/A |
| — front | 320mm (12.6in) dual floating discs 4-piston caliper |
| — rear | 220mm (8.6in) disc, 2-pistons caliper |

# bimota **SB7**

*Gearbox is a six-speed indirect unit with final drive to the rear wheel via chain and sprocket.*

**Bodywork**
The Bimota's fairing is made from carbon fibre reinforced with fibreglass, which contributes to the bike's overall weight reduction.

**Front forks**
A combination of traditional 46mm (1.8in) front forks with a separate hydraulic cartridge allows above-average damping performance.

**Rear suspension**
Ohlins rear shock is adjustable for both compression and rebound. It can also be adjusted for length to offer either more stability or more feedback, depending on the rider's requirements.

**Front brakes**
The stopping power of Bimota's SB7 is delivered courtesy of twin 320mm (12.6in) floating front discs, with the rotors made from cast iron instead of the more common stainless steel, and Brembo 'Gold Series' four-piston calipers.

**Exhaust system**
The four -into-one-into-two stainless steel exhaust system features twin aluminium alloy silencers and the option to fit a catalytic converter.

**Rear brakes**
Single rear disc, also by Brembo, measures just 210mm (8.3in) because the factory felt a larger one could cause the rear wheel to lock.

SB7

**One of the rarer Bimotas,** *the SB7 is powered by Suzuki's GSXR750 RSP. Combine that with Bimota's light chassis and you have a great machine. Its close ratio gearbox does not lend itself to around town riding, but blasting down the motorways more than makes up for it. a pity, then that there are so few on the road.*

Electronic system integrates management of the ignition and fuel injection systems in a bid to secure the smallest possible dimensions, lightest weight and an ability to work perfectly at very high revs.

Twin circular headlights were a hallmark of the SB7 and were also incorporated on the related SB6 and SB6R.

The aluminium beam frame is no stranger to many Bimota models and does the job it sets out to do – the lightweight chassis combined with Suzuki's engine gives out some power.

**Fuel tank**
The shapely, capacious fuel tank is incorporated with the single seat to give a one piece unit and was another element designed to save as much weight as possible.

**Rear sub-frame**
Traditionally used to support the rider's weight and rear panels, the rear sub-frame has been completely removed on the SB7 – a move made possible by the self-supporting carbon fibre bodywork.

**Engine**
The heart of this beast is of Japanese origin. Initially propelling Suzuki's GSX-R750 RSP, the in-line four-cylinder four stroke boasts four valves per cylinder and is water-cooled.

**Wheels**
Standard are three spoke cast wheels. The front tyre is a Michelin High-Sport 120/60 ZR17 whilst the rear tyre is a Michelin High-Sport 180/55 ZR17.

# bimota  SB7

# Specifications

**The SB7 was a bike** which Bimota hoped would put it firmly back on centre stage at the highest levels of racing. The formula certainly seemed to have the right ingredients: special race version of Suzuki's acclaimed **GSX-R750** four-cylinder unit, taken from Suzuki's own homologation machine, the **GSX-R750SP**. This was slotted into the Italians' own special aluminium twin spar frame complete with the new 'straight line concept' design, where the spars dropped right down to the swingarm pivot. An exotic, lightweight, all carbon fibre seat unit was fitted, doing away with the need for a rear subframe. As a result of this and the forward sited battery, weight distribution was a very forward biased 55 per cent, unusual even for a race bike.

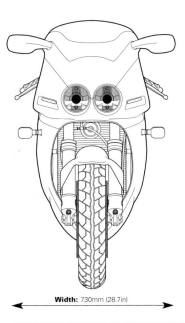

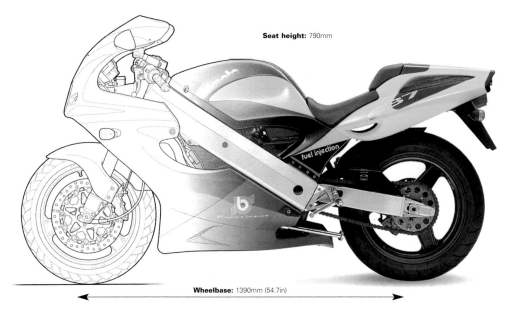

Seat height: 790mm

Width: 730mm (28.7in)

Wheelbase: 1390mm (54.7in)

## ENGINE

| | |
|---|---|
| Type | 4-stroke |
| Layout | in-line 4 |
| Total displacement | 749cc (45.7ci) |
| Bore | 70mm (2.75in) |
| Stroke | 48.7 |
| Compression ratio | 12:1 |
| Valves | 4 per cylinder |
| Fuel system | Weber Marelli fuel injection |
| Ignition | computer controlled engine management |
| Cooling | liquid |
| Maximum power | 35.6kw (99.5 bhp) @ 11,800 rpm |
| Maximum torque | 6.6kg-m (47.7lb-ft) @ 7800 rpm |

## TORQUE

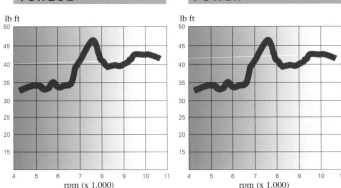

lb ft
rpm (x 1,000)

## POWER

lb ft
rpm (x 1,000)

## TRANSMISSION

| | |
|---|---|
| Primary drive | gear |
| Clutch | wet multiplate |
| Gearbox | 6-speed |
| Final drive | O-ring chain |

## WEIGHTS & CAPACITIES

| | |
|---|---|
| Tank capacity | 16l (4.2gals) |
| Dry weight | 170 kg |
| Weight distribution | |
| — front | 55% |
| — rear | 45% |
| Wheelbase | 1390mm (54.7in) |
| Overall length | 1990mm (78.3in) |
| Overall width | 730mm (28.7in) |
| Overall height | 1060mm (41.7in) |
| Seat height | 790mm (31/1in) |

## CYCLE PARTS

| | |
|---|---|
| Frame | twin spar aluminium |
| Rake/trail | both variable |
| Front suspension | 46mm telescopic forks |
| Travel | 270mm (10.7in) |
| Adjustment | spring preload, rebound and compression damping |
| Rear suspension | rising rate monoshock |
| Travel | 300mm (11.8in) |
| Adjustment | ride height, spring preload, rebound and compression damping |
| Tyres | |
| — make | Michelin/Bridgestone |
| — front | 130/70 x 17 |
| — rear | 180/55x17 |
| Brakes | |
| — make | Brembo |
| — front | 2 x 320mm (12.6in) discs, 4-piston calipers |
| — rear | 1 x 230mm (9.1in) steel disc, 2-piston caliper |

Independent test measurements (above) differ from the manufacturer's claimed maximum power and maximum torque figures.

# bimota  YB8

*Wide and flat, the seat is comfortable enoughfor most. Nor will shorties find it too challenging.*

**Instruments**
The clocks may have everything you need but are hard to read, and, like the bike itself, some people find them tasteless.

**Headlamps**
The twin headlights sit nicely in the moulded fairing, giving the front end a very classy (although some say outdated) look.

**Bodywork**
Even today it is nice to look at. The full fairing is moulded into the tank.

**Carburettors**
4x38mm (1.5in) Mikuni carbs do the job nicely.

**Front suspension**
You either need to get used to it or get it worked on. The 46mm (1.8in) Paoli forks are stiff and uncompromising. It feels as though Bimota has deliberately chosen the hardest springs it could find.

**Tyres**
At the front the Bimota has a TX11 Hi-Sport 180/55 ZR17 while at the rear sits a TX23 Hi-Sport 180/55 ZR17.

**Rear suspension**
At the rear, the YB8 is equipped with an excellent fully adjustable Ohlins monoshock system, which is unfortunately let down by the front end.

# YB8

*There are less than a thousand of these bikes worldwide, but Bimota has only itself to blame. The price, at the time of its launch in 1991, was just plain ridiculous, even for a handbuilt Bimota. But, having said this, you do get something very special and something that even today will leave a lot of bikes in your wake. This is an incredibly awesome and powerful machine. Getting your hands on a YB8 would not be the worst thing you could do.*

*Clocks feature white lettering on red faces. Certainly different from the vast majority of sports bikes both old and new.*

*Short rear subframe looks unusual and contributes to weight saving, which along with the lightweight main spars gives the YB8 a formidable power-to-weight ratio.*

*The rectangular section alloy beam frame is **Bimota**'s own, of course, and as such should be admired, especially for its light weight, which gives the bike an overall dry weight figure of 185kg (408lb) with a wheelbase of 1420mm (55.9in). The combination of light chassis and EXUP engine is what gives this bike its awesome power.*

**Fuel tank**
Holds 14l (3.6gals) and, although it looks good, has a cap which is difficult to unscrew without doing some minor harm to yourself.

**Seat**
The single seat has a height of 780mm (3.1in) so almost everyone could have a chance with this one.

**Brakes**
The single 230mm (9.1in) disc with Brembo two-piston caliper at the rear gives superb stopping power when combined with the win front disc.

**Engine**
The Bimota uses the well-proven Yamaha EXUP engine. The 1002cc (61.1ci) in-line four cylinder DOHC motor is water-cooled and has a bore and stroke of 75.5 X 56 mm. (2.97 x 2.20in).

**Gearbox**
The five-speed gearbox performs well with no unpleasant clunks. Compression ratio is 12.1:1.

# Specifications

**The YB8 is very much** a case of Bimota doing what it does best – taking a top Japanese engine and rehousing it within a handbuilt, lightweight and uncompromising single seat chassis designed solely for going very fast. The Furano's motive power comes courtesy of Yamaha's landmark **FZR1000 EXUP** motor, fitted with Weber Marelli fuel injection in place of the original's carburettors to Bimota's own specification. Bimota claimed a rather optimistic 122kW (164bhp) for the beast, but we found a still-respectable 104kW (139bhp) lurking beneath the bodywork. Still more than enough...

Rake: 24.5°

Height: 960mm (37.8in)

Seat height: 790mm (31.1in)

Length: 2095mm (82.5in)

## ENGINE

| | |
|---|---|
| Type | 4-stroke |
| Layout | DOHC in-line four |
| Total displacement | 1002cc (61ci) |
| Bore | 75.5mm (2.97in) |
| Stroke | 56mm (2.20in) |
| Compression ratio | 12:1 |
| Valves | 5 per cylinder |
| Fuel system | Weber Marelli fuel injection |
| Ignition | Weber Marelli digital |
| Cooling | liquid |
| Maximum power | 104kW (139bhp) @ 10350 rpm |
| Maximum torque | 9.95kg-m (72lb-ft) @ 9300 rpm |

## TRANSMISSION

| | |
|---|---|
| Primary drive | gear |
| Clutch | wet multiplate |
| Gearbox | 5-speed |
| Final drive | O-ring chain |

## WEIGHTS & CAPACITIES

| | |
|---|---|
| Tank capacity | 17l (4.5gals) |
| Dry weight | 180kg (397lb) |
| Weight distribution | |
| — front | N/A |
| — rear | N/A |
| Wheelbase | 1420mm (55.9in) |
| Overall length | 2095mm (82.5in) |
| Overall width | 710mm (27.9in) |
| Overall height | 960mm (37.8in) |
| Seat height | 790mm (31.1in) |

## CYCLE PARTS

| | |
|---|---|
| Frame | twin spar aluminium |
| Rake/trail | 24.5°/95mm |
| Front suspension | 43mm inverted telescopic forks |
| Travel | 112mm (4.4in) |
| Adjustment | Spring preload, rebound and compression damping |
| Rear suspension | rising rate monoshock |
| Travel | 110mm (4.3in) |
| Adjustment | Spring preload, rebound and compression damping |
| Tyres | |
| — front | 120/70 x 17 |
| — rear | 180/55 x 17 |
| Brakes | |
| — front | 2 x 320mm (12.6in) discs, 4-piston calipers |
| — rear | 1 x 230mm (9in) disc, 2-piston caliper |

# bimota **SB6R**

**Instrument panel**
Features a 185mph (298im/h) speedometer in 5mph (87km/h) increments, 13,000 rpm tachometer with the redline at 11,500 rpm, fuel, neutral, oil, indicator and main beam warning lights, and a digital water temperature/trip mileage readout which is toggled by a discreet button mounted in the centre of the top yoke. The rev ceiling is reached at 12,000 rpm, where a limiter cuts in.

*The front brakes are opposed four-piston Brembo calipers biting twin 320mm (12.6in) discs. Braided steel hose comes as standard.*

**Mirrors**
Too narrow and small to be of much use.

**Right handlebar**
Sports the engine kill switch, electric start button, off/park/on light switch and a four-way span adjustable front brake lever.

**Headlamps**
Twin lights lie beneath a single cover and provide adequate light for night riding. Only one headlamp works on dip.

**Left handlebar**
Plays host to the headlamp's hi/lo beam switch, indicator and horn buttons, manual choke lever, pass light switch and four-way span hydraulic clutch lever.

**Fairing**
Looking almost stretched, in traditional Bimota style, its inner edge closely follows the frame to ensure that the thick, aluminium alloy twin spar unit is fully exposed for maximum viewing effect.

**Chain guard**
Features a large cutaway, which can allow riders' heels to briefly rub the chain.

**Carbon fibre**
Used to fashion the rear hugger/chain guard, front mudguard, and part of the rear panelling.

## SB6R

**Its engine may come** *from Suzuki, but there is no doubting Bimota's own frame. It is eye-catchingly different to anything else you are likely to see, with the two aluminium spars wrapping tightly around each side of the engine. Italian exotica? Definitely. But is it one of Bimota's finest examples? You will have to make your own mind up about that – it is a question of what you want from a bike.*

**Tyres**
Standard rubber is a 120/70 x ZR17 front and 190/50 x ZR17 rear Michelin Hi-Sport.

The 4-into-2-into-1-into-2 system has been designed to give a good power boost at high revs and features shorter downpipes than those fitted to the forerunning *SB6*. Style points go to the twin underseat silencers, although their shape is not to everyone's taste.

**Opposed two-piston Brembo** caliper bites a single 230mm (9.1in) disc at the rear.

The massive slab-sided aluminium alloy twin spar frame is ultra-strong and rigid. Unusually, however, there is no subframe on this single seater. Tapered swingarm (10mm/0.39in longer than previous SB6's) is a visual work of art.

**Engine**
Taken from the last incarnation of Suzuki's GSX-R1100, it displaces 1074cc (65.5ci), has a bore and stroke of 75.5mm x 60mm (2.9 x 2.4in), a compression ratio of 11.2:1 and four valves per cylinder. The DOHC in-line four makes its power slightly differently to the old GSX-R by way of a one-off, huge airbox fitted at the Bimota factory and a different exhaust system.

**Seat**
Solo design, making passenger accommodation impossible, it is surprisingly roomy and comfortable.

**Fuel tank**
Huge 22l (5.8galls) tank is made of toughened plastic to help reduce weight.

**Front suspension**
Italian-made 46mm (1.8in) Paioli forks are adjustable for preload, plus rebound and compression damping, and have a maximum travel of 120mm (4.7in).

**Wheels**
Antera rims are 89mm (3.5in) wide front and 140mm (5.5in) rear.

**Wheelbase**
At 1400mm (55.1in), it is just 5mm longer than the Yamaha YZF-R1's.

**Rear suspension**
Horizontally-mounted Ohlins monoshock with remote gas reservoir is adjustable for preload and ride height, as well as rebound and compression damping and allows maximum wheel travel of 120mm (4.7in).

# bimota **TESI**

**Impressive, but...**
Almost like something out of the future to look at, it does not, unfortunately, behave in that manner. There is little steering lock, a badly-positioned sidestand and useless mirrors...

**Dashboard**
A comprehenisve electronic dashboard uses a set of LCD indicators and digital readouts instead of traditional analogue dials.

**Braking**
The hub-centre design means hardly any of the braking forces are carried through to the suspension, allowing you to brake harder (with less dramatic results) than on a conventional bike.

**Swingarm**
The swingarm lookalike front had an amazing steering-cum-suspension system built into it, and it did eliminate the dive which has always been the bane of conventional telescopic forks.

## TESI

### The Bimota Tesi promised
*to be a revolutionary motorcycle, and it was, but unfortunately this was not enough to make it a success. Many bike designers over the years have sought to improve on telescopic forked front ends. Perhaps the most exotic of these designs was Bimota's Tesi.*

*The impressive to look at LCD console is unreliable and difficult to read.*

*The Tesi uses a pair of milled aluminium plates either side of the Ducati engine to mount its front and rear swingarms. Steel tube subframes support the seat, bodywork and steering gear.*

**Bodywork**
Even the body panels are very poorly lined up. What a waste of what could have been a truly great bike.

**Engine**
A specially-tuned version of Ducati's 851, bored out to 904cc (55.2ci), powers the awesome Tesi.

# BMW

# F650 FUNDURO

**BMW has fitted two side-mounted grab handles instead of the usual single rail. Its design allows a natural extension into a luggage rack that locates flush against the stepped rear seat.**

**Mirrors**
Square-shaped and mounted on spindly stalks, but impervious to wind blast and vibration.

**Headlamp**
Square-shaped design and power of the light brings no complaints.

## F650 FUNDURO

*The BMW F650 has been a successful attempt by the German marque to enter into the lucrative trailie market. With subtle, elegant styling and an Aprilia-based engine combined with the traditional strengths of reliability and build quality, it is a worthy addition to BMW's line-up. It may not set your pulse racing immediately, but it is the type of bike which grows on you. Shame about the price tag.*

**Front suspension**
The 41mm (1.6in) leading axle telescopic forks are softly sprung and feature huge travel, yet respond well to normal road-riding input. Bumps, ruts and ripples are easily tackled, ensuring a supremely comfortable ride under tricky road circumstances. Off-road, though, they are not up to anything heavier than green-laning.

**Stone guard**
Just like its bigger R1100GS and R1150GS stablemates, the baby trailie features a guard to trap stones thrown up by the rear tyre into the path of following vehicles. Useful on shale roads and mounted from the tapered rear swingarm.

**Footpegs**
Rubber-covered footpegs isolate both the rider's and passenger's feet from otherwise barely perceptible vibration.

High-mounted, left-side silencer features heat shields to protect the passenger's leg. Still not good news for anyone wanting to use throw-over panniers, though.

Overall, this is a pretty good chassis with good handling and suspension, which soaks up almost everything. The steering also cannot really be faulted and it corners well. The main problem is ground clearance; it really should be higher.

Half-fairing is both robust in a crash and big enough to offer normal-sized riders real weather protection. Style points are gained by its seamless interaction with the tank.

**Wheels**
Both the 483mm (19in) front and 432mm (17in) rear wire-spoked wheels are rebuildable. More importantly, however, their sizing allows a brilliant choice of trailie-inspired rubber.

**Engine**
The 652cc (39.7ci) engine is similar to the unit in Aprilia's Pegaso, but employs a four-valve head. The impact of this, combined with weight and aerodynamic differences, is an 8.5 per cent deficit in top speed and weaker acceleration. However, BMW claims the single cylinder motor, which has a 100 x 83mm (3.9 x 3.3in) bore and stroke and a five speed gearbox, makes just ).75kW (1bhp) less than the Aprilia's 49.

# Specifications

*Although now overshadowed by the 2000 GS, the 1993–99 F650 should not be overlooked. It is still a great bike. The fact that it remained on sale for seven years goes to show what a capable machine it was in the beginning. The 653cc (39.7ci) single features a four valve head and is mated to a five-speed gearbox. The chassis is strong and stiff and although the suspension is fairly softly sprung, this does not come at the expense of on-road handling. Furthermore it is quite capable off-road and boasts decent stone guard protection and even rebuildable wheels!*

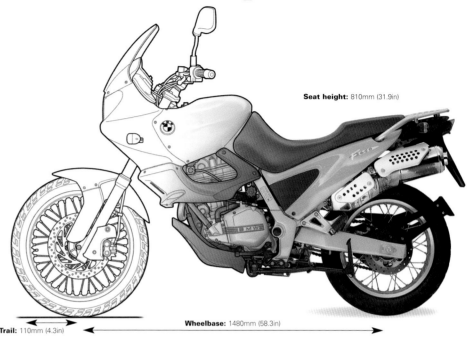

Seat height: 810mm (31.9in)

Width: 880mm (34.6in)

Trail: 110mm (4.3in)

Wheelbase: 1480mm (58.3in)

## ENGINE

| | |
|---|---|
| Type | 4-stroke |
| Layout | DOHC single |
| Total displacement | 653cc (39.7ci) |
| Bore | 100mm (3.9in) |
| Stroke | 83mm (3.3in) |
| Compression ratio | 9.7:1 |
| Valves | 4 |
| Fuel system | 2 x 33mm (1.3in) Mikuni carburettors |
| Ignition | CDI |
| Cooling | liquid |
| Maximum power | 35.6kW (47.7bhp) @ 6442rpm |
| Maximum torque | 5.8kg-m (42lb-ft) @ 5199rpm |

## TORQUE

lb ft

rpm (x 1,000)

## POWER

bhp

rpm (x 1,000)

Independent test measurements (above) differ from the manufacturer's claimed maximum power and maximum torque figures.

## TRANSMISSION

| | |
|---|---|
| Primary drive | gear |
| Clutch | wet multiplate |
| Gearbox | 5-speed |
| Final drive | chain |

## WEIGHTS & CAPACITIES

| | |
|---|---|
| Tank capacity | 17.5l (4.6gals) |
| Dry weight | 170kg (375lb) |
| Weight distribution | |
| — front | N/A |
| — rear | N/A |
| Wheelbase | 1480mm (58.3in) |
| Overall length | 2180mm (85.8in) |
| Overall width | 880mm (34.6in) |
| Overall height | 1180mm (46.5in) |
| Seat height | 810mm (31.9in) |

## CYCLE PARTS

| | |
|---|---|
| Frame | single loop tubular steel |
| Rake/trail | 24.5°/110mm (4.3in) |
| Front suspension | 41mm (1.6in) telescopic forks |
| Travel | 170mm (6.7in) |
| Adjustment | none |
| Rear suspension | progressive linkage, monoshock |
| Travel | 165mm (6.5in) |
| Adjustment | spring preload, rebound damping |
| Tyres | |
| — make | varies |
| — front | 100/90 x 19 |
| — rear | 130/80 x 17 |
| Brakes | |
| — make | Brembo |
| — front | 300mm (11.8in) disc two-piston caliper |
| — rear | 240mm (9.5in) disc single-piston floating caliper |

# BMW R1100S

**Front end**
The neat and compact front end is further enhanced by the bike's sport windscreen, black indicator and hand protector units.

**Exhaust system**
Increased volume was designed to reduce counter-pressure and help boost power and performance without sacrificing the Boxer's distinctive sound. A first for BMW, the twin silencers rest directly beneath the tail section.

**Suspension**
The suspension geometry of the R1100S was designed to reflect the bike's sporting abilities, with an increased wheelbase of 1478mm (58.1in) and BMW's Telelever front wheel suspension system.

**Brakes**
The R1100S carries ABS brakes as an option, the advanced braking technology first introduced by BMW to the motorcycle market in 1988. Since that time, the factory has built more than 200,000 motorcycles with ABS.

**Wheels**
The R1100S features sporty-looking five-double-spoke design wheels, which take 120/70 ZR17 front tyres and 170/60 ZR17 rear tyres.

## R1100S

**In 1998, BMW launched the R1100S,** following the success of its other Boxer twins. And it is exactly what you would expect from BMW in terms of reliability and it is also what some would expect in terms of looks. It has been called downright ugly, and although it could never be described as beautiful, does that matter when the finish is so good and the power delivery so smooth?

BMW's trademark 'twin kidney' grille, as seen on its entire range of cars, also adorns the R1100S.

*The four-piece frame was all-new for the introduction of the 1998 R1100S, featuring a die-cast aluminium front, welded aluminium main frame and a steel pipe rear section.*

*A first for BMW, the fully controlled three-way catalytic converter was fitted as a standard item on the R1100S worldwide.*

**Bars**
The standard bars on the BMW are noticeably compact, but BMW offers a higher 'comfort' handlebar as an option, which comes in conjunction with a taller windscreen.

**Seat**
Seat height is 800mm (31.5in) and the elongated passenger seat cover stretches the BMW's apparent dimensions.

**Engine**
The 1085cc (66.2ci) horizontally opposed twin is air/oil cooled, has a compression ratio of 11.3:4 and puts out a claimed 72.3kW (97bhp) at the rear wheel, and once the rider is used to it, this can really work on the road. The torque curve is flat which means a smooth power delivery.

**Sidestand**
You might think that BMW would get with the programme and offer a centre stand – but no, only a side stand is available on the BMW R1100S.

# Specifications

**Upon introducing the machine** *in 1999, BMW billed the 1100S as the most powerful, lightest and agile of the twin cylinder family... the most dynamic Boxer BMW has ever built. As with all BMWs, claimed power is impressively accurate, in this case 73kW (98bhp). Based on the previous R1100RS, the increase comes from the adoption of four valves per cylinder instead of two, an increase in compression ratio and improved intake breathing. A new exhaust system also reduces back-pressure, while retaining the twin's throaty sound.*

Rake: 25°

Seat height: 800mm

Length: 2,180mm

## ENGINE

| | |
|---|---|
| Type | 4 -stroke |
| Layout | horizontally-opposed twin |
| Total displacement | 1085cc (66.2ci) |
| Bore | 99mm (3.9in) |
| Stroke | 70.5mm (2.8in) |
| Compression ratio | 11.3:1 |
| Valves | 4 per cylinder |
| Fuel system | Bosch Motronic fuel injection |
| Ignition | digital |
| Cooling | air/oil cooled |
| Maximum power | 73kW (98 bhp) @ 7500 rpm |
| Maximum torque | 9.9kg-m (71.5 lb-ft) @ 5750 rpm |

## TRANSMISSION

| | |
|---|---|
| Primary drive | gear |
| Clutch | single plate, dry, contra-rotating |
| Gearbox | 6-speed |
| Final drive | shaft |

## WEIGHTS & CAPACITIES

| | |
|---|---|
| Tank capacity | 18l (4.75gals) |
| Dry weight | 215kg (474lb) |
| Weight distribution | |
| — front | N/A |
| — rear | N/A |
| Wheelbase | 1478mm (58.1in) |
| Overall length | 2180mm (85.8in) |
| Overall width | 880mm (34.6in) |
| Overall height | N/A |
| Seat height | 800mm (31.5in) |

## CYCLE PARTS

| | |
|---|---|
| Frame | cast aluminium and tubular space frame |
| Rake/trail | 25°/100mm (3.9in) |
| Front suspension | BMW Telelever |
| Travel | 110mm (4.3in) |
| Adjustment | rebound damping |
| Rear suspension | BMW Paralever |
| Travel | 130mm (5.1in) |
| Adjustment | preload, rebound damping |
| Tyres | |
| — front | 120/70-ZR17 |
| — rear | 170/60-ZR17 |
| Brakes | |
| — front | 2 x 305mm (1.2in) disc, 4-piston floating calipers |
| — rear | 1 x 276mm (10.8in) disc, twin piston floating caliper |

# BMW **R1100GS**

**The anti-tilt handlebar mountings are a bit of a bonus when covering long distances or going dirt-riding.**

**Indicators**
Horrible push-to-cancel dual switches can be tricky to locate on the move.

**Wet weight**
BMW does not quote dry figures, preferring to list the R1100GS at 243kg (534.6lb) unladen, but ready for the road.

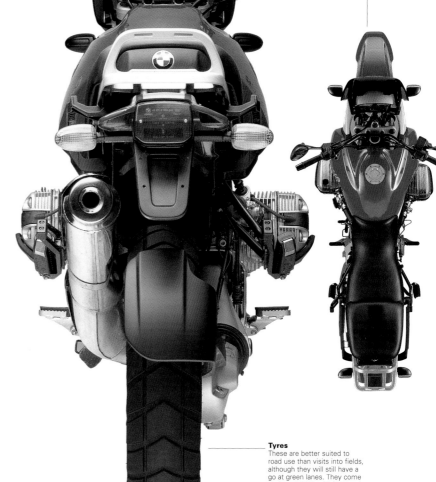

**Front suspension**
Some BMWs might have a reputation for being old farts' machines, but the factory is actually quite adventurous. The unusual Telelever fork set-up connects the front end with the engine block and frame (the latter by way of a load-absorbing externally sprung monoshock running from a central strut), the idea being increased stability under braking. It works. Four-stage spring preload adjustment and 190mm (7.5in) of suspension travel soak up on and off-road bumps well.

*R1100GS*

*Like the R850GS,* the 1100 is a go-anywhere machine. Aimed at those who enjoy long distance riding or travelling through unfamiliar and rough terrains, this BMW copes with it all easily. A lot of it comes down to whether you like BMWs, but those who have never tried one should get down to their local dealer now and ask for a test ride on the 1100 or the new 1150GS.

**Front brakes**
Twin 305mm (12in) disc and four-piston opposed Brembo caliper system offers something rare on bikes but beloved of most who have tried it – optional antilock stopping. The system can be manually turned off for dirt riding (preventing the sensor 'thinking' that lock-up is imminent almost all the time, with the result that stopping is impaired).

**Tyres**
These are better suited to road use than visits into fields, although they will still have a go at green lanes. They come in sizes 110/80 x 19 front and 150/70 x 17 rear.

The luggage rack underneath the removable pillion seat is standard. The bike can carry a payload of up to 200kg (440lb).

If you plan on a bit of 'rough' riding, the standard cylinder guards and undertray will withstand quite a bit of 'abuse'.

'Tuned for midrange' version of BMW's long-running Boxer engine, the horizontally-opposed flat twin motor has a 1085cc (66.2ci) capacity, four valves per cylinder, a bore and stroke of 99 x 70.5mm (3.9 x 2.7in), five-speed gearbox, and closed-loop three-way catalytic convertor. Some markets (not the UK) also have the option of an 848cc R850GS model.

**Fuel tank**
Holds 24l (6.3 gals), of which 4l (1 gal) is the reserve.

**Seat**
Adjusts to either 800mm (31.5in) or 840mm (33.1in) height to accommodate various sizes of riders. Comfort is superb.

**Stone guard**
Looks neat, and does a good job of stopping dirt escaping the rear tyre and hitting following riders.

**Rear suspension**
Hard to see quite how it works, but it clearly does. The R1100GS's Paralever system incorporates shaft drive, the duties of a swingarm and a method of managing 'torque reaction', and looks decidedly odd.

# Specifications

*Introduced in 1994, the BMW R1100GS*

*became a best-seller almost overnight until it was discontinued at the end of 1999. It continued practically unchanged in that period, proving **BMW** knew when it was onto a good thing. Its appeal lies in the fact that it can be used comfortably both on and off road and was not only the largest enduro around but also, in terms of torque, the most powerful off-roader. **BMW** really went the whole hog with this one, allowing both the windscreen and seat to be adjusted to suit the rider.*

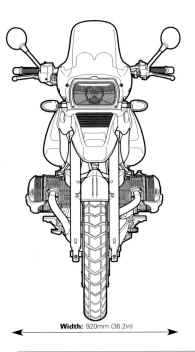

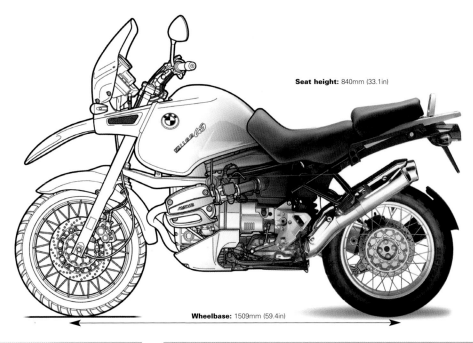

**Seat height:** 840mm (33.1in)

**Width:** 920mm (36.2in)

**Wheelbase:** 1509mm (59.4in)

## ENGINE

| | |
|---|---|
| Type | 4-stroke |
| Layout | Boxer flat twin |
| Total displacement | 1085cc (66.2ci) |
| Bore | 99mm (3.9in) |
| Stroke | 70.5mm (2.7in) |
| Compression ratio | 10.3:1 |
| Valves | 4 per cylinder |
| Fuel system | Motronic fuel injection |
| Ignition | electronic |
| Cooling | air |
| Maximum power | 59.6kw (79.9bhp) @ 6600rpm |
| Maximum torque | 9.7kg-m (70.1lb-ft) @ 5650rpm |

## TRANSMISSION

| | |
|---|---|
| Primary drive | gear |
| Clutch | dry, single-plate |
| Gearbox | 5-speed |
| Final drive | shaft |

## WEIGHTS & CAPACITIES

| | |
|---|---|
| Tank capacity | 25l (6.6 galls) |
| Dry weight | 243kg (535lb) |
| Weight distribution | |
| — front | N/A |
| — rear | N/A |
| Wheelbase | 1509mm (59.4in) |
| Overall length | 2196mm (86.5in) |
| Overall width | 920mm (36.2in) |
| Overall height | N/A |
| Seat height | 840mm (33.1in) |

## CYCLE PARTS

| | |
|---|---|
| Frame | tubular space |
| Rake/trail | N/A |
| Front suspension | telelever |
| Travel | 190mm (7.5in) |
| Adjustment | five-way |
| Rear suspension | paralever |
| Travel | 200mm (7.9in) |
| Adjustment | hydraulic, infinite |
| Tyres | |
| — make | N/A |
| — front | 110/80 x 19 |
| — rear | 150/70 x 17 |
| Brakes | |
| — make | |
| — front | 305mm (12.1in) dual disc |
| — rear | 276mm (10.8in) single disc |

## TORQUE

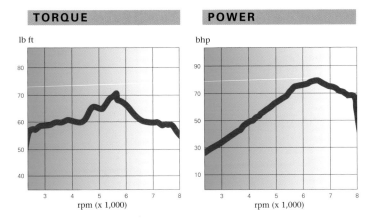

lb ft

rpm (x 1,000)

## POWER

bhp

rpm (x 1,000)

Independent test measurements (above) differ from the manufacturer's claimed maximum power and maximum torque figures.

# BMW R1150GS

**Handlebar width is 903mm (35.6in), so make sure your side alley's wide enough if you live in a terraced house.**

**Handlebar switches**
Redesigned for '99 but still carrying a version of BMW's rather tricky individual indicator buttons. Switching the winkers on is easy enough, turning them off (with yet another switch, this time beside and below the throttle) can be difficult if you have short fingers.

**Windshield**
Adjust to three positions, according to how you like your buffeting, or remove altogether for that flies-in-the-teeth feeling.

**Headlights**
Out with the old rectangular job, in with asymmetric dual ones instead. Looks neat and does the job at night too.

**Gearbox**
The six-speed unit initially introduced on the R1100S has been drafted in to replace the R1100GS's old five-speed box. The first five ratios are close, the top becomes a lazy overdrive (and improves fuel consumption as a result).

**Brakes**
ABS or not, the choice is yours. Ticking the 'yes' box means paying £750 extra. New sintered pads work very well.

**Exhaust**
BMW claims the redesigned chrome-plated exhaust system, with manifolds measuring 45mm (1.7in) diameter instead of the previous model's 38mm, contributes half of the extra claimed (5bhp) the R1150GS enjoys over the R1100GS.

**Wheels**
Spoked, and therefore rebuildable, and come in 2.5x19-inch front and 4x17-inch rear sizes. Tyres are 110/80 and 150/70, with Bridgestone Trail Wings appearing as standard for the UK.

**R1150GS**

**Only the protruding engine** tells you this is a *BMW*. Otherwise you would be forgiven for thinking it's a Japanese marque with its 'into the new millennium' styling. Very good at what it sets out to do, which is to let the rider have a taste of off-road riding while still behaving well on the road. Always good mannered and great fun off-road. Well worth a second look.

Up 45cc (2.7in) over the preceeding R1100GS motor, it is not just a case of extra capacity. The cylinder heads and crankshaft have been taken from the R1100S, the cylinder head covers are made of magnesium (same for all future Boxer engines), a larger oil cooler first used on the R1100RT makes an appearance and there are new camshafts and pistons too. The increased capacity is due to R1200C-based cylinders which extend the bore from 99 to 101mm (3.8–3.9in).

*The paralever swingarm features an enlarged housing to accommodate the six-speed gearbox, and a length of 506mm (19.9in) compared with the R1100GS's 520mm (20.5in). However, other geometrical changes ensure the proven 1509mm (59.4in) wheelbase remains unaltered.*

**Colours**
The yellowy one is arguably the best, although BMW itself appears to favour 'Night Black'. Or you could try 'Titanium Silver', the first metallic option on a BMW, if you are feeling futuristic.

Dry, the weight of the R1150GS is 219kg (481.8lb), oiled and fuelled it is 249kg (547.8lb). The maximum permissible all-up load is 450kg (990lb).

**Fuel tank**
Holds 22.1l (5.8 gals), and comes with a 'roll-over' valve to keep petrol inside following a crash. We tested it off-road and it works!

**Front suspension**
A 'light' version of BMW's famous telelever front end has been introduced and does improve handling. Adjustment is by means of five-position spring adjustment on the front-mounted monoshock. Standard spring travel is 190mm (7.5in).

**Engine management system**
Motronic MA 2.4 digital unit is the same as the R1100S and R1200C's and works with a three-way catalytic converter to ensure minimal emissions but strong performance.

# Specifications

*More of an upgrade* than a new bike, the R1150GS has, however, been endowed with some very useful improvements. It is certainly an improvement on the R1100, though further changes could have been made. Still, it is a typically reliable BMW – a good thing, contrary to the belief of those who still see BMWs as 'boring'. But BMW is one of the most innovative companies around – in technology if not in looks. So do not write off the R1150GS – take a look.

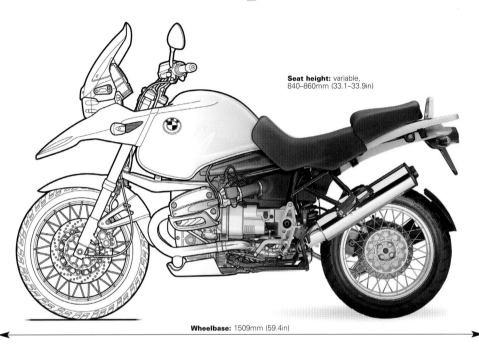

**Seat height:** variable, 840–860mm (33.1–33.9in)

**Width:** 903mm (35.6in)

**Wheelbase:** 1509mm (59.4in)

## ENGINE

| | |
|---|---|
| Type | 4-stroke |
| Layout | horizontal twin |
| Total displacement | 1130cc (68.9ci) |
| Bore | 101mm (3.9in) |
| Stroke | 73mm (2.9in) |
| Compression ratio | 10.3:1 |
| Valves | 4 per cylinder |
| Fuel system | Motronic MA 2.4 |
| Ignition | digital |
| Cooling | air/oil, twin frame-integrated oil coolers |
| Maximum power | 56.6kW (76 bhp) @ 6750rpm |
| Maximum torque | 9.7kg-m (70.4 lb-ft) @ 5900rpm |

## TORQUE

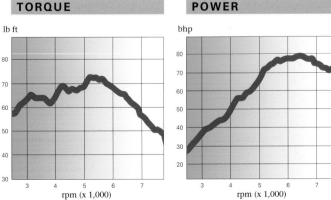

lb ft / rpm (x 1,000)

## POWER

bhp / rpm (x 1,000)

Independent test measurements (above) differ from the manufacturer's claimed maximum power and maximum torque figures.

## TRANSMISSION

| | |
|---|---|
| Primary drive | gear |
| Clutch | dry, single plate |
| Gearbox | 6-speed |
| Final drive | shaft |

## WEIGHTS & CAPACITIES

| | |
|---|---|
| Tank capacity | 22.1l (5.8gal) |
| Dry weight | 219kg (481.8lb) |
| Weight distribution | |
| — front | N/A |
| — rear | N/A |
| Wheelbase | 1509mm (59.4in) |
| Overall length | 2340mm (92.1in) |
| Overall width | 903mm (35.6in) |
| Overall height | 1366mm (53.8in) |
| Seat height | variable, 840–860mm (33.1–33.9in) |

## CYCLE PARTS

| | |
|---|---|
| Frame | independent front/rear subframes, engine/transmission are stressed members |
| Rake/trail | N/A |
| Front suspension | Telelever with central suspension strut |
| Travel | 190mm (7.5in) |
| Adjustment | 5-step spring preload |
| Rear suspension | Paralever |
| Travel | 200mm (7.9in) |
| Adjustment | spring preload, plus rebound damping |
| Tyres | |
| — make | Bridgestone Trail Wing |
| — front | 110/80 x 19 |
| — rear | 150/70 x 17 |
| Brakes | |
| — make | Brembo |
| — front | 2 x 305mm (12in) discs, 4-piston fixed calipers |
| — rear | 285mm (11.2in) disc, 2-piston floating caliper |

# BMW   K1200LT

**Reverse**
An electric reversing aid is is activated by the electric starter and also has a gear connecting the starter to the gearbox drive shaft. The reversing aid can be activated only with the engine running and the gearbox in idle.

**Clutch**
The LT is fitted with a hydraulic clutch and the lever is adjustable to four different positions.

**Screen**
The electrically adjustable screen is undoubtedly a bonus and looks good too. When in its lower position, it gives the LT a sporting appearance from the front. It comes in two heights with the taller version 180mm (7in) higher.

**Radiators**
The K1200LT has two radiators, which BMW claims are arranged for an optimum flow of air rushing by. Whenever necessary, two fans are switched on automatically.

**Lights**
The cluster of lights at the rear is fitted flush, forming one unit together with the indicators.

**Bumper**
The bumper and impact system fitted to the K1200LT prevents the bike from falling all the way to its mirrors. The front bumper and impact cover extends out of the fairing on both sides.

**Gearbox**
The five-speed gearbox is new for this model with the fifth gear serving as an overdrive.

## K1200LT

**Introduced in 1999,** BMW's K1200LT was launched as a heavyweight tourer, which it undoubtedly is – and a good one at that. It has everything anyone could want for touring and is bound to be a rival for Honda's well-established Gold Wing. As they are both good performers and similarly priced, it will come down to personal preference.

**Brakes**
Not surprisingly, the 1200 sports an ABS 2 anti-lock braking system with 305mm (1.2in) dual disc, four piston calipers at the front and a 285mm (11.2in) disc, four piston caliper at the rear.

**Wheels**
The 1200 is fitted with extra light 43.1cm (17in) five-spoke cast aluminium wheels. The front wheel has been reinforced to take up the extra load and weight.

The top box will take two full-face helmets while the side panniers have a standard baggage allowance of 35l (2136ci) each. The topcase and panniers are not removable.

At the heart of the K1200LT lies a 1171cc 16 valve horizontal in line four cylinder with a bore and stroke of 70 x 75mm (2.7 x 2.9in).

This is the same frame concept as the RS. The engine is not connected rigidly to the frame as a load-bearing element but instead rests in a central, ultra-stiff cast aluminium frame to avoid unnecessary vibration. On the LT, however, the fairing, fuel tank, seats, panniers, topcase and exhaust system are all integral parts of the all-inclusive bike body.

**Cockpit**
Well-structured with a speedo, rev counter, fuel gauge, water temperature gauge, gear indicator, digital clock and map reading light.

**Seat**
Available with a pull-out knob beneath the left hand case cover to set the seat height at either 770mm (30.3in) or 800mm (31.5in). The seat is wide with the passenger sitting higher and having the added benefit of a backrest which can also be moved by 25mm (1in).

**Front end**
A big bike such as this one benefits from BMW's Telelever system, which soaks up most of the bumps and prevents any unnecessary dive when applying the brakes.

**Rear brake**
The new rear wheel brake comes with a four-piston caliper and a 285mm (11.2in) floating disc.

# Specifications

*When the K1200LT entered* the market in 1999, BMW's *press release made great claims for this bike – and it has lived up to most of them. On this bike, it is only the styling that will make some people think twice. If they go by overall performance only – handling, braking and comfort – they would be laying down the not inconsiderable amount of almost £13,000 ($22,000) immediately upon return of their test ride. The thing with a bike like this is that you really have to want a big tourer to pay this sort of money ,and it appears enough people do, because according to BMW the K1200LT is selling extremely well.*

**Seat height:** 770/800mm (30.03in/31.2in)

**Width:** 1080mm (42.12in)

**Trail:** 109mm (4.3in)

**Wheelbase:** 1633mm (63.6in)

## ENGINE

| | |
|---|---|
| Type | 4- stroke |
| Layout | in line four |
| Total displacement | 1171cc (71.5ci) |
| Bore | 70.5mm (2.7in) |
| Stroke | 75mm (2.9in) |
| Compression ratio | 10:8 |
| Valves | 4 per cylinder |
| Fuel system | electronic Motronic MA 2.4 |
| Ignition | electronic |
| Cooling | liquid |
| Maximum power | 87.17 bhp @ 6200rpm |
| Maximum torque | 86.54 bhp @ 4600rpm |

## TRANSMISSION

| | |
|---|---|
| Primary drive | gear |
| Clutch | dry, single plate |
| Gearbox | 5-speed |
| Final drive | shaft |

## WEIGHTS & CAPACITIES

| | |
|---|---|
| Tank capacity | 23.4l (6.1gal) |
| Wet weight | 378kg (833lb) |
| Weight distribution | |
| — front | N/A |
| — rear | N/A |
| Wheelbase | 1633mm (63.6in) |
| Overall length | 2508mm (97.8in) |
| Overall width | 1080mm (42.12in) |
| Overall height | N/A |
| Seat height | 770/800mm (30.03/31.2in) |

## CYCLE PARTS

| | |
|---|---|
| Frame | cast aluminium |
| Rake/trail | 26°/109mm |
| Front suspension | 35mm Telelever |
| Travel | 102mm (4.3in) |
| Adjustment | none |
| Rear suspension | Paralever |
| Travel | 130mm (5.1in) |
| Adjustment | preload |
| Tyres | |
| — make | N/A |
| — front | 120/70 x 17 |
| — rear | 160/70 x 17 |
| Brakes | |
| — make | BMW ABS |
| — front | 305mm dual disc, four-piston calipers |
| — rear | 285mm (11.2in) floating disc, four-piston caliper |

## TORQUE

## POWER

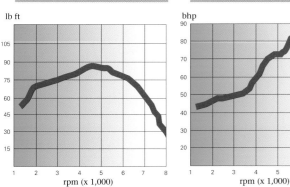

lb ft / bhp — rpm (x 1,000)

**Independent test measurements (above) differ from the manufacturer's claimed maximum power and maximum torque figures.**

**BMW** **K1200RS**

*BMW's first six-speed gearbox has a higher top ratio than ever before and is significantly slicker than many previous five-speed offerings.*

**Screen**
Adjustable, although most riders leave it in the lowest position, such is the bike's efficiency at wind protection.

**Steering damper**
A two-stage damper to ensure maximum stability is fitted as standard. It goes unnoticed in sweepers and fast turns and only makes its presence felt in tight, low speed turns.

**Adjustability**
The K1200RS features adjustable clip-ons, gear lever and footpegs, to ensure it ergonomically suits the majority who ride it.

**Weight**
The K1200RS tips the scales at 286.4kg (630lb) – not a bad result for a bike with so much on board.

**Rear frame**
As is to be expected, BMW's world-famous Paralever suspension and shaft drive combo makes an appearance.

**Brakes**
Tried and tested combination of four-piston Brembo calipers, floating discs and BMW's second generation anti-lock system inspires confidence and works tremendously in the wet.

**Offset**
The K1200RS' rear wheel has been offset by 5mm (0.2in) to accommodate a small but imperceptible weight bias to the right of the bike.

*K1200RS*

*With all the attributes* *you would expect from BMW, namely quality, reliability and superb engineering, plus a few more you might not – water cooled in-line motor, stylish looks and adjustable bars and footpegs – the K1200RS is designed to appeal to the broadest cross-section of buyers. From our impressions, it looks like BMW's succeeded.*

All-enclosing bodywork has been subjected to hundreds of hours of wind-tunnel testing in BMW's quest to rid the K-series of its flying brick image.

The massive fuel tank holds a substantial 25l (6.6gal). Range is perfectly suited for touring – 312km (194 miles).

Chassis design is an aluminium box section, which connects the front and rear suspension assemblies. Engine vibrations were a major reason for sticking with a separate frame.

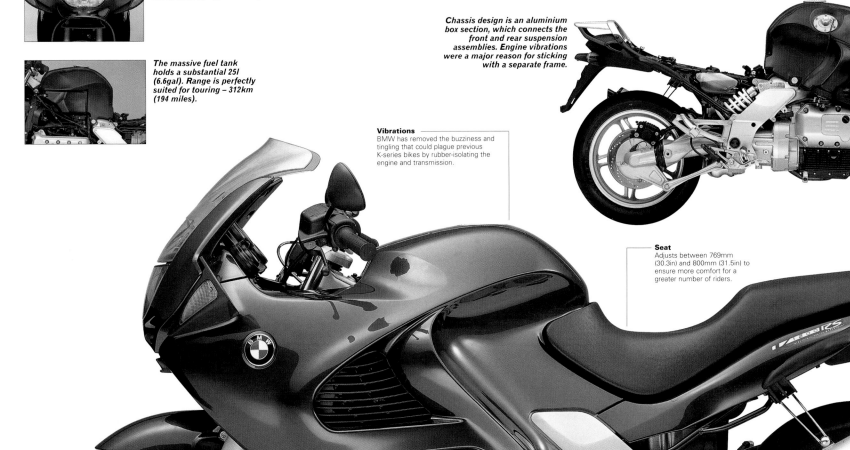

**Vibrations**
BMW has removed the buzziness and tingling that could plague previous K-series bikes by rubber-isolating the engine and transmission.

**Seat**
Adjusts between 769mm (30.3in) and 800mm (31.5in) to ensure more comfort for a greater number of riders.

**Engine**
Liquid and oil-cooled in-line four sports a 70.5 x 75mm (2.7 x 2.9in) bore and stroke, 1171cc (71.5ci) capacity and Bosch Motronic fuel injection. It is noted for its incredible mid-range torque.

**Wheelbase**
Lengthy 1549mm (61in) wheelbase ensures the K1200RS will have bags of stability but less ability to steer quickly through corners. This is as BMW intended for the sports-tourer model.

# Specifications

*The bike which finally* saw off the K-series' 'flying brick' image, the K1200RS, is a surprisingly quick sports tourer and a worthy alternative to Italian and Japanese machines. The in-line four sets it apart from most other BMWs, though this is one major element which contributes to the bike's weight – at 285kg (628lb) topped up, it is no bantam. This, and the bike's ride quality, may put some off, but these factors aside, the K1200RS is a highly sophisticated tourer with outstanding ergonomics and elegant looks, which might just appeal to non traditional BMW fans too.

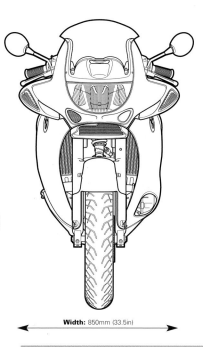

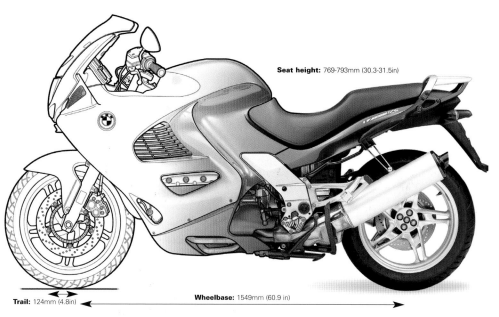

**Seat height:** 769-793mm (30.3-31.5in)

**Width:** 850mm (33.5in)

**Trail:** 124mm (4.8in)

**Wheelbase:** 1549mm (60.9 in)

## ENGINE

| | |
|---|---|
| Type | 4-stroke |
| Layout | in-line four |
| Total displacement | 1171cc (71.5ci) |
| Bore | 70.5mm (2.7in) |
| Stroke | 75mm (2.9in) |
| Compression ratio | N/A |
| Valves | 4 per cylinder |
| Fuel system | Bosch Motronic MA2.4 with throttle cut-off |
| Ignition | digital electronic |
| Cooling | liquid |
| Maximum power | 84.5kW (113.3bhp) @ 8100rpm |
| Maximum torque | 11.1kg-m (80.4 lb-ft) @ 6900rpm |

## TORQUE

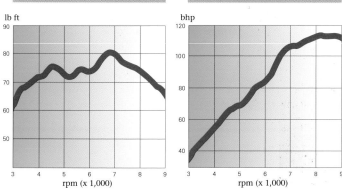

lb ft

rpm (x 1,000)

## POWER

bhp

rpm (x 1,000)

*Independent test measurements (above) differ from the manufacturer's claimed maximum power and maximum torque figures.*

## TRANSMISSION

| | |
|---|---|
| Primary drive | gear |
| Clutch | wet, multiplate |
| Gearbox | 6-speed |
| Final drive | shaft |

## WEIGHTS & CAPACITIES

| | |
|---|---|
| Tank capacity | 22l (4.99gal) |
| Wet weight | 285kg (628lb) |
| Weight distribution | |
| — front | N/A |
| — rear | N/A |
| Wheelbase | 1549mm (60.9in) |
| Overall length | 2250mm (88.5in) |
| Overall width | 850mm (33.5in) |
| Overall height | N/A |
| Seat height | 769–793mm (30.3–31.5in) |

## CYCLE PARTS

| | |
|---|---|
| Frame | cast aluminium, vibration decoupled engine mounting |
| Rake/trail | 37.25°/124mm (4.8in) |
| Front suspension | Telelever, centrally-mounted |
| leading link | |
| Travel | 115mm (4.5in) |
| Adjustment | N/A |
| Rear suspension | Paralever |
| Travel | 150mm (5.9in) |
| Adjustment | N/A |
| Tyres | |
| — make | varies |
| — front | 120/70 x 17 |
| — rear | 170/60 x 17 |
| Brakes | |
| — make | BMW |
| — front | 2 x 305mm (12in) floating discs, 4-piston floating calipers, ABS |
| — rear | 285mm (11.2in) disc, 2-piston fixed caliper, ABS |

# BMW R1200C

*BMW is proud of its quality of finish, and understandably so. The firm uses a specialist application technique and insists on at least two layers of clear topcoat lacquer. Rigorous inspections are carried out on the assembly and production lines.*

**Fuel tank**
Holds 17l (4.5gal).

**Engine**
Classic 'Boxer' design, but heavily updated. The bore and stroke is up from BMW's usual 99 x 70.5mm (3.9 x 2.7in) to 101 x 73mm (4 x 2.9in); the inlet and exhaust valves shrink from 36 to 34mm (1.6 to 1.3in) and 31 to 29mm (1.2 to 1.1in) respectively; there is a new camshaft configuration with shorter duration and stroke; and the electronic engine management system has been overhauled. Peak torque occurs at just 3000rpm.

**Clutch and gearbox**
Hydraulically operated single-plate dry clutch joins forces with a new five-speed gearbox design. The 'box is based on the six-speed unit fitted to the K1200RS. BMW is so confident of its design that the unit's service intervals have been extended from 20,000 to 40,000km (12,425 to 24,850 miles).

**Catalytic convertor**
As standard in all countries, and claimed to filter out up to 85 per cent of carbon monoxide, hydrocarbon and nitric oxide emissions. It is made of stainless steel and is finished in high-shine chrome.

**Silencers**
BMW says the utilisation of a Monolever rear end also allows the firm to use exactly the kind of silencers it wanted to on the R1200C. They say they could not have done it with the Paraleve. The R1200C became the first new BMW motorcycle to hit the market in over a decade with two silencers running on either side!

*R1200C*

**BMW is justifiably proud** *of its R1200C – now its best-selling bike. Very individual in its design, it appeals to both diehard BMW fans and cruiser fans of any ilk. The classic 'Boxer' engine has been updated and its riding position made more comfortable than most others by its long wheelbase.*

No pillion? Turn the seat into a rider's backrest, then. There are three different angles to choose from, and flipping it vertical also allows access to a chrome-plated aluminium rack. Excellent!

In keeping with the rest of the bike, the 'instrument panel' is very individual. Its minimalistic look will surprise many.

'Dynamically styled' cast aluminium is the order of the day for the front end of the frame, while the rear gets plain old steel tubing. The engine is used as a stressed member and the frame's front also serves as a mounting point for the Telelever suspension assembly.

**Riding position**
Utilising a long (1650mm [65in]) wheelbase meant giving the rider more room – so it is good of BMW to take advantage of this and push the rider's seat further rearward than usual while simultaneously shifting the footpegs further forward. The result is one of serene comfort for almost everyone.

**Brakes**
R1100GS stainless steel discs measuring 305mm (12in) have been used in conjuction with fixed four-piston Brembo calipers up front. The rear gets a 285mm (11.2in) disc and two-piston floating caliper, again just like the R1100GS. ABS is an optional extra.

**Monolever rear suspension**
The swingarm has been extended by 90mm (3.5in) to increase the wheelbase, which has allowed BMW's designers and engineers to swop back to the firm's old Monolever instead of Paralever design. The philosophy behind the move is that a long Monolever assembly "is just as efficient in balancing the reaction of the shaft drive" as a shorter and more complex double-joint Paralever.

**BMW** *R1200C*

# Specifications

*It is a bit of a mystery* as to why this is *BMW's biggest selling bike, especially since the German firm now has so many good two-wheelers on the road. Although the designers are supposed to have worked hard on the R1200C, many might be justified in wondering just what they were working on.*
*As a cruiser, it is not bad, but it is by no means overly good: suspension is harsh, steering is slow, anyone of even average height finds it uncomfortable and it vibrates terribly at anything resembling a high speed. But its brakes are reasonably good and the finish is good. For BMW fans only.*

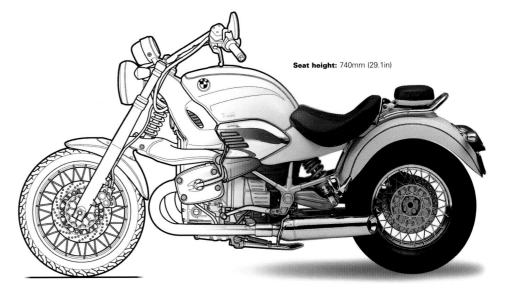

Seat height: 740mm (29.1in)

Width: 1050mm (41.3in)

Wheelbase: 1650mm (64.9in)

## ENGINE

| | |
|---|---|
| Type | 4-stroke |
| Layout | Boxer flat twin |
| Total displacement | 1170cc (71.4ci) |
| Bore | 101mm (4in) |
| Stroke | 73mm (2.9in) |
| Compression ratio | 10.0 |
| Valves | 4 per cylinder |
| Fuel system | Motronic |
| Ignition | electronic |
| Cooling | air/oil |
| Maximum power | 43kW (57.8bhp) @ 4700rpm |
| Maximum torque | 12.2kg-m (88.4lb-ft) @ 4500rpm |

## TRANSMISSION

| | |
|---|---|
| Primary drive | shaft |
| Clutch | dry, single-plate |
| Gearbox | 5-speed |
| Final drive | Monolever |

## WEIGHTS & CAPACITIES

| | |
|---|---|
| Tank capacity | 17.5l (4.6gal) |
| Dry weight | 256kg (564lb) |
| Weight distribution | |
| — front | N/A |
| — rear | N/A |
| Wheelbase | 1650mm (64.9in) |
| Overall length | 2340mm (92.1in) |
| Overall width | 1050mm (43.1in) |
| Overall height | N/A |
| Seat height | 740mm (29.1in) |

## CYCLE PARTS

| | |
|---|---|
| Frame | tubular space |
| Rake/trail | N/A |
| Front suspension | telelever |
| Travel | 144mm (5.6in) |
| Adjustment | spring |
| Rear suspension | paralever |
| Travel | 100mm (3.9in) |
| Adjustment | hydraulic spring |
| Tyres | |
| — make | N/A |
| — front | 100/90 x 18 |
| — rear | 170/80 x 15 |
| Brakes | |
| — make | N/A |
| — front | 305mm dual disc (12in) |
| — rear | 285mm (11.2in) single disc |

## TORQUE

## POWER

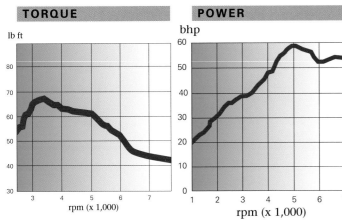

Independent test measurements (above) differ from the manufacturer's claimed maximum power and maximum torque figures.

# Buell  *X1 LIGHTNING*

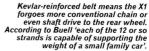

*Kevlar-reinforced belt means the X1 forgoes more conventional chain or even shaft drive to the rear wheel. According to Buell 'each of the 12 or so strands is capable of supporting the weight of a small family car'.*

*The underslung Showa monoshock unit looks odd but makes sense, allowing a shorter wheelbase while ensuring there are few maintenance-intensive linkages.*

**Headlight**
The headlight is lower than on previous Buells, and this, together with the taller windscreen, gives a more aggressive look.

**Airbox**
Buell is known for its huge and ugly airboxes, which are designed more with performance than aesthetics in mind. The X1's slims dramatically over previous models, however, and now looks almost as though it belongs to the bike.

**Brakes**
The front setup can fail suddenly after high numbers of quickly repeated hard stops from high speed (unlikely in normal use). Stopping to allow the huge 340mm (13.4in) disc, six-piston caliper and the fluid to cool down restores bite. This appears to be a fluid problem.

**X1 LIGHTNING**

*If you are looking for a fight,* look no further than Buell's new beast. From every aspect, it looks as though it is waiting to pounce on the next unsuspecting bike to come its way. Yes, it looks diffferent, but so what? And its performance is great – certainly not what you might be expecting.

**Fuelling**
New-for-'99, the X1's 'Dynamic Digital Fuel Injection' replaces the carburettor used on 1998's hot-shot White Lightning, and is made by a subcontracted firm in Milwaukee, the home of Buell. It worked poorly on pre-production models and is still not fully sorted now, metering fuel efficiently only from 3500 rpm and above. Below this, throttle lag and misfires sometimes occur.

**Front suspension**
The X1 uses Showa units instead of the White Lightning's WP forks, but there is still something of flaw: the upside-downers are adjustable only for compression and rebound damping. And there is no preload. That said, they work brilliantly.

**Weight distribution**
Buell claims a 52 per cent bias toward the rear, yet the X1 can still feel a fraction nose-heavy in corners.

**Dry weight**
No fairy at 440 lb (200 kg), the X1 is a full 15 lb (6.8 kg) heavier than the White Lightning.

The redesigned rear header pipe now runs closer to the engine (courtesy of a redesigned frame which allows this), thus meaning that riding a Buell no longer equals a cooked lower right leg.

Chrome-moly tubing, based on previous Buells but now widened (and, crucially, lengthened) where it counts – around the engine. This allows the exhaust downpipes to be resituated.

**Seat**
Wider for '99, thanks partly to the redesigned frame, it is just 75cm (29.5in) tall and places the rider in a comfortable position in relation to the handlebars and modestly rear-set footpegs. A small storage area hides below.

**Planted**
Despite a rake angle of only 23˚ and just 88.9mm (3.5in) trail, plus a short wheelbase of 1397mm (54.9in), the X1 is remarkably stable on almost all road surfaces and particularly through corners.

**Engine**
Made by parent company Harley-Davidson to Buell's own specification, the air-cooled 'Thunderstorm' V-twin motor displaces 1203cc (73.4ci) and makes a claimed 70kW (95bhp) @ 6200 rpm and 11.8kg-m (86lb-ft) of torque @ 5600 rpm.

**Swingarm**
The cast swingarm not only looks far better than previous spindly offerings, but is claimed to be stronger and more rigid too.

# Buell X1 LIGHTNING

# Specifications

*The styling of any Buell* is distinctive, due in no small part to the design of the stainless steel header pipes. It is the ultimate streetfighter in appearance, and its performance should not be sniffed at either. For 2000, there have been relatively few changes, but all significant. Many Buell owners will be pleased to see a recalibrated engine control module introduced to overcome the teething problems of the Dynamic Digital Fuel Injection system. And Buell is offering a free upgrade of this system to all owners of fuel injected 1999 Buells. The transmission and braking system have also been upgraded and the engine is now fitted with a stronger, straight crank pin and smaller valve lifters to reduce inertia.

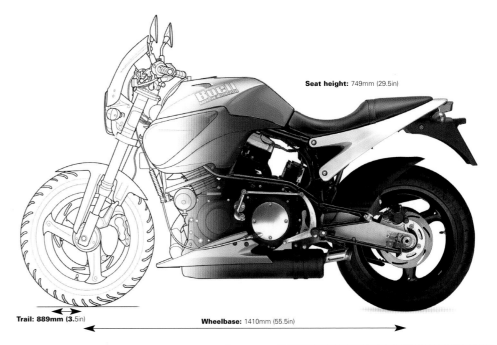

Seat height: 749mm (29.5in)

Width: 760mm (29.64in)

Trail: 889mm (3.5in)

Wheelbase: 1410mm (55.5in)

## ENGINE

| | |
|---|---|
| Type | 4-stroke |
| Layout | 54° V-twin |
| Total displacement | 1203cccc |
| Bore | 88.8mm (3.5in) |
| Stroke | 96.8mm (3.8in) |
| Compression ratio | 10:1 |
| Valves | 2 per cylinder |
| Fuel system | digital fuel injection |
| Ignition | electronic |
| Cooling | air |
| Maximum power | 55kW (73.77 bhp) @ 5600 rpm |
| Maximum torque | 9.75kg-m (70.55 lb-ft) @ 5300 rpm |

## TORQUE

## POWER

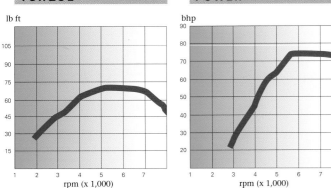

Independent test measurements (above) differ from the manufacturer's claimed maximum power and maximum torque figures.

## TRANSMISSION

| | |
|---|---|
| Primary drive | chain |
| Clutch | wet, multiplate |
| Gearbox | five-speed, constant mesh |
| Final drive | Kevlar belt |

## WEIGHTS & CAPACITIES

| | |
|---|---|
| Tank capacity | 16.33l (4.3gal) |
| Dry weight | 200kg (440lb) |
| Weight distribution | |
| — front | N/A |
| — rear | N/A |
| Wheelbase | 1410mm (55.5in) |
| Overall length | 2070mm (80.73in) |
| Overall width | 760mm (29.64in) |
| Overall height | 1170mm (45.63in) |
| Seat height | 749mm (29.5in) |

## CYCLE PARTS

| | |
|---|---|
| Frame | tubular perimeter chrome-moly, vibration isolation system |
| Rake/trail | 23°/889mm (3.5in) |
| Front suspension | Showa inverted forks |
| Travel | 119mm (4.7in) |
| Adjustment | compression and rebound damping |
| Rear suspension | Showa extension type damper |
| Travel | 11.7cm (4.6in) |
| Adjustment | compression and rebound damping, spring preload |
| Tyres | |
| — make | Dunlop |
| — front | 120/70 x 17 |
| — rear | 170/60 x 17 |
| Brakes | |
| — make | N/A |
| — front | 340mm (13.3in) floating rotor, 6-piston caliper |
| — rear | 230mm (9in) rotor, single piston caliper |

# CAGIVA GRAN CANYON 900

*The headlamps are minimalist in keeping with the bike's bodywork design. Only one works on dip; main beam is good, but not great, and is a limiting factor in fast night riding.*

**Fairing screen**
A token effort in keeping with the rest of the styling., this offers adequate wind protection to shorter riders, although six-footers may find that at high speed an unwelcome blast intrudes upon the ride.

**Clutch**
Operated by a four-way span adjustable lever, its action is pleasant and light, though clutch slip can be a problem after repeated wheelies when the engine is running hot. Waiting 20 minutes or so restores full bite, although this definitely shows up a weakness.

**Steering lock**
Poor, which can mean three point turns in the middle of the road.

**Front mudguard**
Its close proximity to the tyre is a clear indication (together with tyre choice) that the Gran Canyon is not intended as a proper off-road bike. Hit mud and the whole lot will clog in a second.

**Exhausts**
À la Ducati 916, only not quite as trick, the under seat pipe layout helps minimize the bike's lines at the rear. Grunty sound under power.

**GRAN CANYON 900**

**Wheels**
Thankfully standard-sized 43.2cm (17in) items, the spoked hoops allow a huge range of tyres to be fitted. The standard Pirellis are acceptable, but road riders would be better off opting for stickier, sportier rubber if riding hard is the intended purpose.

**Grab rail**
Doubles as a sandwich box carrier, looks odd, but actually serves passengers well.

*What the Gran Canyon really, really wants is to go blasting down twisty, beaten-up back roads or twisty main roads. Off-road, this is fantastic fun and wants to take you absolutely anywhere, while in town the tall seat gives the rider an advantage in traffic. Many believe it to be overpriced, and it certainly does not come cheap, but it would make a great second bike.*

*The speedo is displayed in 20km/h (12.4miles) increments to 220km/h (137mph). Countries which require mph readouts simply get a tacky overlay sticker which displays speeds up to 70mph (130km/h) only. Rev counter displays a maximum readout of 11,000 rpm, with a redline of 9000 rpm. Ignition cut-out is at 9750 rpm.*

*The 904cc 90° V-twin is simply a fuel-injected version of Ducati's 900SS Supersport powerplant. It is air-cooled and has a bore and stroke of 92 x 68mm (3.6 x 2.7in).*

**Suspension**
Front 45mm (1.7in) forks and rear Boge monoshock offer a decent range of adjustment and are set-up to cope with bumpy roads admirably well. Component finish quality at both ends is high.

**Seat**
Superbly comfortable for the rider and acceptably so for passengers, it is both broad and well-padded.

**Bash plate**
The underslung engine guard looks the part but, unless you are fond of riding up kerbs quickly, it will not be needed, since the Gran Canyon is pretty hopeless off road.

**Wheelbase**
About right for its intended class at 1530mm (60.2in), it aids stability but, combined with the Gran Canyon's lowish centre of gravity and rear weight bias, compromises the bike's abilities to manage trailie-ubiquitous stoppies.

# CAGIVA GRAN CANYON 900

# Specifications

*It is widely seen as the new trailie on the block, but the Gran Canyon is, in fact, a difficult bike to categorize. And that is not a fault; quite the reverse, because what it means is that this 900 can do almost anything. It is good in traffic, will take the motorways with ease, but get it out on back lanes and tight, twisty roads and it is in its element. Great styling, good handling and, best of all, brilliant fun. Read on and allow your eyes to be opened to the facts and figures making up this winning machine.*

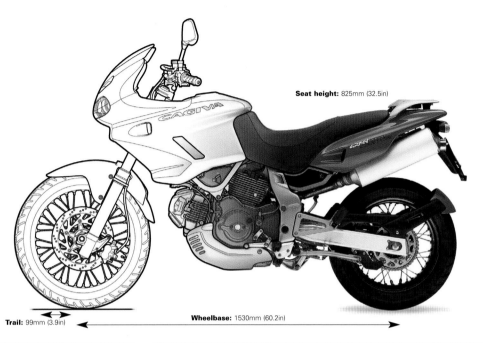

**Seat height:** 825mm (32.5in)

**Width:** 790mm (31in)

**Trail:** 99mm (3.9in)

**Wheelbase:** 1530mm (60.2in)

## ENGINE

| | |
|---|---|
| Type | 4-stroke |
| Layout | 90° |
| Total displacement | 904cc (55ci) |
| Bore | 92mm (3.6in) |
| Stroke | 68mm (2.7in) |
| Compression ratio | 9:2:1 |
| Valves | 2 per cylinder |
| Fuel system | Weber fuel injection, one injector per cylinder |
| Ignition | electronic |
| Cooling | air/oil |
| Maximum power | 48kW (64.4bhp) @ 7400rpm |
| Maximum torque | 7.3kg-m (52.7lb-ft) @ 5200rpm |

## TORQUE

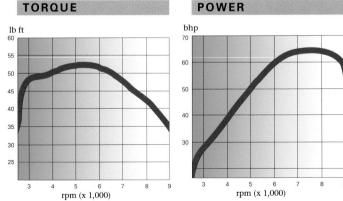

lb ft

rpm (x 1,000)

## POWER

bhp

rpm (x 1,000)

**Independent test measurements (above) differ from the manufacturer's claimed maximum power and maximum torque figures.**

## TRANSMISSION

| | |
|---|---|
| Primary drive | gear |
| Clutch | dry, multiplate |
| Gearbox | 6-speed |
| Final drive | chain |

## WEIGHTS & CAPACITIES

| | |
|---|---|
| Tank capacity | 20l (5.3 galls) |
| Dry weight | 218kg (479.6lb) |
| Weight distribution | |
| — front | N/A |
| — rear | N/A |
| Wheelbase | 1530mm (60.2in) |
| Overall length | 2200mm (86.6in) |
| Overall width | 790mm (31.1in) |
| Overall height | N/A |
| Seat height | 825mm (32.5in) |

## CYCLE PARTS

| | |
|---|---|
| Frame | single tube cradle |
| Rake/trail | 99mm (3.9in) |
| Front suspension | 45mm (1.7in) Marzocchi telescopic forks |
| Travel | 170mm (6.7in) |
| Adjustment | |
| Rear suspension | Boge monoshock |
| Travel | 170mm (6.7in) |
| Adjustment | spring preload, rebound damping |
| Tyres | |
| — make | Dunlop D604/ Pirelli MT80/ Metzeler Enduro/ Michelin T66/ Bridgestone Trail Wing |
| — front | 110/80 x 19 (Dunlop, Pirelli, Metzeler), 110/90 x 19 (Michelin, Bridgestone) |
| — rear | 150/70 x 17 |
| Brakes | |
| — make | Nissin |
| — front | 2 x 296mm (11.7in) discs, 2-piston calipers |
| — rear | 240mm (9.5in) disc, 2-piston caliper |

# CAGIVA *RAPTOR*

**Handlebars**
The Raptor's wide handlebars and sit-up riding position put the rider right in control. Cagiva also produced a V-Raptor, with a small nose cone and lower handlebars.

**Front brakes**
The front Brembo brakes use dual four-piston calipers. Braided steel hoses give a firm feel at the lever and strong stopping power.

**Suspension**
The rear double-sided swingarm is made from extruded aluminium. It operates an adjustable rear monoshock.

**Exhaust**
The stainless steel system is a two-into-two design, with a pair of large-volume silencers. Oval-shaped exhausts give extra ground clearance for faster cornering.

**Tyres**
Wide, sticky radial sports tyres are fitted to lightweight, cast-aluminium alloy wheels.

# *RAPTOR*

***The Cagiva Raptor is a*** *machine which combines the best of both worlds: Italian flair in chassis design and styling, and Japanese efficiency in a reliable, powerful engine. Designed by the man who created Ducati's Monster, the Cagiva Raptor is a high-performance city roadster, with Japanese power courtesy of a Suzuki TL1000S engine.*

*Stripped down, the minimalistic steel tube trellis frame of the Raptor can be seen. It is much stiffer than it looks. The chassis also features radical design elements, with angular footrest hangers, sharp-edged bodywork and, in the V-Raptor variant, an aggressive nose cone.*

**Engine**
The Raptor's 996cc (60.7ci) water-cooled, eight-valve 90° V-twin engine is a re-badged TL1000S item, with Cagiva's own fuel injection and exhaust systems.

**Steering head**
The Raptor has a steep steering head angle, which allows quick turning. But this can lead to instability over bumpy surfaces, and many owners fit a steering damper.

**Seat**
The Raptor has a single-piece dual seat for rider and pillion. It comes with a plastic rear seat cover, for use when there is no passenger.

# CCM  604E

*Opinions vary about the comfort of the seat. Most find it very hard but some reckon it is comfortable. The bodywork is also very basic and some consider it more plain than is necessary.*

**Throttle**
Throttle response is amazingly quick – and we do mean quick. Any tiny mistaken movement of the throttle may send you lurching forward. Beware!

**Headlight**
The very small headlight is, again, only there to make it road legal. This is not a bike you should be riding at night.

**Suspension**
In addition to the very good forks, the CCM is equipped with the excellent White Power shocks at the rear. Put them together and you are in for a smooth ride – most of the time.

## 604E

**The CCM 604E may be road legal,**
*but do not assume that makes it a bike suited to the road. It certainly is not – not by any stretch of the imagination, although it will perform adequately enough on the tarmac. The point is that this is a true enduro machine and is made to be ridden hard, but off the road, not on it.*

**Brakes**
A single disc at the fornt and another disc at the rear. The brakes are pretty sharp and will not let you down.

**Tyres**
In keeping with the rest of the bike's components, the CCM is equipped with good tyres in the form of Corsa compound Pirelli Dragons, which work super-well in the dirt.

**Wheelbase**
With a wheelbase of 1512mm (59.5in) and a dry weight of 132kg (354lb), this is an easy bike to chuck around, as it should be. And picking it up after you have dropped it is no sweat at all.

*This is as good as it gets on the CCM. You will not see any of the myriad of clocks we have become accustomed to on bikes. If it is not absolutely necessary, the CCM will not have it – which is no bad thing on a bike such as this.*

*The headlight and rear light are both little better than useless. Never try to ride this at night – they are fitted strictly for legality purposes.*

*The engine on the CCM is a lot peakier than you might expect. It is powerful and very, very responsive. The lightweight crankshaft and drive train transmit power instantly through to the back tyre.*

**Seat**
Expect nothing at all from this. It is there simply because a bike has to have a seat. Anyway, when off the road, you are likely to be standing on the pegs more often than sitting on that hard little blue thing.

**Front end**
46mm (1.8in) Paioli forks contribute to the good feeling you get from the suspension, especially for road use.

**Wheels**
53.3cm (21in) at the front and 48.2cm (18in) at the rear, the wheels are wire spoked. Wire spokes may suit the look of the bike but are no help after a heavy day in the dirt when you are trying to clean them.

**Cooling**
The CCM is air-cooled but also has help from oil running through the frame, which acts like a giant radiator.

**Engine**
The 597cc (36.4ci) single cylinder air-cooled four stroke is strong and a lot smoother than you might expect, with an edge to it which you should enjoy.

**CCM** *604E*

# Specifications

*If you are looking for some* mad, wild fun, take a look at this piece of kit! This is the bike which will encourage you to go right to the edge – but only off road. You can be completely manic in traffic, though this is not advisable despite the fact that it handles and brakes very well.
*It has a rough edge to it, and the noise it makes just may attract unwanted attention on the road. Nor is it built for that. This is a competition bike which is only just road legal. Take it on the tarmac only when on your way to do some serious off-roading.*

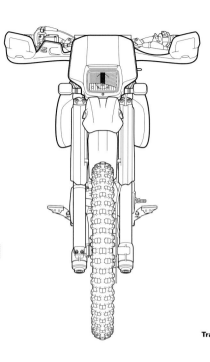

**Seat height:** 925mm (36.4in)

**Trail:** 114.3mm (4.5in)

**Wheelbase:** 1530mm (60.2in)

## ENGINE

| | |
|---|---|
| Type | 4-stroke |
| Layout | single cylinder |
| Total displacement | 597cc (36.4ci) |
| Bore | 97mm (3.8in) |
| Stroke | 81mm (3.1in) |
| Compression ratio | 10:1 |
| Valves | 4 per cylinder |
| Fuel system | Dellorto VHSB 39 flat slide carbs |
| Ignition | electronic CDI |
| Cooling | air |
| Maximum power | 26.5kW (35.5bhp) @ 7400rpm |
| Maximum torque | 3.6kg-m (26.2lb-ft) @ 6700rpm |

## TRANSMISSION

| | |
|---|---|
| Primary drive | N/A |
| Clutch | wet, multiplate |
| Gearbox | 5-speed |
| Final drive | chain |

## WEIGHTS & CAPACITIES

| | |
|---|---|
| Tank capacity | 13.6l (3.6gal) |
| Dry weight | 130kg (287lb) |
| Weight distribution | |
| — front | N/A |
| — rear | N/A |
| Wheelbase | 1530mm (60.2in) |
| Overall length | N/A |
| Overall width | N/A |
| Overall height | N/A |
| Seat height | 925mm (36.4in) |

## CYCLE PARTS

| | |
|---|---|
| Frame | twin cradle |
| Rake/trail | 27.5/114.3mm (4.5in) |
| Front suspension | 46mm (1.8in) conventional fork |
| Travel | N/A |
| Adjustment | compression, rebound |
| Rear suspension | piggy-back shock |
| Travel | N/A |
| Adjustment | preload, compression, rebound |
| Tyres | |
| — make | Pirelli Dragon |
| — front | 120/70 x 17 |
| — rear | 150/60 x 17 |
| Brakes | |
| — make | |
| — front | 320mm (1.3in) disc, two-piston caliper |
| — rear | 220mm (8.6in) disc, two-piston caliper |

## TORQUE

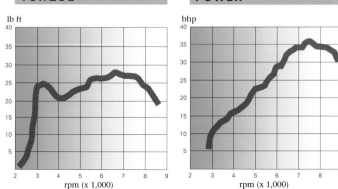

lb ft — rpm (x 1,000)

## POWER

bhp — rpm (x 1,000)

Independent test measurements (above) differ from the manufacturer's claimed maximum power and maximum torque figures.

# DUCATI M600 DARK

*At the front, braking is provided by a single 320mm (12.6in) disc, mounted on the left side and wearing a two-piston caliper. Performance is adequate and no more.*

**Mirrors**
Mounted exactly where they need to be for decent rear view. Blur from intrusive vibration is present, but not in any great quantity.

**Instrument panel**
The standard array of idiot lights is there, but reading it can be difficult in bright sunshine. The bulbs are not strong enough.

**Headlamp**
Adequate beam that can spend half of its time in the air thanks to the M600's wheelie potential. Occasionally works loose after a bad landing, but easily cured with two turns of an Allen key.

**Horn**
Hidden above the front cylinder and mounted horizontally from the frame. Ours sounded like a croaky duck in distress.

**Rear mudguard**
Many people do not even notice the mudguard thanks to its black colour and tyre-hugging fit – and advantage in the winter months.

**M600 DARK**

**With its exposed trellis** *frame and dark hue, the Monster Dark looks every inch the sinister motorcycle. It also has a certain style, and along with its bigger brothers, is begining to attain a cult status. But it not only looks the part, it goes too, especially when the road opens up. With the 583cc (35.6ci) V-twin making a claimed 38kW (51bhp), you will have no problem seeing the far side of 177km/h (110mph).*

**Tyres**
Dunlops are favoured as standard, in the UK anyway, and come in 120/60 x 17 front and 160/60 x 17 rear sizes. They cope well with the bike's standard power output, but changing to stickier rubber allows more aggressive powering out of corners.

**Exhausts**
As stylish as ever, but still plagued by the ground clearance problems of its bigger 750cc (45.7ci)and 900cc (54.9ci) stablemates. Chamfered silencers say it all.

Just 770mm (30.3in) tall, making the Monster Dark attractive to shorter riders and women. Comfort is good too, though hanging on at top speed can be a chore thanks to the bike's naked design.

Trick, or what? Inverted 40mm (1.6in) front suspension looks the business, provides acceptable damping, and offers a fairly standard 120mm (4.7in) of travel. Sadly, they are not adjustable.

Another Ducati trait, the instantly recognizable tubular steel trellis frame. It enhances the bike's mysterious tones, bringing realism to its 'Dark' name.

**Fuel tank**
Holds 16.5l (4.4gal).

**Pillion comforts**
There are none! Jump on, lean forward and suffer. Anyone with long limbs will find the footpegs mounted too high and there is little room for the bottom!

**Engine**
90° V-twin, as you would espect from Ducati, is air-cooled, uses twin 38mm carburettors, makes a claimed 51bhp at the crank and has a 583cc (35.6ci) displacement. The two valves per cylinder are desmodromically-operated, there's a bore and stroke of 80 x 58mm (3.1 x 2.3in), a 10.7:1 compression ratio and five-speed gearbox.

**Rear suspension**
Progressive linkage monoshock has spring preload as well as rebound damping adjustment and fairly long travel at 144mm (5.7in).

# DUCATI M600 DARK

# Specifications

**The baby Monster might** look identical to its bigger brothers, but there are measurable differences, as our specifications panel reveals.

The engine's a 90° V-twin, as is to be expected from Ducati, air-cooled with two desmodromically-operated valves per cylinder. The frame is Ducati's instantly recognizable tubular steel trellis with inverted 40mm (1.6in) forks, which suit the bike down to the ground. As mentioned before, this has become something of a cult bike, due mainly to its looks.

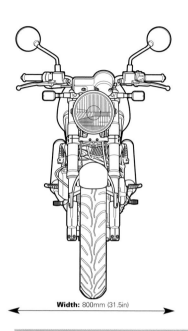

Width: 800mm (31.5in)

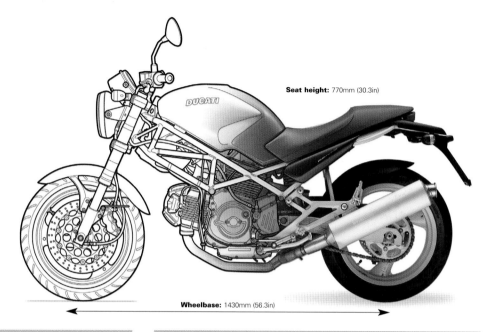

Seat height: 770mm (30.3in)

Wheelbase: 1430mm (56.3in)

## ENGINE

| | |
|---|---|
| Type | 4-stroke |
| Layout | 90° V-twin |
| Total displacement | 583cc (35.6ci) |
| Bore | 80mm (3.1in) |
| Stroke | 58mm (2.28in) |
| Compression ratio | 10.7:1 |
| Valves | 2 per cylinder |
| Fuel system | 2 x 38mm carburettors |
| Ignition | digital electronic |
| Cooling | air |
| Maximum power | 35.6kW (47.8bhp) @ 7800rpm |
| Maximum torque | 4.7kg-m (34.3lb-ft) @ 5900rpm |

## TRANSMISSION

| | |
|---|---|
| Primary drive | gear |
| Clutch | dry, multiplate |
| Gearbox | 5-speed |
| Final drive | chain |

## WEIGHTS & CAPACITIES

| | |
|---|---|
| Tank capacity | 16.5l (4.4gal) |
| Dry weight | 174kg (384lb) |
| Weight distribution | |
| — front | N/A |
| — rear | N/A |
| Wheelbase | 1430mm (56.3in) |
| Overall length | 2070mm (81.5in) |
| Overall width | 800mm (31.5in) |
| Overall height | 1030mm (40.6in) |
| Seat height | 770mm (30.3in) |

## CYCLE PARTS

| | |
|---|---|
| Frame | tubular steel trellis |
| Rake/trail | N/A |
| Front suspension | inverted 40mm (1.6in) forks |
| Travel | 120mm (4.7in) |
| Adjustment | none |
| Rear suspension | progressive linkage, monoshock |
| Travel | 144mm (5.7in) |
| Adjustment | preload, plus rebound damping |
| Tyres | |
| — make | Dunlop / varies |
| — front | 120/60 x 17 |
| — rear | 160/60 x 17 |
| Brakes | |
| — make | Brembo |
| — front | 320mm (12.6in) disc, single caliper |
| — rear | 245mm (9.7in) disc, single caliper |

## TORQUE

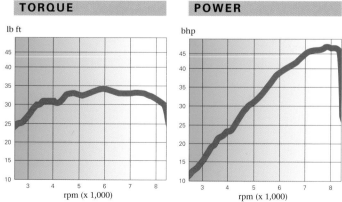

lb ft

rpm (x 1,000)

## POWER

bhp

rpm (x 1,000)

Independent test measurements (above) differ from the manufacturer's claimed maximum power and maximum torque figures.

# DUCATI 748 BIPOSTO

*Virtually unique thanks to its lack of graphics, the fuel tank holds 17l (4.5gal). Beware blocked breather pipes, which can create a tank-denting vacuum.*

**Fuel system**
Electronic fuel injection works glitch-free for the most part and has proved to be ultra-reliable. Though responsive, it thankfully does not deliver the kind of instant snap that can cause tyre traction problems while getting back on the gas exiting corners.

**Mirrors**
Shorter riders may find them acceptable; taller owners often complain of visible bodyparts blocking the rear view. Often the first things to go if the bike falls off its stand, they are expensive to replace.

**Forks**
Inverted 43mm (1.7in) forks look the business and handle brilliantly too. Many riders are staggered by the grip, feel and behaviour of the 748's front end, which holds an excellent line through corners and feeds copious information back to the user every time.

**Fairing**
As with the 916, the beautifully sculpted fairing panels help make the bike a true style icon. Minimalist graphics are either loved or loathed. Recent spares price reductions mean bodywork replacement costs are no longer massive in the event of a spill.

**Tyres**
Fat 120/60 front and 180/55 rear tyres are ZR-rated for speeds over 240km/h (150mph). Many owners opt for the stickiest but quickest-wearing compounds in a bid to let them take their bikes to the very edge in relative safety. Popular sizes mean a huge choice is available.

**Rear suspension**
Set firmly at the factory, the Showa unit, which is fully-adjustable, may take a little getting used to. Once acquainted, owners will find it's as good as the outstanding front forks. What more can be said?

## 748

***Introduced in 1995**, the 748 didn't seem much – just a 916 copy with less power. However, since then it has made a bit of a hit amongst punters, not least because of the individual character of its engine and its superb chassis. It may lack the outright power of a four-cylinder 600, but it is not much slower out on the road. For anyone who likes Italian styling, this is a bike worthy of attention.*

*Mounted across the front of the tank instead of, more usually, to one side of the frame, the steering damper can damage paintwork if not correctly aligned.*

*The silencers exit from under the seat rather than to the side of the bike, helping the 748 to keep its minimalist lines. Many owners say they are the best-looking components on the bike. They are often replaced by aftermarket units, with a carbon fibre finish proving popular.*

*Basically a smaller version of Ducati's 916 motor, the 748's 90° V-twin packs beautiful low-range grunt and is blessed with a gearbox with excellent ratios for the road. Ducati claims it makes 72kW (97bhp) @ 11,000 rpm compared with the 916's 84kW (112 bhp) @ 8500rpm.*

**Seat**
Many owners initially complain of the firmness and also of extreme riding position, but quickly become accustomed to it to the point where riding other sportsters can feel strange. For all its race orientation, however, riding long distances is still possible.

**Front brakes**
The twin Brembo caliper, pad, and 320mm (12.6in) disc combination at the front behaves differently to many Japanese sportster arrangements. While Asian machines often have tremendous initial bite, which, arguably, could catch lesser-experienced riders unawares in an emergency, the 748's stoppers grab gently at first but still have plenty of power.

**Sidestand**
Self-retracting once the bike's weight is removed, many owners choose to modify them to prevent this. Bolt-on plates to adjust the spring's returning properties are commonly available.

**Swingarm**
Single-sided swingarm facilitates quick wheel changes, looks great and confuses non-bikers viewing the 748 from its right hand side. It is heavy, though.

# DUCATI 748 BIPOSTO

# Specifications

*Similar in looks to its* revered 996 bigger brother, the Ducati 748 utilizes the same fine blend of chassis and engine technology. So we have the exquisite eight-valve V-twin *Desmo*, but in smaller capacity mode; and the reduced displacement, lighter flywheels and a higher compression ratio, allowing the Italian Supersport contender to peak at 11,000 rpm. A great trackday machine, the 748 is often likely to surprise those who would dismiss it on the strength of its horsepower output. Do not underestimate the 748.

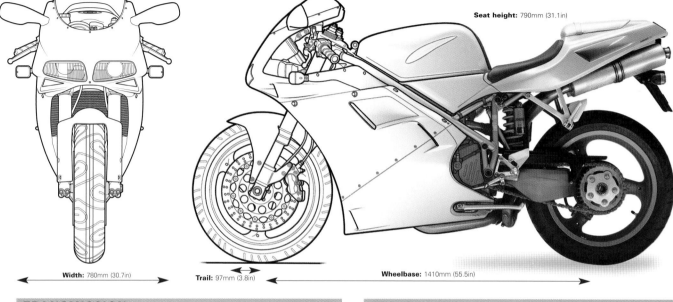

**Seat height:** 790mm (31.1in)

**Width:** 780mm (30.7in)  **Trail:** 97mm (3.8in)  **Wheelbase:** 1410mm (55.5in)

## ENGINE

| | |
|---|---|
| Type | 4-stroke |
| Layout | 90° V-twin |
| Total displacement | 748cc (45.6ci) |
| Bore | 88mm (3.5in) |
| Stroke | 61.5mm (2.4in) |
| Compression ratio | N/A |
| Valves | 4 per cylinder |
| Fuel system | electronic fuel injection |
| Ignition | digital electronic |
| Cooling | liquid |
| Maximum power | 70kW (94.1bhp) @ 10,838rpm |
| Maximum torque | 7.4kg-m (53.5lb-ft) @ 8600rpm |

## TORQUE

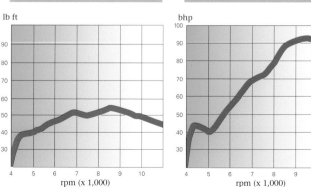

lb ft

rpm (x 1,000)

## POWER

bhp

rpm (x 1,000)

## TRANSMISSION

| | |
|---|---|
| Primary drive | gear |
| Clutch | dry, multi-plate |
| Gearbox | 6-speed |
| Final drive | chain |

## WEIGHTS & CAPACITIES

| | |
|---|---|
| Tank capacity | 17l (4.4gal) |
| Dry weight | 196kg (432lb) |
| Weight distribution | |
| — front | N/A |
| — rear | N/A |
| Wheelbase | 1410mm (55.5in) |
| Overall length | 2030mm (79.9in) |
| Overall width | 780mm (30.7in) |
| Overall height | 1080mm (42.5in) |
| Seat height | 790mm (31.1in) |

## CYCLE PARTS

| | |
|---|---|
| Frame | tubular steel trellis |
| Rake/trail | 24°/97mm (3.8in) |
| Front suspension | inverted 43mm forks |
| Travel | 127mm (5.0in) |
| Adjustment | preload, plus compression and rebound damping |
| Rear suspension | progressive linkage, monoshock |
| Travel | 130mm (5.1in) |
| Adjustment | preload, plus compression and rebound damping |
| Tyres | |
| — make | varies |
| — front | 120/60 x 17 |
| — rear | 180/55 x 17 |
| Brakes | |
| — make | Brembo |
| — front | 2 x 320mm (12.6in) discs, opposed 2-piston calipers |
| — rear | 220mm (8.6in) disc, single caliper |

**Independent test measurements (above) differ from the manufacturer's claimed maximum power and maximum torque figures.**

# DUCATI 748R

The gold-coloured titanium nitride coating on the Showa front fork stanchions reduces static friction or 'stiction'. This improves finesse and feel from the fully adjustable suspension components.

**Ergonomics**
Fabulous fairing design and wicked looking twin headlight arrangement in the self-same mould as its big brother, the 996 give this Ducati an air of purpose and understated aggression. The instrumentation is comprehensive and well thought out – everything is where you would expect it to be.

**Fuel system**
Cylinders fire by way of an electronic ignition that works in conjunction with an indirect-type Marelli electronic fuel injection system. This system uses 50mm (2in) throttle bodies with each cylinder fed by one nozzle, and requires at least 92-octane fuel to ensure proper combustion.

**Brakes**
The brakes on the 748R are hydraulic, twin 320mm (12.6in) floating discs squeezed by four-piston calipers up front with a single 220mm (8.6in) disc and two-piston caliper residing out back. The discs are mounted to lightweight three (or five)-spoke alloy rims that do a good job of highlighting the beautiful single-sided swing arm.

**Riding position**
Small slim tank, high and firm seat and handlebars that throw your weight forward on to your wrists. Straightaway, you know that you are riding something special, designed for one thing and one thing only – going fast.

## 748R

***This Ducati is a strange manifestation** in the 916 mould. A seven-fifty from a name like **Ducati** should be pretty impressive, but the pieces just do not fit in this case. For those who ever ridden a 916, the first ride proves a notable disappointment! Although it has all the looks, it fails to come up to scratch as far as power is concerned!*

*A single seat unit and no pillion footrests confirm the 748R as a machine for solo pleasures only.*

*The classically engineered, and typically Ducati, frame is of the trestle type constructed of 'ALS 450' chrome moly steel alloy tubes. It is rigid and well proven on the 996; this is Italian engineering that even Ferrari should admire.*

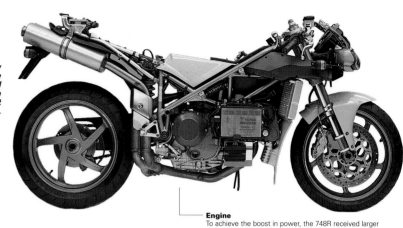

**Engine**
To achieve the boost in power, the 748R received larger valves than its predecessor. NC-machined cylinder heads, similar to those found in the competition 996, are also a new addition and 54mm (2.1in) throttle bodies with new injectors raised above the air intake tracts.

**Power**
Power noticeably rushes in at 7500rpm, but not with the sudden punch of Supersport in-line fours with similar peak-power numbers. This twin revs slower than the average in-line motor, but not as slow as Ducati's 750 Supersport.

**Style**
A classic racing style for the pipes gives the 748R the finished look in terms of its aspirations, but the seat is uncomfortable and the peg positioning could be better.

DUCATI

desmoquattro
**748**

# DUCATI 748R

# Specifications

*The specifications for the* 748R *tell the whole story –* this is a sports bike built to win races, especially the Supersport World Championship, and the refinements made to it for 2001mean that Ducati is surely moving down the right road. It now has a lighter flywheel and crankshaft and the piston has also been lightened for greater acceleration and higher speeds. The gearbox for the new model has adopted a vacuum precision-cast Desmodromic gear selector drum, again for lighter weight and better accuracy. The power delivery remains the same.

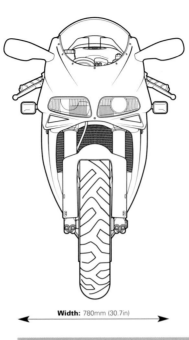

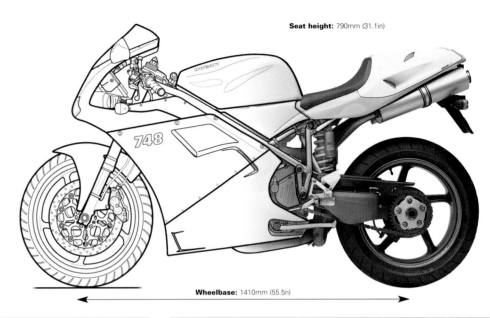

**Seat height:** 790mm (31.1in)

**Width:** 780mm (30.7in)

**Wheelbase:** 1410mm (55.5n)

## ENGINE

| | |
|---|---|
| Type | 4-stroke |
| Layout | Desmodromic V-twin |
| Total displacement | 748cc (45.5ci) |
| Bore | 88mm (3.46in) |
| Stroke | 61.5mm (2.4in) |
| Compression ratio | 11.3:1 |
| Valves | 2 per cylinder |
| Fuel system | electronic fuel injection |
| Ignition | electronic |
| Cooling | liquid |
| Maximum power | 75kW (100.2bhp) @ 9100rpm |
| Maximum torque | 7.3kg-m (52.6lb-ft) @ 11,200rpm |

## TRANSMISSION

| | |
|---|---|
| Primary drive | straight cut gear |
| Clutch | dry, multiplate |
| Gearbox | 6-speed |
| Final drive | chain |

## WEIGHTS & CAPACITIES

| | |
|---|---|
| Tank capacity | 17l (4.5gal) |
| Dry weight | 192kg (423 lb) |
| Weight distribution | |
| — front | N/A |
| — rear | N/A |
| Wheelbase | 1410mm (55.5in) |
| Overall length | 2030mm (79.9in) |
| Overall width | 780mm (30.7in) |
| Overall height | 1080mm (42.5in) |
| Seat height | 790mm (31.1in) |

## CYCLE PARTS

| | |
|---|---|
| Frame | tubular steel trellis |
| Rake | 23.5°-24.5° |
| Front suspension | upside down fork |
| Travel | 120mm (4.7in) |
| Adjustment | full |
| Rear suspension | progressive cantilever, monoshock |
| Travel | 130mm (5.1in) |
| Adjustment | full |
| Tyres | |
| — make | N/A |
| — front | 120/60 x 17 |
| — rear | 180/55 x 17 |
| Brakes | |
| — make | Brembo |
| — front | 320mm (12.6in) dual semi-floating discs,4-piston caliper |
| — rear | 220mm (8.6in) disc, 2-piston caliper |

## TORQUE

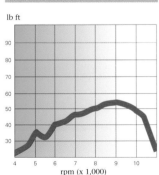

lb ft

rpm (x 1,000)

## POWER

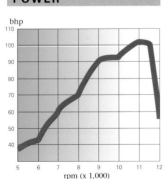

bhp

rpm (x 1,000)

**Independent test measurements (above) differ from the manufacturer's claimed maximum power and maximum torque figures.**

# DUCATI 851

**Body work**
The first 851 Strada models produced in late 1987 and 1988 suffered from poor handling, but later models were improved by fitting 43cm (17in) wheels and even better quality suspension. In 1992, Ducati switched to Japanese Showa suspension for the standard 851. The rather boxy bodywork, with its square headlight, quickly dated, but was at the cutting edge of design in the late 1980s.

**Fuel injection**
The 851 used a Weber Marelli fuel injection system, based on a system used on the Ferrari F40 and Ford Sierra RS Cosworth sportscars, among other cars.

**Exhaust**
A desmodromic valve system uses a camshaft to positively close as well as open the engine's poppet inlet and exhaust valves. This positive closing system, rather than using return springs, allows more radical valve movements and perfect valve control at high engine speeds.

**Front forks**
The front forks are upside-down Showa parts. Earlier models used Marzocchi forks.

DUCATI 851

## The ancestor of the massively

*successful 916 range, Ducati's 851 superbike brought water-cooled desmoquattro power to the racetrack, in a classic, winning package. The roots of Ducati's incredible success throughout the last decade of the twentieth century lay with the 851. First conceived in the mid-1980s by Ducati engineer Massimo Bordi, it was an answer to the impending obsolescence of the air-cooled, two-valve engines then used by Ducati.*

Stripped down, air intakes can be
seen either side of the headlight.
These direct cool air onto the
cylinder head area, helping power
production. The trellis frame and
large battery are also visible.

**Engine**
The 851 engine was developed from a 748cc
(45.6ci) design, built by Ducati engineer
Massimo Bordi. Bordi had championed the idea
of a four-valve, desmodromic cylinder head
since his days at university, and the engine
also featured belt-driven double overhead
cams, fuel injection and water-cooling.

**Fuel tank**
The aluminium fuel
tank holds 20l
(5.2gal). Later fuel
tanks were steel.

**Rear suspension**
An extruded aluminium
swingarm pivots on the rear
of the engine's crankcases.

# DUCATI MONSTER 900

Monster 900

**Way back in 1992,** Ducati's designers surprised everyone with the launch of the Monster 900. Its unusual look immediately attracted buyers, who bought it by the thousands, many customizing their machines to give them an even more individual look. Even now, it remains one of the most original looking machines around.

Basic speedo and odometer is fitted into the left side of a plastic shroud mounted above and to the rear of the headlamp. The square warning panel, which includes neutral, indicator, fuel, lights on and main beam bulbs, is difficult to read in sunlight.

The rear single Brembo caliper and 245mm (9.7in) disc combination works averagely well, but lacks a little feel.

**Front Brakes**
Twin four-piston Brembo calipers in gold finish meet 320mm (12.6in) discs to provide good stopping power with decent feel. Initial bite is not as strong as on many Japanese machines, but the set-up is arguably more progressive. Right handlebar-mounted lever is four-way span adjustable.

**Silencers**
Ducati obviously knows something other manufacturers do not, as the inspired note from the silencers manages to remain booming and deep, yet still passes stringent noise tests. Chamfers on the lower edge have been introduced to help boost ground clearance, although spirited riding will still result in contact with the road.

**Rear Shock**
The progressive Boge monoshock linkage has rebound damping and preload adjustment and a maximum 144mm (5.7in) of wheel travel.

**Tyres**
Dunlop D204s suit the Monster's handling and power characteristics quite well, but are often replaced by even stickier rubber by sporting owners.

**Front Mudguard**
One of only three painted bodywork parts on the Monster, it has a close-fitting profile and conventional four bolt attachment arrangement. The limited edition M900S comes with a carbon fibre mudguard as standard.

*Although visually similar to the 916 Biposto's silencers, the cans fitted to the 996 have been tweaked to make the most of the extra power coming from the 80cc (5.3ci) larger engine.*

*The fuel tank holds 16.5l (4.2gal), is sculpted to allow close fitment of the seat and is quickly removed by undoing one clasp.*

*The tubular steel trellis design is now synonymous with Ducati's roadsters and sports machines, and is not only strong and good-looking in its own right, but also serves to ensure maximum exposure of the engine, resulting in clean and uncomplicated lines.*

**Headlamp**
Adequate – and no more – it is easily repositioned according to individual tastes. M900S gets a fly screen which wraps around the light to provide limited windblast protection. This does not appear on the standard Monster.

**Forks**
The inverted 41mm (1.6in) Showa forks look particularly beefy on the diminutive Monster, work well, and are adjustable for compression and rebound damping, plus preload. They have a maximum travel of 120mm (4.7in).

**Seat**
At 770mm (30.3in), it is low enough for almost all riders and is one reason why Monsters have proven so popular with women. It is also comfortable, but not particularly well-padded.

**Pillion Comforts**
With a tiny seat hidden under a removable cover and high-placed footrests, passengers will not want to travel very far on the back of a Monster. Handling two-up is not overly bad, though ground clearance becomes even more of an issue.

**Rear Mudguard**
Close-fitting hugger design guard prevents road debris, salt and muck from flying onto the shock absorber and rear engine cylinder and exhaust header pipe. Limited edition M900s get re-profiled guards, which look prettier.

**Engine**
The 90°, two-valve per cylinder motor has a bore and stroke of 92 x 68mm (3.6 x 2.7in), compression ratio of 9.2:1 and is air and oil-cooled. It is fed by two 38mm (1.5in) carburettors. The gearbox has six speeds. Claimed maximum power at the crankshaft is 53kw (71bhp) at 7000rpm (a special edition version, the M900S, makes a claimed 55kW/74bhp at the same revs).

# DUCATI MONSTER 900

# Specifications

**Many riders have fallen** *for the bare, aggressive look of the Monster, making a change from the retro-look bikes of some other manufacturers. It is good-looking and just unusual enough to make people sit up and take notice as you ride by or when the bike is parked at the kerb. It is not good for going long distances (although many owners do), but it handles very well on smooth roads. Ducati does it again!*

**Seat height:** 770mm (30.3in)

**Width:** 800mm (31.5in)

**Trail:** 104mm (4in)

**Wheelbase:** 1430mm (56.3in)

## ENGINE

| | |
|---|---|
| **Type** | 4-stroke |
| **Layout** | 90° V-twin |
| **Total displacement** | 904cc |
| **Bore** | 92mm (3.6in) |
| **Stroke** | 68mm (2.7in) |
| **Compression ratio** | 9.2:1 |
| **Valves** | 2 per cylinder |
| **Fuel system** | 2 x 38mm (1.5in) carburettors |
| **Ignition** | CDI |
| **Cooling** | air/oil |
| **Maximum power** | 58kW (78bhp) @ 7025rpm |
| **Maximum torque** | 8.3kg-m (60lb-ft) @ 5370rpm |

## TRANSMISSION

| | |
|---|---|
| **Primary drive** | gear |
| **Clutch** | dry multiplate |
| **Gearbox** | 6-speed |
| **Final drive** | chain |

## WEIGHTS & CAPACITIES

| | |
|---|---|
| **Tank capacity** | 16.5l (3.63gal) |
| **Dry weight** | 185kg (407lb) |
| **Weight distribution** | |
| — front | N/A |
| — rear | N/A |
| **Wheelbase** | 1430mm (56.3in) |
| **Overall length** | 2080mm (81.9in) |
| **Overall width** | 800mm (31.5in) |
| **Overall height** | 1030mm (40.6in) |
| **Seat height** | 770mm (30.3in) |

## CYCLE PARTS

| | |
|---|---|
| **Frame** | tubular steel trellis |
| **Rake/trail** | 23°/104mm (4in) |
| **Front suspension** | inverted 41mm (1.6in) Showa forks |
| **Travel** | 120mm (4.7in) |
| **Adjustment** | spring preload, plus rebound and compression damping |
| **Rear suspension** | Boge monoshock |
| **Travel** | 144mm (5.7in) |
| **Adjustment** | spring preload, plus rebound damping |
| **Tyres** | |
| — make | Dunlop D204 |
| — front | 120/70 x 17 |
| — rear | 170/60 x 17 |
| **Brakes** | |
| — make | Brembo |
| — front | 2 x 320mm (12.6in) discs, opposed 4-piston calipers |
| — rear | 245mm (9.6in) disc, single caliper |

## TORQUE

## POWER

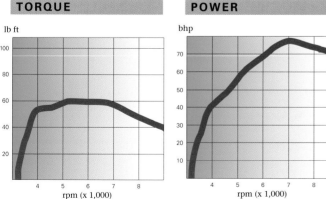

Independent test measurements (above) differ from the manufacturer's claimed maximum power and maximum torque figures.

# DUCATI 900SS

*Although the brake calipers are the same as those fitted to the 916 and ST2, the 900SS master cylinder is all new and helps give much better feedback.*

**New clothes**
Ducati design chief Pierre Terblanche has worked wonders with the the new bodywork. The slabby, dull panes and tank on the old 900SS have been replaced by aggressive, swooping in-your-face works of art. Non-bikers just stop and stare.

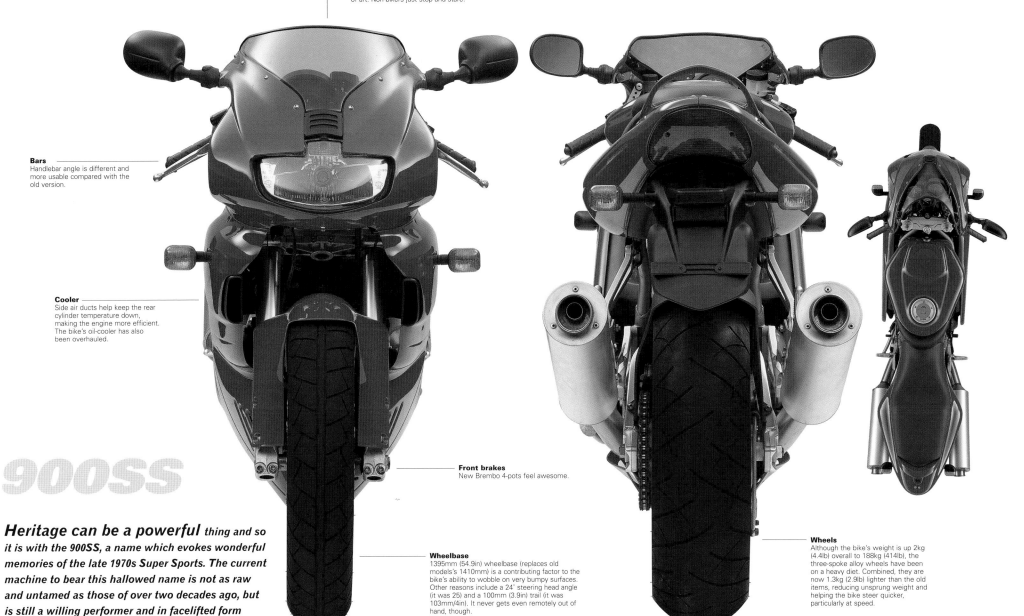

**Bars**
Handlebar angle is different and more usable compared with the old version.

**Cooler**
Side air ducts help keep the rear cylinder temperature down, making the engine more efficient. The bike's oil-cooler has also been overhauled.

**Front brakes**
New Brembo 4-pots feel awesome.

**Wheelbase**
1395mm (54.9in) wheelbase (replaces old models's 1410mm) is a contributing factor to the bike's ability to wobble on very bumpy surfaces. Other reasons include a 24° steering head angle (it was 25) and a 100mm (3.9in) trail (it was 103mm/4in). It never gets even remotely out of hand, though.

**Wheels**
Although the bike's weight is up 2kg (4.4lb) overall to 188kg (414lb), the three-spoke alloy wheels have been on a heavy diet. Combined, they are now 1.3kg (2.9lb) lighter than the old items, reducing unsprung weight and helping the bike steer quicker, particularly at speed.

## 900SS

*Heritage can be a powerful* thing and so *it is with the 900SS, a name which evokes wonderful memories of the late 1970s Super Sports. The current machine to bear this hallowed name is not as raw and untamed as those of over two decades ago, but is still a willing performer and in facelifted form simply stunning to look at.*

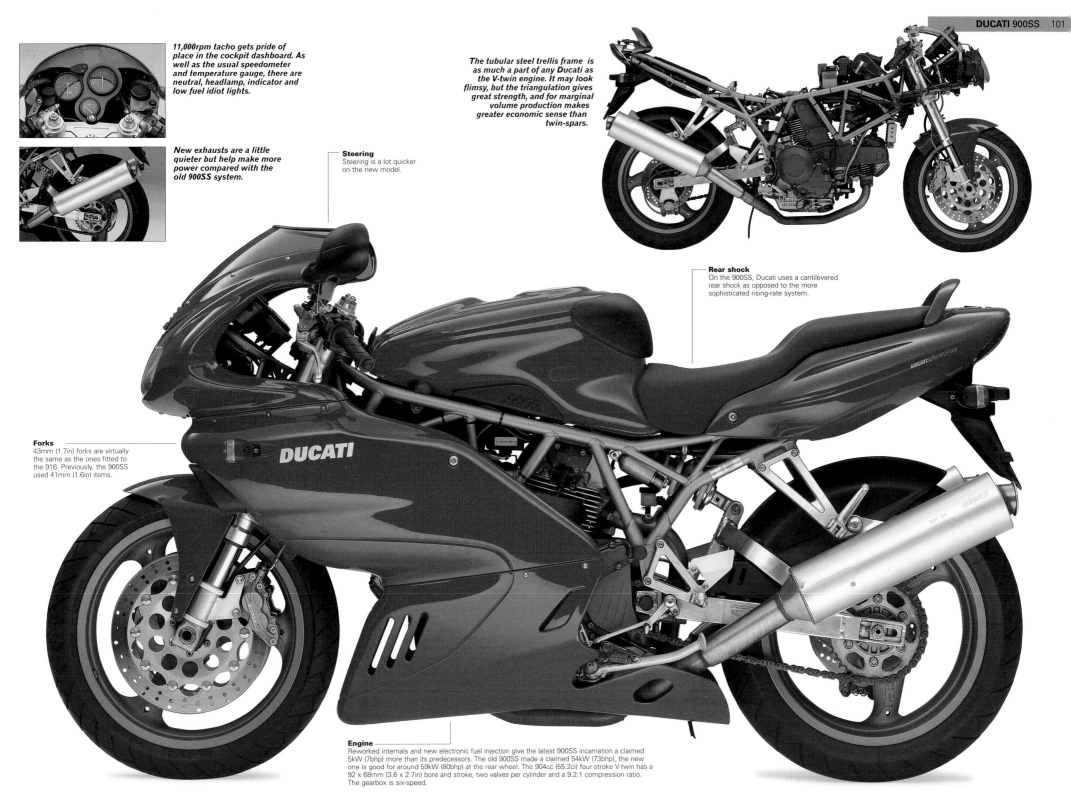

**11,000rpm tacho gets pride of place in the cockpit dashboard. As well as the usual speedometer and temperature gauge, there are neutral, headlamp, indicator and low fuel idiot lights.**

**New exhausts are a little quieter but help make more power compared with the old 900SS system.**

**The tubular steel trellis frame is as much a part of any Ducati as the V-twin engine. It may look flimsy, but the triangulation gives great strength, and for marginal volume production makes greater economic sense than twin-spars.**

**Steering**
Steering is a lot quicker on the new model.

**Rear shock**
On the 900SS, Ducati uses a cantilevered rear shock as opposed to the more sophisticated rising-rate system.

**Forks**
43mm (1.7in) forks are virtually the same as the ones fitted to the 916. Previously, the 900SS used 41mm (1.6in) items.

**Engine**
Reworked internals and new electronic fuel injection give the latest 900SS incarnation a claimed 5kW (7bhp) more than its predecessors. The old 900SS made a claimed 54kW (73bhp), the new one is good for around 59kW (80bhp) at the rear wheel. The 904cc (55.2ci) four-stroke V-twin has a 92 x 68mm (3.6 x 2.7in) bore and stroke, two valves per cylinder and a 9.2:1 compression ratio. The gearbox is six-speed.

# DUCATI 900SS

# Specifications

**The engine that powers** *the 900SS is a direct descendant of the one which powered the Ducati Pantah, which has also been used in many other Ducatis, including the 750F1 of the mid-1980s and Cagiva's Elefant. In other words, a well-proven and reliable engine, which we expect from Ducati anyway. Since 1998, it has been fuel-injected – sourced from Marelli – and is integrated with the ignition system to give full control. Other changes have brought the bike firmly into the 21st century while still retaining the charm of its 1970s' predecessor.*

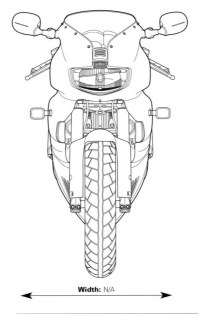

**Width:** N/A

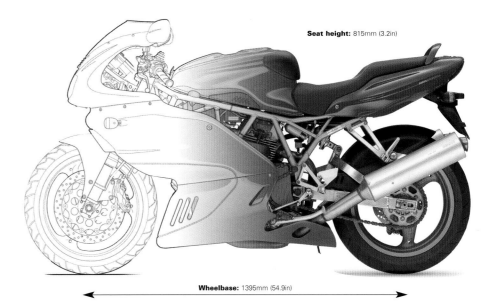

**Seat height:** 815mm (3.2in)

**Wheelbase** 1395mm (54.9in)

## ENGINE

| | |
|---|---|
| **Type** | 4-stroke |
| **Layout** | Desmodromic V-twin |
| **Total displacement** | 904cc (55.2ci) |
| **Bore** | 92mm (3.6in) |
| **Stroke** | 68mm (2.7in) |
| **Compression ratio** | 9.2:1 |
| **Valves** | 2 per cylinder |
| **Fuel system** | electronic injection |
| **Ignition** | electronic |
| **Cooling** | air |
| **Maximum power** | 58.2kW (78.1bhp) @ 8100rpm |
| **Maximum torque** | 7.7kg-m (56.2lb-ft) @ 6050rpm |

## TORQUE

## POWER

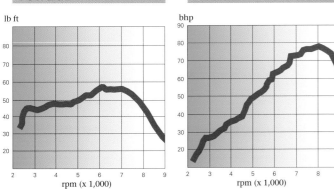

Independent test measurements (above) differ from the manufacturer's claimed maximum power and maximum torque figures.

## TRANSMISSION

| | |
|---|---|
| **Primary drive** | straight cut gears |
| **Clutch** | dry multiplate, hydraulic control |
| **Gearbox** | 6-speed |
| **Final drive** | chain |

## WEIGHTS & CAPACITIES

| | |
|---|---|
| **Tank capacity** | 16l (4.2gal) |
| **Dry weight** | 188kg (504lb) |
| **Weight distribution** | |
| — front | N/A |
| — rear | N/A |
| **Wheelbase** | 1395mm (54.9in) |
| **Overall length** | N/A |
| **Overall width** | N/A |
| **Overall height** | N/A |
| **Seat height** | 815mm (3.2in) |

## CYCLE PARTS

| | |
|---|---|
| **Frame** | tubular steel trellis |
| **Rake** | 24° |
| **Front suspension** | 43mm (1.7in) Showa upside-down fork |
| **Travel** | 120mm (4.7in) |
| **Adjustment** | full |
| **Rear suspension** | Sachs cantilever linkage |
| **Travel** | 136mm (5.4in) |
| **Adjustment** | monoshock and stroke depending damping |
| **Tyres** | |
| — make | N/A |
| — front | 120/70 x 17 |
| — rear | 170/60 x 17 |
| **Brakes** | |
| — make | N/A |
| — front | 2 x 320mm (1.6in) semi-floating discs, 4-piston caliper |
| — rear | 245mm (9.6in) disc, 2-piston caliper |

# DUCATI 916 BIPOSTO

**Instruments**
A cable-driven speedometer and trip meter, electronic tachometer, temperature gauge, warning lights for neutral, high beam, turn, low fuel and generator. An oil pressure light is in the tachometer face.

**Exhaust**
The characteristic high-level system features a pair of silencers beneath the seat attached to stainless steel pipes. A crossover pipe behind the engine improves harmonics and boosts mid-range power.

**Handlebar controls**
On the right are the engine kill and electric start buttons, while on the left are the lights on, dip/main, headlamp flash and indicator switches. The dip/main switch is unusual in being a push button rather than the more common sliding type. Clutch and front brake levers are both span-adjustable.

**Bodywork**
Designed by Massimo Tamburini, the styling has set new industry standards. The bike has a distinctive feminine shape when viewed from above, narrowing significantly at the waist. The fairing and seat unit are constructed from injection-moulded plastic while the fuel tank is made from pressed steel.

**Cooling system**
The engine is fully liquid-cooled with a gear-driven water pump. The radiator is curved to increase surface area without adding to the overall width.

**Headlights**
The left headlight is for dipped beam, the right for main beam. The dipped beam is a projector lamp, which means that the glass lens focuses the light (as in a slide projector) rather than the light being focused by a reflector behind the bulb. The projector method produces a more accurate light pattern.

**Forks**
The Japanese-made 43mm (1.7in) diameter Showa forks are built to finer engineering tolerances than those used on Japanese production bikes, and the fork yokes are machined in pairs to ensure perfect alignment and therefore reduced friction, giving better performance.

**Swingarm**
The single-sided swingarm is cast from aluminium and mounted directly to the back of the engine's crankcases to minimize the bike's length. This also allows the swingarm bearings to be lubricated by engine oil rather than grease, making maintenance easier. A single-sided arm is heavier than a conventional double-sided item, but Ducati engineers made this sacrifice for the sake of enhancing the bike's looks.

**Fuel injection**
The standard 916 has a single injector per cylinder using the indirect injection system. This means that the injector pumps fuel into the inlet tract rather than squirting it directly into the cylinder, as on many diesel engines. The high-pressure injector pump is sited inside the fuel tank, and the control unit is under the seat.

**Wheels**
The three-spoke aluminium wheels are slightly heavier than five-spoke wheels of the same strength, but they were chosen partly for their good looks.

*916*

***The Ducati 916** is the superbly successful result of Ducati's intention to create a motorcycle with the qualities needed to take it to the very top of the supersport class, but with a style that reflects the bike's feline grace and agility. Its appeal lies not only in its svelte curves but also in its thrilling performance and enormous race track potential. **D**ucati has developed a bike which is already hailed by motorcyclists the world over as a true modern classic.*

**Tyres**
Pirelli Dragon Corsa or Michelin Hi-Sport tyres are fitted as standard in sizes 120/70 x 17 front and a giant 190/50 x 17 at the rear. The large-section rear tyre was chosen by the engineers partially for its visual impact, as a slightly narrower version would improve the rate of turn with no significant loss of grip.

*The bell mouths, which draw in the pressurized air uniformly, look so good that it is a pity the tank has to be removed to see them.*

*Ducati's use of the desmo engine allows the toothed belt driving the 916 to be more narrow than is usual.*

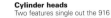

*Much of the Ducati's bodywork is held in place by Dzus fasteners, making it easily removable.*

*With the airbox removed, one can see the two fuel-injector bodies. Fuel injection, of course, gives better performance, economy and reduced emissions.*

**Engine**
With its 94mm x 66mm (3.7 x 2.6in) cylinder dimensions, the 90° V-twin motor is very over-square and thus capable of high revs (11,000rpm) despite its large capacity.

**Cylinder heads**
Two features single out the 916 as rare in the motorcycle world. One is the use of toothed belts to drive the overhead camshafts – these require no lubrication, are lightweight and almost silent in operation. The second, and most famous, is the use of desmodromic valve operation, where the valves are pulled closed by secondary rocker arms rather than relying on springs.

**Frame**
Made from tubular chrome-molybdenum steel, the frame includes the engine as a crucial integral component, minimizing overall chassis weight.

**Brakes**
Made by Italian company Brembo, the front brakes feature semi-floating discs. This means that the pins securing the 320mm (1.6in) diameter rotors to the central carriers, leave some play to allow for the different expansion rates of the steel rotors and aluminium carriers, which get hot in use. The calipers are opposed four-piston units.

**Clutch**
Unusually for a road bike, the 916 uses a dry clutch whereas most run in a bath of oil. A dry clutch is lighter than a wet one, but it overheats easier during heavy low-speed use, such as in traffic, and after repeated fast getaways.

**Gearbox**
Contains conventional constant mesh gears, meaning all gears are permanently meshed together and the drive is engaged by dogs on the sides of the gear pinions. The six ratios must be selected in sequence so, for example, third gear can be reached only through second or fourth gear.

# DUCATI 916 BIPOSTO

# Specifications

**DUCATI'S distinctive desmodromic valve** *system operating within the 90° V-twin engine is one of the most distinctive points of the 916 – along with the styling. The frame is tubular steel lattice, the clutch a dry multi-plate unit and the suspension the high-quality Japanese Showa you would expect with a bike such as this. One minor let-down is the brakes, which, despite improvements, still demand a higher than usual lever pressure. Still, the 916 does come pretty close to perfection.*

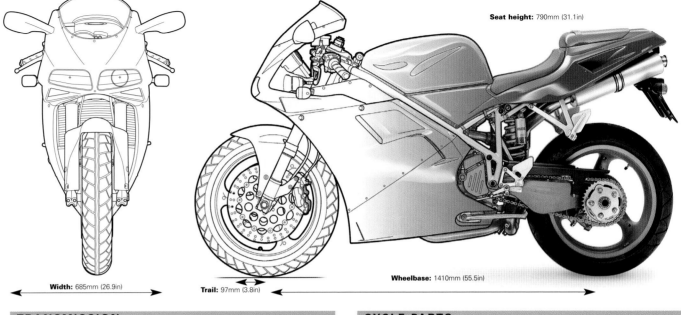

**Seat height:** 790mm (31.1in)

**Wheelbase:** 1410mm (55.5in)

**Width:** 685mm (26.9in)

**Trail:** 97mm (3.8in)

## ENGINE

| | |
|---|---|
| Type | 4-stroke |
| Layout | V-twin |
| Total displacement | 916cc (55.9ci) |
| Bore | 94mm (3.7in) |
| Stroke | 66mm (2.6in) |
| Compression ratio | 11.5:1 |
| Valves | 4 per cylinder |
| Fuel system | Weber IAW1.6M fuel injection with one injector per cylinder |
| Ignition | electronic fuel injection |
| Cooling | liquid |
| Maximum power | 78kW (105bhp) @ 9000rpm |
| Maximum torque | 8.8kg-m (64lb-ft) @ 8500rpm |

## TORQUE

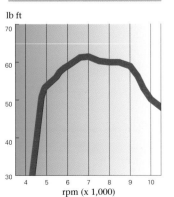

lb ft

rpm (x 1,000)

## POWER

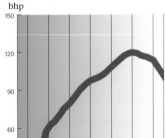

bhp

rpm (x 1,000)

Independent test measurements (above) differ from the manufacturer's claimed maximum power and maximum torque figures.

## TRANSMISSION

| | |
|---|---|
| Primary drive | straight-cut gears |
| Clutch | dry multi-plate |
| Gearbox | 6-speed |
| Final drive | DiD O-ring chain |

## WEIGHTS & CAPACITIES

| | |
|---|---|
| Tank capacity | 17l (3.74gal) |
| Dry weight | 203kg (447.5lb) |
| Weight distribution | |
| — front | 47% |
| — rear | 53% |
| Wheelbase | 1410mm (55.5in) |
| Overall length | 2050mm (80.7in) |
| Overall width | 685mm (26.9in) |
| Overall height | 1090mm (42.9in) |
| Seat height | 790mm (31.1in) |

## CYCLE PARTS

| | |
|---|---|
| Frame | steel trellis |
| Rake/trail | 24°/97mm (3.8in) |
| Front suspension | Showa 43mm (1.7in) inverted forks |
| Travel | 127mm (4.9in) |
| Adjustment | preload, compression, rebound |
| Rear suspension | single-sided swingarm with rising rate monoshock |
| Travel | 135mm (5.3in) |
| Adjustment | preload, compression, rebound |
| Tyres | |
| — make | Michelin Hi Sport or Pirelli Dragon |
| — front | 120/70 ZR17 |
| — rear | 180/55 ZR17 or 190/50 ZR17 |
| Brakes | |
| — make | Brembo |
| — front | 2 x 320mm (1.6in) floating discs with 2-piston calipers |
| — rear | 220mm (8.7in) disc with 2-piston caliper |

# DUCATI 916SPS

*Improved battery charging, courtesy
of a new regulator, was another
change made during 1997.*

**Racing stance**
It is derived from a race bike, but the
916 SPS' forward set bars and whopping
780mm (30.7in) seat height means this is
no machine for shorties and a forward
crouch is mandatory at all times. As a result
riding around town is often a painful
experience.

**Front suspension**
Twin 43mm (1.7in) Showa forks are crafted to Ducati
specifications and are adjustable for spring preload,
plus compression and rebound damping. The yokes are
designed to match a specific pair of forks, resulting in
greater steering response. An Ohlins steering damper
(fitted from late 1997 onwards) helps further still.

**Exhaust**
Twin Termigoni carbon
fibre exhaust cans were
standard equipment on
the SPS, as they were
originally on the limited
production Senna
(which appeared before
the SPS). They came in
a box and had to be
installed by the dealer
or owner (for legal
reasons).

**Gearbox**
Transmission is a six-speed indirect
constant mesh gearbox with, as per
Ducati tradition, a dry multiplate clutch.

## 916 SPS

**At a glance, it appears almost** indistinguishable from
a standard 916 Biposto, but a closer look reveals a different
tailpiece, with no provision for a pillion. After a bit more
investigation, you soon realize that the motor does not displace
916cc (55.9ci) at all, but has been bored out to 996cc (60.8ci)!
Confused? The SPS is basically a WSB homologation model and
boasts a larger, more powerful engine and uprated running gear.

*Clocks are identical to the standard 916, though an overlay on the speedometer gives a clue to this bike's continental origins. Ohlins steering damper indicates it is a late version.*

*Dual 320mm (1.6in) Brembo discs are gripped by opposed four-piston floating calipers. In late 1997, the SPS got uprated items.*

*Stylish, timeless trellis steel frame still lokss absolutely stunning and its triangualtion makes it bvery strong and stiff, as does utilizing the engine as a stressed member. From 1997, the SPS got an even lighter and stiffer frame.*

**Fuel tank**
Beautifully sculptured fuel tank holds 17l (4.5gal), giving a range of just under 270km/h (168miles) between filling stations.

**Seat:**
Short and narrow, the seat is unsuitable for very tall riders, nor very short ones either, thanks to its relationship with the footpegs and foot-operated controls.

**Wheels:**
Three-spoke rims are identical to the standard 916 and the design was chosen, mainly for looks. The latter Carl Fogarty replica and 996 SPS use lighter five-spoke wheels.

**Engine:**
Legendary liquid-cooled 90° V-twin and called a 916, but the SPS motor actually displaces 996cc (the first of them), with a bigger bore (98mm/3.9in) versus 96mm (3.8in) on the original 916. The stroke remains unchanged. Power is also up to a claimed 92kW (123bhp) from 81kW (109), thanks to the larger cylinders and also to recalibrated fuel injection with two injectors per cylinder and metering.

**Rear suspension:**
Single rising rate monoshock, also supplied by Showa, features adjustable preload, compression and rebound damping.

# DUCATI 916SPS

# Specifications

**The 916 SPS is, in fact,** equipped with a 996cc (60.8ci) engine, and at the time of its launch in 1996 there were many who found it odd that it should be named the 916. However, that changed in October of 1998 when Ducati discontinued the 916 model and launched the 996SPS, which is just a newer version of the 916. Distinguishable at the rear from others in the 916/996 range by its white panels, the SPS ensures its exclusivity with its price of around £17,000 ($26,000). Surprising just how many you see on the roads, however.

Seat height: 790mm (31.1in)

Length: 2030mm (79.9in)

## ENGINE

| | |
|---|---|
| Type | 4-stroke |
| Layout | 90° V-twin |
| Total displacement | 996cc (60.8ci) |
| Bore | 98mm (3.9in) |
| Stroke | 66mm (2.6in) |
| Compression ratio | 11.5:1 |
| Valves | 4 per cylinder |
| Fuel system | electronic injection |
| Ignition | electronic |
| Cooling | liquid |
| Maximum power | 87.7kW (117.6bhp) @ 9750rpm |
| Maximum torque | 9.5kg-m (68.6lb-ft) @ 7750rpm |

## TRANSMISSION

| | |
|---|---|
| Primary drive | gear |
| Clutch | dry multiplate |
| Gearbox | 6-speed |
| Final drive | chain |

## WEIGHTS & CAPACITIES

| | |
|---|---|
| Tank capacity | 17l (4.5gal) |
| Dry weight | 190kg |
| Weight distribution | |
| — front | N/A |
| — rear | N/A |
| Wheelbase | 1410mm (55.1in) |
| Overall length | 2030mm (79.9in) |
| Overall width | 780mm (30.7in) |
| Overall height | 1080mm (42.5in) |
| Seat height | 790mm (31.1in) |

## CYCLE PARTS

| | |
|---|---|
| Frame | tubular steel trellis |
| Rake/trail | N/A |
| Front suspension | 43mm (1.7in) inverted forks |
| Travel | 127mm (4.9in) |
| Adjustment | compression, rebound and preload |
| Rear suspension | progressive linkage with monoshock |
| Travel | 130mm (5.1in) |
| Adjustment | compression, rebound and preload |
| Tyres | |
| — make | N/A |
| — front | 120/70 x 17 |
| — rear | 190/50 x 17 |
| Brakes | |
| — make | N/A |
| — front | 2 x 320mm (1.6in) floating discs |
| — rear | 220mm (8.7in) disc |

# DUCATI ST4

*The 257km/h (160mph) speedo face is marked in 20mph increments and features white markings against a black background. Unusually for bikes, the speedo under-reads at near maximum performance, indicating 140mph (225km/h) while the true speed is actually 148mph (238km/h).*

**Mirrors**
Spring-mounted mirrors fold in briefly to allow access to narrow garages and alleys, but expand again as soon as manual pressure is relieved.

*Redesigned after criticism from owners of other Ducati models, the sidestand still retracts whenever the bike is lifted, but now has a more sure-footed standing.*

**Right handlebar**
Home to the electric starter button, kill switch and a brembo-branded non-adjustable brake lever (the lack of span sizing comes in for criticism from some owners).

**Left handlebar**
Houses the high/low headlamp beam switch, off/park/on light switch, pass light button, indicators switch, horn button and choke lever. The non-span adjustable clutch lever is brembo-branded.

**Ignition barrel**
Unusually mounted in plastic fascia on front of petrol tank.

**Clutch**
The trademark rattle and jangle of the dry Ducati clutch remains on the ST4, making owners fear it is about to go pop while the reality is it probably never will.

**Footpegs**
Both rider and pillion footpegs use rubber topping to help isolate feet from vibration.

**Exhausts**
How come Ducati can make its exhausts produce so much evocative noise and still pass stringent worldwide regulations? With owners of other bikes exchanging their stock pipes as much for increased sound as for performance, many firms could learn a thing or two from Ducati.

**Mudguard**
Standard rear hugger ensures road crud cannot reach the bike's underside.

*ST4*

*Introduced in October 1998, the ST4 is basically an uprated version of the ST2 but with a 916 engine. Although it has been on the market for a short time, it is proving fairly popular with bikers, who approve of both its power and looks. And it has that unmistakeable Ducati sound booming out from the exhaust. Ducati fans are unlikely to be disappointed.*

*Essential on any sports tourer, the ST4's grab rail does not disappoint.*

*The dry weight increases by 8kg (17.6lb) over the ST2 to total 215kg (473lb). This is largely due to the 916-derived engine weighing more than its stablemate's.*

**Petrol tank**
Holds 21l (5.5gal) in total, while reserve holds 6l (1.6gal).

**Seat height**
At 820mm (32.28in), it is identical to the ST2's.

**Engine**
While the ST2 has a 944cc (57.6ci), two-valves-per-cylinder lump, Ducati has opted to lower capacity for the ST4. However, as this is a retuned version of the legendary 916's four-valves-per-cylinder engine, power is increased , the ST4 making a claimed 78kW (105bhp) against the ST2's 62kW (83bhp).

**Mainstand**
An underrated accessory which, just like the ST2's, is easy to operate and a real boon when it comes to chain lubrication and adjustment.

# DUCATI ST4

# Specifications

*The ST4 combines the* ST2 *chassis with the* 916 *engine, so you know from the beginning that you cannot go far wrong. The engine has few changes to the established and well-respected 916 – just refinements. Its 238km/h (148mph) top speed is no disgrace nor its 0–96km/h (0–60mph) in 3.5 seconds; it is a delight to tour on, commute or just enjoy. It is only a pity the* ST2 *came first – Ducati could have forgotten about that and just released the* ST4.

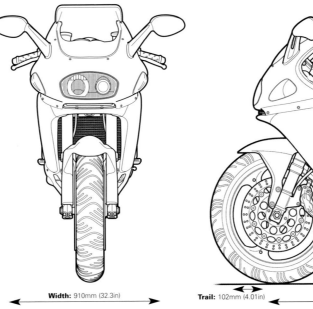

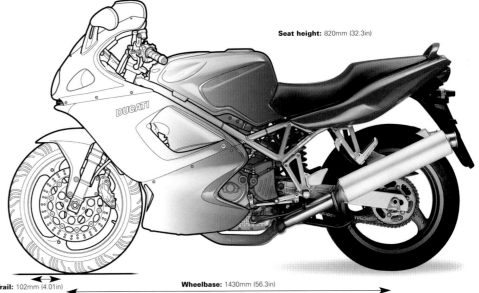

**Seat height:** 820mm (32.3in)

**Width:** 910mm (32.3in)

**Trail:** 102mm (4.01in)

**Wheelbase:** 1430mm (56.3in)

## ENGINE

| | |
|---|---|
| **Type** | 4-stroke |
| **Layout** | 90° DOHC V-twin |
| **Total displacement** | 916cc (55.9ci) |
| **Bore** | 94mm (3.7in) |
| **Stroke** | 66mm (2.6in) |
| **Compression ratio** | 11:1 |
| **Valves** | 4 per cylinder |
| **Fuel system** | electronic fuel injection |
| **Ignition** | CDI |
| **Cooling** | liquid |
| **Maximum power** | 77kW (103.5bhp) @ 9000rpm |
| **Maximum torque** | 8.7kg-m (63.2lb-ft) @ 7000rpm |

## TRANSMISSION

| | |
|---|---|
| **Primary drive** | gear |
| **Clutch** | dry, multi-plate |
| **Gearbox** | 6-speed |
| **Final drive** | chain |

## WEIGHTS & CAPACITIES

| | |
|---|---|
| **Tank capacity** | 21l (5.5gal) |
| **Dry weight** | 215kg (473lb) |
| **Weight distribution** | |
| — front | N/A |
| — rear | N/A |
| **Wheelbase** | 1430mm (56.3in) |
| **Overall length** | 2070mm (81.5in) |
| **Overall width** | 910mm (35.8in) |
| **Overall height** | 1180mm (46.5in) |
| **Seat height** | 820mm (32.3in) |

## CYCLE PARTS

| | |
|---|---|
| **Frame** | tubular steel trellis |
| **Rake/trail** | 24°/102mm (4.01in) |
| **Front suspension** | 43mm (1.7in) telescopic forks |
| **Travel** | 130mm (5.1in) |
| **Adjustment** | preload, plus compression and rebound damping |
| **Rear suspension** | monoshock |
| **Travel** | 148mm (5.8in) |
| **Adjustment** | preload, plus compression and rebound damping |
| **Tyres** | |
| — make | Metzeler or Michelin |
| — front | 120/70 x ZR17 |
| — rear | 170/60 x ZR17 |
| **Brakes** | |
| — make | Brembo |
| — front | twin 320mm (12.6in) discs, |
| — rear | single 245mm (9.6in) disc, |

## TORQUE

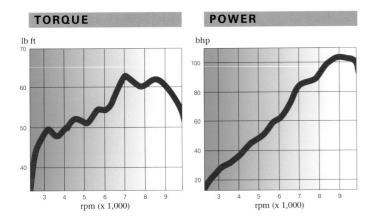

lb ft

rpm (x 1,000)

## POWER

bhp

rpm (x 1,000)

Independent test measurements (above) differ from the manufacturer's claimed maximum power and maximum torque figures.

# DUCATI ST2

**Marelli electronic fuel injection provides a precise mixture under all conditions, giving increased performance and fuel economy.**

*Excellent Brembo brakes. The two 320mm (1.6in) discs up front, and single 245mm (9.6in) disc at the rear, ensure the short braking distances that are to be expected from the ST2.*

**Mirrors**
The mirrors might seem to stick out like alien antennae, but the slightly extended stalks mean your rear view is enhanced – you will see the road rather than your elbows.

**Protection**
The fairing screen's pronounced lip helps keep wind and rain off the rider. Wind blast can become annoying above 200km/h (125mph) unless your head is tucked behind the bubble.

**Headlights**
The very powerful headlamp lights up the road, but can sometimes dazzle oncoming drivers, even on dip.

**Indicators**
Front indicators are integrated into the bodywork and look superb.

**Stands**
The ST2 gets a stable main stand as standard, which is just as well because this machine is no different to other Ducatis in that the sidestand is terrible. Yes, it will hold the bike, but because of its 'flip-up' style and its location, it is almost impossible to operate while on the bike. You need both patience and practice.

**Touchdown**
Belt the bike hard around left handers and the sidestand can just scrape. You would have to be riding hard to do this, though.

## ST2

**The name gives the game** away: the letters **ST** stand for **S**ports **T**ourer. And this is one of the few bikes of its breed which actually does what it is supposed to do – lets you tour comfortably without having to settle for a cruiser-type machine while still retaining that sporty look and feel which will let you mix it with other sports bikes. The **ST2** was, according to Ducati, conceived and built in the tradition of the 'Grand Turismo' cars of Europe – a combination of performance and useability.

**Front tyre**
Metzeler MEZ4 sport/touring tyre is the first radial ever released for front wheels and is ultra stable, combining longevity with control. The ST2 is quite a tyre-sensitive bike.

**Novel idea**
Pivoting exhaust mounts allow the silencers to be raised out of the way for hard scratching, or lowered to accommodate purpose-built Ducati panniers.

*Featuring, of course, the now classic V-Twin Ducati desmo engine with electronic fuel injection and a steel trellis frame, the ST2 behaves exactly as it should – a sports bike with Italian pedigree.*

*The ST2 uses a version of Ducati's tried-and-tested tubular steel trellis frame. This example has its roots in the firm's old 851.*

**Instruments**
The 916-inspired instrument panel is very functional, with the speedo and tacho positioned forward. The fuel level, coolant temperature and clock information are all integrated into one easy-to-see digital display.

**Fuel tank**
Sculpted, stylish and capable of holding a useful 21l (5.5gal).

**Comfy**
Unlike Ducati's race reps, the ST2's ride is actually very smooth thanks to a softer rear shock absorber.

**Pillion**
Pillions reckon the rear seat is comfy and also give top marks to the relationship between footpegs and grab rail. Hundreds of miles can be covered in a day in total comfort on the back.

**Front end**
Monster 43mm (1.7in) upside-down forks have excellent damping and springing at any speed and are part of the reason the ST2 can cut it equally well as a sportster or tourer. In fact, the bike handles better than some early 1990s dedicated race replicas.

**Engine**
The 944cc (57.6ci) engine has its origins in Ducati's old 907iE Paso motor and is a four stroke, 90° V-twin with two valves per cylinder, desmodromic valve gear and Marelli fuel injection. Cooling is liquid and the compression ratio is 10.2:1. Mid-range grunt is impressive.

**Footpegs**
Hard cornering can grind the right-side one out. The left is unlikely to touch down because the sidestand will beat it to it. The lower footpegs combined with higher handlebars do help with comfort, though.

# DUCATI ST2

# Specifications

DUCATI has made such *big advances in both design and build quality over the last few years that worries about reliability and quality are now hardly worse than with Japanese bikes. The ST2 is an accomplished sports tourer, which handles very well, is extremely comfortable and just eats up those miles so easily.*

*It may not look as gorgeous as the 996, but this is mainly because the sports tourer needs to be taller in order to protect the rider better, which means it loses that certain sleekness of pure sports bikes. But the ST2 holds its own in its class.*

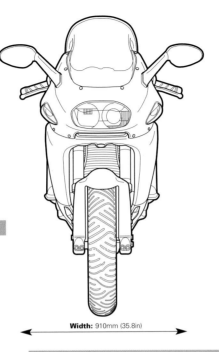

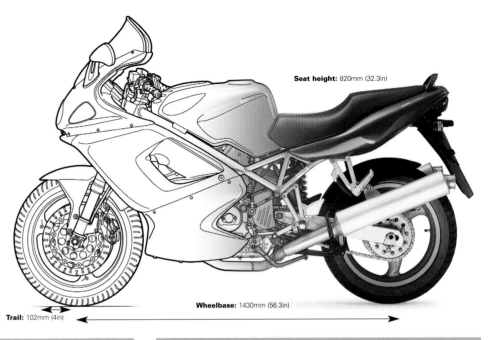

**Seat height:** 820mm (32.3in)

**Width:** 910mm (35.8in)

**Trail:** 102mm (4in)

**Wheelbase:** 1430mm (56.3in)

## ENGINE

| | |
|---|---|
| Type | 4-stroke |
| Layout | 90° SOHC V-twin |
| Total displacement | 944cc (57.6ci) |
| Bore | 94mm (3.7in) |
| Stroke | 68mm (2.7in) |
| Compression ratio | 10.2:1 |
| Valves | 2 per cylinder |
| Fuel system | electronic fuel injection |
| Ignition | CDI |
| Cooling | liquid |
| Maximum power | 61kW (82bhp) @ 8560rpm |
| Maximum torque | 8.6kg-m (62.2lb-ft) @ 6500rpm |

## TORQUE

lb ft / rpm (x 1,000)

## POWER

bhp / rpm (x 1,000)

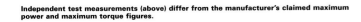

**Independent test measurements (above) differ from the manufacturer's claimed maximum power and maximum torque figures.**

## TRANSMISSION

| | |
|---|---|
| Primary drive | gear |
| Clutch | dry multiplate |
| Gearbox | 6-speed |
| Final drive | chain |

## WEIGHTS & CAPACITIES

| | |
|---|---|
| Tank capacity | 21l (4.62gal) |
| Dry weight | 209kg (459.8lb) |
| Weight distribution | |
| — front | N/A |
| — rear | N/A |
| Wheelbase | 1430mm (56.3in) |
| Overall length | 2070mm (81.5in) |
| Overall width | 910mm (35.8in) |
| Overall height | 1320mm (52.0in) |
| Seat height | 820mm (32.3in) |

## CYCLE PARTS

| | |
|---|---|
| Frame | tubular steel trellis |
| Rake/trail | 24°/102mm (4in) |
| Front suspension | 43mm (1.7in) telescopic forks |
| Travel | 130mm (5.1in) |
| Adjustment | preload, plus compression and rebound damping |
| Rear suspension | monoshock |
| Travel | 148mm (5.8in) |
| Adjustment | preload, plus compression and rebound damping |
| Tyres | |
| — make | Metzeler or Michelin |
| — front | 120/70 x ZR17 |
| — rear | 170/60 x ZR17 |
| Brakes | |
| — make | Brembo |
| — front | twin 320mm (1.6in) discs |
| — rear | single 245mm (9.6in) disc |

# DUCATI 996 BIPOSTO

*The 996 Biposto uses the front Brembo brake calipers originally fitted to the 996SPS rather than the lower-spec ones on the 916 Biposto. A master cylinder from the new 900SS is used too.*

**Clutch**
Ducati has fitted a revised clutch master cylinder to help beef up the 996BP.

**Width**
With a maximum width of just 780mm (30.7in), the 996 will fit down most narrow alleys and passageways for storage.

**Racing position**
The footpeg height combined with a seat height of 790mm (31.1in) and far-forwardly placed handlebars means riders are immediately forced into a committed crouch on the 996. It makes sense for high speed riding, but can be a pain (quite literally on wrists and neck) at other times.

**Footpegs**
As with every member of the 916 family, the only way you'll ever scrape a 996's footpegs is by crashing – the front ones are a whopping 390mm (15.35in) off the deck!

**Tyres**
Ducati has chosen to equip the 996BP with Michelin Hi-Sport II tyres instead of the better mark III versions. They work well on the road, but could be a limiting factor to very experienced riders on trackdays. Sizes are 120/70-ZR17 front and 190/50-ZR17 rear.

**Shapely**
The 996 Biposto's styling follows the curvaceous lines first designed into the 916 Strada in 1993. Viewed from above, the bike's form is supposed to resemble a woman's.

## 996

***Ducati's master stroke** has been to breathe new life into what was the 916. By adding 80cc (4.9ci), fitting extra fuel injectors, revising the exhaust system, brakes and clutch, the Italian firm has created the 996 Biposto. It matters little that it had to be done to keep up with the competition; what matters is that it has been done so beautifully.*

Although visually similar to the 916 Biposto's silencers, the cans fitted to the 996 have been tweaked to make the most of the extra power coming from the 80cc (4.9ci) larger engine.

Not only does the tried-and-tested steel tube trellis frame make the bike instantly recognizable as a Ducati, it also works well with little flex and precise road manners in conjunction with other chassis parts. To get the most from the handling, rake can be adjusted between 23°30' and 24°30', while trail is adjustable between 91mm (3.58in) and 97mm (3.82in).

The four-stroke, 90°, V-twin engine displaces 996cc (60.8ci), 80cc (4.9ci) more than the forerunning 916BP version. It has a 98mm (3.9in) bore, 66mm (2.6in) stroke and an average compression ratio of 11.5:1. There are four valves per cylinder, the usual desmodromic valve gear, straight-cut primary gears, a dry multiplate clutch and a six-speed gearbox.

**Tank**
The beautifully sculpted but arguably overly plain petrol tank holds 17l (4.5gal), which is fractionally less than most sportsters.

**Revealing**
At first glance, the only way to tell the 996 Biposto apart from its smaller 916cc (55.9ci) cousin is the discreet fairing capacity logo. A dual seat and red all-over bodywork reveals it is a Biposto instead of an SPS or SP model.

**Better fit**
The mountings for the seat have been revised to make it more secure compared with previous models.

**Front suspension**
The beautifully-crafted, inverted 43mm (1.7in) Showa forks are adjustable for rebound and compression damping, as well as preload. They have a maximum 127mm (5in) of travel.

**Low**
Even more so than many sports bikes, the 996's fairing bellypan is close to the ground with just 150mm (5.91in) clearance. You will not scrape it while cornering, but beware of kerbs!

**Rear suspension**
Showa also supplies the progressive linkage monoshock rear suspension, which is adjustable for rebound and compression damping, plus spring preload. The vertically-mounted unit has a maximum 71mm (2.8in) of travel.

# DUCATI 996 BIPOSTO

# Specifications

*Adding just 80cc (5ci) to* what is essentially a 916BP engine and fitting extra fuel injectors plus a revised exhaust system and governing computer chip has given Ducati a new lease of life with the 996BP engine. In this guise it is more than capable of taking on Aprilia's new RSV1000 Mille, and slaughters other twins such as Honda's VTR1000 FireStorm and both Suzuki TL1000s. And it's still the sexiest-looking bike on the market, even though the design has been around since 1993!

**Seat height:** 790mm (31in)

**Width:** 780mm (30.7in)

**Trail:** 91mm/97mm (3.6/3.8in)

**Wheelbase:** 1410mm (55.5in)

## ENGINE

| | |
|---|---|
| **Type** | 4-stroke |
| **Layout** | 90° V-twin |
| **Total displacement** | 996cc (60.8ci) |
| **Bore** | 98mm (3.9in) |
| **Stroke** | 66mm (2.6in) |
| **Compression ratio** | 11.5:1 |
| **Valves** | 4 per cylinder |
| **Fuel system** | 2 injectors per cylinder |
| **Ignition** | electronic with Nippon Denso starter motor |
| **Cooling** | liquid, curved radiator |
| **Maximum power** | 84.5kW (113.3bhp) @ 8630rpm |
| **Maximum torque** | 10kg-m (72.2lb-ft) @ 6910rpm |

## TORQUE

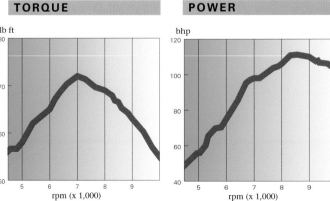

lb ft
rpm (x 1,000)

## POWER

bhp
rpm (x 1,000)

**Independent test measurements (above) differ from the manufacturer's claimed maximum power and maximum torque figures.**

## TRANSMISSION

| | |
|---|---|
| **Primary drive** | straight-cut gears |
| **Clutch** | dry multiplate |
| **Gearbox** | 6-speed |
| **Final drive** | sealed D.I.D 525 HV O-ring chain |

## WEIGHTS & CAPACITIES

| | |
|---|---|
| **Tank capacity** | 17l (4.5gal) |
| **Dry weight** | 198kg (435.6lb) |
| **Weight distribution** | |
| — front | N/A |
| — rear | N/A |
| **Wheelbase** | 1410mm (55.5in) |
| **Overall length** | 2030mm (79.9in) |
| **Overall width** | 780mm (30.7in) |
| **Overall height** | 1080mm (42.5in) |
| **Seat height** | 790mm (31.1in) |

## CYCLE PARTS

| | |
|---|---|
| **Frame** | steel tube trellis |
| **Rake/trail** | adjustable between 23° 30' and 24° 30'/adjustable between 91mm (3.6in) and 97mm (3.8in) |
| **Front suspension** | 43mm (1.7in) USD fork |
| **Travel** | 127mm (5in) |
| **Adjustment** | rebound and compression damping, preload |
| **Rear suspension** | progressive linkage monoshock |
| **Travel** | 71mm (2.8in) |
| **Adjustment** | rebound and compression damping, preload |
| **Tyres** | |
| — make | Michelin Hi-Sports |
| — front | 120/70 x 17 |
| — rear | 190/50 x 17 |
| **Brakes** | |
| — make | Brembo |
| — front | 2 x 320mm (1.6in) steel floating discs, opposed four-piston calipers |
| — rear | 220mm (8.7in) steel disc, two-piston caliper |

# DUCATI 996 SPS

**Racing pedigree**
As with the 916SPS, Ducati produced a limited edition 'Foggy Replica' 996SPS to celebrate the success of its WSB rider, Carl Fogarty. Featuring a race-replica paint scheme, 150 bikes were produced in 1999. Troy Bayliss won the 2001 World Superbike championship on a factory-supported 996R, the 2001 model year successor to the 996SPS.

**Suspension**
Both the fully adjustable rear monoshock and the steering damper are high-quality parts by Swedish manufacturer Ohlins.

**Front forks**
The Ohlins forks shown here were fitted for the 2000-model bike. Their inner stanchion tubes are coated in gold-coloured titanium nitride, a hard, slippery substance that reduces friction in the forks, improving their operation.

**Wheels**
The wheels were high-specification five-spoke Marchesinis, lighter than the standard three-spoke designs featured on the standard 996.

DUCATI 996SPS

**Ducati's range-topping flagship**
sports bike from 1998–2000, the 996SPS, is one of the most highly developed race replica machines ever produced. The 'SPS' suffix to the 996 model name stands for 'Sport Production Special' and denotes a very high specification variant of the standard Ducati 996 machine. Launched in 1998 as a replacement to the 916SPS model (which, confusingly, used a 996cc/60.8ci engine), the Ducati 996SPS featured higher specification engine and chassis components than those that were used on the standard 996.

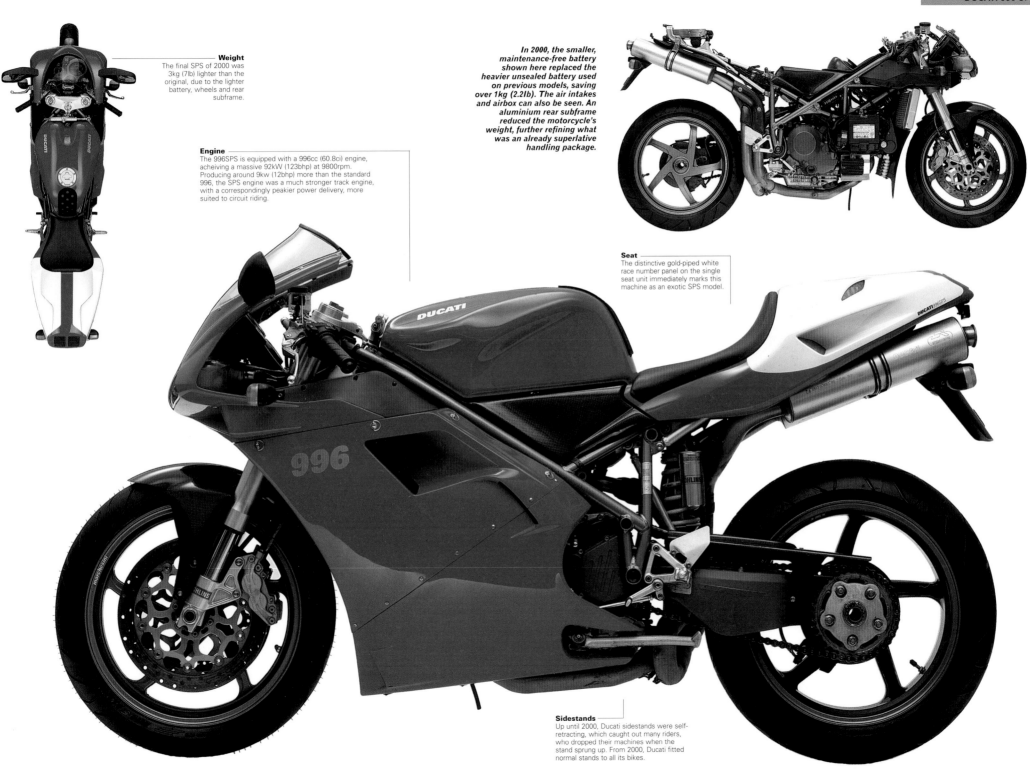

**Weight**
The final SPS of 2000 was 3kg (7lb) lighter than the original, due to the lighter battery, wheels and rear subframe.

*In 2000, the smaller, maintenance-free battery shown here replaced the heavier unsealed battery used on previous models, saving over 1kg (2.2lb). The air intakes and airbox can also be seen. An aluminium rear subframe reduced the motorcycle's weight, further refining what was an already superlative handling package.*

**Engine**
The 996SPS is equipped with a 996cc (60.8ci) engine, acheiving a massive 92kW (123bhp) at 9800rpm. Producing around 9kw (12bhp) more than the standard 996, the SPS engine was a much stronger track engine, with a correspondingly peakier power delivery, more suited to circuit riding.

**Seat**
The distinctive gold-piped white race number panel on the single seat unit immediately marks this machine as an exotic SPS model.

**Sidestands**
Up until 2000, Ducati sidestands were self-retracting, which caught out many riders, who dropped their machines when the stand sprung up. From 2000, Ducati fitted normal stands to all its bikes.

# HARLEY-DAVIDSON 883 SPORTSTER

*The valanced rear mudguard is a real echo from the 1950s, and its lines are not spoiled by a pillion seat.*

**Controls**
The right cluster holds the engine kill switch, starter button and right indicator. On the left are the lights dip/main switch, horn and left indicator. There is no lights on/off switch, as they come on with the ignition.

**Brakes**
Single 292.1mm disc (11.5in) at the front and exactly the same at the rear.

**Indicators**
Unusually, the indicators are suspended from the handlebars instead of being fixed to the fork legs between the top and bottom yokes.

**Low seat**
At just 711mm (28in), the 883's seat is fairly low, making it easy to cope with the bike's relatively heavy weight and popular with new riders lacking the confidence to tackle taller machines.

**Rear suspension**
The twin rear shock absorbers worked by the tubular steel swingarm are heavily chromed and adjustable for preload only, by turning a notched collar at the base.

**Forks**
The 883's 39mm (1.5in) forks are plain and simple, with the only adjustment option being the weight of oil you decide to use. Maximum suspension travel is 175.3mm (6.1in).

**Wheels and tyres**
The wheels are available either laced or the more usual 13 spoke aluminium cast. Tyres are 100/90 x 19 front and 130/90 x 16 rear with Dunlop Elite being the preferred choice.

**Slim profile**
The Harley's V-twin engine and a total lack of bodywork keep the bike extremely slim, making it ideal for nipping through gaps in heavy city traffic. If the wide handlebars can slip through, you know you have room.

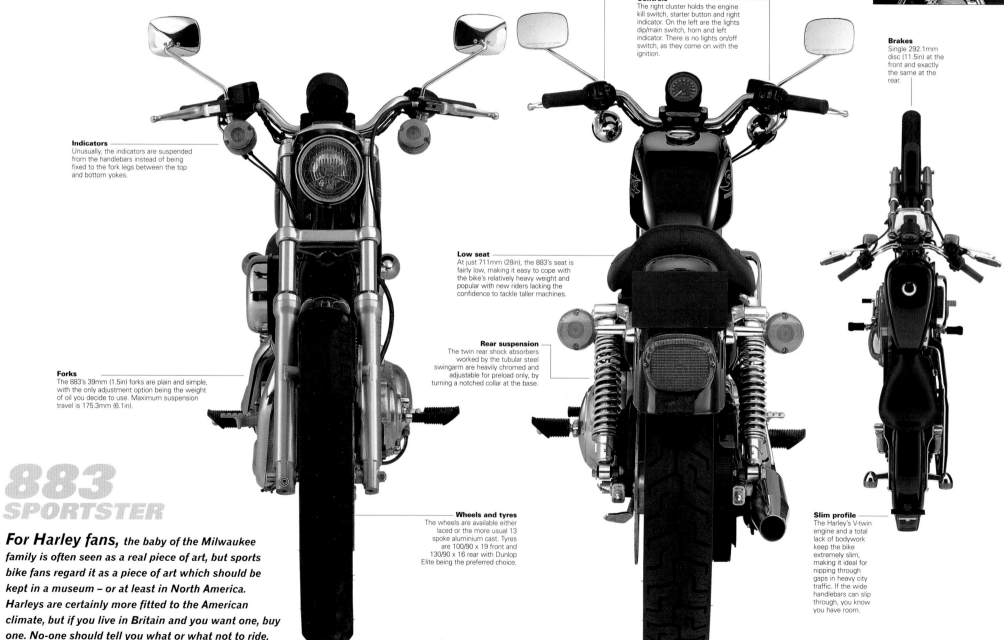

# 883 SPORTSTER

**For Harley fans,** *the baby of the Milwaukee family is often seen as a real piece of art, but sports bike fans regard it as a piece of art which should be kept in a museum – or at least in North America. Harleys are certainly more fitted to the American climate, but if you live in Britain and you want one, buy one. No-one should tell you what or what not to ride.*

*The footrests are covered in thick rubber, which helps damp out the motor's considerable vibrations.*

*The large upright speedo and single bank of warning lights give the bike a clean and classic look when viewed from the saddle.*

*The 883's engine is fed by a standard issue carb, breathing through an oval 'race track' air filter.*

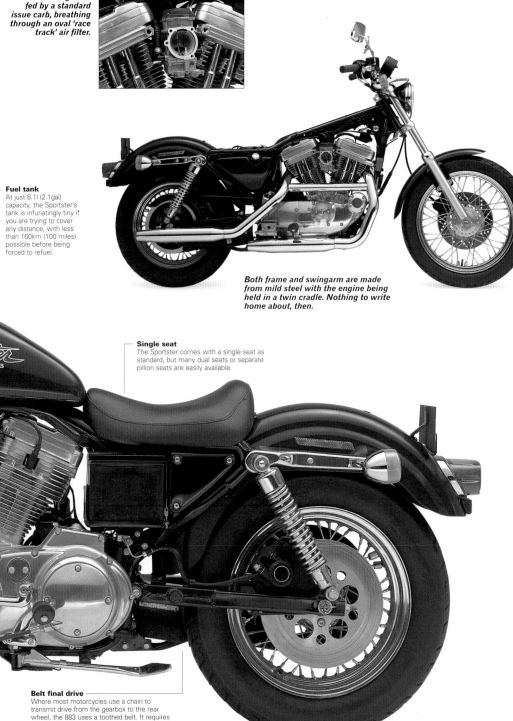

*Both frame and swingarm are made from mild steel with the engine being held in a twin cradle. Nothing to write home about, then.*

**Fuel tank**
At just 8.1l (2.1gal) capacity, the Sportster's tank is infuriatingly tiny if you are trying to cover any distance, with less than 160km (100 miles) possible before being forced to refuel.

**Single headlight**
The quartz halogen 55 watt low beam/60 watt high beam light is cased in a domed chrome retro-style shell. It isn relatively weak, so night riding is best kept to short distances.

**Single seat**
The Sportster comes with a single seat as standard, but many dual seats or separate pillion seats are easily available.

**Engine**
The 883cc (54ci) Evolution V-twin is standard across the Harley band. Service intervals are: first at 805km (500 miles) and every 8050km (5000 miles) thereafter.

**Belt final drive**
Where most motorcycles use a chain to transmit drive from the gearbox to the rear wheel, the 883 uses a toothed belt. It requires less maintenance than a chain and is quieter, but could not handle superbike power.

# HARLEY-DAVIDSON 883 SPORTSTER

# Specifications

*It has been all change* at *Harley-Davidson for 2000 and the Sportster has not missed out, with new brakes and transmission internals, among other features. This is one Harley that appeals to a wider audience than just Harley fans. Could be because it has remained uncluttered and with a simplicity of style that appeals to even those who swear they would never ride a Harley.*

*It was also the only bike available to shorter riders years before the Japanese manufacturers saw the potential market for cruisers. Still, it remains a popular choice for many.*

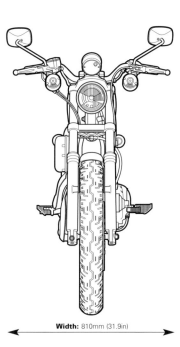

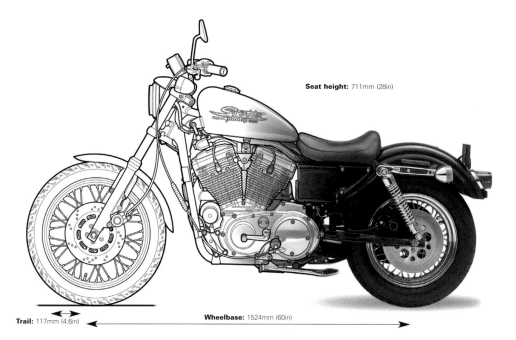

**Seat height:** 711mm (28in)

**Width:** 810mm (31.9in)

**Trail:** 117mm (4.6in)

**Wheelbase:** 1524mm (60in)

## ENGINE

| | |
|---|---|
| **Type** | 4-stroke |
| **Layout** | 45° V-twin |
| **Total displacement** | 883cc (54ci) |
| **Bore** | 76.2mm (3in) |
| **Stroke** | 96.8mm (3.8in) |
| **Compression ratio** | 9.0:1 |
| **Valves** | 2 per cylinder |
| **Fuel system** | single constant velocity carburettor |
| **Ignition** | battery-powered spark, electric |
| **Cooling** | air |
| **Maximum power** | 26kW (35bhp) @ 6000rpm |
| **Maximum torque** | 5.1kg-m (36.9lb-ft) @ 2400rpm |

## TORQUE

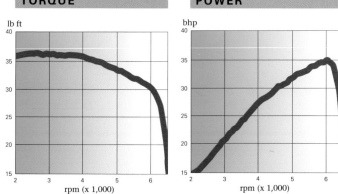

lb ft
rpm (x 1,000)

## POWER

bhp
rpm (x 1,000)

## TRANSMISSION

| | |
|---|---|
| **Primary drive** | chain |
| **Clutch** | wet, multi-plate |
| **Gearbox** | 5-speed |
| **Final drive** | belt |

## WEIGHTS & CAPACITIES

| | |
|---|---|
| **Tank capacity** | 12.5l (3.3gal) |
| **Dry weight** | 222.3kg (489lb) |
| **Weight distribution** | |
| — front | N/A |
| — rear | N/A |
| **Wheelbase** | 1524mm (60in) |
| **Overall length** | 2235mm (88in) |
| **Overall width** | 810mm (31.9in) |
| **Overall height** | 1150mm (45.3in) |
| **Seat height** | 711mm (28in) |

## CYCLE PARTS

| | |
|---|---|
| **Frame** | steel twin cradle |
| **Rake/trail** | 29.6°/117mm (4.6in) |
| **Front suspension** | 39mm (1.5in) telescopic forks |
| **Travel** | N/A |
| **Adjustment** | preload |
| **Rear suspension** | twin shock |
| **Travel** | 175mm (6.9in) |
| **Adjustment** | preload |
| **Tyres** | |
| — make | Dunlop |
| — front | 100/90 x 19 |
| — rear | 130/90 x 16 |
| **Brakes** | |
| — make | |
| — front | single 292mm (11.5in) disc, fixed 4-piston caliper |
| — rear | single 292mm (11.5in) disc, fixed 4-piston caliper |

**Independent test measurements (above) differ from the manufacturer's claimed maximum power and maximum torque figures.**

## HARLEY-DAVIDSON DYNA SUPERGLIDE SPORT

*Clocks are minimalist and to the point; they feature an electronically-operated speedometer, a tacho, fuel gauge, and trip meter. The 'idiot light' cluster comprises high beam, neutral, oil and indicator bulbs.*

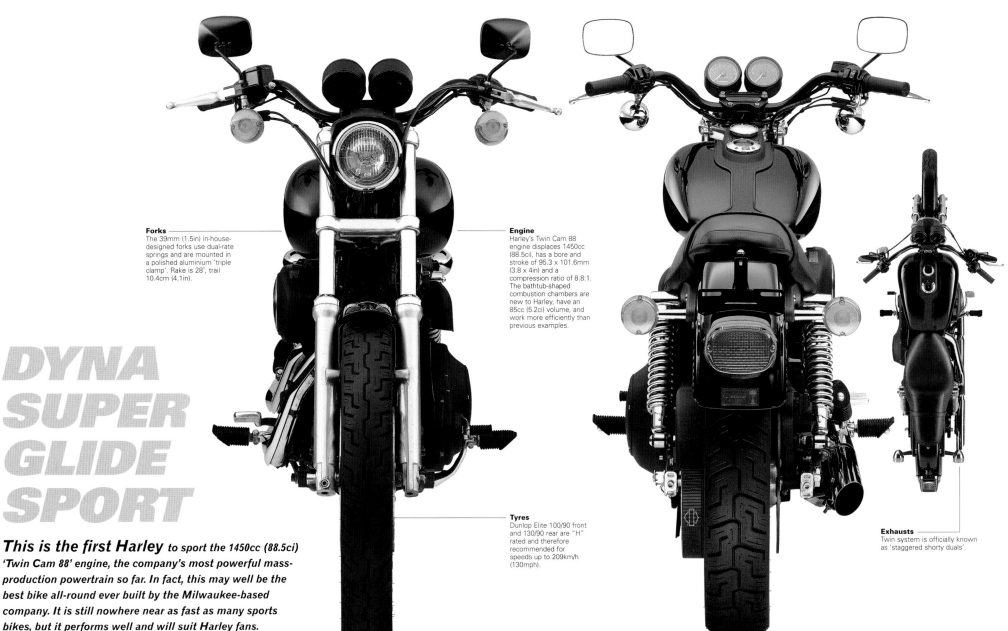

**Forks**
The 39mm (1.5in) in-house-designed forks use dual-rate springs and are mounted in a polished aluminium 'triple clamp'. Rake is 28°, trail 10.4cm (4.1in).

**Engine**
Harley's Twin Cam 88 engine displaces 1450cc (88.5ci), has a bore and stroke of 95.3 x 101.6mm (3.8 x 4in) and a compression ratio of 8.8:1. The bathtub-shaped combustion chambers are new to Harley, have an 85cc (5.2ci) volume, and work more efficiently than previous examples.

**Tyres**
Dunlop Elite 100/90 front and 130/90 rear are "H" rated and therefore recommended for speeds up to 209km/h (130mph).

**Exhausts**
Twin system is officially known as 'staggered shorty duals'.

## DYNA SUPER GLIDE SPORT

**This is the first Harley** to sport the 1450cc (88.5ci) 'Twin Cam 88' engine, the company's most powerful mass-production powertrain so far. In fact, this may well be the best bike all-round ever built by the Milwaukee-based company. It is still nowhere near as fast as many sports bikes, but it performs well and will suit Harley fans.

*The 45° V-twin has 50 per cent bigger cooling fins, new, forged flywheels and stronger connecting rods. Bore distortion should be a thing of the past thanks to a new metal-to-metal joint marrying the crankcases and cylinders.*

*The 292mm (11.5in) twin disc set-up may not look much, but what do looks matter when you have stopping power like this? The rider will feel little bite, but this Harley will stop from 160km/h (100mph) in just 118.2m (388ft) – not at all bad.*

*The Harley frame uses a rectangular-section backbone and twin downtubes, married to a rectangular-section swingarm, all fashioned from mild steel.*

**Fuel tank**
Holds 18.57l (4.9gal) and has an average fuel consumption of 55km/pg (37.5 mpg).

**Seat**
The slim Badlander seat helps set the Sport aside from other models in the range and is just 686mm (27in) high. Pillion comfort in the stepped and short rear platform is poor over long distances.

**Brakes**
Harley's brakes are the butt of many jokes, but these work remarkably well on the Sport, stopping the bike completely from 160km/h 100mph in 118metres (388ft) – just 3m (9.8ft) shy of Honda's VFR800 sports tourer!).

**Wheels**
Laced rims come in 19 x 63.5mm (2.5in) front and 16 x 7.6mm (3in) rear.

**Wheelbase**
The wheelbase is 1623mm (63.9in).

# HARLEY-DAVIDSON  *DYNA SUPERGLIDE SPORT*

# Specifications

*At the heart of the* Super Glide Sport lies the 'Twin Cam 88' engine – the most powerful mass-produced motor Harley-Davidson has ever produced. However, despite its 1450cc displacement, it fails to offer the performance of a Japanese or European machine – but that is not what Harleys are about. With the bike's weight, stopping power has to be good – and it is. Although the 292mm (11.5in) front discs do not look impressive, they are certainly effective. The chassis is typical Harley, with a mild steel rectangular backbone and downtubes married to a rectangular-section swingarm.

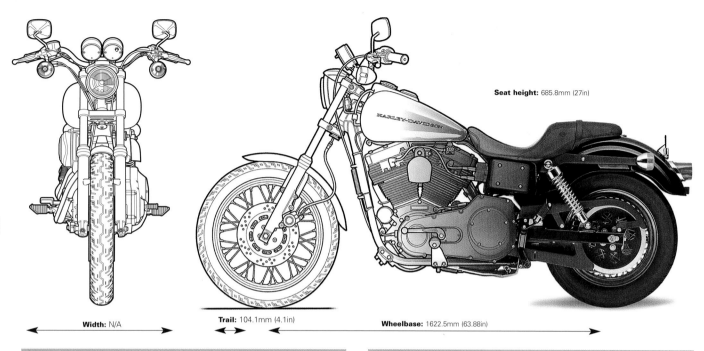

**Seat height:** 685.8mm (27in)

**Width:** N/A

**Trail:** 104.1mm (4.1in)

**Wheelbase:** 1622.5mm (63.88in)

## ENGINE

| | |
|---|---|
| Type | 4-stroke |
| Layout | 45° V-twin |
| Total displacement | 1450cc (88.5ci) |
| Bore | 95.2mm (3.75in) |
| Stroke | 101mm (4in) |
| Compression ratio | 8.9:1 |
| Valves | 2 per cylinder |
| Fuel system | 40mm (1.6in) CV carburettor |
| Ignition | electronic |
| Cooling | air |
| Maximum power | 19.8kW (53.6bhp) @ 5300rpm |
| Maximum torque | 9.3kg-m (67lb-ft) @ 3090rpm |

## TRANSMISSION

| | |
|---|---|
| Primary drive | double row chain |
| Clutch | wet, multiplate |
| Gearbox | 5-speed |
| Final drive | belt |

## WEIGHTS & CAPACITIES

| | |
|---|---|
| Tank capacity | 18.6l (4.1gal) |
| Dry weight | 300kg (660lb) |
| Weight distribution | |
| — front | N/A |
| — rear | N/A |
| Wheelbase | 1622.5mm (63.88in) |
| Overall length | 2539mm (92.88in) |
| Overall width | N/A |
| Overall height | N/A |
| Seat height | 685.8mm (27in) |

## CYCLE PARTS

| | |
|---|---|
| Frame | mild steel, rectangular backbone, twin downtubes |
| Rake/trail | 28°/104.1mm (4.1in) |
| Front suspension | 39mm forks |
| Travel | N/A |
| Adjustment | none |
| Rear suspension | twin shock |
| Travel | preload |
| Adjustment | |
| Tyres | |
| — make | Dunlop Elite |
| — front | 100/90 x 19 |
| — rear | 130/90 x 16 |
| Brakes | |
| — make | Harley-Davidson |
| — front | 292mm (11.5in) discs |
| — rear | 292mm (11.5in) discs |

## TORQUE

## POWER

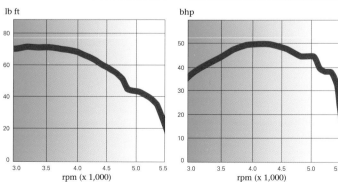

Independent test measurements (above) differ from the manufacturer's claimed maximum power and maximum torque figures.

# HONDA *NC30*

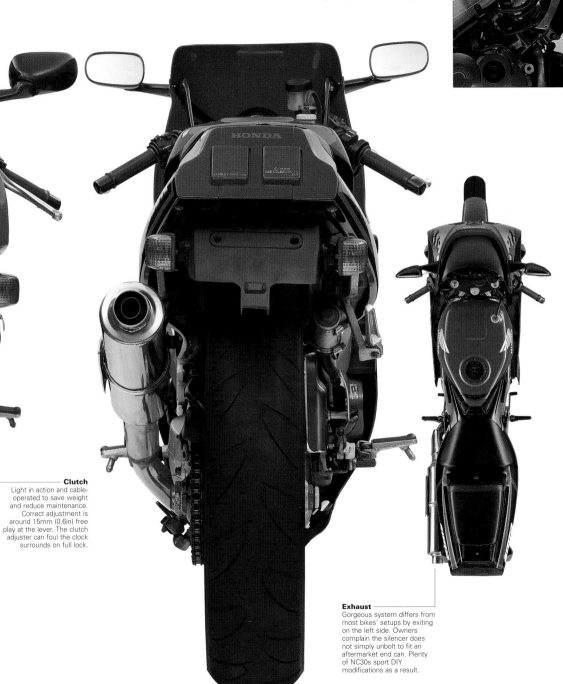

*Honda recommends two heat ranges of spark plugs, according to how hard the bike will be ridden. Many owners fit 'high speed' plugs, only to have them foul at low to moderate speed. Removal of the plugs is described by many owners as a nightmare.*

**Carburettors**
Can go out of balance quickly, which means another tricky job for the home mechanic because of the way the engine and its peripherals are so tightly packed into the frame. With the carbs seated between the vee of the cylinders, access is difficult, while the location of the adjuster screws and vacuum plugs (on the underside) means screwdrivers with universal joints are usually needed.

**Clutch**
Light in action and cable-operated to save weight and reduce maintenance. Correct adjustment is around 15mm (0.6in) free play at the lever. The clutch adjuster can foul the clock surrounds on full lock.

**Exhaust**
Gorgeous system differs from most bikes' setups by exiting on the left side. Owners complain the silencer does not simply unbolt to fit an aftermarket end can. Plenty of NC30s sport DIY modifications as a result.

## *NC30*

*If you have never* considered anything smaller than a 600 before, take a look at Honda's NC30. Packed full of race-bred technology, it comes into its own on the twisties and will surprise more than a few riders of bigger machinery. Best of all, it is exclusive, something which cannot be said about too many sports bikes these days, unless you are prepared to pay well over the odds.

With the speedo, the most obvious detail difference between grey and 'officially' imported NC30s is the speedometer. British and American bikes come with **MPH** clocks while continentally sourced imports have **KPH** clocks.

Fuel tank holds 15l (4gal), of which 2l (0.5gal) is reserve. The reserve fuel tap is awkwardly shaped and placed, making its operation tricky on the move.

Tyres are narrow by some standards, but ideally suited to the NC30. They come in 120/60 x 17 and a more unusual 150/60 x 18 rear fitment. Rubber choice is slightly restricted.

**Rake/trail**
Sporty figures of 25.2° and 96mm (3.8 in) show how race-oriented the NC30 is.

**Seat**
Small and low and necessitates a sporty posture, its great for short distance scratching and track riding, but uncomfortable for longer periods.

**Swingarm**
The NC30 is one of the very few bikes to sport a single-sided swingarm. It not only boosts looks, but makes rear wheel removal easier too. A specific-fit paddock stand is needed.

# Specifications

*Available as an import* for only the first half of its lifespan, the VFR4OOR NC30, Honda's stunning mini-racer, has captivated the hearts of tens of thousands worldwide since its introduction back in 1989. The jewel-like V-four engine, with its gear-driven cams, packs plenty of torque for its size and blends seemlessly with a stunning chassis.
A short wheelbase, superb suspension and sticky tyres make the NC30 the perfect back-road scratching tool and an ideal diminutive track racer straight from the crate.

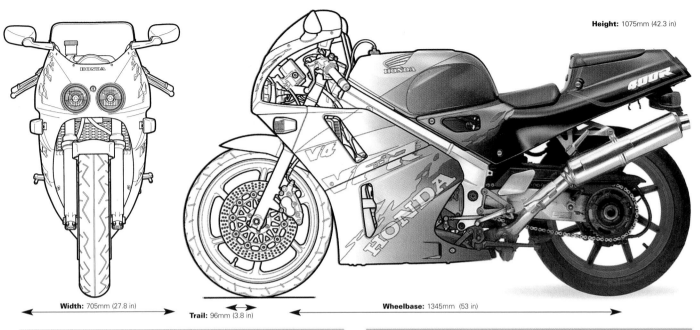

**Height:** 1075mm (42.3 in)

**Width:** 705mm (27.8 in)

**Trail:** 96mm (3.8 in)

**Wheelbase:** 1345mm (53 in)

## ENGINE

| | |
|---|---|
| Type | 4-stroke |
| Layout | 90° V-four |
| Total displacement | 399cc (24.3ci) |
| Bore | 55mm (2.2in) |
| Stroke | 42mm (1.7in) |
| Compression ratio | 11.3:1 |
| Fuel system | 4 x constant velocity carburettors |
| Ignition | digital electronic |
| Cooling | liquid |
| Maximum power | 42.4ci (56.8bhp) @ 12,500rpm |
| Maximum torque | 3.7kg-m (26.7lb-ft) @ 9800rpm |

## TRANSMISSION

| | |
|---|---|
| Primary drive | gear |
| Clutch | wet multiplate |
| Gearbox | 6-speed |
| Final drive | chain |

## WEIGHTS & CAPACITIES

| | |
|---|---|
| Tank capacity | 15l (3.3gal) |
| Dry weight | 175kg (385lb) |
| Weight distribution | |
| — front | N/A |
| — rear | N/A |
| Wheelbase | 1,345mm (52.95in) |
| Overall length | 1985mm (78. 1in) |
| Overall width | 705mm (28in) |
| Overall height | 1075mm (42.3in) |
| Seat height | N/A |

## CYCLE PARTS

| | |
|---|---|
| Frame | backbone |
| Rake/trail | 25.2 /96mm (3.8in) |
| Front suspension | telescopic forks |
| Travel | 120mm (4.7in) |
| Adjustment | preload, compression and rebound damping |
| Rear suspension | Single-sided swingarm |
| Travel | 120mm (4.7in) |
| | |
| Tyres | |
| — make | varies |
| — front | 120/60 x 17 |
| — rear | 150/60 x 18 |
| Brakes | |
| — make | Nissin |
| — front | twin discs |
| — rear | single disc |

## TORQUE

## POWER

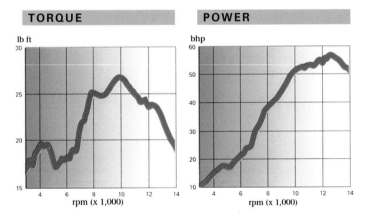

**Independent test measurements (above) differ from the manufacturer's claimed maximum power and maximum torque figures.**

# HONDA **CB400 FOUR**

*Unlike the bigger 750, the 400 had a six-speed gearbox and a wet, multiplate clutch.*

**Bars**
Flat, making for a sporty look and a comfortable ride.

**Handlebars**
The flat handlebars were a trademark of the 400 Four.

**Brakes**
The front disc was powerful enough, but for hard stopping the rear drum was needed.

**Engine**
The 408cc (24.9ci) air-cooled four was smooth, satisfying and ultra reliable by the standards of the mid-1970s.

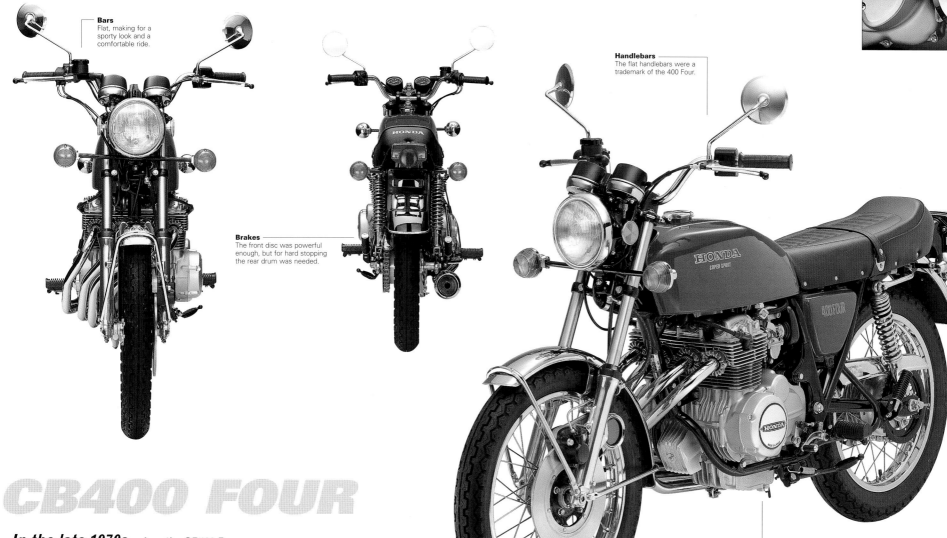

## CB400 FOUR

*In the late 1970s, when the CB400 Four was launched, most Japanese performance roadsters followed a similar layout. This near-universal design was based around an air-cooled, four-cylinder engine, mounted transversely in a steel tube cradle frame, with front disc brakes, rear drum brake, conventional forks and twin rear shocks.*

*On early models, the paintwork was scarlet or deep blue.*

*A tubular steel cradle with a single front downtube split to two tubes under the engine.*

**Exhaust**
The four-into-one exhaust was the perfect touch with the downpipes slanting diagonally across the front of the engine.

**Clocks**
Simple, clean and easy to read.

**Engine**
The 408cc (24.9ci) air-cooled eight-valve engine used a central chain to a single overhead cam.

# HONDA CB600 HORNET S

**Fuel tank**
A small-capacity tank which, when combined with the engine's surprising thirst, means the Hornet is handicapped by a limited fuel range – hard riding can easily have you searching for a filling station after as little as 160km (100 miles).

**Fairing**
A basic frame-mounted fairing designed to expand the Hornet's ability as a higher-speed, long-distance machine. The protection it offers is not great, but it fends off the worst of the windblast and adds considerably to the bike's practicality for that reason alone.

**Front suspension**
Fairly basic conventional telescopic forks, which offer no facility for adjusting either the damping or the spring preload. But they are still a reasonable quality, so a lot of riders will not miss having the relevant knobs to fiddle with.

## HORNET S

**The Hornet S differs from** the Hornet only in having the frame-mounted half fairing. The bike's attractive styling was originally seen on the Hornet 250, a model sold only in Japan. It has translated extremely well to the bigger 600cc (36.6ci) version, although the engine, which is derived from the superb **CBR600F,** has made the move to the new bike less effectively.

*An old-fashioned steel spine-type frame designed to be unobtrusive visually and to be relatively cheap to make. It shows off the engine and gives the bike a more traditional look, although there is a penalty to pay in the extra weight compared to an aluminium frame.*

**Front brakes**
At first, these look like state-of-the-art four-piston calipers, but closer inspection shows them to be the cheaper floating two-piston kind. These flex more when the brakes are used hard, which reduces feedback to the rider and gives the lever a more wooden sensation.

**Swingarm**
A simple box-section design, but it does make one concession to improving the bike's performance by being made of aluminium. This is disproportionately beneficial as the reduction in weight is in unsprung mass, which improves suspension performance considerably.

**Gearbox**
Based on the CBR600F unit, which means it is a variation on Honda's general gearbox design, with all the clunkiness that comes with it. This was improved in the mid-1990s, but is still below average in feel and ease of operation.

**Engine**
Absolutely typical Japanese four-cylinder unit, based on the excellent CBR600F motor, which means four carburettors, double overhead camshafts and so on. Age is given away by the use of steel cylinder liners rather than the more modern ceramic-coated all-aluminium cylinders.

# HONDA **CB600 HORNET S**

# Specifications

**The Hornet followed the** *pattern set by Suzuki and Yamaha in using the engine from a supersports 600 and adapting it to suit a streetbike chassis, thus creating a budget middleweight machine which does not lose out too much in performance terms to the genuine supersports bikes. And the pattern continues with the Hornet S, which like many bikes of this type has followed up the original naked version with the addition of a half fairing. This expands the bike's capabilities by taking the effort out of long distance, high speed work, fending off the windblast which on the naked option has the rider hanging on and stressing his neck and arm muscles.*

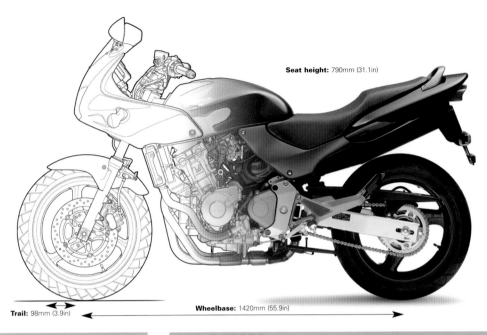

Seat height: 790mm (31.1in)

Width: 730mm (28.7in)

Trail: 98mm (3.9in)

Wheelbase: 1420mm (55.9in)

## ENGINE

| | |
|---|---|
| Type | 4-stroke |
| Layout | inline 4 |
| Total displacement | 599cc (37ci) |
| Bore | 65mm (2.6in) |
| Stroke | 45.2mm (17.8in) |
| Compression ratio | 12:1 |
| Valves | 4 per cylinder |
| Fuel system | 4 x 34mm (1.3in) slanted flat-slide CV carbs |
| Ignition | computer controlled digital |
| Cooling | liquid |
| Maximum power | 70.4kW (94.4bhp) @ 11,817rpm |
| Maximum torque( | 6.6kg-m (47.75lb-ft) @ 9569rpm |

## TRANSMISSION

| | |
|---|---|
| Primary drive | gear |
| Clutch | wet multiplate |
| Gearbox | 6-speed |
| Final drive | O-ring chain |

## WEIGHTS & CAPACITIES

| | |
|---|---|
| Tank capacity | 16l (4.2gal) |
| Dry weight | 180kg (396.8lb) |
| Weight distribution | |
| — front | N/A |
| — rear | N/A |
| Wheelbase | 1420mm (55.9in) |
| Overall length | 2090mm (82.3in) |
| Overall width | 730mm (28.7in) |
| Overall height | 1060mm (41.7in) |
| Seat height | 790mm (31.1in) |

## CYCLE PARTS

| | |
|---|---|
| Frame | steel box-section spine |
| Rake/trail | 25°/98mm (3.9in) |
| Front suspension | 41mm (1.6in) telescopic forks |
| Travel | 128mm (5in) |
| Adjustment | none |
| Rear suspension | monoshock |
| Travel | 128mm (5in) |
| Adjustment | 7-way preload |
| Tyres | |
| — make | Michelin/Bridgestone |
| — front | 130/70 x ZR16 |
| — rear | 180/55 x ZR17 |
| Brakes | |
| — make | Nissin |
| — front | 2 x 296mm (11.7in) discs, 2-piston calipers |
| — rear | 1 x 220mm (8.7in) disc, 1-piston caliper |

## TORQUE

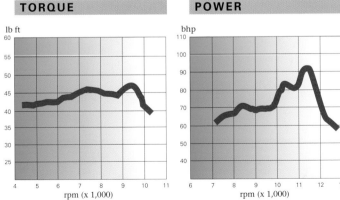

lb ft

rpm (x 1,000)

## POWER

bhp

rpm (x 1,000)

Independent test measurements (above) differ from the manufacturer's claimed maximum power and maximum torque figures.

# HONDA *CBR600F*

*Too many bikes these days do not have a mainstand. The handy little Honda does, though.*

**Handlebars**
Clip-on bars are higher than you would expect and this, combined with the footpeg position, means that the rider is balanced in a fairly sedate position, which is comfortable over long distances.

**Cooling system**
The radiator on the CBR600 is curved, giving a greater surface area for maximum cooling efficiency.

*Direct Air Induction is Honda's ram air system. Note the duct in the fairing below the headlight.*

**Screen and mirrors**
Screen offers good protection because of its shape. The mirrors are large enough to offer a good view

**Forks**
41mm (1.6in) telescopic forks are adjustable for preload and rebound damping, but the springs are relatively soft.

**Front brakes**
Twin 296mm (11.7in) steel discs with Nissin dual piston calipers. The discs are drilled to give better heat dissipation and to sweep away the layer of brake dust that forms on the pad under braking.

*Screw head is the rebound damping adjuster for a front fork and below it is the preload adjuster.*

**Rear suspension**
Honda Pro-link rising rate linkage with Kayaba monoshock. Fully adjustable for rebound and compression damping and preload. Firm, responsive, good all round.

**Rear brake**
220mm (8.7in) disc with a single piston caliper using sintered metal pads.

**Tyres**
Original equipment Michelin Macadams on 43.2cm (17in) five-spoke wheels perform only averagely. Hard riders should consider changing them for stickier rubber once they wear out.

# CBR600F

## The CBR600F has been a world

*favourite since its introduction just over a decade ago. It is fast and it handles well, but what makes it stand out? The package – the balance of power, handling and braking is superb. And this is not just a bike for the road. It has achieved enormous success in the 600cc (36.6ci) class on the track – a truly formidable opponent and one of the great motorcycles of the last 20 years.*

Instrumentation is simple – speedometer, tachometer and water temperature gauge. Redline is at 13,500rpm.

Stripped of its bodywork, you can see the CBR's ageing but still effective chassis. Above the swingarm is a rear wheel hugger and chain guard, which helps to keep dirt and oil off the rear shock.

**Engine**
The 13,500rpm engine pulls strongly from just 4000rpm, giving a wide spread of useable power. It makes around 71kW (95bhp) on the dyno.

**Fuel and ignition system**
The fuel/air mixture is fed to the cylinders via four 36mm (1.4in) Keihin carburettors. Ignition is controlled by a computerized digital ignition system using a conventional coil.

**Grab-rail**
A rare item on modern sports bikes. Features like these add to the CBR's reputation as the most accomplished all-rounder.

**Headlamp**
This is a conventional reflector unit – the light beam is focused by a concave reflecting plate behind the bulb.

**Fairing**
It has never strayed far from the original concept – just become more stylish over the years.

**Chassis**
The twin spar frame may be made of steel while many newer sports bikes are using aluminium, but the rideability impresses.

# Specifications

*Although Honda's CBR600F had* always sold in huge numbers, the launch of Yamaha's **R6** and the success of Suzuki's **GSX-R600** and Kawasaki's **ZX-6R** meant that the company decided it was time for a change.
*And what a change! This is a totally redesigned bike with a more powerful engine, great handling and absolutely superb brakes. An aluminium chassis replaced the steel one and weight was reduced by an astounding 16kg (35.2lb). This sharp all-rounder should satisfy anyone.*

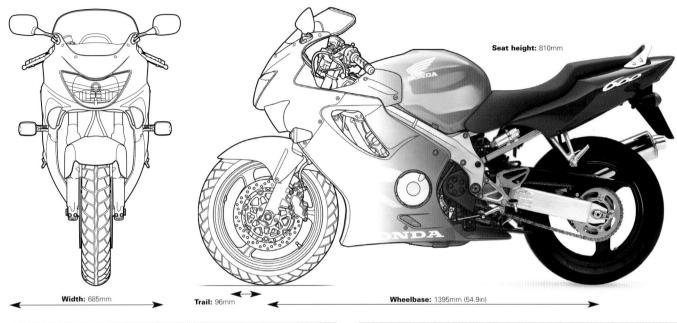

**Seat height:** 810mm

**Width:** 685mm

**Trail:** 96mm

**Wheelbase:** 1395mm (54.9in)

## ENGINE

| | |
|---|---|
| Type | 4-stroke |
| Layout | DOHC in-line four |
| Total displacement | 599cc (37ci) |
| Bore | 67mm (2.6in) |
| Stroke | 42.5mm (16.7in) |
| Compression ratio | 12:1 |
| Valves | 4 per cylinder |
| Fuel system | 4 x 36.5mm slanted flat-slide CV carburettors |
| Ignition | CDI |
| Cooling | liquid |
| Maximum power | 98bhp @ 12,000rpm |
| Maximum torque | 45.6lb-ft @ 10,100rpm |

## TORQUE

lb ft

rpm (x 1,000)

## POWER

bhp

rpm (x 1,000)

Independent test measurements (above) differ from the manufacturer's claimed maximum power and maximum torque figures.

## TRANSMISSION

| | |
|---|---|
| Primary drive | gear |
| Clutch | wet multiplate |
| Gearbox | 6-speed |
| Final drive | chain |

## WEIGHTS & CAPACITIES

| | |
|---|---|
| Tank capacity | 18l (3.96gal) |
| Dry weight | 170kg (374lb) |
| Weight distribution | |
| — front | N/A |
| — rear | N/A |
| Wheelbase | 1395mm (54.9in) |
| Overall length | 2,060mm (81.1in) |
| Overall width | 685mm (27.0in) |
| Overall height | 1,130mm (44.5in) |
| Seat height | 810mm (31.9in) |

## CYCLE PARTS

| | |
|---|---|
| Frame | aluminium twin spar |
| Rake/trail | 24°/96mm |
| Front suspension | 43mm (1.7in) telescopic forks |
| Travel | 120mm (4.7in) |
| Adjustment | preload, plus rebound and compression damping |
| Rear suspension | monoshock |
| Travel | 120mm (4.7in) |
| Adjustment | preload, plus rebound and compression damping |
| Tyres | |
| — make | varies (Michelin, Bridgestone, Dunlop) |
| — front | 120/70 x ZR17 |
| — rear | 180/55 x ZR17 |
| Brakes | |
| — make | Nissin |
| — front | 2 x 296mm discs, opposed 4-piston calipers |
| — rear | 220mm (8.7in) disc, 1-piston caliper |

# **HONDA** CBR600FS

**Fairing**
Although diminutive and equipped with a low screen, it actually offers reasonable weather protection, although you'd still need waterproofs to keep dry in the rain.

**Tail light**
The fitting of two bulbs means rearwardly-approaching vehicles can still see you if one bulb succumbs to vibration.

**Engine**
A large part of the package which has made the '99 CBR 16kg (35.2lb) lighter than its predecessor, it has been almost totally changed. New crankcases (which are used as a stressed member to anchor the swingarm), cylinders, pistons, head, valves, crankshaft and clutch are among the major features.

**Mirrors**
The stalks are longer than on many faired bikes, which means a decent rear view devoid of a rider's arms or shoulders is offered. They don't blur with excessive vibration at any speed and can be folded against the fairing to aid mobility through narrow passages.

**Air induction system**
Racers of previous CBRs have criticised the bike for a throttle response which sometimes suffered as a result of less than optimal air metering. New pipework between the fairing-mounted scoops and the carbs helps, as does introducing new auxiliary air intake channels which run independently of the main ducts and feed directly to the floatbowls.

**Front suspension**
The 43mm (1.7in) conventional telescopic forks are well set-up as standard, but offer full adjustability so riders can taper handling performance to their own needs. Minor adjustments can be clearly felt so a big deviation away from stock is unlikely to be necessary. They have exactly 120mm (4.7in) of travel.

**Footpegs**
Thankfully, Honda hasn't moved the footpegs into a more sporty position. Their placement means even the tallest riders can travel good distances without suffering cramp. Combined with the seat height and excellent handlebar position, they make both fast sports and sedate touring riding a pleasure.

**Silencer**
Raised enough to make contact with the road unlikely when cornering, it can be easily removed too. Expect a wide range of aftermarket offerings for both race and road to hit the shops soon.

**Tyres**
The 180/55 rear and 120/70 front tyres are the widest combination yet fitted to any CBR600. The front has been designed specifically to complement the 1999 model, while the rear uses already proven technology. Both are Michelin TX Hi-Sport radials and offer outstanding grip well suited to fast trackday use. They won't last as long as other, harder compounds though.

*In 1999 a new era dawned for Honda's CBR600F. This was not just a slightly revamped model but an all-new machine. A lighter but more powerful engine combined with a lighter aluminium frame focused even more attention on performance. It aimed to be one of the lightest, strongest and fastest machines in its class.*

*Wide, chunky and ideally placed, the grab rail offers passengers a superb comfort and safety aid.*

*The front stoppers are now identical to those fitted to the FireBlade and offer a big improvement over previous designs, resulting in much better feel and increased stopping power. Although the caliper, disc and pad combination doesn't excel on the heavier 'Blade, it suits the lighter 600 very well.*

*Replacing the steel chassis fitted to all previous CBR600s with aluminium has given the 1999 machine a major new lease of life. Combined with a new, lighter swingarm, this component part now weighs in at a staggering 7kg (15.4lb) less than the 1998 bike's version. This means easier and less tiring turning and a reduced workload for the suspension – something which pays dividends down bumpy roads.*

**Fuel tank**
Riding at 70 mph in top gear returns around 48 mpg which, combined with a 3.96 gallon fuel tank, gives a range of 190 miles. The tank's design allows magnetic bags to be easily attached and is so slim at the rear that it almost feels as though it's not there.

**Seat**
The padding is more than comfortable enough to make riding between fuel stops a joy. The seat height of 810mm (31.9in) is just right for most riders and the pillion perch is flat enough to prevent passengers sliding around under hard acceleration or braking. There's space for a U-lock underneath.

**Headlight**
Good enough for swift riding in the rain thanks to a new multi-reflector design, it's still not the best on offer and can definitely be improved.

**Wheels**
The front is 8cm (3.5in) wide, the rear 13cm (5.5in). Both are 17in in diameter and are of a hollow-section triple-spoke cast aluminium design. The new rear rim size opens up a wider range of slicks for racers.

**Wheelbase**
At 1395mm (54.9in), it's short enough to be sporty and long enough to offer stability. The result is a bike which holds its line well but isn't the quickest turning on the planet.

# Specifications

*Although Honda's **CBR600FS** had* always sold in huge numbers, with the launch of Yamaha's **R6** and the success of Suzuki's **GSX-R600** and Kawasaki's **ZX-6R** the company obviously (and rightly) decided it was time for a change.
And what a change! This is a totally redesigned bike with a more powerful engine, great handling and absolutely superb brakes. An aluminium chassis replaced the steel one and weight was reduced by an astounding 35.2lb (16kg). It is a sharp all-rounder which should satisfy anyone.

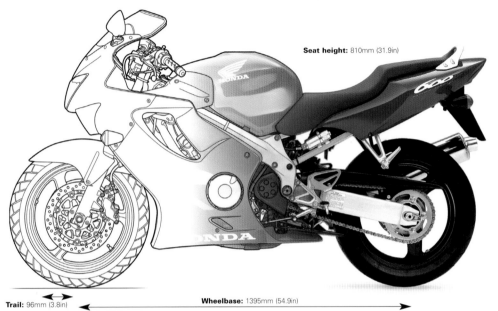

**Seat height:** 810mm (31.9in)

**Width:** 685mm (27in)  **Trail:** 96mm (3.8in)  **Wheelbase:** 1395mm (54.9in)

## ENGINE

| | |
|---|---|
| Type | 4-stroke |
| Layout | DOHC in-line four |
| Total displacement | 599cc (37ci) |
| Bore | 67.0mm |
| Stroke | 42.5mm (16.7in) |
| Compression ratio | 12:1 |
| Valves | 4 per cylinder |
| Fuel system | 4 x 36.5mm (14.4in) slanted flat-slide CV carburettors |
| Ignition | CDI |
| Cooling | liquid |
| Maximum power | 73kw (98bhp) @ 12,000rpm |
| Maximum torque | 6.3kg-m (45.6lb-ft) @ 10,100rpm |

## TORQUE

## POWER

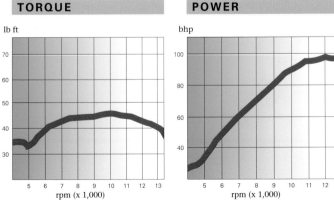

lb ft

bhp

rpm (x 1,000)

rpm (x 1,000)

**Independent test measurements (above) differ from the manufacturer's claimed maximum power and maximum torque figures.**

## TRANSMISSION

| | |
|---|---|
| Primary drive | gear |
| Clutch | wet multiplate |
| Gearbox | 6-speed |
| Final drive | chain |

## WEIGHTS & CAPACITIES

| | |
|---|---|
| Tank capacity | 18l (4.8gal) |
| Dry weight | 170kg (374lb) |
| Weight distribution | |
| — front | N/A |
| — rear | N/A |
| Wheelbase | 1395mm (54.9in) |
| Overall length | 2060mm (81.1in) |
| Overall width | 685mm (27in) |
| Overall height | 1130mm (44.5in) |
| Seat height | 810mm (31.9in) |

## CYCLE PARTS

| | |
|---|---|
| Frame | aluminium twin spar |
| Rake/trail | 24°/96mm (3.8in) |
| Front suspension | 43mm (1.7in) telescopic forks |
| Travel | 120mm (4.7in) |
| Adjustment | preload, plus rebound and compression damping |
| Rear suspension | monoshock |
| Travel | 120mm (4.7in) |
| Adjustment | preload, plus rebound and compression damping |
| Tyres | |
| — make | varies (Michelin, Bridgestone, Dunlop) |
| — front | 120/70 x ZR17 |
| — rear | 180/55 x ZR17 |
| Brakes | |
| — make | Nissin |
| — front | 2 x 296mm discs, opposed 4-piston calipers |
| — rear | 220mm (8.7in) disc, 1-piston caliper |

# HONDA CBR600RR

**The CBR600RR's** high-tech electronic display incorporates a large analogue tachometer with a digital LCD speedometer. An **LCD** fuel gauge and clock also feature, as well as a gearchange light, which flashes when engine revs approach the redline.

**Ram-air intakes**
The twin air intakes on the front edge of the fairing feed cool, dense, high-pressure air to the CBR's large air box. Special chambers in the intake tracts boost midrange power and reduce intake noise from the engine.

**Mirrors**
The CBR's mirrors feature a super-light resin construction.

**Engine**
Mostly hidden behind the fully enclosed fairing, the CBR600RR's engine is a conventional inline-four, 16-valve design, albeit very compact and powerful.

**Silencer**
The CBR600RR features a 'Centre-Up' exhaust design, with an underseat silencer replacing the conventional side-mounted design of earlier models. This improves ground clearance and aerodynamics, while giving a clean 'racing' style to the rear end.

**Headlights**
The CBR600RR uses Honda's Line Beam headlight technology, which allows a brighter, sharper beam from a smaller headlight aperture. Only one light is illuminated on dip beam.

**Tail light**
Conventional incandescent bulbs have been replaced on the CBR600RR by a sealed LED unit. This saves weight and cuts maintenance; LEDs never burn out like normal bulbs. The LED brake light also illuminates quicker, improving safety.

**Gearbox**
The CBR's gearbox uses a 'stacked' layout to shorten the engine, allowing a more compact chassis.

## CBR600RR

**Designed to dominate** World Superport racing, as well as win showroom sales, Honda's **CBR600RR** took a different direction from previous **CBR600** models. The **RR** suffix denotes a no-compromise performance machine, and the **CBR** borrowed design cues from Honda's awesome **RC211V** MotoGP champion. Superlative handling and a powerful 85.8kW (115bhp) engine ensured success for Honda – Australian rider Chris Vermeulen won the 2003 **WSS** championship on the **CBR600RR**, and it topped sales charts worldwide.

**Forks**
An advanced 45mm (1.8in) cartridge-type front fork provides superb damping and control, as well as high levels of rigidity, improving handling.

**Rear tyre**
Honda fitted a sticky 180/55 section rear tyre to the CBR600RR.

*The CBR's massive aluminium rear swingarm uses Honda's Unit Pro-Link system, which mounts the rear shock completely in the swingarm. It combines massive stiffness with light weight.*

**Frame**
Honda developed a new casting process to produce the CBR's frame, which is made up from cast sections welded together.

**Exhaust**
Small link pipes between the exhaust header pipes improve midrange power delivery. The main collector pipe passes up the side of the swingarm to the underseat silencer.

**Pillion seat**
The CBR600RR is primarily a sports machine, so the passenger accomodation is rather limited. The small pillion pad sits high behind the rider, and the small footpegs make for an uncomfortable ride. The pillion seat can be swapped for a plastic cover for use with a rider only.

**Fuel injection**
Hidden under the fuel tank, the CBR600RR uses a sophisticated fuel injection system, with two fuel injectors for each cylinder, improving power delivery at low and high engien speeds.

**Fuel tank**
What looks like a conventional fuel tank is in fact a plastic cover. The fuel tank is situated partly below the rider's seat, the front part of the space under the cover being taken by the large air box.

**Screen**
The CBR's race design means the screen is low, and the rider has to be in a tight crouch to tuck in behind at speed.

**Front brakes**
The CBR uses dual 310mm (12.2in) floating discs and Nissin four-piston hydraulic calipers, providing excellent stopping power and control.

# HONDA XL600V TRANSALP

The silencer has a trick appearance thanks to twin over-and-under end caps. Escaping sound is more like that from a busy sewing machine, however.

**Hand guards**
Honda has a tendency to go for cheap plastic hand guards, and what a boon they are. Made of the kind of stuff that can take a thousand crashes, they also do a brilliant job at keeping hands dry and reasonably warm too. A real boon for the winter distance rider.

**Carburettors**
The simple and low-powered engine design is happily fed by two 34mm (1.3in) carburettors.

**Rear brake**
Single 240mm (9.5in) disc and single-piston caliper assembly lacks feel but packs good power.

**Tank**
Holds 18l (4.8gal), giving a potential range of 254km (158 miles) at a sedate pace. The filler cap screws off.

**Gearbox**
5-speed transmission is precise, if a little clunky. Neutral selection occasionally proves tricky when the engine is hot.

**Front suspension**
41mm (1.6in) leading-axle fork set-up has 200mm (7.9in) travel, giving the bike some, albeit limited, opportunity for gentle off-road use. The damping action is soft under all conditions.

**Rear suspension**
Pro-Link design gives 190mm (7.5in) of axle travel, allowing relaxed green lane riding.

**Swingarm**
Alignment markings for chain adjustment are notoriously inaccurate. Correct true is best checked manually.

## XL600V TRANSALP

**On the continent,** the Transalp would go down well, but in Britain this type of machine is usually seen as second best to any sports bike. Numerous updates have been introduced since its launch in 1987, but the constantly low price has ensured its popularity with its intended buyers. The Transalp excels at nothing, but as an all-round, everyday, versatile bike there are not many as easy to live with as this.

The liquid-cooled, four-stroke, single overhead cam engine is of V-twin design but uses a 'non-conventional' 52° angle between cylinders. Bore and stroke is 75 x 66mm (3 x 2.6in), compression ratio is 9.2:1 and total displacement measures 583cc (35.6ci).

Front 256mm (10.1in) discs and dual-piston calipers look weedy – and are. Our testers could only manage a best stop of 122.7m (402.5ft) from 160km/h (100mph). Feedback through the handlebars and lever is, however, very good.

**Grab handles**
Side-mounted grab handles help boost passenger safety and comfort and tie-up with Honda's mini luggage rack, which will be used by owners far more frequently than they might think.

**Seat**
Acceptably comfortable and 33.5in (850mm) tall at the rider's end, it is virtually stepless toward the rear, allowing passengers to tuck in snugly.

**Gaitors**
Cheap 'concertina' fork covers not only help the bike look the part, but extend fork seal life and protect the chrome of the inner legs as well. These particular ones are prone to splitting over a year or two, but are easily replaced by generic items costing only a few pounds.

**Bashplate**
Standard equipment on most true off-roaders, and often seen on hopeless wannabe imitators too. Its sole job is to protect the engine sump from damage by rocks, logs and other obstacles.

**Gear lever**
Mounted proud of the bashplate, it is in a prime spot for damage in the event of an off-road tumble.

# Specifications

*Honda's Transalp has been* around, for what seems like an eternity – almost 14 years in fact, which is a good indication of how popular this trailie has been with the buying public. Its sales potential was recognized from the beginning, and as a result it has received numerous updates during the course of its life span. Its grunty 35.8kW (48bhp), 583cc (35.6ci) V-twin has enough power to satisfy most and the XLV's inherent toughness and ease of maintenance make it a good choice for new riders and those not afraid to get into the dirt.

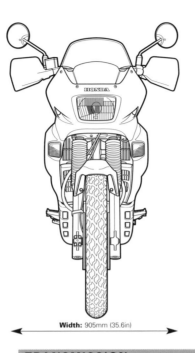

**Width:** 905mm (35.6in)

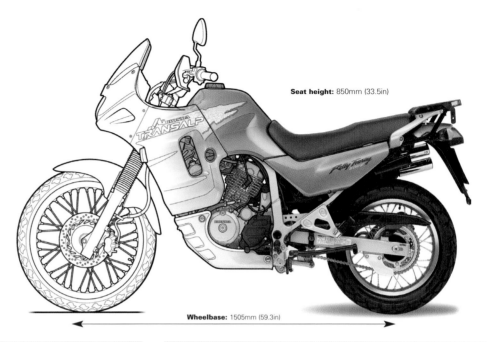

**Seat height:** 850mm (33.5in)

**Wheelbase:** 1505mm (59.3in)

## ENGINE

| | |
|---|---|
| Type | 4-stroke |
| Layout | V-twin |
| Total displacement | 583cc (35.6ci) |
| Bore | 75mm (3in) |
| Stroke | 66mm (2.6in) |
| Compression ratio | 9.2:1 |
| Valves | 2 per cylinder |
| Fuel system | 2 x 34mm (1.3in) carburettors |
| Ignition | digital transistorized withelectronic advance |
| Cooling | liquid |
| Maximum power | 35.5kW (47.6bhp) @ 7759rpm |
| Maximum torque | 5.2kg-m (37.6lb-ft) @ 5964rpm |

## TRANSMISSION

| | |
|---|---|
| Clutch | wet, multiplate |
| Gearbox | 5-speed |
| Final drive | 'O' ring chain |

## CYCLE PARTS

| | |
|---|---|
| Frame | steel mono-backbone |
| Rake/trail | N/A |
| Front suspension | 41mm (1.6in) leading-axle fork |
| Travel | 200mm (7.9in) |
| Adjustment | none |
| Rear suspension | Pro-link |
| Travel | 190mm (7.5in) |
| Adjustment | none |
| Tyres | |
| — make | Varies |
| — front | 90/90 x 21 |
| — rear | 120/90 x 17 |
| Brakes | |
| — make | N/A |
| — front | 2 x 256mm (10in) discs, dual-piston calipers, sintered metal pads |
| — rear | 240mm (9.4in) hydraulic disc, single-piston caliper |

## WEIGHTS & CAPACITIES

| | |
|---|---|
| Tank capacity | 18l (4.8gal) |
| Dry weight | 196kg (432lb) |
| Weight distribution | |
| — front | N/A |
| — rear | N/A |
| Wheelbase | 1505mm (59.3in) |
| Overall length | 2265mm (89.2in) |
| Overall width | 905mm (35.6in) |
| Overall height | 1300mm (52.4in) |
| Seat height | 850mm (33.5in) |

## TORQUE

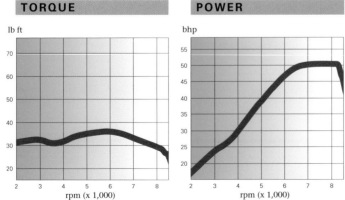

lb ft

rpm (x 1,000)

## POWER

bhp

rpm (x 1,000)

Independent test measurements (above) differ from the manufacturer's claimed maximum power and maximum torque figures.

# HONDA *SLR650*

*The 41mm (1.6in) leading axle forks have 190mm (7.5in) of travel, are softly sprung, and have no scope for adjustment whatsoever.*

**Mirrors**
Cheap build-quality, but low vibration and fair field of vision.

**Fuel tank**
Short and stubby tank holds just 13l (2.86gal).

**Front brake**
Single 276mm (10.9in) disc is grabbed by a two-piston caliper wearing sintered metal pads. Hard application causes the forks to dive, then buck, and fade becomes apparent after a few runs. They work okay, but are not particularly confidence-inspiring.

**Rear suspension**
Cheap monoshock with Pro-Link linkage feels bargain-basement but is actually a sturdy and robust component. Travel is a hefty 170mm (6.7in).

**Wheels**
Just like its rival, Aprilia's Pegaso, Honda has gone for typical trailie 48.3cm (19in) front and 43.2cm (17in) rear rim sizes. They take 100/90 and 120/90 size tyres respectively. Rims are aluminium.

# *SLR650*

## There is nothing special *about this one.*

*Only produced from 1996 to 1999 with basic but uninspiring hardware and variable build quality, the SLR650 is unlikely to be remembered with affection in years to come. Although its specs look weak on paper, you may be pleasantly surprised when you get it out on the road or in the dirt.*

Rear brake – 220mm (8.7in) disc and one-piston caliper, with non-asbestos resin mould pads combination, has a progressive feel and reasonable power. Better than the rear of many sportsbikes, in fact.

Uninspiring black sidecovers hide a mass of tightly crammed electrics and help protect pillion's legs from the exhaust's heat.

A no frills, tubular steel design the chassis, like the rest of the bike is designed for minimal maintenance. However, flexing is quite noticeable and build quality only average compared to most Hondas.

**Seat**
At 845mm (33.3in), the SLR's seat height is, again, identical to the Pegaso. Comfort and is roomy enough for two.

**Mudguard**
One glance at its proximity to the front tyre shows how unsuited this trailie is to actual off-road work.

**Engine**
No-frills basics here. The air-cooled SOHC single four-stroke has a 644cc (39.3ci) capacity, bore and stroke of 100 x 82mm (3.9 x 3.2in), and lowly compression ratio of 8.3:1. Fuel is supplied by a single 40mm (1.6in) carburettor. Gearbox is five-speed.

**Ground clearance**
Bashguard-protected underside has 200mm (7.9in) of clearance.

**HONDA** *SLR650*

# Specifications

*If you have only ever* ridden sports bikes along the lines of Honda's **CBR600F** or FireBlade, Yamaha's **YZF-R1**, Suzuki's **GSX-R750** – well, the SLR650 will only disappoint.

But if you are into something different or are a fairly new rider, this is not a bad bike to own. Its weight and seat height mean it suits almost everybody and it is quick off the mark too – ideal for city traffic. But highway riding will only serve to frustrate; stick to minor roads on this one because it has a top speed of only 155km/h (96.5 mph). Basic but fun.

**Seat height:** 845mm (333in)

**Wheelbase:** 1440mm (56.7in)

**Width:** 765mm (29.8in)

## ENGINE

| | |
|---|---|
| Type | 4-stroke |
| Layout | 4 valve, single cylinder |
| Total displacement | 644cc |
| Bore | 100mm (3.9in) |
| Stroke | 82mm (3.2in) |
| Compression ratio | 10:1 |
| Valves | 4 per cylinder |
| Fuel system | 40mm (1.6in) carburettor |
| Ignition | transistorized electronic |
| Cooling | air |
| Maximum power | 23.8kW (31.9bhp) @ 6150rpm |
| Maximum torque | 4.3kg-m (31.2lb-ft) @ 4250rpm |

## TORQUE

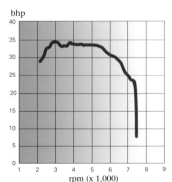

## POWER

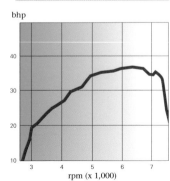

Independent test measurements (above) differ from the manufacturer's claimed maximum power and maximum torque figures.

## TRANSMISSION

| | |
|---|---|
| Primary drive | chain |
| Clutch | wet |
| Gearbox | 5-speed |
| Final drive | 'O'-ring sealed chain |

## WEIGHTS & CAPACITIES

| | |
|---|---|
| Tank capacity | 13l (3.4gal) |
| Dry weight | 161kg (354.2lb) |
| Weight distribution | |
| — front | N/A |
| — rear | N/A |
| Wheelbase | 1440mm (56.7in) |
| Overall length | 2185mm (85.2in) |
| Overall width | 765mm (29.8in) |
| Overall height | 1140mm (44.4in) |
| Seat height | 845mm (33.3in) |

## CYCLE PARTS

| | |
|---|---|
| Frame | steel mono backbone |
| Rake/trail | N/A |
| Front suspension | 41mm (1.6in) telescopic forks |
| Travel | 190mm (7.5in) |
| Adjustment | none |
| Rear suspension | Pro-Link |
| Travel | 170mm (6.6in) |
| Adjustment | preload |
| Tyres | |
| — make | Varies |
| — front | 110/90 x 19 |
| — rear | 120/90 x 17 |
| Brakes | |
| — make | N/A |
| — front | 276mm single hydraulic, dual piston caliper, sintered metal pads |
| rear | 220mm (8.7in) hydraulic disc, single piston caliper, non-asbestos resin mould pads |

# HONDA **CB750**

**Clocks**
As concise and unobtrusive as possible, staying true to the minimalist styling of the 1960s and 1970s.

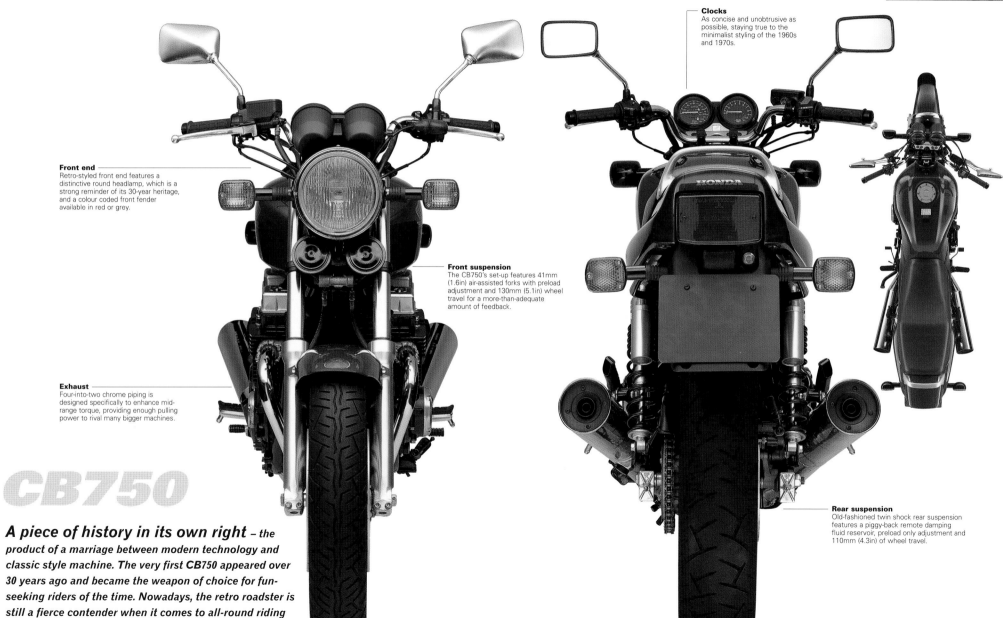

**Front end**
Retro-styled front end features a distinctive round headlamp, which is a strong reminder of its 30-year heritage, and a colour coded front fender available in red or grey.

**Front suspension**
The CB750's set-up features 41mm (1.6in) air-assisted forks with preload adjustment and 130mm (5.1in) wheel travel for a more-than-adequate amount of feedback.

**Exhaust**
Four-into-two chrome piping is designed specifically to enhance mid-range torque, providing enough pulling power to rival many bigger machines.

**Rear suspension**
Old-fashioned twin shock rear suspension features a piggy-back remote damping fluid reservoir, preload only adjustment and 110mm (4.3in) of wheel travel.

## CB750

***A piece of history in its own right*** – the product of a marriage between modern technology and classic style machine. The very first **CB750** appeared over 30 years ago and became the weapon of choice for fun-seeking riders of the time. Nowadays, the retro roadster is still a fierce contender when it comes to all-round riding with its durable engine and responsive suspension.

The aluminium grab rail is stylish and different from the usual body colour of black. Yet another subtle, and retro, touch.

At the front, a pair of 296mm (11.7in) solid discs and two-piston calipers provide the stopping power. At the rear is a single 240mm (9.4in) disc.

*Not particularly exciting, but the CB750's tubular steel chassis is strong and stiff, helping to give good stability and predictable handling.*

**Tank**
Classically sculpted 20 l (5.3gal) fuel tank gives reasonable range depending on the style of riding, and is ergonomically designed to allow the rider to sit snugly against the bike.

**Seat**
Noted by many for its exceptional comfort, whether on short-distance outings or long-haul excursions. The 790mm (31.1in) seat height makes the bike accessible to riders of all but the shortest leg length.

**Wheels**
43.2cm (17in) six spoke cast aluminium wheels finished in black give the CB750 a solid-looking, aggressive street appeal.

**Engine**
Based on the old 16 valve CBX750 power unit of the mid-1980s, with high-revving 67 x 53mm (2.6 x 2.1in) bore and stroke dimensions. The 747cc (45.6ci) in-line four cylinder DOHC engine is air-cooled, features a five-speed indirect gearbox and uses four 34mm (1.3in) constant velocity carburettors. It makes a claimed 54.4kW (73bhp) at 8500rpm.

**Wheelbase**
The 1495mm (59in) wheelbase offers a reasonable blend of stability and agility, which makes the CB750 an easy-to-ride machine for experienced and novice riders alike and enhances the bike's already-ample all-round capabilities.

# Specifications

*Although the CB750 has been around, in one form or another, for three decades – and obviously the model launched in 1992 is a great improvement on its predecessor – some would still describe it as 'average'. It cannot be over-criticized: although it performs and handles as it should, it certainly lacks the excitement factor, and when put against others in the 750 class, its school report would definitely be marked as 'could do better'.*

Height: 1100mm (43.3in)

Seat height: 795mm (31.3in)

Length: 2155mm (84.8in)

## ENGINE

| | |
|---|---|
| Type | 4-stroke |
| Layout | in-line four |
| Total displacement | 747cc (45.6ci) |
| Bore | 67mm (2.6in) |
| Stroke | 53mm (2.1in) |
| Compression ratio | 9.3:1 |
| Valves | 4 per cylinder |
| Fuel system | 4 x 34mm (1.3in) VE-type carburettors |
| Ignition | fully transistorised electronic |
| Cooling | air |
| Maximum power | 51.8kW (69.3bhp) @ 84000rpm |
| Maximum torque | 6kg-m (43.7lb-ft) @ 7000rpm |

## TRANSMISSION

| | |
|---|---|
| Primary drive | gear |
| Clutch | wet multiplate |
| Gearbox | 5-speed |
| Final drive | 'O' ring sealed chain |

## WEIGHTS & CAPACITIES

| | |
|---|---|
| Tank capacity | 20l (5.3gal) |
| Dry weight | 215kg |
| Weight distribution | |
| — front | N/A |
| — rear | N/A |
| Wheelbase | 1495mm |
| Overall length | 2155mm (84.8in) |
| Overall width | 780mm (30.7in) |
| Overall height | 1100mm (43.3in) |
| Seat height | 795mm (31.3in) |

## CYCLE PARTS

| | |
|---|---|
| Frame | twin cradle |
| Rake/trail | N/A |
| Front suspension | 41mm (1.6in) air-assisted forks |
| Travel | 130mm (5.1in) |
| Adjustment | none |
| Rear suspension | remote reservoir dampers |
| Travel | 110mm (4.3in) |
| Adjustment | spring preload |
| Tyres | |
| — make | N/A |
| — front | 120/70 x 17 |
| — rear | 150/70 x 17 |
| Brakes | |
| — make | N/A |
| — front | 296mm (11.7in) dual disc, dual piston calipers |
| — rear | 240mm (9.4in) single disc, single piston caliper |

*Includes a white-faced rev counter, digital speed and tripmeter, and a nickel, silver and carbon fibre ignition key. If you want to throw your key on the bar to impress anyone, this is the one to have.*

**Bodywork**
In a brilliant red ,the contours are very, very sexy. The silencers are integrated into the bodywork, the nose tips slightly forward – a Honda showpiece alright.

**Brakes**
Four-piston calipers on twin 310mm (12.2in) discs will haul the bike up quickly from any speed, although you may feel it in your arms. There is hardly any fork dive, though.

**Suspension**
Front and rear suspension is fully adjustable, as you would expect from this bike.

*NR750*

*You are looking at one of* the most rare and desirable motorcycles in the known universe. For sheer mystique and technical wizadry, the NR750 is without peers. Unfortunately for Honda, the price put many would-be buyers off and most around today are closeted and cosseted, so you are unlikely to see them on the road where they belong.

The 747cc (45.6ci) 32-valve *DOHC*, liquid-cooled engine was extremely innovative with its oval-pistoned V-four arrangement. It is worth noting, however, that many years before the Honda it was Triumph who first developed this. Bore and stroke is 101.2 x 50.6mm (3.9 x 1.9 in).

Five spoke, lightweight rims are racing spec items. The rear features quick release nut to minimize time in the pits on the racing circuit.

Nothing new here. A traditional twin spar frame wraps around the engine with a similar architecture to the RC30. The welding on all parts visible can only be described as delicate. It is no lightweight at 222.5kg (489.5lb), but is balanced well with near-perfect weight distribution.

**Steering**
Spot-on: it is stable and feedback is very good. Could be put down to the 24.5° rake and the 40.6cm (16in) front wheel. It will change direction with no effort at all.

**Forks**
Traditional 45mm (1.8in) upside-down forks, but with the NR750 distinctive in that they are finished in gold alumite.

**Engine**
A smoothie, this one. No power band, just a smooth, controlled power delivery all the way.

# Specifications

*This is a bike with* the most exotic specification of any road motorcycle in recent history. Not all of it comes across in the figures below, and in fact much of it does not seem at all special considering that it was introduced at the same time as the epochal FireBlade. That, of course, was the NR's big problem, along with the fact that Honda deliberately limited its power output to 93.2kW (125bhp) when it was capable of making much more – as much as 119.3kW (160bhp), said some insiders. Nor will the numbers give you an idea of the influence that the NR's styling had on many subsequent bikes, including most significantly Ducati's 916, which underwent a complete styling revamp after the NR was unveiled.

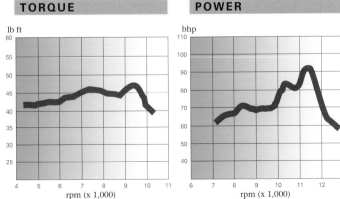

**Seat height:** 787mm (30.9in)

**Width:** 810mm (31.8in)

**Trail:** 87mm (3.4in)

**Wheelbase:** 1433mm (56.4in)

## ENGINE

| | |
|---|---|
| Type | 4-stroke |
| Layout | 90° V-4 |
| Total displacement | 747.7cc (45.6ci) |
| Bore | 75.3mm (2.9in) |
| Stroke | 42mm (1.7in) |
| Compression ratio | 11.7:1 |
| Valves | 8 per cylinder |
| Fuel system | Weber Marelli fuel injection |
| Ignition management | computer controlled engine |
| Cooling | liquid |
| Maximum power | 93.2kW (125bhp) @ 14,000rpm |
| Maximum torque | 6.9kg-m (50.5lb-ft) @ 11,500rpm |

## TORQUE

lb ft

rpm (x 1,000)

## POWER

bhp

rpm (x 1,000)

Independent test measurements (above) differ from the manufacturer's claimed maximum power and maximum torque figures.

## TRANSMISSION

| | |
|---|---|
| Primary drive | gear |
| Clutch | wet multiplate |
| Gearbox | 6 speed |
| Final drive | O-ring chain |

## WEIGHTS & CAPACITIES

| | |
|---|---|
| Tank capacity | 17.3l |
| Dry weight | 222.5kg |
| Weight distribution | |
| — front | N/A |
| — rear | N/A |
| Wheelbase | 1433mm (56.4in) |
| Overall length | 2110mm (83in) |
| Overall width | 810mm (31.8in) |
| Overall height | 1060mm (41.7in) |
| Seat height | 787mm (30.9in) |

## CYCLE PARTS

| | |
|---|---|
| Frame | twin spar aluminium |
| Rake/trail | 24°-30°/87mm (3.4in) |
| Front suspension | 45mm (1.8in) telescopic forks |
| Travel | N/A |
| Adjustment | spring preload, rebound and compression damping |
| Rear suspension | rising rate monoshock |
| Travel | N/A |
| Adjustment | ride height, spring preload, rebound and compression damping |
| Tyres | |
| — make | Michelin |
| — front | 130/70 x 16 |
| — rear | 180/55 x 17 |
| Brakes | |
| — make | Nissin NR |
| — front | 2 x 310mm (12.2in) discs, 4-piston caliper |
| — rear | 220mm (8.7in) disc, 2-piston caliper |

# HONDA RC45

The speedo is numbered in 20mph (32km/h) increments, although 5mph (8km/h) markers are used as well. The tacho displays its highest revs at its tallest point to save racers both that vital fraction of a second and the movement of the neck needed to check it out. The cluster of idiot lights and the temperature gauge can be difficult to view when your head is on the tank, thanks to the prominent front brake master cylinder.

**Mirrors**
For such a sporty bike, the mirrors actually do a good job at showing what is going on behind. Although taller riders may find their view a little blocked, average height people usually have no complaint.

*Unusual because it is mounted on the left, the quickly unbolted muffler is raised high to provide serious ground clearance.*

**Engine**
The 90° four-stroke V4 engine displaces 749.2cc (45.7ci), has a bore and stroke of 72 x 46mm (2.8 x 1.8in), a compression ratio of 11.5:1 and elicits a gorgeous howl.

**Forks**
Showa's 41mm (1.6in) upside-down forks with 120mm (4.7in) of travel, spring preload adjustment, and variable compression and rebound damping, are near perfect both on the road and track.

**Footpegs**
It is quite normal for riders above 1.8m (6ft) tall to find the bike cramped, thanks to raised, rearset footpegs which contort long limbs on anything more than a short spin.

**Swingarm**
In keeping with the bike's intended use on the race track, the swingarm is of a single-sided design to facilitate ultra-quick wheel changes. Its pay-off is extra weight, however, and this part alone goes a long way toward explaining the RC45's serious rearward weight distribution.

**Rear suspension**
The Showa rising rate monoshock is fully adjustable, sports 130mm (5.1in) of travel, and lets riders know exactly what is going on at the rear. Slightly stiff as standard, it is a world apart from the monoshock systems fitted to many other race replicas.

**Tyres**
The RC45 comes with Dunlop D204s as standard, although riders often change to their own particular favourites. Unusually, the front has a diameter of just 40.6cm (16in) instead of the more usual 43.2cm (17in), helping it turn more quickly.

## RC45

***Since its introduction*** at the end of 1993, comparatively few RC45s have been sold. The high price tag means that it has met competition from bikes such as Honda's FireBlade and Yamaha's YZF-R1, which are almost as good and about half the price. This, however, does not make the RC45 any less special.

*The RC45's brakes lack the outright power and initial sharpness of some setups, but manage to feed back plenty of information to the rider about what is going on between tyre and road.*

Honda has moved the RC45 away from the typical weight bias which normally results in near equal distribution front and rear. Instead, the bike's weight lies 56 per cent to the rear and 44 per cent to the front. Because first gear is ultra-tall, acceleration up to 112km/h (70mph) is less brisk than many sportsters which, in turn, means the weight distribution does not have as much front wheel-lifting effect as might be expected.

**Tank**
More rounded than curvy, it is nonetheless acceptably narrow at the crucial point toward the rear, where legs and body meet machine. It holds the industry standard 18l (4.8gal).

**Seat**
True race bikes like this one do not offer a perch for pillions. The rider's padding is thin but surprisingly comfortable for some and, at just 770mm (30.31in), low enough for most.

**Headlights**
The front lights throw out a decent beam, but are too reminiscent of the units once fitted to now out-of-date sportsters. They were designed to allow endurance racers to angle one of them to give an early view through rapidly approaching corners at night.

**Wheelbase**
At 1410mm (55.51in), it is sporty but not excessively so. Stability is no problem on the RC45.

**Clutch**
The wet, multi-plate clutch is built particularly strong to cope with the RC45's stupendously tall first gear and the resulting abuse that is needed to launch the bike quickly off the line.

# Specifications

*Other than its race-replica* style, the RC45 stands apart from the rest, thanks mainly to the chassis. The suspension is great – it continues to work and feed back information to the rider well beyond the limits of most other machines. The 41mm (1.6in) upside-down forks and rising-rate rear both offer good adjustability, allowing the bike to be set up for both road and track. The valve train is gear-driven, the connecting rods are made of titanium and the cylinder sleeves are now made of a lightweight, composite material. You may have to ride hard to enjoy it, but it is well worth it.

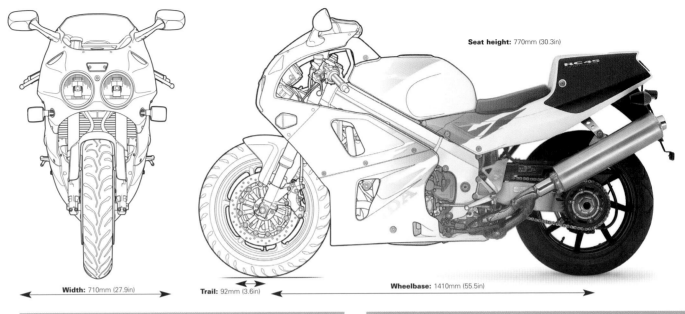

Seat height: 770mm (30.3in)
Width: 710mm (27.9in)
Trail: 92mm (3.6in)
Wheelbase: 1410mm (55.5in)

## ENGINE

| | |
|---|---|
| Type | 4-stroke |
| Layout | 90° V-four |
| Total displacement | 749.2cc (45.7ci) |
| Bore | 72mm (2.8in) |
| Stroke | 46mm (1.8in) |
| Compression ratio | 11.5:1 |
| Valves | 4 per cylinder |
| Fuel system | injection, one injector per cylinder |
| Ignition | digital electronic |
| Cooling | water |
| Maximum power | 79.7kw (106.9bhp) @ 12,000rpm |
| Maximum torque | 7.3kg-m (52.8lb-ft) @ 10,000rpm |

## TORQUE

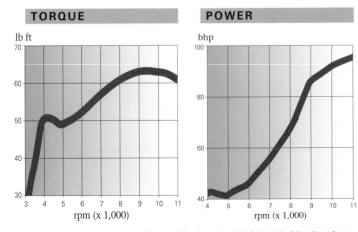

lb ft

rpm (x 1,000)

## POWER

bhp

rpm (x 1,000)

Independent test measurements (above) differ from the manufacturer's claimed maximum power and maximum torque figures.

## TRANSMISSION

| | |
|---|---|
| Primary drive | straight-cut gears |
| Clutch | wet multiplate |
| Gearbox | 6-speed |
| Final drive | sealed O-ring chain |

## WEIGHTS & CAPACITIES

| | |
|---|---|
| Tank capacity | 18l (4.8gal) |
| Dry weight | 189kg (415.8lb) |
| Weight distribution | |
| — front | 44% |
| — rear | 56% |
| Wheelbase | 1410mm (55.5in) |
| Overall length | 2110mm (83.1in) |
| Overall width | 710mm (27.9in) |
| Overall height | 1100mm (43.3in) |
| Seat height | 770mm (30.3in) |

## CYCLE PARTS

| | |
|---|---|
| Frame | aluminium twin spar |
| Rake/trail | 24°/92mm (3.6in) |
| Front suspension | 41mm (1.6in) Showa upside-down forks |
| Travel | 120mm (4.7in) |
| Adjustment | compression and rebound damping, plus preload |
| Rear suspension | Showa rising rate monoshock |
| Travel | 130mm |
| Adjustment | compression and rebound damping, plus preload |
| Tyres | |
| — make | Dunlop D204 |
| — front | 130/70-16 |
| — rear | 190/50-17 |
| Brakes | |
| — make | Nissin |
| — front | twin 4-piston calipers, 310mm (12.2in) discs |
| — rear | single 2-piston caliper, 220mm (8.7in) disc |

# HONDA XRV750 AFRICA TWIN

Features such an electronic trip-meter, digital timer and three mileage accumulators, make it easier to calculate hourly averages or follow rally road maps.

*Twin, bug-eye design is synonymous with the Africa Twin and offers a decent beam on both dip and main.*

*The brakes on the Paris–Dakar-styled machine are strong thanks to dual 276mm (10.9in) discs, dual-piston calipers and sintered metal pads.*

**Carburettors**
Generously sized at 36mm (1.4in), the two CV carbs are of the responsive flat-slide design.

**Sump guard**
Affords ground clearance of 215mm (8.5in), protects the engine and is made of durable aluminium.

**Pillion handles**
Take a bit of getting used to, but work effectively. They also incorporate bungee-attaching hooks.

**Front suspension**
43mm (1.7in) forks feature 220mm (8.7in) of travel, making them useful for light off-road use. There is no adjustment, but this is not essential anyway – the springing rate is reasonably on course from the start. Plastic reinforcing protects the sleeves.

**Seat**
Not overly tall for a bike of this type at 33.9in (860mm), although pre-1993 models measure in at 34.5in (875mm).

## XRV750

*Never tried a dual-purpose sports bike before?* *Well, get down to your nearest Honda dealer and ask for a go on the Africa Twin. It has to be doing something right – after all, it has been around for a decade and is still selling. For those who think bikes such as the CBR600F are the only ones to have fun on, the XRV750 will prove them wrong. And those who have tried it, need no-one to tell them what the fun is all about!*

The tank holds 23l (9.1gal), giving a range of around 322km (200 miles) at a push. Its position was altered in 1993, when the factory moved it further back and closer to the centre of gravity. This brought the added benefit of improved handling and agility – at all speeds.

**Fairing**
The current version owes much to a rethink in 1996, when a higher screen and resdesigned sides were introduced to boost rider comfort and protection.

The original motor featured a slightly bored-out version of the Transalp's powerplant, but this was dropped in 1990. The factory decided to up capacity to 750cc (45.8ci) but because the Transalp lump could not be taken out this far, a new engine had to be introduced. Today, it is a liquid-cooled 52° V-twin sporting a total of six valves, a single overhead cam design, 742cc (45.3ci), a 9:1 compression ratio and a bore and stroke of 81 x 72mm (3.2 x 2.8in).

**Wheels**
Aluminium rims use strong steel spokes and take a 90/90 x 21 bias ply front and 140/80 x 17 radial rear tyre.

**Rear brake**
Powerful, but offers decent feel too. The 256mm (10.1in) disc is grabbed by a single-piston caliper and resin mould pads.

# Specifications

*If you are looking for* a good dual-purpose bike, Honda's Africa Twin is probably as good a machine as any to start off with. It is a decent enough performer with a top speed of 174km/h (108mph). Nothing to get too excited about perhaps, but it does cruise along nicely at 160km/h (100mph).

It is when you get it off-road that you will really appreciate it. This Paris–Dakar replica will have you falling in love with both it and the dirt. And it looks good too.

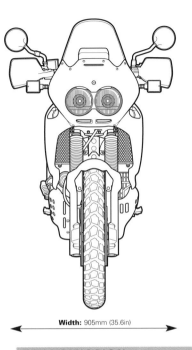

**Width:** 905mm (35.6in)

**Seat height:** 860mm (33.9in)

**Wheelbase:** 1565mm (61.6in)

## ENGINE

| | |
|---|---|
| Type | 4-stroke |
| Layout | SOHC 52° V-twin |
| Total displacement | 742cc (45.3ci) |
| Bore | 81mm (3.2in) |
| Stroke | 72mm (2.8in) |
| Compression ratio | 9:1 |
| Valves | 3 per cylinder |
| Fuel system | 2 x 36mm (1.4in) flat-slide carburettors |
| Ignition | digital electronic |
| Cooling | liquid |
| Maximum power | 38.7kW (52bhp) @ 7200rpm |
| Maximum torque | 60.8kg-m (44lb-ft) @ 5400rpm |

## TRANSMISSION

| | |
|---|---|
| Primary drive | gear |
| Clutch | wet, multiplate |
| Gearbox | 5-speed |
| Final drive | chain |

## WEIGHTS & CAPACITIES

| | |
|---|---|
| Tank capacity | 23l (5.06gal) |
| Dry weight | 207.5kg (456.5lb) |
| Weight distribution | |
| — front | N/A |
| — rear | N/A |
| Wheelbase | 1565mm (61.6in) |
| Overall length | 2320mm (91.3in) |
| Overall width | 905mm (35.6in) |
| Overall height | 1430mm (56.3in) |
| Seat height | 860mm (33.9in) |

## CYCLE PARTS

| | |
|---|---|
| Frame | cradle |
| Rake/trail | N/A |
| Front suspension | 43mm (1.7in) forks |
| Travel | 220mm (8.7in) |
| Adjustment | none |
| Rear suspension | Pro-Link, aluminium swing arm |
| Travel | 220mm (8.7in) |
| Adjustment | preload |
| Tyres | |
| — make | Bridgestone TW101 (f), TW152 (r), Michelin T66 (f), T66X (r) |
| — front | 90/90 x 21 |
| — rear | 140/80 x 17 |
| Brakes | |
| — make | Nissin |
| — front | dual 276mm (10.9in) discs, 2-piston calipers |
| — rear | 256mm (10.1in) disc, single-piston caliper |

## TORQUE

## POWER

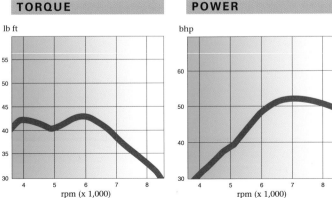

Independent test measurements (above) differ from the manufacturer's claimed maximum power and maximum torque figures.

# **HONDA** *VFR800*

*Though slightly bland in appearance, the instrumentation is nonetheless well laid out for ease of use. The white-faced rev counter, which displays its readout in 500rpm markings and 1000rpm numerals, takes pride of place in the centre, while the 274km/h (170mph) black-faced speedo lives on the left. A digital display on the right reveals a clock, trip meter, odometer and temperature gauge, among other features.*

**Mirrors**
Perfectly placed for most riders and, thankfully, almost vibration-free.

**Fuel injection**
Just as the engine is based on the one in Honda's track-conquering RC45 superbike, so is the injection system. Its setup ensures a clean response, without excessively sharp uptake, at any throttle opening position, which further reinforces the bike's ethos of being easy to ride.

**Fairing**
Love or hate its styling,, it is certainly practical and, being quite angular when viewed from the front, distinctive and a little different too. Recesses cut into the side panels (below the fuel tank) are there to give long-limbed riders more leg room.

**Left clip-on**
Houses the clutch lever, pass-light, main/dip beam switch, indicator button, and choke lever.

**Gearbox**
Six-speed box has well-chosen ratios and outputs power through a sealed O-ring chain.

**Right clip-on**
Plays host to the throttle grip, span-adjustable front brake lever, engine kill switch, electric start button and lights off/park/on switch.

**Brakes**
Honda's 'Dual Combined' system is used and links the twin front 296mm (11.7in) discs and three-piston calipers with the single rear 256mm (10.1in) disc and three-piston caliper. Sintered metal pads are fitted as standard. Front discs are 4.5mm (0.17in) thick, the rear 6mm (0.24in).

**Wheels**
Both the six-spoke front and five-spoke rear hoops have a 43.2cm (17in) diameter and are made of cast aluminium.

# *VFR800*

*When Honda announced it would add 50cc (3.1ci) to the much-loved VFR in 1998, almost everybody believed it would be an unbeatable machine. Unfortunately, they reckoned without Ducati's ST4 and Triumph's Sprint ST. Still, the VFR is such a good bike that it takes a lot of work and riding ability for anything to come near it.*

Each cylinder's downpipe is routed below or along the right side of the bike, before meeting at a collector box connecting to the single, right-side silencer. Some owners would have liked the silencer to exit on the left, allowing the rear wheel (which is mounted on a left-side single-sided swingarm) to be totally exposed from the right. Space and engineering considerations made it an impossibility on this model, though.

Side-mounted because the V-four motor's front two cylinders occupy most of the chassis' given engine bay space, the radiators are now in a position where flying stones and chippings can do no harm. Fairing slots allow for extraction of heat-exchanged air.

The ubiquitous aluminium twin spar frame is not only a beautiful looker (though sadly half hidden behind the fairing side panels), it is well up to the job too, allowing the sports-side of the bike's nature to shine through on twisty roads.

**Tank**
Holds 21l (5.5gal), giving a tank range of 214–291km (133–181 miles), depending on how it is ridden.

**Grab handles**
Can be unbolted and removed in seconds and are made from a material that does not feel overly cold to the touch.

**Seat**
Stepped design affords excellent rider and reasonable pillion space and is well padded. Rider seat height is 805mm (31.7in).

**Tyres**
ZR-rated (approved for speeds in excess of 240km/h (150 mph), the front fitment is a 120/70, the rear 180/55.

**Engine**
The extra 33.7cc (2.1ci) capacity which the new 781.7cc (47.7ci) VFR800 has over its 748cc (45.6ci) VFR750 predecessor has transformed the performance from excellent to outstanding. The flexibility to pull strongly from almost any revs in any gear is vital in any top-line sports-tourer and the liquid-cooled, four-stroke, 16-valve, DOHC, 90˚ V-four powerplant manages this well for a bike which really falls into the 750cc (45.8ci) class.

**Swingarm**
Single-sided and bearing to the left, it allows quick wheel changes and boosts styling, yet is heavier than a conventional twin spar design.

# Specifications

**The VFR800 is Honda's** *answer to demands for a large capacity mile-eater with ample sporting pretentions, and it achieves this through a mix of specifications and measurements designed to create a balanced, all-round machine. Introduced to replace the ageing VFR750, which has served Honda riders since 1986, the VFR88 has been trimmed of substantial weight and its dimensions have been tightened up. In essence, this is a new bike, rather than one that has been merely blessed with a minor capacity increase. However, the degree of user-friendliness associated with the VFR is not diminished; it remains as versatile and easy to ride as ever before.*

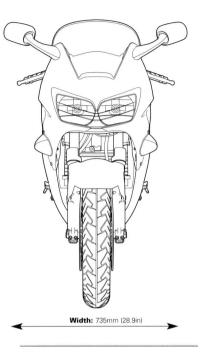

Width: 735mm (28.9in)

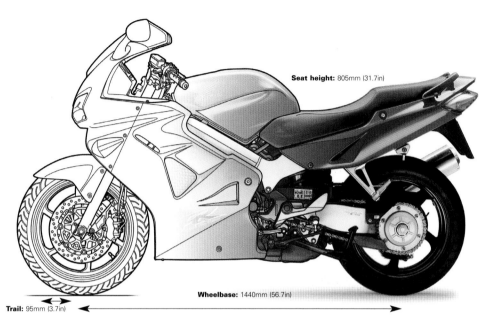

Seat height: 805mm (31.7in)

Wheelbase: 1440mm (56.7in)

Trail: 95mm (3.7in)

## ENGINE

| | |
|---|---|
| Type | 4-stroke |
| Layout | DOHC 90° V-four |
| Total displacement | 781.7cc (47.7ci) |
| Bore | 72mm (2.8in) |
| Stroke | 48mm (1.8in) |
| Compression ratio | 11.6:1 |
| Valves | 4 per cylinder |
| Fuel system | PGM-F1 electronic fuel injection |
| Ignition | digital electronic |
| Cooling | liquid |
| Maximum power | 82kW (110bhp) @ 10,281rpm |
| Maximum torque | 8.5kg-m (61.5lb-ft) @ 8,549rpm |

## TRANSMISSION

| | |
|---|---|
| Primary drive | chain |
| Clutch | wet multiplate |
| Gearbox | 6-speed |
| Final drive | sealed O-ring chain |

## WEIGHTS & CAPACITIES

| | |
|---|---|
| Tank capacity | 21l (5.5gal) |
| Dry weight | 208kg (457.6lb) |
| Weight distribution | |
| — front | N/A |
| — rear | N/A |
| Wheelbase | 1440mm (56.7in) |
| Overall length | 2095mm (82.5in) |
| Overall width | 735mm (28.9in) |
| Overall height | 1190mm (46.85in) |
| Seat height | 805mm (31.7in) |

## CYCLE PARTS

| | |
|---|---|
| Frame | aluminium twin spar |
| Rake/trail | 25.5°/95mm (3.7in) |
| Front suspension | 41mm (1.6in) telescopic forks |
| Travel | 109mm (4.3in) |
| Adjustment | preload |
| Rear suspension | Pro-Arm mono-arm system, gas charged damper |
| Travel | 120mm (4.7in) |
| Adjustment | preload, plus rebound damping |
| Tyres | |
| — make | varies |
| — front | 120/70 x ZR17 |
| — rear | 180/55 x ZR17 |
| Brakes | |
| — make | Nissin |
| — front | 2 x 296mm (11.7in) discs, dual combined three piston calipers |
| — rear | single 256mm (10in) disc, dual combined three piston caliper |

## TORQUE

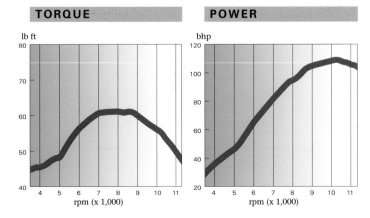

lb ft — rpm (x 1,000)

## POWER

bhp — rpm (x 1,000)

Independent test measurements (above) differ from the manufacturer's claimed maximum power and maximum torque figures.

# HONDA CBR900RR

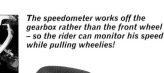

**The speedometer works off the gearbox rather than the front wheel – so the rider can monitor his speed while pulling wheelies!**

**The braced and tapered swingarm gives easy access to adjust settings on the rear shock.**

**Handlebar controls**
The engine kill switch and start buttons are on the right clip-on. On the left are the lights on, headlight dip/main, flash and indicator switches. Tiny dowels locate the plastic bodies to the handlebars.

**Cooling system**
The engine is fully liquid cooled. Problems with the radiator and water pump are extremely rare.

**Clutch**
The beefy, wet multiplate clutch fitted to all FireBlades has proved robust and resilient to abuse such as fast getaways and wheelies. However, under hard use it can become grabby.

**Forks**
Though feeling 'sticky' to some riders, the 45mm (1.8in) telescopic forks give good feel and feedback, together with full adjustment for compression and rebound damping and preload.

**Wheels**
The FireBlade is unusual in having a 40.6cm (16in) front wheel and specially-made tyre with a 43.2cm (17in) tyre's profile. The idea behind a smaller wheel is to reduce gyroscopic force and aid fast turning.

**Headlights**
The FireBlade is easily recognized by its characteristic Fox-eye headlights, introduced in December 1993 to mark the model's third incarnation. Although since modified, they retain their distinctive look.

**Swingarm**
The twin-sided braced swingarm has proved flex-free under almost all conditions. The finish is highly resistant to weather and corrosion.

**Tyres**
Bridgestone BT56 tyres are fitted as standard in 130/70 x 16 front and 180/55 x 17 rear. The front tyre's profile means the tread continues up onto the tyre sidewall, making it impossible to run out of tread.

**Bodywork**
The angular panels are expensive to replace following a spill. They are made of light plastic to keep weight down, but this also makes them relatively flimsy.

**Exhaust**
The black paint flaked off the silencer on pre-1996 models, often while still under warranty. 1997's model was supplied with a plain alloy finish. Most FireBlade owners swap the silencer for a louder, lighter, slimmer and more stylish aftermarket one.

**Rear suspension**
Showa monoshock with rising-rate linkage is adjustable for compression and rebound damping as well as preload. Shocks can lose much of their damping qualities in under 10,000 miles and would even blow seals on early models.

## CBR900RR
## FIREBLADE

**The Honda FireBlade** redefined the supersports class at its launch in March 1992. The bike had the power of a 1000cc (61ci) engine but was closer to a 600cc (36.6ci) in terms of weight. Journalists were amazed at the bike's abilities, but some thought it too radical for the ordinary road rider. However, the FireBlade became a huge sales success. Now road bike performance standards have been pushed higher by Yamaha's YZF-R1.

The twin headlights use conventional reflectors. The shape has been tweaked for 1998 to make them look even meaner.

Four Mikuni carbs and a huge airbox provide instant throttle response while returning around 38mpg. Power-boosting aftermarket Dynojet carb needle kits are popular.

The 1998 FireBlade's frame, swingarm and suspension collectively weigh 5kg (11.23lb) less than on previous models. Many owners fit carbon-fibre protectors to prevent knocks and scratches.

**Brakes**
The twin, four-piston Nissin front calipers on the 1998 model are among the best on any road bike. The brakes on previous models were widely slated for lacking feel and feedback at the lever. Discs on early models could crack between the drilled holes.

**Engine**
Originally 893cc (54.5ci) then 918cc (56ci) and with 80 per cent of the internals modified for 1998, the in-line four-cylinder four-stroke produces a claimed 95.4kW (128bhp). Bikes with essentially identical engines can vary in power by 3.7kW (5bhp), though generally stay within nine per cent of the claimed figure.

**Gearbox**
Six-speed gearbox with a conventional 'one down, five up' selection, with neutral between first and second. It is competent, but has a coarse feel compared with many similar bikes.

# Specifications

**The FireBlade is a** *superbly compact sports motorcycle which stunned the biking world with its light weight, sharp steering and stunning power at its 1992 launch.*
*For 1998, the FireBlade is lighter than ever at 180.2kg (397lb). Honda has achieved this by shaving weight from many of the bike's components, such as the clutch mechanism, exhaust system and engine internals. With just 24° of rake and a 1404mm (55.3in) wheelbase, this quick-steering machine still rates as one of the most highly-focused, radical and exciting road bikes you can buy.*

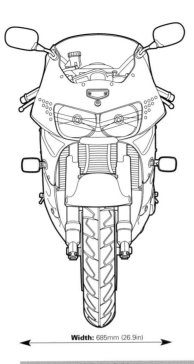

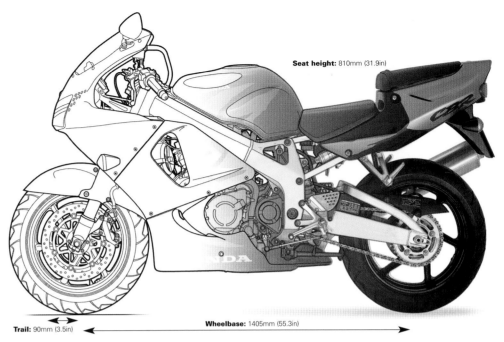

**Seat height:** 810mm (31.9in)

**Width:** 685mm (26.9in)   **Trail:** 90mm (3.5in)   **Wheelbase:** 1405mm (55.3in)

## ENGINE

| | |
|---|---|
| Type | 4-stroke |
| Layout | DOHC in-line four |
| Total displacement | 918cc (56ci) |
| Bore | 71mm (2.8in) |
| Stroke | 58mm (2.3in) |
| Compression ratio | 11.1:1 |
| Valves | 4 per cylinder |
| Fuel system | 4 x 38mm (1.5in) Mikuni carburettors |
| Ignition | digital electronic |
| Cooling | liquid |
| Maximum power | 91.2kW (122.3bhp) @ 10,720rpm |
| Maximum torque | 9.1kW (66lb-ft) @ 8,350rpm |

## TORQUE

lb ft
(graph, rpm x 1,000)

## POWER

bhp
(graph, rpm x 1,000)

**Independent test measurements (above) differ from the manufacturer's claimed maximum power and maximum torque figures.**

## TRANSMISSION

| | |
|---|---|
| Primary drive | straight-cut gears |
| Clutch | wet multiplate |
| Gearbox | 6-speed |
| Final drive | sealed O-ring chain |

## WEIGHTS & CAPACITIES

| | |
|---|---|
| Tank capacity | 18l (3.96gal) |
| Dry weight | 180.2kg (397lb) |
| Weight distribution | |
| — front | 51% |
| — rear | 49% |
| Wheelbase | 1405mm (55.3in) |
| Overall length | 2040mm (80.3in) |
| Overall width | 685mm (26.9in) |
| Overall height | 1135mm (44.7in) |
| Seat height | 810mm (31.9in) |

## CYCLE PARTS

| | |
|---|---|
| Frame | aluminium alloy twin spar |
| Rake/trail | 24°/ 90mm (3.5in) |
| Front suspension | 45mm (1.8in) Kayaba telescopic forks |
| Travel | 120mm (4.7in) |
| Adjustment | preload, compression and rebound damping |
| Rear suspension | Showa monoshock with rising rate linkage |
| Travel | 125mm (4.9in) |
| Adjustment | preload, compression and rebound damping |
| Tyres | |
| — make | Bridgestone BT56 |
| — front | 130/70 x 16 |
| — rear | 180/55 x 17 |
| Brakes | |
| — make | Nissin |
| — front | 2 x 310mm (12.2in) steel semi-floating discs, opposed four-piston calipers |
| — rear | 220mm (8.7in) steel disc, opposed two-piston caliper |

# HONDA CBR900RR 1999

Up front, the bars are higher than most and the clocks and switches are the usual Honda quality – well thought out. The mirrors work ok, as is usual with sports bikes they show a lot of shoulder and arm but are relatively vibration free.

**CBR900RR**
**FIREBLADE**

**The new Honda FireBlade has been** designed to win back the sports crown first taken by Yamaha's R1 and then Suzuki's GSX-R1000. It's a tall order, but the 10 year old blade still has a few tricks up its sleeve that the other two could learn from. It may not be the out and out 'nutter' bike it was in the early nineties and it may no longer be the bike to be seen on, but it is still an excellent riding package.

**Body**
At 170kg (374lbs), the Fireblade is one of the most lightweight sports bikes on the market – lighter than most 600cc sportsbikes, including Honda's own CBR600F. It is extremely compact, making it feel incredibly manageable and user friendly.

**Rear suspension**
The back end has a whole new swing arm and shock absorber arrangement supporting a 220mm (8.6in) rear disc and twin pot calliper. The swing arm actually hangs off the back of the engine and, strangely, does not attach to the frame.

**Seat**
The seating position is relatively comfortable, and even the saddle seems to have a rare amount of padding on it. Honda seem to have realised that people ride bikes for fun and comfort is important, most sports bike manufacturers sacrifice everything for speed.

*Some enthusiasts modify the bike by changing the Fireblade's heavy chain for a lighter one, saving up to 2kg (5lb) in weight.*

**Chassis**
The 1999 model uses a semi-pivotless frame, with aluminium plates to hold the swing-arm in place. This gives a reduction in the high stresses at the end of th swing arm borrowed from off-road technology.

**Fairing**
The bodywork is beautifully put together – as you would expect from Honda, one of the most consistently high-quality manufacturers. The panel fit is good and the nuts and bolts do not go furry on your first meeting with rain and spray! The graphics are understated making the bike seem less aggressive than the competition.

**Front tyre**
The new 43cm (17in) front wheel has been called for by almost everyone who has ever owned a Blade. Honda have finally caught up with the idea and the new layout has made for a very quick steering machine, but one that doesn't turn in sharply like the old 40cm (16in) version.

**Brakes**
The brakes are fantastic, the four pot Nissin callipers and bigger than ever 330mm (12in) discs can bite harder than most and longer than any, before any fade begins to rear it's ugly head. The FireBlade only weighs 170kgs (455lbs) and with these stoppers on board you can land it on a pinhead!

**Engine**
Our Blade puts out 123bhp at the rear wheel giving away a fair bit to the competition. The Blade motor really has to be revved hard to get the most from it and the fuel injection makes the motor feel harsh. The power delivery is smooth though and, in conjunction with the six speed gearbox, works very well.

# *Specifications*

*When the boys at Honda decided to update the Fireblade, they did not go down the usual gradual, evolvement route, but opted instead for a cut-and-thrust dramatic change. With the emphasis on loosing weight, most of the modifications were made to the engine, but the chassis and bodywork did not miss out either. The result is a sharper, stronger and more powerful bike with the stability and handling to match.*

Rake: 23.8°

Height: 1135mm (44.7in)

Seat height: 815mm (32in)

Length: 2040mm (80.3in)

## ENGINE

| | |
|---|---|
| Type | 4-stroke |
| Layout | DOHC in-line four |
| Total displacement | 929cc (56.7ci) |
| Bore | 74mm (2.9in) |
| Stroke | 54mm (2.1in) |
| Compression ratio | 11.3:1 |
| Valves | 4 per cylinder |
| Fuel system | PGM-FI |
| Ignition | computer controlled |
| Cooling | liquid |
| Maximum power | 113.3kW (152bhp) @ 11,000rpm |
| Maximum torque | 10.4kg-m (75lb-ft) @ 9000rpm |

## TRANSMISSION

| | |
|---|---|
| Primary drive | gear |
| Clutch | wet multiplate |
| Gearbox | 6-speed |
| Final drive | 'O' ring sealed chain |

## WEIGHTS & CAPACITIES

| | |
|---|---|
| Tank capacity | 18l (4.8gal) |
| Dry weight | 170kg (375lb) |
| Weight distribution | |
| — front | N/A |
| — rear | N/A |
| Wheelbase | 1400mm (55.1in) |
| Overall length | 2040mm (80.3in) (80.3in) |
| Overall width | 685mm (44.8in) |
| Overall height | 1135mm (44.7in) |
| Seat height | 815mm (32in) |

## CYCLE PARTS

| | |
|---|---|
| Frame | twin spar aluminium alloy |
| Trail | 23.8°/97mm (3.8in) |
| Front suspension | 43mm (1.7in) inverted HMAS telescopic fork |
| Travel | 120mm (4.7in) |
| Adjustment | spring preload, compression and rebound |
| Rear suspension | Pro-Link HMAS damper |
| Travel | 135mm (5.3in) |
| Adjustment | spring preload and compression and rebound |
| Tyres | |
| — front | 120/70 x 17 |
| — rear | 190/50 x 17 |
| Brakes | |
| — front | 330mm dual disc, 4-piston calipers |
| — rear | 220mm (8.7in) single disc, single piston caliper |

# HONDA CBR1000F

**Gearbox**
Six-speed design allows maximum speeds in each gear of 1st 86.3km/h (68.7mph); 2nd 145.2km/h (90.2mph); 3rd 181km/h (112.5mph); 4th 216km/h (134.2 mph); 5th 237km/h (147.3mph); 6th 246km/h (152.9mph). Changing through the lower ratios can be a notchy experience. Final drive is by a sealed O-ring chain.

**Engine**
998cc (60.9ci), liquid-cooled, 16-valve, DOHC, in-line, four 4-stroke motor has a bore and stroke of 77 x 53.6mm (3 x 2.1 in), a compression ratio of 10.5;1, and breathes through a bank of four 38mm (1.5in) carburettors. Power was more than acceptable when the bike first appeared in 1987, but could be considered to be lacking now. It is still smooth and suited to a sports-tourer role, though.

**Bodywork**
Hassle to remove and refit, but all-enclosing, which helps ensure hidden components remain free of road grime and accompanying corrosion. Styling is similar to, but less rounded than, early CBR600s.

**Exhaust**
Header pipes are prone to rotting over time, while the stubby silencers will never win awards for their good looks as standard. Many CBR1000s feature replacement systems that were pricey in the early days but which continue to become ever more affordable as demand falls.

**Front suspension**
41mm (1.6in) cartridge forks feature a pneumatic chamber to damp out road vibes and aid handling and 130mm (5.1in) of axle travel. Now feels vague by comparison to others in its class.

**Dry weight**
235kg (517lb)

CBR1000F

**It was first launched in 1987** *and since then has obviously done very well for it still to be on Honda's fleet after only minor changes. A comfortable bike that would probably best serve the needs of a long-distance commuter or tourer, it is also pretty nimble in the traffic. It may look a bit of a heavy beast, but if you're not comfortable with the likes of Yamaha's YZF-R1 or Honda's FireBlade, this may be the bike for you.*

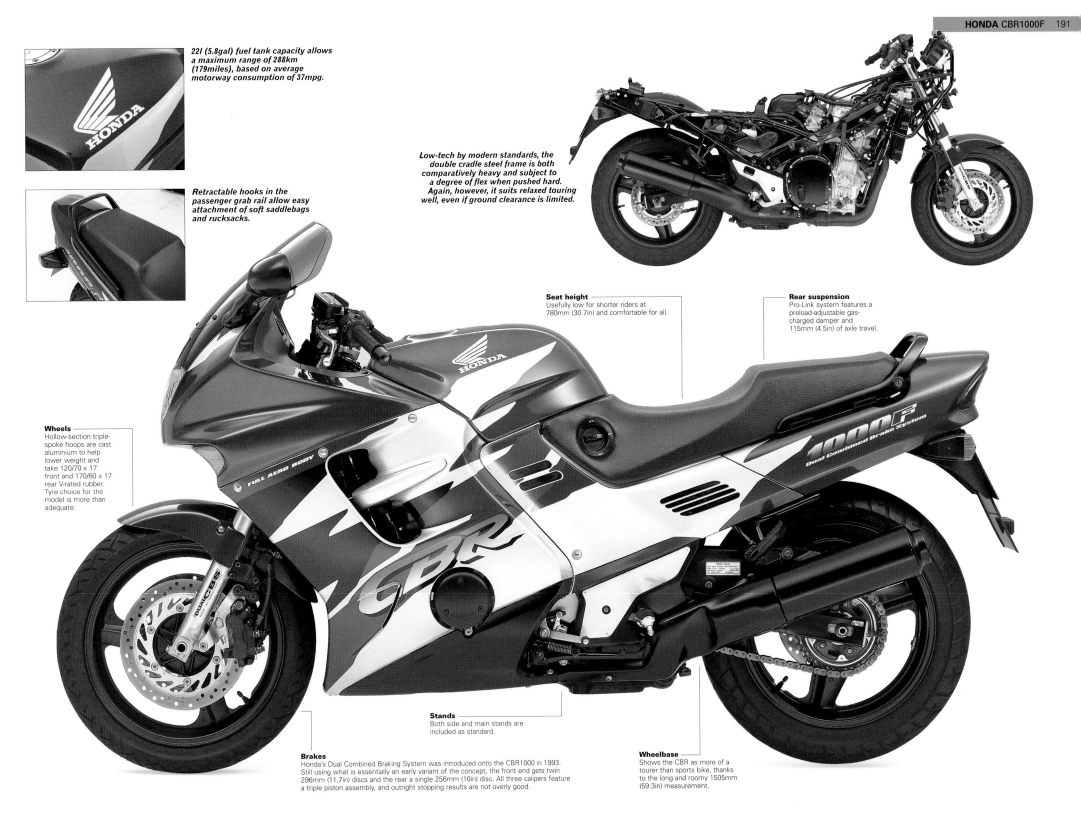

*22l (5.8gal) fuel tank capacity allows a maximum range of 288km (179miles), based on average motorway consumption of 37mpg.*

*Retractable hooks in the passenger grab rail allow easy attachment of soft saddlebags and rucksacks.*

*Low-tech by modern standards, the double cradle steel frame is both comparatively heavy and subject to a degree of flex when pushed hard. Again, however, it suits relaxed touring well, even if ground clearance is limited.*

**Seat height**
Usefully low for shorter riders at 780mm (30.7in) and comfortable for all.

**Rear suspension**
Pro-Link system features a preload-adjustable gas-charged damper and 115mm (4.5in) of axle travel.

**Wheels**
Hollow-section triple-spoke hoops are cast aluminium to help lower weight and take 120/70 x 17 front and 170/60 x 17 rear V-rated rubber. Tyre choice for the model is more than adequate.

**Stands**
Both side and main stands are included as standard.

**Brakes**
Honda's Dual Combined Braking System was introduced onto the CBR1000 in 1993. Still using what is essentially an early variant of the concept, the front end gets twin 296mm (11.7in) discs and the rear a single 256mm (10in) disc. All three calipers feature a triple piston assembly, and outright stopping results are not overly good.

**Wheelbase**
Shows the CBR as more of a tourer than sports bike, thanks to the long and roomy 1505mm (59.3in) measurement.

**HONDA** *CBR1000F*

# Specifications

**The CBR1000F was one** *of the first motorcycles in the modern era to feature fully enclosed bodywork, which led to accusations that it looked like a mobile bathroom suite. But, despite its oddball looks (which were later toned down), the CBR1000F remained Honda's flagship – and the company's fastest bike until the launch of the FireBlade in 1992. The CBR1000F was also significant in that it marked the factory's return to conventional in-line fours, after an experiment with V-fours failed because the bikes proved too costly and cumbersome.*

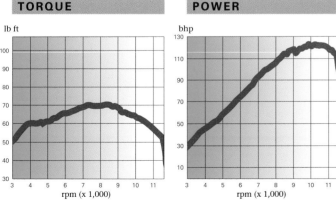

**Width:** 40mm (29.1in)  **Trail:** 110mm (4.3in)  **Wheelbase:** 1505mm (59.3in)

## ENGINE

| | |
|---|---|
| Type | 4-stroke |
| Layout | in-line four |
| Total displacement | 998cc (60.9ci) |
| Bore | 77mm (3in) |
| Stroke | 53.6mm (2.1in) |
| Compression ratio | 10.5:1 |
| Valves | 4 per cylinder |
| Fuel system | 4 x 38mm (1.5in) CV-type carburettors |
| Ignition | computer-controlled digital transistorized with electronic advance |
| Cooling | liquid |
| Maximum power | 91.4kW (122.6bhp) @ 9850rpm |
| Maximum torque | 9.7kg-m (70.2lb-ft) @ 8600rpm |

## TORQUE

lb ft

rpm (x 1,000)

## POWER

bhp

rpm (x 1,000)

**Independent test measurements (above) differ from the manufacturer's claimed maximum power and maximum torque figures.**

## TRANSMISSION

| | |
|---|---|
| Primary drive | helical cut gears |
| Clutch | wet, multiplate |
| Gearbox | 6-speed |
| Final drive | chain |

## WEIGHTS & CAPACITIES

| | |
|---|---|
| Tank capacity | 22l (5.8gal) |
| Dry weight | 235kg (517lb) |
| Weight distribution | |
| — front | N/A |
| — rear | N/A |
| Wheelbase | 1505mm (59.3in) |
| Overall length | 2,235mm (88.0in) |
| Overall width | 40mm (29.1in) |
| Overall height | 1215mm (47.8in) |
| Seat height | N/A |

## CYCLE PARTS

| | |
|---|---|
| Frame | steel double cradle |
| Rake/trail | 27°/110mm (4.3in) |
| Front suspension | 41mm (1.6in) air-assisted cartridge-type fork |
| Travel | 130mm (5.1in) |
| Adjustment | preload, plus rebound damping |
| Rear suspension | pro-link with hydraulic gas charged damper |
| Travel | 115mm (4.5in) |
| Adjustment | preload, plus rebound damping |
| Tyres | |
| — make | Bridgestone, Dunlop |
| — front | 120/70 VR17 |
| — rear | 170/60 VR17 |
| Brakes | |
| — make | Nissin |
| — front | 296mm (11.7in) dual discs with dual combined three piston caliper and sintered metal pads |
| — rear | 256mm (10in) dual combined three piston caliper and single disc with sintered metal pads |

# HONDA **CBX1000**

**Power**
At the time of its launch, no other bike could match the Honda for its smoothness and raw six-cylinder engine. In 1978, this 1047cc (63.9ci) air-cooled, 24-valve, transverse six had a claimed top speed of 217km/h (135mph). which it reached smoothly.

**Brakes**
At the front sat a pair of ventilated discs, which not many customers complained about as they were capable enough of stopping the big across-the-frame six.

**Exhaust**
Six shiny downpipes protruded from the angled-forward cylinders to run into an impressive-looking silencer at the rear.

## CBX1000

**HONDA** *released this now legendary machine in 1978 as an example of the company's ability to build powerful motorbikes. It was designed as an out-and-out sports bike by Shoichiro Irimajiri, the former grand prix engineer, but unfortunately it was not particularly successful at the time, although there are many around today (and also CBX1000 owners clubs).Perhaps it was just too powerful for its time; after it was detuned in 1981, fitted with a fairing and better suspension and sold as the CBX-B, it sold well as a sports tourer.*

**Suspension**
Some journalists of the day complained about the handling of the CBX, but it is now widely agreed that the firm suspension helped give the bike its good handling.

*The steel tubular spine frame was designed in such a manner as to show the huge engine off to best effect.*

**Front end**
Very reminiscent of its day was the look of the front end, which had a single round headlamp with one indicator light on either side, a close-fitting front guard and telescopic forks.

**Engine**
One of the most powerful bikes of its time the CBX1000 was equipped with a 1047cc (63.9ci) air-cooled, 24-valve, DOHC, transverse six engine with a bore and stroke of 64.5 x 53.4mm (2.5 x 2.1in).

# HONDA VTR1000 FIRESTORM

The 996cc (60.8ci), 90°, V-twin four-stroke engine has four valves per cylinder, double overhead cams, a 98 x 66mm (3.9 x 2.6in) bore and stroke, and a six-speed gearbox.

Honda has departed from the norm with the use of side-mounted radiators. This enables the steep-steering head angle of 25° to be used and keeps the VTR looking slim.

**Mirrors**
You get an excellent view on the VTR1000. However, some riders complain of vibration.

*The steering is good for sports touring because it is fairly slow while providing tremendous stability. The stability and the power of the engine make this a quicker bike than you might expect.*

**Footpegs**
Well positioned for most and surprisingly vibration-free. However, it is a different story for pillions, as taller passengers might just find the footrests a little too high.

**Headlamp**
Heavier riders may find the main beam points at the sky, thanks to the slightly squat back end.

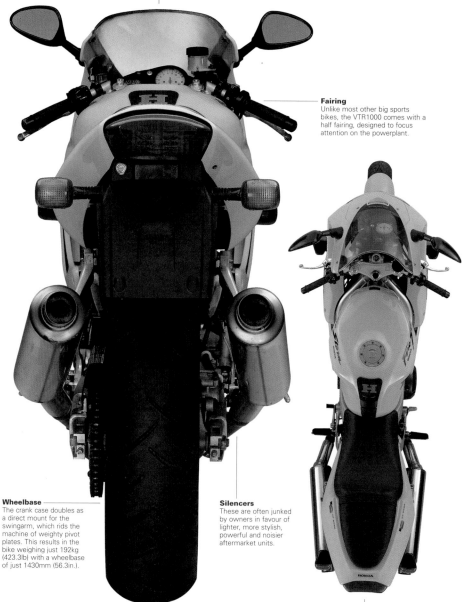

**Fairing**
Unlike most other big sports bikes, the VTR1000 comes with a half fairing, designed to focus attention on the powerplant.

**Front brakes**
296mm (11.7in) dual hydraulic disc with four-piston calipers and sintered metal pads.

**Wheelbase**
The crank case doubles as a direct mount for the swingarm, which rids the machine of weighty pivot plates. This results in the bike weighing just 192kg (423.3lb) with a wheelbase of just 1430mm (56.3in.).

**Silencers**
These are often junked by owners in favour of lighter, more stylish, powerful and noisier aftermarket units.

**Passenger comfort**
The removable seat hump reveals fairly plush pillion accommodation.

## VTR1000

**HONDA introduced the FireStorm** at the beginning of 1997 after seeing the success achieved by Ducati with the 916 and 900SS V-twins. Although never been able to see off its Italian rival, the VTR has done well against Suzuki's TL1000S, a bike in much the same mould. As an all-round machine for those who wish to mix sports riding with touring, it is an excellent and capable machine.

The slanted 48mm (1.9in) flat-valve carbs are the largest ever used on a Honda engine and the computer-controlled ignition system provides optimum performance throughout the rev range.

The engine is a stressed member of the twin spar aluminium chassis, creating exceptional rigidity. Aftermarket bellypans, which replace the tiny stock protector, are available for the VTR.

**Fuel tank**
Holds only 16l (4.2gal), which, if you are travelling long distances regularly, could become an irritation. Although the paint everywhere is generally thick, the tank is easily scuffed, so it pays to use a protective tank pad.

**Seat height**
At 810mm (31.9in), the FireStorm is a reasonably good height for short riders.

**Wheels and rubber**
Dunlop D204 tyres come in 120/70 front and 180/55 rear sizes. As for the wheels, the three-spoke hoops have a 43.2cm (17in) diameter front and rear.

# HONDA VTR1000 FIRESTORM

# Specifications

*Slim, stylish, powerful, and* that is just the engine. Honda's FireStorm has enjoyed serious sales success since its launch in early 1997, snatching the limelight from Suzuki's TL1000S which, although superior on paper, has received some very bad press. Of course, it is not THE V-twin most riders lust after – that accolade belongs to Ducati's 916/996 family – but as a budget offering it makes a brilliant start.

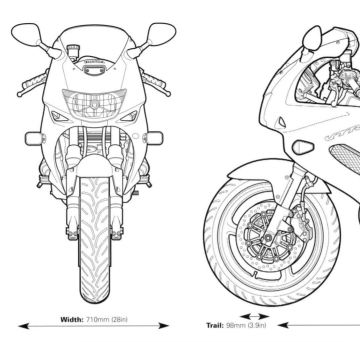

**Seat height:** 810mm (31.9in)

**Width:** 710mm (28in)

**Trail:** 98mm (3.9in)

**Wheelbase:** 1430mm (56.3in)

## ENGINE

| | |
|---|---|
| Type | 4-stroke |
| Layout | 90° V-twin |
| Total displacement | 996cc (60.8ci) |
| Bore | 98mm (3.9in) |
| Stroke | 66mm (2.6in) |
| Compression ratio | 9.4:1 |
| Valves | 4 per cylinder |
| Fuel system | 2 x 48mm (1/9in) CV-type slanted flat-side |
| Ignition | Digital transistorized, electronic advance |
| Cooling | liquid |
| Maximum power | 85kW (114bhp) @ 8700rpm |
| Maximum torque | 10.3kg-m (74.5lb-ft) @ 6636rpm |

## TORQUE

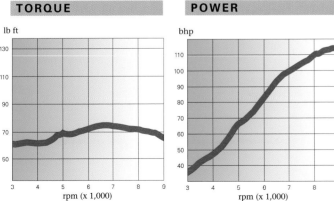

lb ft

rpm (x 1,000)

## POWER

bhp

rpm (x 1,000)

**Independent test measurements (above) differ from the manufacturer's claimed maximum power and maximum torque figures.**

## TRANSMISSION

| | |
|---|---|
| Primary drive | gear |
| Clutch | wet, multiplate |
| Gearbox | 6-speed |
| Final drive | chain |

## WEIGHTS & CAPACITIES

| | |
|---|---|
| Tank capacity | 16l (4.2gal) |
| Dry weight | 192kg (422.4lb) |
| Weight distribution | |
| — front | |
| — rear | |
| Wheelbase | 1430mm (56.3in) |
| Overall length | 2050mm (80.7in) |
| Overall width | 710mm (28.0in) |
| Overall height | 1155mm (45.5in) |
| Seat height | 810mm (31.9in) |

## CYCLE PARTS

| | |
|---|---|
| Frame | aluminium twin-spar |
| Rake/trail | 25°/98mm (3.9in) |
| Front suspension | 41mm (1.6in) forks |
| Travel | 109mm (4.3in) |
| Adjustment | preload, plus rebound damping |
| Rear suspension | Pro-Link, monoshock |
| Travel | 124mm (4.9in) |
| Adjustment | preload, plus rebound damping |
| Tyres | |
| — make | varies |
| — front | 120/70 x 17 |
| — rear | 180/55 x 17 |
| Brakes | |
| — make | Nissin |
| — front | 2 x 296mm (11.7in) discs, opposed 4-piston calipers |
| — rear | 220mm (8.7in) disc, single piston caliper |

# HONDA XL1000 VARADERO

The 2-into-1-into-2 system has been designed to maximize mid-range efficiency and is made of stainless steel for long-lasting durability. Because the twin 4.5l (275ci) silencers exit under the seat and are shrouded by rear bodywork, large panniers can be used without fear of melting. The silencers detach at the collector box.

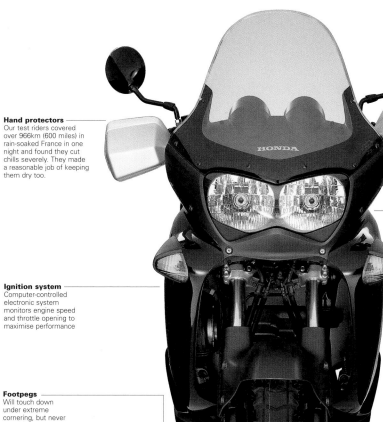

**Hand protectors**
Our test riders covered over 966km (600 miles) in rain-soaked France in one night and found they cut chills severely. They made a reasonable job of keeping them dry too.

**Ignition system**
Computer-controlled electronic system monitors engine speed and throttle opening to maximise performance

**Footpegs**
Will touch down under extreme cornering, but never a problem.

**Headlamps**
The best Honda has ever made? The dual multi-reflector design throws out an awesome beam that is strong on dip and a revelation on main.

**Carburettors**
With 42mm (1.7in) venturi sizes, each of the bank of slanted flat-valve downdraft CV carbs is 6mm (0.2in) smaller than those fitted to the FireStorm. Honda felt their size was the best balance of 'strong low-to-mid-range performance and swift, linear response for the type of riding the Varadero is geared toward'.

**Brakes**
As also featured on Honda's CBR1000F, ST1100 Pan European, CBR1100XX Super Blackbird and VFR, the Varadero gets a dual combined system, by which operating the front also partly operates the rear and vice versa. The front wears dual 296mm (11.7in) discs, while the rear gets a 256mm (10in) item.

**Mirrors**
Rounded design is set up wide enough to afford a decent rear view.

**Tail light**
Dual bulb design means if one blows, you still have the other.

**XL1000V VARADERO**

***Honda's Varadero** turned out to be quite a bit different to what those 'in the know' had been expecting. Instead of an insane wheelie machine, Honda has brought out a bike with manners. Still able to wheelie, it will also tour and commute in a very civilised manner. Not to everyone's taste, but still worth a good, hard look before making up your mind.*

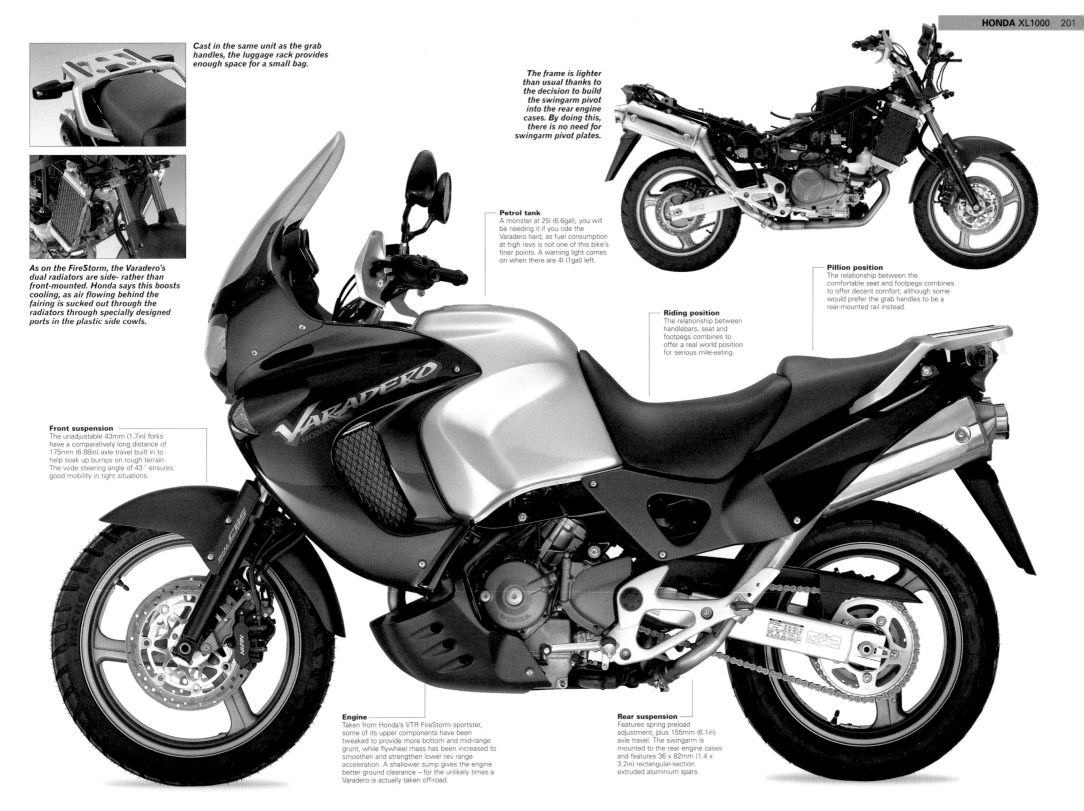

*Cast in the same unit as the grab handles, the luggage rack provides enough space for a small bag.*

*As on the FireStorm, the Varadero's dual radiators are side- rather than front-mounted. Honda says this boosts cooling, as air flowing behind the fairing is sucked out through the radiators through specially designed ports in the plastic side cowls.*

*The frame is lighter than usual thanks to the decision to build the swingarm pivot into the rear engine cases. By doing this, there is no need for swingarm pivot plates.*

**Petrol tank**
A monster at 25l (6.6gal), you will be needing it if you ride the Varadero hard, as fuel consumption at high revs is not one of this bike's finer points. A warning light comes on when there are 4l (1gal) left.

**Riding position**
The relationship between handlebars, seat and footpegs combines to offer a real world position for serious mile-eating.

**Pillion position**
The relationship between the comfortable seat and footpegs combines to offer decent comfort, although some would prefer the grab handles to be a rear-mounted rail instead.

**Front suspension**
The unadjustable 43mm (1.7in) forks have a comparatively long distance of 175mm (6.88in) axle travel built in to help soak up bumps on rough terrain. The wide steering angle of 43° ensures good mobility in tight situations.

**Engine**
Taken from Honda's VTR FireStorm sportster, some of its upper components have been tweaked to provide more bottom and mid-range grunt, while flywheel mass has been increased to smoothen and strengthen lower rev range acceleration. A shallower sump gives the engine better ground clearance – for the unlikely times a Varadero is actually ridden off-road.

**Rear suspension**
Features spring preload adjustment, plus 155mm (6.1in) axle travel. The swingarm is mounted to the rear engine cases and features 36 x 82mm (1.4 x 3.2in) rectangular-section extruded aluminium spars.

# Specifications

*Honda's Varadero is one* of the most comfortable long-distance bikes ever built and a genuine alternative to routine, conventionally-styled tourers.

It is a more civilized machine than was first imagined by those who had heard the rumours before its launch, but this pseudo-trailie bike, which is nimble enough to use as an everyday commuter, has attracted quite a few buyers. Here we examine the raw technical ingredients that go into such a fine creation.

**Width:** 880mm (34.7in)

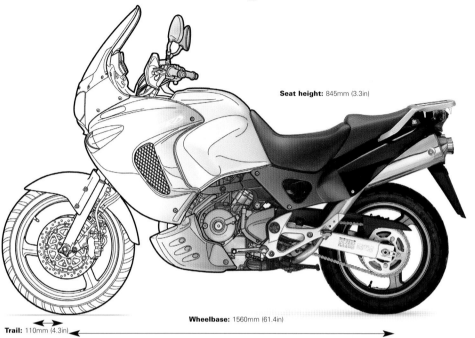

**Seat height:** 845mm (3.3in)

**Wheelbase:** 1560mm (61.4in)

**Trail:** 110mm (4.3in)

## ENGINE

| | |
|---|---|
| Type | 4-stroke |
| Layout | DOHC 90° V-twin |
| Total displacement | 996cc (60.8ci) |
| Bore | 98mm (3.9in) |
| Stroke | 66mm (2.6in) |
| Compression ratio | 9:1 |
| Valves | 4 per cylinder |
| Fuel system | 2 x 42mm (1.7in) slanted flat-slide CV carburettors |
| Ignition | CDI |
| Cooling | liquid |
| Maximum power | 68.6kW (92bhp) @ 7500rpm |
| Maximum torque | 9.9kg-m (72lb-ft) @ 5900rpm |

## TRANSMISSION

| | |
|---|---|
| Primary drive | gear |
| Clutch | wet multiplate |
| Gearbox | 5-speed |
| Final drive | chain |

## CYCLE PARTS

| | |
|---|---|
| Frame | box-section steel tube semi-cradle |
| Rake/trail | 27°/110mm (4.3in) |
| Front suspension | 43mm (1.7in) forks |
| Travel | 175mm (6.9in) |
| Adjustment | none |
| Rear suspension | Pro-Link, monoshock |
| Travel | 155mm (6.1in) |
| Adjustment | spring preload |
| Tyres | |
| — make | Michelin T65/varies |
| — front | 110/80 x 19 |
| — rear | 150/70 x 17 |
| Brakes | |
| — make | Nissin |
| — front | 2 x 296mm (11.7in) discs, 3-piston 'Dual Combined' calipers |
| — rear | 256mm (10in) disc, 3-piston 'Dual Combined' caliper |

## TORQUE

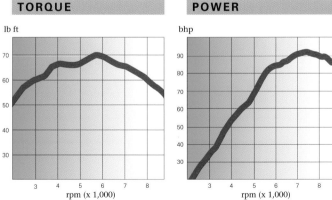

lb ft

rpm (x 1,000)

## POWER

bhp

rpm (x 1,000)

## WEIGHTS & CAPACITIES

| | |
|---|---|
| Tank capacity | 25l (6.6gal) |
| Dry weight | 220kg (484lb) |
| Weight distribution | |
| — front | N/A |
| — rear | N/A |
| Wheelbase | 1560mm (61.4in) |
| Overall length | 2295mm (90.4in) |
| Overall width | 880mm (34.7in) |
| Overall height | 1460mm (57.5in) |
| Seat height | 845mm (33.3in) |

**Independent test measurements (above) differ from the manufacturer's claimed maximum power and maximum torque figures.**

# HONDA CBR1100XX SUPER BLACKBIRD

*The grab rail is essential on a bike which can rip from 0 to 160km/h (100mph) in 5.9 seconds and reaches 240km/h (150mph) in just 15.2 seconds!*

*As with most sports tourers, the Blackbird is equipped with an easy-to-use main stand, which makes wheel removal and chain maintenance easy.*

**Mirrors**
Well-placed to provide an excellent rear view, they also incorporate the front indicators, further enhancing the Blackbird's aerodynamic design.

**Headlamps**
Ugly as they are, the piggyback headlights do a great job at turning night into day. The beam is strong and properly diffused to make fast riding on twisty roads possible at any time.

**Clutch**
The 1999 versions get a clutch with a new seven-plate design and a reworked master cylinder; older examples have a nine-plate system, which is heavier to operate.

**Fairing**
The Blackbird's fairing is claimed to have the most 'slippery' shape in the world, although Suzuki's new GSX1300R Hayabusa will certainly dispute this. Hard riding will grind the fairing lowers out on both sides.

**Screen**
Thankfully, Honda has fitted a screen that works well enough to keep the rider dry in light showers. Legs get wet from the knees down, though.

*CBR1100XX
SUPER BLACKBIRD*

**HONDA'S Super Blackbird** *proved an instant success when launched in 1996. Although chunkier than other sports tourers, the CBR1100XX's top speed of 280km/h (175mph) was enough to make thousands fall over themselves to buy it. The Blackbird handles well, is a great tourer and still remains one of Honda's most popular machines.*

**Wheelbase**
At 1490mm (58.66in), it is average for its class and certainly precludes the Blackbird from having super-fast handling. Stability is excellent, though.

*Despite a heavy revision for 1999, Honda has retained the Blackbird's unpopular linked brake system, which really only provides benefit to inexperienced riders. Operating the front calipers also works the rear's pistons to a degree, and vice versa. It takes a bit of getting used to.*

*No startling design revelation here, just a standard, strong aluminium twin spar chassis. It is heavy, though, and contributes considerably towards the bike's claimed dry weight of 223kg (490.6lb).*

**Fuel tank**
Already a useful 22l (4.9gal) in 1998, it has grown to 24l (5.4gal) for 1999.

**Knock sensor**
A computer circuit constantly monitoring the engine adjusts the ignition timing according to the internal conditions. It retards the ignition when it senses detonation is looming and advances it again once it has stopped, maximizing combustion efficiency and power output.

**Seat**
The rider's seat height is 810mm (31.89in), but feels slightly taller, thanks to a reasonably wide design. Comfort for both rider and pillion is not an issue, although some passengers feel the footrests are placed a little too high.

**Engine**
Honda claims 122kW (164bhp) at the crank from the 1137cc (69.4ci), 16-valve, liquid-cooled motor. Most analytical tests reveal 114–118kW (153–158bhp) is more likely. Rear wheel dyno readouts tend to record 105–109kW (141–146bhp). The engine is based on an overbored design of the best-selling FireBlade.

**Fuel system**
Last year's model had a bank of 42mm (1.7in) Keihin carbs, while new-for-'99 machines feature a PGM fuel injection system (with 42mm/1.7in throttle bodies) based on Honda's RC45 works racers. As well as smoothing power delivery, it helps cut fuel consumption and exhaust emissions too by constantly monitoring inlet pressure, air temperature, throttle position and engine temperature and adjusting the rate of fuel flow to maximize combustion.

# CBR1100XX SUPER BLACKBIRD

# Specifications

*More of a hawk* than a blackbird, the streamlined *CBR1100XX* needed, and got, an advanced aerodynamic design to encourage it to its awesome top speeds. It also got an engine based on the conquering *FireBlade's* just to make doubly sure. Unfortunately for *Honda, Suzuki* came up with the *Hayabusa*, but, while some may want to trade in the *Blackbird* for the new fast bike on the block, there will be many who will stay loyal to the machine which has given them so much pleasure.

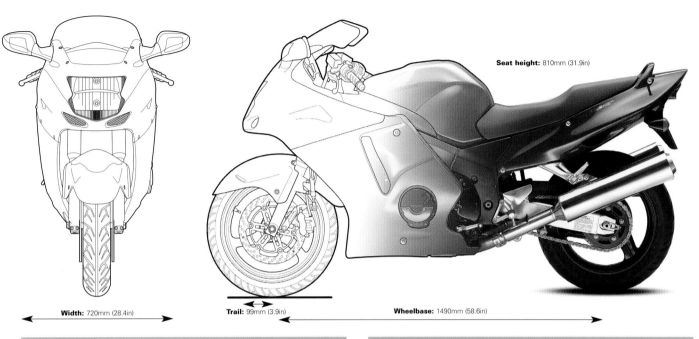

**Seat height:** 810mm (31.9in)

**Width:** 720mm (28.4in)   **Trail:** 99mm (3.9in)   **Wheelbase:** 1490mm (58.6in)

## ENGINE

| | |
|---|---|
| Type | 4-stroke |
| Layout | DOHC in-line four |
| Total displacement | 1137cc (69.4ci) |
| Bore | 79mm |
| Stroke | 58mm |
| Compression ratio | 11:1 |
| Valves | 4 per cylinder |
| Fuel system | 4 x 42mm (1.7in) carburettors |
| Ignition | digital transistorized |
| Cooling | liquid |
| Maximum power | 112kw (150.4bhp) @ 9539rpm |
| Maximum torque | 12.3kg-m (89lb-ft) @ 7281rpm |

## TRANSMISSION

| | |
|---|---|
| Primary drive | gear |
| Clutch | wet multiplate |
| Gearbox | 6-speed |
| Final drive | chain |

## WEIGHTS & CAPACITIES

| | |
|---|---|
| Tank capacity | 22l (4.84gal) |
| Dry weight | 223kg (490.6lb) |
| Weight distribution | |
| — front | N/A |
| — rear | N/A |
| Wheelbase | 1490mm (58.6in) |
| Overall length | 2160mm (85.0in) |
| Overall width | 720mm (28.4in) |
| Overall height | 1170mm (46.1in) |
| Seat height | 810mm (31.9in) |

## CYCLE PARTS

| | |
|---|---|
| Frame | aluminium twin spar |
| Rake/trail | 25°/99mm |
| Front suspension | 43mm (1.7in) telescopic forks |
| Travel | 120mm (4.7in) |
| Adjustment | none |
| Rear suspension | Pro-Link, monoshock |
| Travel | 120mm (4.7in) |
| Adjustment | preload, plus rebound damping |
| Tyres | |
| — make | varies |
| — front | 120/70 x ZR17 |
| — rear | 180/55 x ZR17 |
| Brakes | |
| — make | Nissin |
| — front | 2 x 310mm (12.2in) discs, opposed 3-piston 'Dual Combined' calipers |
| — rear | 256mm (10in) disc, opposed 3-piston 'Dual Combined' caliper |

## TORQUE

## POWER

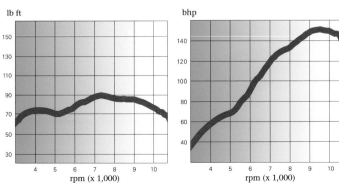

**Independent test measurements (above) differ from the manufacturer's claimed maximum power and maximum torque figures.**

# HONDA ST1100A PAN EUROPEAN

**Luggage storage beneath the seat complements the integral panniers and will enable you to carry everything but the kitchen sink.** Simply undo the locks on either side of the seat to access it.

**Paintwork**
The Pan European is available in plenty of colours and you are unlikely to have any trouble with the paintwork. Expect it to stay as good as new.

**Mirrors**
The wide mirrors, offer excellent rearward visibility and are faired to minimize aerodynamic drag. They also incorporate the front indicators.

**Fairing**
Ideally suited to those who would buy the Pan European is the fully integrated fairing, which protects both rider and passenger well.

**Brakes**
Two models available, one with ABS and one without. The latter has 316mm (12.4in) dual discs at the front and a 316mm (12.4in) dual piston caliper disc at the rear. The ABS model has smaller 296mm (11.7in) discs with Dual Combined three piston calipers.

**Panniers**
The solid, lockable panniers come as standard. They are not overly big, but are well-designed and more weatherproof than most.

## ST1100A
## PAN EUROPEAN

***It may not be a motorcycle** which stirs the soul, but then again it was not designed to do so. What Honda sought with the Pan European (introduced towards the end of 1989) was a fast, powerful, practical touring machine that covered vast distances, but which could also be fun for the rider. Like many of its bikes, Honda succeeded in its goal.*

*The silencers you see here were modified in 1995 to comply with new regulations. If you are not happy with them, you can always accessorize the bike yourself.*

*You have almost everything you could need here. The anti-glare controls are topped by a row of easy-to-see indicators, which include a digital clock and a control allowing the rider to adjust the height of the headlamp beam.*

*Completely encased, the tubular steel cradle frame is not the best looking and, by modern standards, is rather heavy.*

**Headlights**
The single glass headlamp is adjustable for differing loads.

**Tyres**
There are plenty of tyre choices with the Pan European (well, three really). Sizes are 110/80 x 18 at the front and 160/70 x 17 at the rear. ABS models differ in that they are fitted with 120/70 x 18 at the front, but the rear stays the same.

**Fuel tank**
The tank holds 28l (7.4gal) which includes a 4l (1.1gal) reserve that is perfect for the touring purpose it has been designed for.

**Seat**
At 800mm (31.5in), it is not overly tall for most and is wide and comfortable for both rider and pillion, even on long stretches.

**Engine**
The arrangement for the 1084cc (66.2ci) engine is a 90° longitudinal V4, which Honda chose for the low centre of gravity it allows with the high cubic capacity. It has four valves per cylinder and power is smooth and progressive at all speeds.

**Ground clearance**
You have 145mm (5.7in) of clearance – and you will never need any more.

# Specifications

*Some motorcycles are here* today, gone tomorrow, but not Honda's ST1100 Pan European. Launched way back in 1989 and already over a decade old, this capable machine has seen few changes during its lifespan. The 1084cc (66.2ci), electronic fuel-injected V-four packs a considerable punch and is one of the most reliable powerplants out there. The engine – combined with the bike's sound stability and braking ability, courtesy of its 1555mm (61.2in) wheelbase and 316mm (12.4in) disc front and rear – makes it easy to see why the Pan European has remained popular for so long.

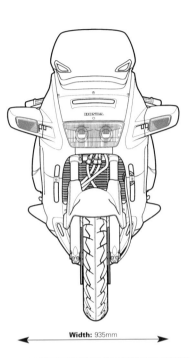

Width: 935mm

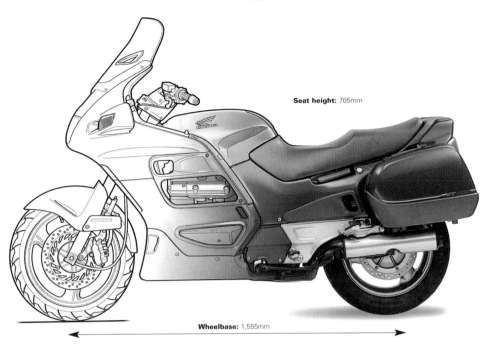

Seat height: 705mm

Wheelbase: 1,555mm

## ENGINE

| | |
|---|---|
| Type | 4-stroke |
| Layout | V-four |
| Total displacement | 1084cc (66.2ci) |
| Bore | 73mm (2.9in) |
| Stroke | 64.8mm (2.6in) |
| Compression ratio | 10:1 |
| Valves | 4 per cylinder |
| Fuel system | electronic |
| Ignition | computer controlled digital transistorized |
| Cooling | liquid |
| Maximum power | 74.6kw (100bhp) @ 7500rpm |
| Maximum torque | 11.2kg-m (81lb-ft) @ 6000rpm |

## TORQUE

## POWER

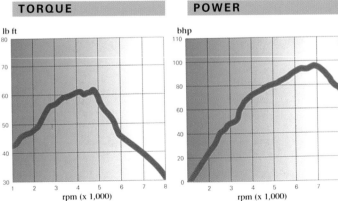

Independent test measurements (above) differ from the manufacturer's claimed maximum power and maximum torque figures.

## TRANSMISSION

| | |
|---|---|
| Primary drive | chain |
| Clutch | dry |
| Gearbox | 5-speed |
| Final drive | shaft |

## WEIGHTS & CAPACITIES

| | |
|---|---|
| Tank capacity | 28l (7.4gal) |
| Dry weight | 287kg (632lb) |
| Weight distribution | |
| — front | not available |
| — rear | not available |
| Wheelbase | 1555mm (61.2in) |
| Overall length | 2285mm (89.9in) |
| Overall width | 935mm (36.8in) |
| Overall height | 1395mm (54.9in) |
| Seat height | 795mm (31.3in) |

## CYCLE PARTS

| | |
|---|---|
| Frame | tubular steel cradle |
| Rake/trail | N/A |
| Front suspension | 41mm (1.6in) telescopic forks |
| Travel | 140mm (5.5in) |
| Adjustment | none |
| Rear suspension | Single sided |
| Travel | 120mm (4.7in) |
| Adjustment | preload and rebound |
| Tyres | |
| — make | Various |
| — front | 110/80 x 18 |
| — rear | 160/70 x 17 |
| Brakes | |
| — make | N/A |
| — front | 316mm (12.4in) dual discs, sintered metal pads |
| — rear | 316mm (12.4in) dual piston caliper disc, sintered metal pads |

*Muscular tank fairing adds to the streetfighter appeal of the X11. The tank can swallow 22l (5.8gal), enabling riders to cover a more than respectable 288km (179 miles) between fill-ups.*

**Cockpit shroud**
This mini-cowl might not look like much, but its clever design makes all the difference at speeds above 115km/h (70mph-), diverting disturbed air above and around the rider's head. We have even been to above 240km/h (150mph) on it without a fairing, without problems. Definitely a first for naked streetbikes.

**Fuel injection**
Honda's legendary PGM-FI system makes delivery glitch-free at almost all revs. A rev idler adjuster situated to the right side of the bike acts like a secondary choke if needed. Stuntmen have already discovered it can help them perform ultra-low speed manoeuvres.

**Radiator shroud**
The controversial component which some say makes the X11, when viewed from the front, look like a fridge. But Honda allegedly spent significant sums of money developing it – its primary functions being protection, improved downforce for increased stability at speed and increased airflow to keep the engine cool. It also diverts windblast out and around the rider's legs, making fast work far less fatiguing.

**Security**
The X11 is one of an increasing number of new Honda's to sport HISS – Honda Ignition Security System. It works by electronically matching a chip in the key to the bike's on board 'brain'. The common rideaway crime is now said to be impossible.

**Front suspension**
The 43mm (1.7in) forks have 120mm (4.7in) of axle travel, but are not adjustable. The springing and damping set as standard allows comfortable tourer and sports-style riding.

**Brakes**
The combination of three-piston Nissin calipers and twin 310mm (12.2in) discs up front, coupled with a 256mm (10in) disc to the rear, looks usual enough. But the X11 is the latest Honda to sport the firm's Dual Combined System, where operating the rear also partly operates the front, and vice versa. The system has its fans (aids stability, suits novices) and critics (can take away an element of control).

*X11*

*Take the 1137cc (69.4ci) engine from the Super Blackbird, tune it for more mid-range grunt, place it in a tough twin-spar chassis – and you have the X11. It may seem pointless and in some respects controversial, but for those who want a naked, gut-wrenching torque monster, which can still be ridden like a 600, Honda might just have found the ideal mix.*

*Monoshock design features seven-way adjustable spring preload to accommodate pillions and heavier riders plus 120mm (4.7in) of axle range.*

*Orange-red inlays give the speedo and rev counter displays a welcome, fresh appearance, but work poorly at night. The odometer is digital, and the cluster of idiot lights lives in a central display.*

*Closely based on the Super Blackbird's twin spar design rather than the spine assembly the industry first assumed it would sport, it visually adds to the X11's air of brutality and is seriously stronger than the hefty output of the engine. Flex will not be a problem.*

**Seat**
795mm (31.3in) makes the X11's perch averagely tall. But it is amazingly comfortable, as a 800km (500 mile) trip through France eventually showed.

**Engine**
The engine is directly based on the awesome Super Blackbird's, but has received minor work to ensure the emphasis on power delivery is in the mid-range. The 1137cc (69.4ci), DOHC in-line-four sports four valves per cylinder, a bore and stroke of 79 x 54mm (3.1 x 2.1in), an 11:1 compression ratio, and makes a claimed 103kW (138bhp).

**Exhausts**
Thin catalysers routed in the pipes help reduce emissions, but cause the silencers' exterior to become remarkably hot.

# Specifications

*Honda's main aim, the* company states, in producing the *X11 was to have a bike ready for the new millennium in both styling and power. And it has done it.*
*The engine is based closely on that of the CBR1100XX, but the X11 is a naked sports bike with power, strength and oodles of style. Sure, you are not going to almost break your neck on a fully faired machine of this capacity, but then you don't get that incredible rush when you grab a handful of throttle, either.*

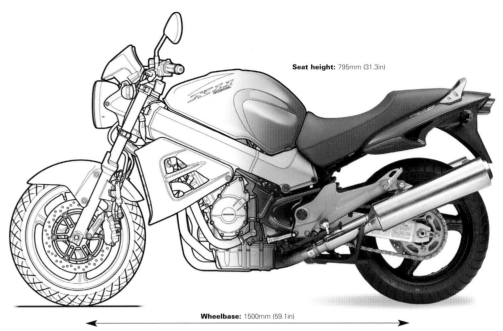

**Seat height:** 795mm (31.3in)

**Width:** 750mm (29.5in)

**Wheelbase:** 1500mm (59.1in)

## ENGINE

| | |
|---|---|
| Type | 4-stroke |
| Layout | in-line four |
| Total displacement | 1137cc (69.4ci) |
| Bore | 79mm (3.1in) |
| Stroke | 54mm (2.1in) |
| Compression ratio | 11:1 |
| Valves | 4 per cylinder |
| Fuel system | electronic fuel injection |
| Ignition | computer controlled digital transistorized with electronic advance |
| Cooling | liquid |
| Maximum power | 92.4kW (123.9bhp) @ 9500rpm |
| Maximum torque | 10.8kg-m (77.9lb-ft) @ 7400rpm |

### TORQUE

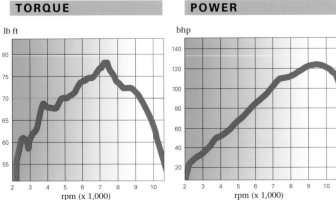

### POWER

## TRANSMISSION

| | |
|---|---|
| Primary drive | gear |
| Clutch | wet, multiplate |
| Gearbox | 5-speed |
| Final drive | 'O'ring chain |

## WEIGHTS & CAPACITIES

| | |
|---|---|
| Tank capacity | 22l (5.8gal) |
| Dry weight | 222kg (489.4lb) |
| Weight distribution | |
| — front | N/A |
| — rear | N/A |
| Wheelbase | 1500mm (59.1in) |
| Overall length | 2145mm (84.4in) |
| Overall width | 750mm (29.5in) |
| Overall height | 1115mm (43.9in) |
| Seat height | 795mm (31.3in) |

## CYCLE PARTS

| | |
|---|---|
| Frame | aluminium twin-spar beam |
| Rake/trail | N/A |
| Front suspension | 43mm (1.7in) telescopic forks |
| Travel | 120mm (4.7in) |
| Adjustment | none |
| Rear suspension | monoshock |
| Travel | 120mm (4.7in) |
| Adjustment | 7-way spring preload |
| Tyres | |
| — make | Michelin Macadam/Bridgestone |
| — front | 120/70 x 17 |
| — rear | 180/55 x 17 |
| Brakes | |
| — make | Nissin |
| — front | twin 310mm (12.2in) discs, Combined 3-piston calipers, sintered metallic pads |
| — rear | single 256mm (10in) disc, Combined 3-piston caliper, sintered metallic pads |

**Independent test measurements (above) differ from the manufacturer's claimed maximum power and maximum torque figures.**

# HONDA **FC6 VALKYRIE**

*Honda's five-speed gearbox offers real world ratios and an acceptably clunk-free change in both directions. Final drive is by low-maintenance shaft.*

**Tank**
A big cruiser needs a big tank. The Valkyrie's holds 20l (5.3gal).

*The rear suspension features dual shocks. These have five-way preload adjustment and 120mm (4.7in) of travel.*

**Engine**
Closely-based on the legendary Gold Wing's, but nestling in a lighter chassis, it provides astonishing acceleration for what is, after all, a massive custom cruiser. The flat six cylinder design with 12 valves and a whopping 1520.3cc (92.8ci) capacity gives a distinctive engine note. Compression is a lowly (by modern standards) 9.8:1, and six 28mm (1.1in) carburettors are used to feed the beast.

**Front brakes**
Honda has chosen twin 296mm (11.7in) discs with dual-piston calipers to haul up the F6C. Though larger discs and higher-spec calipers are routinely used on sportsters weighing far less, the Valkyrie has no need of them since it is not intended to make an appearance on the track.

**Mudguards**
Typically American-styled, as the F6C is intended to be, thanks to the wraparound, hugging design, which is also effective at keeping road salt at bay.

## Honda's F6C (Flat Six Custom) is

*big, heavy and laden with chrome. The Gold Wing-based engine is snuggly fitted into a lighter chassis, and you may be surprised by its weight and agility. It zooms from (0–96km/h (0–60mph) in 3.6 seconds and does a very respectable 206km/h (128mph) top speed. Cruisers may never be the same again.*

*Inverted 45mm (1.8in) front forks provide a plush ride, look the business and offer up to 110mm (4.3in) of travel. There is no adjustment.*

**Clocks**
Night-riding has revealed a green back-light up until now. Subsequent F6Cs will boast an easier-to-view orange glow. Instrumentation includes a tacho, water temperature gauge and typical warning lights.

*Prepare to be staggered when it comes to weight – the F6C tips the scales at 309 kg (680lb) dry!*

**Front wheel**
Choosing a 43.2cm (17in) rim means opting for a good combination of both stability and flickability at the fractional expense of authentic style. The standard front tyre has a massive 150/80 profile – the same size as fitted to several big-bore sportsters' rear ends in the 1980s!

**Seat**
With a height of just 740mm (29.1in), the F6C can be easily managed by anyone – as long as they can cope with the bike's sheer weight. For the 2000 model year, the seat's shape and material were both changed. The raked bars provide a relaxing position, allowing the rider to sit comfortably at high speed despite the bike's naked lines.

**Ground clearance**
Careful mounting those kerbs – though there is 155mm (6.1in) of clearance, the sheer length of the wheelbase (1690mm/66.5in) exaggerates the possibility of grinding out.

**Chrome**
Acres of it, and thickly applied too. Poor longevity simply should not be an issue.

# Specifications

*It may be big, it may be heavy, but it is also very popular.
It appeared in 1997 and captured the hearts of many cruiser fans,
and it almost stops the traffic when on the road.
There is so much chrome on this beast, so it is a pity there is not
more ground clearance: with a lean, the silencers touch down
first. And that proves expensive.
But it is solid, stable, comfortable, and will even wheelie! At the
price, though, you have to be in love with it.*

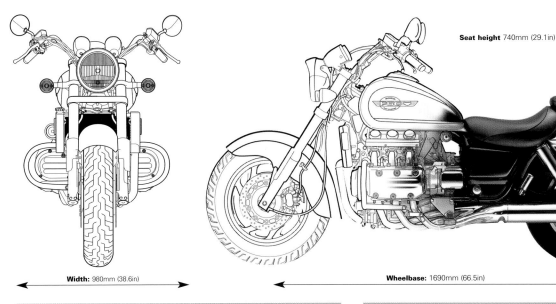

**Seat height** 740mm (29.1in)

**Width:** 980mm (38.6in)

**Wheelbase:** 1690mm (66.5in)

## ENGINE

| | |
|---|---|
| Type | 4-stroke |
| Layout | horizontally opposed six-cylinder |
| Total displacement | 1520cc (92.8ci) |
| Bore | 71mm (2.8in) |
| Stroke | 64mm (2.5in) |
| Compression ratio | 9.8:1 |
| Valves | 2 per cylinder |
| Fuel system | 6 x 28mm (1.1in) CV-type carburettors |
| Ignition | fully transistorized electronic |
| Cooling | liquid |
| Maximum power   65.6kW | (88bhp) @ 5250rpm |
| Maximum torque | 120kg-m (86.9lb-ft) @ 4950rpm |

## TRANSMISSION

| | |
|---|---|
| Primary drive | gear |
| Clutch | hydraulic |
| Gearbox | 5-speed |
| Final drive | shaft |

## WEIGHTS & CAPACITIES

| | |
|---|---|
| Tank capacity | 20l (5.3gal) |
| Dry weight | 309kg (681lb) |
| Weight distribution | |
| — front | N/A |
| — rear | N/A |
| Wheelbase | 1690mm (66.5in) |
| Overall length | 2530mm (99.6in) |
| Overall width | 980mm (38.6in) |
| Overall height | 1185mm (4.7in) |
| Seat height | 740mm (29.1in) |

## CYCLE PARTS

| | |
|---|---|
| Frame | tubular steel cradle |
| Rake/trail | N/A |
| Front suspension | 45mm (1.8in) inverted telescopic forks |
| Travel | 110mm (4.3in) |
| Adjustment | none |
| Rear suspension | dual conventional dampers |
| Travel | 120mm (4.7in) |
| Adjustment | 5-step adjustable spring preload |
| Tyres | |
| — make | Dunlop |
| — front | 150/80 x 17 |
| — rear | 180/70 x 16 |
| Brakes | |
| — make | N/A |
| — front | 296mm (11.7in) dual discs, dual piston calipers |
| — rear | 316mm (12.4in) single disc dual piston caliper |

## TORQUE

lb ft

rpm (x 1,000)

## POWER

bhp

rpm (x 1,000)

Independent test measurements (above) differ from the manufacturer's claimed maximum
power and maximum torque figures.

# HONDA GL1500 GOLD WING

**Honda has introduced another version of integral braking, this time with a system where operating the rear brake also brings one of the front discs and calipers into play. The front set-up incorporates twin 296mm (11.7in) discs and dual-piston calipers, while the rear features a truly massive single 316mm (12.4in) disc and dual-piston caliper.**

**Comprehensive equipment**
It is the features such as the system to manage onboard air temperature, and the compressor to inflate tyres and adjust suspension air settings, that make the Gold Wing such a legend.

**Screen**
Some owners complain that he screen is hard to see through in heavy rain and also a fraction too tall for average height riders to peer over.

**Fuel tank**
Holds 23l (6gal).

**Engine**
Current Gold Wing's sport a 12-valve SOHC 1520cc (92.8ci) flat-6 engine with liquid-cooling. The five-speed gearbox is supplemented by a reverse gear – operated by means of a hand-pull lever to the bike's lower left side. Given the enormous dry weight of 372kg (818.4lb), the slow-moving reverse is arguably invaluable.

**Exhausts**
Similar to the design seen on Gold Wings since 1987, but featuring revised silencers since 1998.

## GL1500 GOLD WING

*Many believe this is more akin to a car than a bike! And it is true that the Gold Wing is most definitely not suited to everybody. In fact, many riders believe that owners are missing out on what biking is all about; but you must not forget that not only are many of them older, but they have also 'been there, done that' and feel it is now time to enjoy a bit of comfort. Good on them for at least staying on two wheels, even if it is a bit of a heavyweight.*

**Final drive**
Shaft drive provides a plush ride and ensures maintenance is kept to a minimum.

**Tyres**
Surprisingly narrow for such a big bike, but then again lean angle and outright grip are not the issue. The front is a 130/70 x 18, the rear 160/80 x 16. They sit on cast-aluminium alloy wheels.

The radio/cassette features quadraphonic sound courtesy of two speakers front and two rear. The main controls are situated on the handlebars, offering volume, tone and speaker balance adjustments. An automatic volume setting feature sets levels according to ambient noise.

The reinforced steel frame is very strong – as it needs to be for a bike of such weight. Considering its size, handling is better than you would imagine, though it will not set pulses racing.

41mm (1.6in) forks are air-assisted to provide a plush ride according to terrain, altitude, temperature and all-up weight.

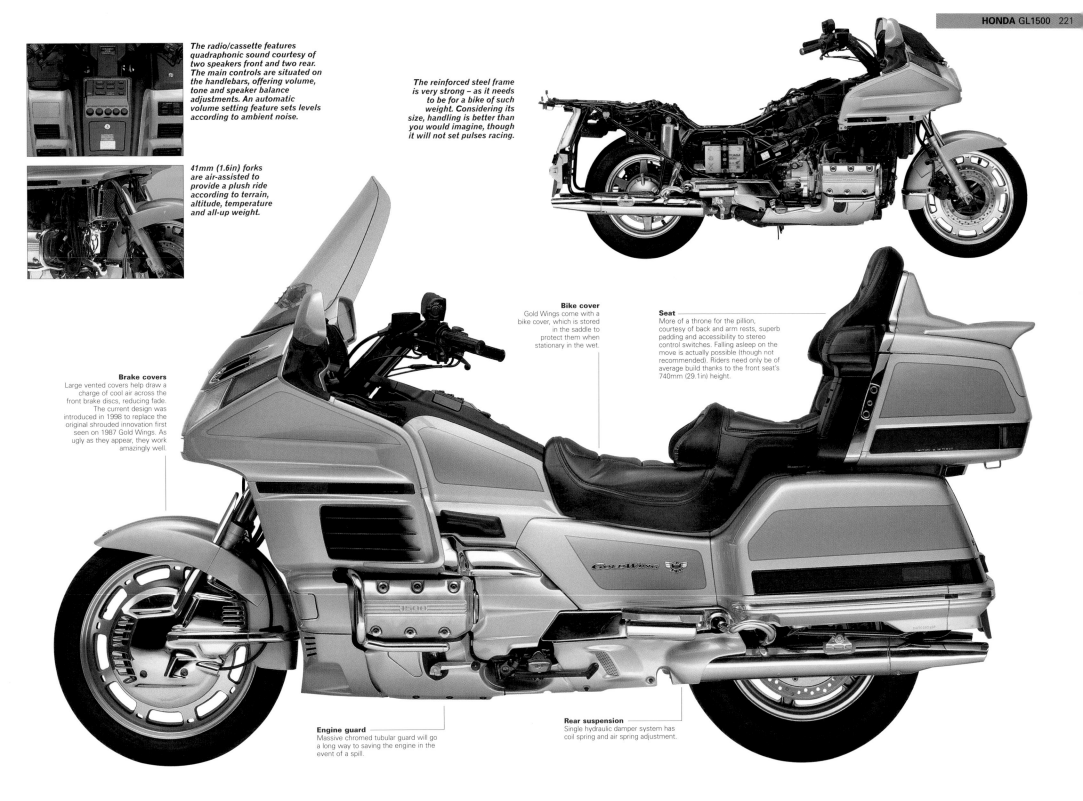

**Bike cover**
Gold Wings come with a bike cover, which is stored in the saddle to protect them when stationary in the wet.

**Seat**
More of a throne for the pillion, courtesy of back and arm rests, superb padding and accessibility to stereo control switches. Falling asleep on the move is actually possible (though not recommended). Riders need only be of average build thanks to the front seat's 740mm (29.1in) height.

**Brake covers**
Large vented covers help draw a charge of cool air across the front brake discs, reducing fade. The current design was introduced in 1998 to replace the original shrouded innovation first seen on 1987 Gold Wings. As ugly as they appear, they work amazingly well.

**Engine guard**
Massive chromed tubular guard will go a long way to saving the engine in the event of a spill.

**Rear suspension**
Single hydraulic damper system has coil spring and air spring adjustment.

# Specifications

*At first glance a* barge, a boat and an oil-tanker all rolled into one, the leviathan *G*old Wing packs the advanced features and carefully-engineered components needed to make a superlative, ultra-reliable tourer.
With six cylinders and plenty of grunt, the hefty Wing will sit at well over the ton for hours and handling and braking are far better than you might expect from a bike of this size and weight. For a sizeable percentage of riders, and for covering vast distances with ease, the GL1500 *G*old Wing is, without question, in a league of its own.

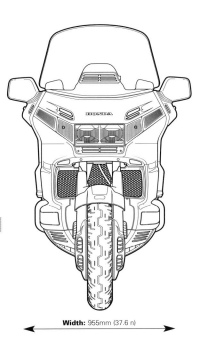

**Width:** 955mm (37.6 n)

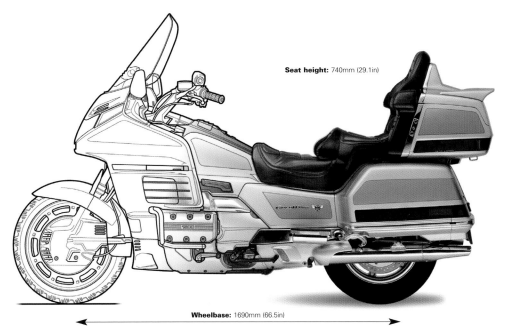

**Seat height:** 740mm (29.1in)

**Wheelbase:** 1690mm (66.5in)

## ENGINE

| | |
|---|---|
| Type | 4-stroke |
| Layout | OHC horizontally opposed six |
| Total displacement | 1520cc (92.8ci) |
| Bore | 71mm (2.8in) |
| Stroke | 64mm (2.5in) |
| Compression ratio | 9.8:1 |
| Valves | 2 per cylinder |
| Fuel system | 2 x 33mm (1.3in) carburettors |
| Ignition | transistorized electronic |
| Cooling | liquid |
| Maximum power | 65.5kW (87.9bhp) @ 5100rpm |
| Maximum torque | 11.9kg-m (85.9lb-ft) @ 4950rpm |

## TRANSMISSION

| | |
|---|---|
| Primary drive | gear |
| Clutch | wet, multiplate |
| Gearbox | 5-speed |
| Final drive | shaft |

## WEIGHTS & CAPACITIES

| | |
|---|---|
| Tank capacity | 23l (6gal) |
| Dry weight | 372kg (818.4lb) |
| Weight distribution | |
| — front | n/a |
| — rear | n/a |
| Wheelbase | 1690mm (66.5in) |
| Overall length | 2615mm (103in) |
| Overall width | 955mm (37.6in) |
| Overall height | 1495mm (58.9in) |
| Seat height | 740mm (29.1in) |

## CYCLE PARTS

| | |
|---|---|
| Frame | steel, reinforced |
| Rake/trail | n/a |
| Front suspension | 41mm (1.6in) forks |
| Travel | 140mm (5.5in) |
| Adjustment | air-assisted |
| Rear suspension | hydraulic damper, coil spring |
| Travel | 105mm (4.1in) |
| Adjustment | preload, air-spring |
| Tyres | |
| — make | varies |
| — front | 130/70 x 18 |
| — rear | 160/80 x 16 |
| Brakes | |
| — make | Nissin |
| — front | 2 x 296mm (11.7in) discs, dual-piston calipers |
| — rear | 316mm (12.4in) disc, dual-piston caliper |

## TORQUE

lb ft

rpm (x 1,000)

## POWER

bhp

rpm (x 1,000)

Independent test measurements (above) differ from the manufacturer's claimed maximum power and maximum torque figures.

# GL1800 GOLD WING

**Screen**
The Gold Wing's massive windshield is manually adjustable to six height positons, to better tailor it to different riders and riding styles. Optional screen extensions further improve protection from wind and weather.

*As well as large analogue tachometer and speedometer displays, a large LCD display indicates sound system information, odometer and trip displays as well as warnings for open trunk and a rear suspension setting display.*

**Aerial**
A large whip aerial is connected to the built-in radio sound system. It folds down for easy storage.

**Indicators**
The turn signals are incorporated into the large rear view mirrors, for better visibility and cleaner aerodynamics.

**Headlights**
Four large headlights give incredible illumination for easy night time progress. Low beams uses two lights, and high beam uses all four bulbs.

**Luggage**
The two large side panniers and massive topbox are fully integrated into the Gold Wing's bodywork. The boxes have a total of 147l (8970ci) of storage space, hold a CD multichanger and are centrally locked by a remote control radio fob.

**Lights**
A large complement of running lights, and high level brake lights make the Gold Wing an impressive sight from behind at night.

## GL1800 GOLD WING

**The most recent version** of Honda's legendary Gold Wing supertourer, the GL1800 is the most advanced touring bike yet built. Using superbike technology to cut weight and improve performance, the aluminium-framed Wing appeared in 2001, and was an instant hit with high-mileage junkies. A super-smooth engine, incredible luxury accommodation and impressive equipment levels make it the choice for crossing continents in days, while the firmer chassis and powerful brakes add a further dash of sporting performance.

**Crash bars**
Tough, chromed steel bars protect the cylinder heads from damage in slow-speed crashes.

**Exhaust**
The six-into-two stainless steel system has six outlet pipes, giving the GL1800 a distinctive, classy exhaust tone.

*The GL1800 incorporates brake-linked anti-dive forks. When operated, brake fluid pressure increases the fork damping effect, via the chamber on front of the fork. This reduces front-end dive under braking, improving stability. This picture also shows the Dual-CBS linkage above the brake caliper.*

*Smooth lines and careful swooping design makes the GL1800 then per cent more aerodynamic than its predecessor, the GL1500 Gold Wing.*

**Swingarm**
The rear Pro-Link swingarm is an aluminium single-sided design, with a computer-adjustable monoshock. This allows pushbutton adjustment of preload, with two preset memory positions.

**Reverse Gear**
The Wing features an electric reverse gear, where the engine's starter motor turns the rear wheel, pushing the bike backwards at low speed for parking.

**Frame**
The dual-spar box-section aluminium frame is a hefty 11kg (22lb) lighter than the steel frame of the GL1500.

**Engine**
The GL1800 engine is a flat-six SOHC 12-valve water-cooled design, with a 1832cc (112ci) capacity. The cylinder heads can clearly be seen from each side. It is a very smooth, powerful and torquey design, perfect for touring duties.

**Transmission**
The Gold Wing uses a five-speed gearbox, driven through a hydraulically-operated clutch, with shaft final drive.

**Seat**
The sculpted riders seat is separated from the pillion seat by a large backrest. Low-mounted footpegs further improve rider and passenger comfort.

**Radiators**
Honda fitted twin side-mounted radiators to improve cooling efficiency and keep heat away from the rider. This also frees up space behind the front wheel compared with a conventional radiator.

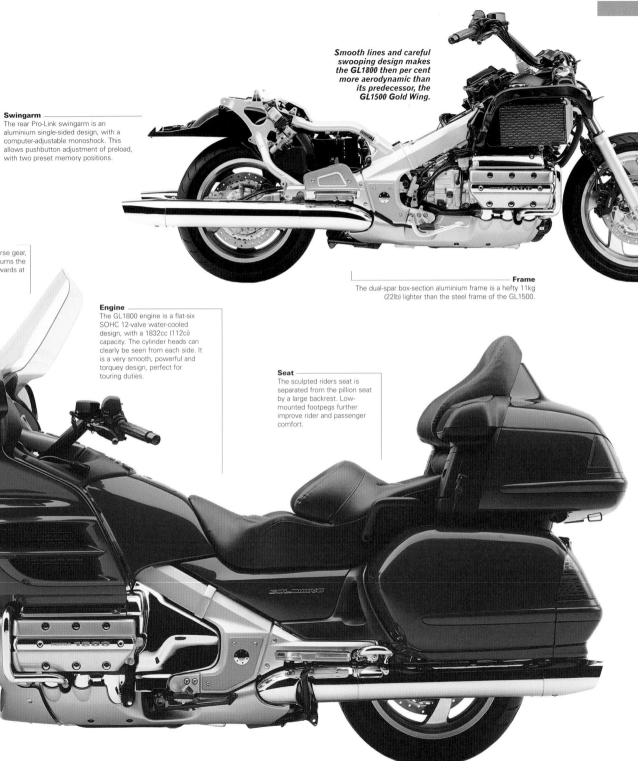

# Kawasaki ZXR400

**Bars**
The low, racing style bars are situated in such a position as to force the rider into a racing crouch. But that is how most who buy this will want to ride it.

**Bodywork**
Kawasaki is renowned nowadays for the excellent finish on most of its bikes, and the ZXR does not let it down. The two paintschemes available nowadays only serve to accentuate the sporty style of the bike. The lime green/white is typical Kawasaki and would be picked out from a crowd as such immediately, while the ebony/metallic eventide looks superb. The green version does, however, give the bike a 'fast' look.

**Forks**
The front end is fitted with 41mm (1.6in) upside down telescopic forks and can be adjusted for rebound damping plus preload.

**Tyres**
At the front, the ZXR is fitted with a 120/60 x 17 tyre; at the rear, the rubber is 160 x 17.

**Exhaust**
The four into one exhaust has just the one alloy end can exiting on the right. Very nice and very efficient

*Kawasaki likes to call this the 'pocket rocket', and for once this is not just manufacturer's blurb. Take the logo off and many would assume this is a 600cc (36.6ci) sports bike, although once they sat on it they would soon notice the difference, with the low seat height and dry weight of only 159kg (351lb). A pity there are not more bikes like the Kawasaki.*

Head on, this looks really, really nice. In the full race fairing, you can see the air ducts and twin hoses that run through the fuel tank.

*The double cradle, perimeter-style frame is clearly visible through the bodywork. It may be over a decade old, but nobody would guess it.*

**Fuel tank**
It holds 16l (4.2gal), about right for a sports bike, and is perfectly moulded for most riders to fit snugly into the bike when in the inevitable crouched, racing position.

*Until 1995, the Kawasaki sported ZXR400 on its tail piece; nowadays it is just 400. The earlier version looked better – Kawasaki should have stuck with it.*

**Seat**
The two-piece race pad style seat is built for speed not comfort, but the rider will be pleasantly surprised at just how comfortable it is. Not so the pillion! And there aren't many riders who will not be able to touch the ground, as it sits at just 760mm (29.9in).

**Wheels**
The 43.2cm (17in) three spoke cast wheels are nothing unusual, but look good.

**Engine**
At the heart of the ZXR sits a 398cc 16 valve in-line four with water cooling and a bore and stroke of 57 x 39mm (2.2 x 1.5in). There is plenty of performance to be had from this motor which gives a top speed of just over 225km/h (140mph). With a 14,500rpm redline, this engine packs as much punch as many 600s.

# Kawasaki ZXR400

# Specifications

*This great little 400* has been around for more than a decade. And it is good to see Kawasaki has not discontinued it, because what other brilliant 400s are there? This is often nicknamed the 'pocket rocket' and just one ride on it tells you why. Get on a good but twisty road and it will see off many a bigger, more powerful bike. It is nimble, has sharp steering and great handling. And it looks brilliant as well.

You can fault little about this bike and perhaps we should be less surprised than we often are that other manufacturers are not putting out their own 400s – after all, the ZXR is a tough act to follow, let alone beat.

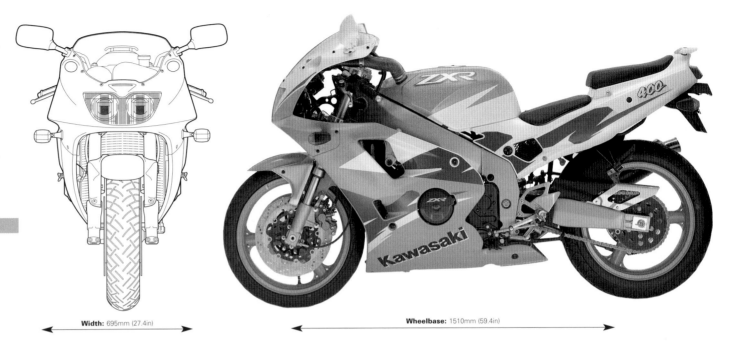

Width: 695mm (27.4in)

Wheelbase: 1510mm (59.4in)

## ENGINE

| | |
|---|---|
| Type | 4-stroke |
| Layout | in-line four |
| Total displacement | 398cc (24.3ci) |
| Bore | 57mm (2.2in) |
| Stroke | 39mm (1.5in) |
| Compression ratio | N/A |
| Valves | 4 per cylinder |
| Fuel system | carburettor |
| Ignition | electric |
| Cooling | water |

## TRANSMISSION

| | |
|---|---|
| Primary drive | gear |
| Clutch | multiplate |
| Gearbox | 6-speed |
| Final drive | chain |

## WEIGHTS & CAPACITIES

| | |
|---|---|
| Tank capacity | 22l (5.8gal) |
| Dry weight | 242kg (534lb) |
| Weight distribution | |
| — front | N/A |
| — rear | N/A |
| Wheelbase | 1510mm (59.4in) |
| Overall length | N/A |
| Overall width | 695mm (27.4in) |
| Overall height | N/A |
| Seat height | 790mm (31.1in) |

## CYCLE PARTS

| | |
|---|---|
| Frame | alloy perimeter |
| Rake/trail | 27°/110mm (4.3in) |
| Front suspension | 41mm (1.6in) telescopic forks |
| Travel | N/A |
| Adjustment | preload, plus rebound damping |
| Rear suspension | Uni-Trak |
| Travel | N/A |
| Adjustment | preload, plus rebound damping |
| Tyres | |
| — front | 120/70 x 17 |
| — rear | 170/60 x 17 |
| Brakes | |
| — front | twin discs |
| — rear | single disc |

# Kawasaki *ER5*

*You do not often see drum brakes on bikes these days but, in truth, these are all the lightweight ER-5 needs to stop. There is enough bite to lock the rear wheel at 112km/h (70mph). If you buy secondhand, make sure the shoes have plenty of life left in them. Otherwise they will wreck the drum's lining.*

**Speedo cable**
This is one of the most frequently failing ER5 parts. Riding with a broken one might save you from recording your increasing mileage, but it is also a road traffic offence.

**Clocks**
Twin chrome clocks look stylish when viewed from head on.

**Headlamp**
Simple, single round headlamp provides enough power for the ER-5's turn of speed.

**Paintwork**
Not the best around, and particularly soft and thin on the fuel tank. Buckles, zips and tankbags can soon take their toll.

**Forks**
Spindly 37mm (1.5in) telescopic forks have no preload or damping adjustment, quickly use up most of their 125mm (4.9in) of travel under braking or on bumpy roads, and are prone to pitting if the bike is not carefully maintained. That said, they do the job – just.

**Engine**
The four-stroke, 498cc (30.4ci), DOHC twin has a bore and stroke of 74 x 58mm (2.9 x 2.3in), a compression ratio of 9.8:1, four valves per cylinder, liquid cooling, and is fed by two Keihin CVK34 carburettors. It is quite revvy and low-powered by nature, which means constant shifting through the gearbox when the wind is blowing hard.

**Silencer**
A factory replacement whisper-quiet silencer is not cheap. Believe it or not, performance aftermarket systems are available for the ER5, though.

**Tyres**
Standard Dunlop D202s are often junked in favour of grippier rubber. Do not be tempted to fit oversize tyres, though, unless the manufacturer specifically recommends it. The standard sizes are 110/70 x 17 front and 130/70 x 17 rear.

*ER5*

**Not a great looker,** *but then how many cheap bikes are? The ER5 is aimed at a specific customer, one that wants simplicity, practicality and economy, and in all three categories the little Kawasaki excels. The componentry is basic, the twin shocks, drum rear brake and single front discs seem pretty dated, yet everything works well enough in relation to the capabilities of the bike. It is certainly a no-frills bike, but it comes at a great price.*

*The twin shock rear suspension comes with built-in bounce and sag on standard settings. Most owners need at least one more click of preload adjustment. Ours handled best with two more. Maximum rear suspension travel is 105mm (4.1in).*

*The lack of fairing lowers means the engine and all its peripherals are open to the ravages of road crud and salt. Careful and correct maintenance is essential to keep the bike looking like new.*

*Tubular steel cradle frame, twin rear shocks, 37mm (1.5in) forks – hardly specifications to set the world on fire. The bike does not excel in any one area, yet the overall package makes for one that is an easy ride.*

**Fuel tank**
16l (4.2gal) tank capacity gives the ER-5 a potential range of 265–274km (165–170 miles).

**Seat height**
At 780mm (30.7in), the ER5's rider perch is low enough for most owners.

**Wheels**
Three-spoke design looks both cute and inoffensive, and is comparatively light.

**Oil level**
The ER5 is one of the few bikes light enough for most people to hold upright while simultaneously crouching on the ground to check the oil level sight glass.

**Chain and sprockets**
Horror stories abound of skint owners fitting ultra-cheap chain kits, only for them to snap shortly after. Don't do it!

# **Kawasaki** *ER5*

# Specifications

*Although the ER5 is* nothing spectacular on paper, it has developed a large and devoted following. When flat-out performance and the ability to flick from left to right in a nano-second do not matter, but ease of use, tractibility and extreme value for money do, *K*awasaki's budget baby fits the bill. *O*ne of the best bikes around to learn on, the ER5 is commonly used by direct access training centres. But experienced riders like it too – for being exactly what it is.

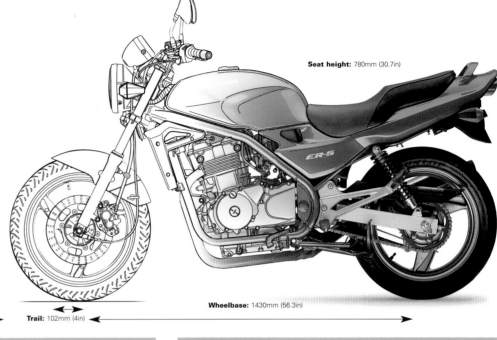

Seat height: 780mm (30.7in)

Width: 730mm (28.7in)  Trail: 102mm (4in)  Wheelbase: 1430mm (56.3in)

## ENGINE

| | |
|---|---|
| Type | 4-stroke |
| Layout | DOHC twin |
| Total displacement | 498cc (30.4ci) |
| Bore | 74mm (2.9in) |
| Stroke | 58mm (2.3in) |
| Compression ratio | 9.8:1 |
| Valves | 4 per cylinder |
| Fuel system | 2 x Keihin CVK34 carburettors |
| Ignition | CDI |
| Cooling | liquid |
| Maximum power | 33.1kW (44.4bhp) @ 8800rpm |
| Maximum torque | 4.2kg-m (30.7lb-ft) @ 7000rpm |

## TRANSMISSION

| | |
|---|---|
| Primary drive | chain |
| Clutch | wet multiplate |
| Gearbox | 6-speed |
| Final drive | chain |

## WEIGHTS & CAPACITIES

| | |
|---|---|
| Tank capacity | 16l (4.2gal) |
| Dry weight | 174kg (382.8 lb) |
| Weight distribution | |
| — front | N/A |
| — rear | N/A |
| Wheelbase | 1430mm (56.3in) |
| Overall length | 2040mm (80.3in) [2070mm (81.5in) Germany, Greece, Norway, Sweden] |
| Overall width | 730mm (28.7in) |
| Overall height | 1070mm (42.1in) |
| Seat height | 780mm (30.7in) |

## CYCLE PARTS

| | |
|---|---|
| Frame | tubular, double-cradle |
| Rake/trail | 27°/102mm (4in) |
| Front suspension | 37mm (1.5in) telescopic forks |
| Travel | 125mm (4.9in) |
| Adjustment | none |
| Rear suspension | twin shock |
| Travel | 105mm (4.1in) |
| Adjustment | preload |
| Tyres | |
| — make | varies |
| — front | 110/70 x 17 |
| — rear | 130/70 x 17 |
| Brakes | |
| — make | N/A |
| — front | single disc, 2-piston caliper |
| — rear | single drum |

## TORQUE

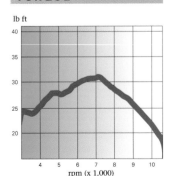

lb ft / rpm (x 1,000)

## POWER

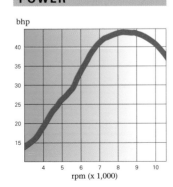

bhp / rpm (x 1,000)

**Independent test measurements (above) differ from the manufacturer's claimed maximum power and maximum torque figures.**

# Kawasaki GPZ500

**Colours**
Only two exterior colour options are listed for the GPZ500, sombre Black Pearl (shown) or the more glitzy Candy Persimmon Red.

**Front suspension**
Twin 37mm (1.5in) telescopic forks feature 130mm (5.1in) of wheel travel. The forks were uprated from 36mm (1.4in) in 1994 and also given revised damping characteristics in a bid to improve the bike's handling and stability.

**Exhaust**
Two-into-two piping with alloy finish end cans features chrome-plated silencers on all post-1994 models, to give a slightly more lustrous appearance to an otherwise visually unscintillating system.

**Rear suspension**
Kawasaki's once state-of-the-art Uni-Trak monoshock rear suspension system features preload only adjustment and 100mm (3.9in) of wheel travel to give a good all-round ride.

**Brakes**
Stopping power is delivered on the UK models (D and F) via a single 280mm (11in) front disc brake with Balanced Actuation Calipers. The 230mm (9in) rear disc brake replaced the original drum brake in 1994.

*GPZ500*

***Inheriting several top-quality** characteristics from its earth-shattering **GPZ900R** relative, the **GPZ500** failed to set the world alight in its own right. Classified as a sports middleweight, the **GPZ500** offers back-to-basics biking at a reasonable cost. It may not make your heart skip a beat, but it will keep experienced riders content and newly qualified riders right side up.*

The cockpit is typically standard Japanese – nothing particularly flash, but the clocks are easy to read and all switches well within arm's reach.

Tyres are fairly narrow – 110 70 x 17 front and 130 70 x 17 rear – but give decent enough grip and are the same as those fitted to the best-selling **ER5**.

**Tank**
An 18l (4.8gal) fuel tank gives reasonable range, but just how reasonable is very much down to your individual style of riding.

Like many other 'budget' bikes, the **GPZ**'s backbone is a straight forward double cradle box section frame, fabricated from mild steel.

**Seat**
The GPZ500's low seat height, at only 775mm (30.5 in), makes the bike an attractive proposition for those who are not so long on the leg.

**Wheels**
The Kawasaki's 43.2cm (17in) three spoke cast aluminium wheels are lightweight but lasting and a 2.5cm (1in) increase from the pre-1994 model's fashionable but less stable 40.6cm (16in) wheels.

**Engine**
Liquid-cooled DOHC eight valve in-line twin is based almost entirely on the factory's 1984 GPZ900R engine, but with two cylinders missing. The GPZ900R motor became the blueprint for many other manufacturers and the GPZ500S inherits many of its quality characteristics.

**Transmission**
Six-speed gearbox includes Kawasaki's renowned 'positive stop neutral finder' mechanism. In layman's terms, when you come to a stop in first gear, the gear lever will only go into neutral, which saves you accidentally slipping it into second and stalling.

# Kawasaki | *GPZ500*

# Specifications

*There is nothing special about* the *GPZ500 – it has been around for three decades and although it was launched as a sports middleweight, it is now in the 'budget bike' class since it has received barely any modifications since 1987.*
*But the reason the GPZ has been around for so long, and is likely to remain in production for a while yet, is that the buyer gets value for money.*
*The GPZ500 does not disappoint: it has a top speed of just over 200km/h (125mph), it does everything it should, and it does it a lot better than you might expect from the price.*

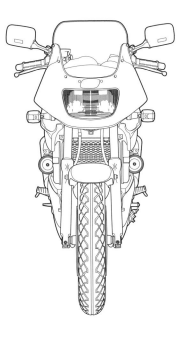

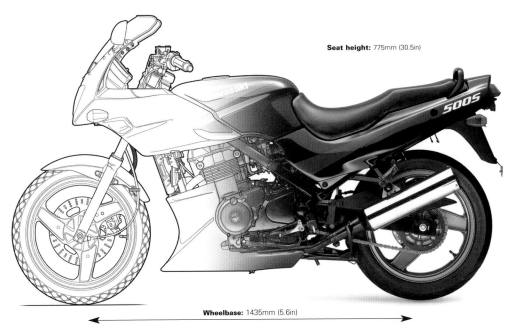

Seat height: 775mm (30.5in)

Wheelbase: 1435mm (5.6in)

## ENGINE

| | |
|---|---|
| Type | four-stoke |
| Layout | inclined parallel twin |
| Total displacement | 498cc (30.4ci) |
| Bore | 74mm (2.9in) |
| Stroke | 58mm (2.3in) |
| Compression ratio | 1.28:1 |
| Valves | four per cylinder |
| Fuel system | digital electronic |
| Ignition | CVK 34mm semi-flat slide carbs |
| Cooling | liquid |
| Maximum power | 38.5kW (51.6bhp) @ 7850rpm |
| Maximum torque | 4.3kg-m (31.2lb-ft) @ 7900rpm |

## TRANSMISSION

| | |
|---|---|
| Primary drive | Helical cut gear |
| Clutch | wet, multiplate |
| Gearbox | 6-speed, indirect constant mesh, |
| Final drive | chain |

## CYCLE PARTS

| | |
|---|---|
| Frame | box section double cradle |
| Rake/trail | 27°/91mm (3.6in) |
| Front suspension | 37mm (1.5in) telescopic forks |
| Travel | N/A |
| Adjustment | spring preload |
| Rear suspension | Uni-Trak |
| Travel | N/A |
| Adjustment | spring preload |
| Tyres | |
| — make | N/A |
| — front | 110/70 x 17 |
| — rear | 130/70 x 17 |
| Brakes | |
| — make | N/A |
| — front | 280mm (11in) single disc, single piston caliper |
| — rear | disc (drum until 1994) |

## WEIGHTS & CAPACITIES

| | |
|---|---|
| Tank capacity | 18l (4.8gal) |
| Dry weight | 176kg (388lb) |
| Weight distribution | |
| — front | N/A |
| — rear | N/A |
| Wheelbase | 1435mm (5.6in) |
| Overall length | N/A |
| Overall width | N/A |
| Overall height | N/A |
| Seat height | 775mm (30.5in) |

## TORQUE

## POWER

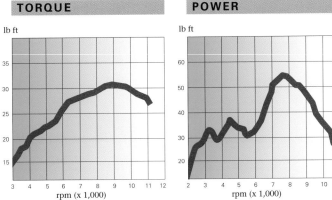

lb ft

rpm (x 1,000)

lb ft

rpm (x 1,000)

Independent test measurements (above) differ from the manufacturer's claimed maximum power and maximum torque figures.

# Kawasaki ZX-6R NINJA

The familiar sports bike layout sees the analogue rev counter take pride of place, with the speedo just offset to the left. The odometer records digitally while, to the right, is the usual cluster of warning lights. Some riders find that the front brake master cylinder obscures their view of this in a racing crouch.

Despite a tiny glitch in the power delivery at 5000rpm, the engine is among the strongest feeling in its class. Useful power can be found all the way through the rev range of the 599cc (36.5ci) four-cylinder, 16-valve lump.

**Mirrors**
Fractionally wider than most others in their class, they offer an excellent, vibration-free rear view for all riders but the very biggest.

**Colours**
Owners tend to prefer the famous green Kawasaki colour scheme, while other riders think the red/black one is best. A third example, black and grey, is available too but less popular. Paint is generally thick and the finish high, although it can succumb to flying chippings.

**Headlight**
Properly integrated and flush-fitting to ensure aerodynamic efficiency, it has a powerful, well diffused main beam and an acceptable dip.

**Clutch**
Stronger and more progressive than the CBR's under repeated race start launches, it is cable-operated and has a four-way adjustable span lever to accommodate most hand sizes.

*ZX-6R*

**IN 1998 Kawasaki's ZX-6R Ninja** *was arguably the best in the 600 range, matching the impressive Honda CBR600F for all-round ability. As popular with riders for its sporting prowess as for its touring capabilities, the Ninja remains a serious contender and is by no means overshadowed by Yamaha's mighty R6 and Honda's almost completely rebuilt CBR600F.*

**Mudguard**
Black plastic side mouldings look odd but actually improve aerodynamic flow by creating a smooth surface to deflect air past the forks with the minimum of impedance.

**Forks**
Monster 46mm (1.8in) conventional telescopic forks are fully adjustable, which means rebound and compression damping, as well as preload can be tinkered with. The standard settings are quite near the mark, though.

**Silencer**
Neat, reasonably light and upswept far enough to prevent contact with the road during fast cornering, it can be quickly removed courtesy of four bolts and a gasket to allow a 'slip-on' aftermarket unit to be used.

**Tyres**
Dunlop D204s come in 120/60-ZR17 front and 170/60 ZR17 rear sizes and provide a good balance between outright grip and wear rate. Many owners swop to something stickier after about 2410km (1500 miles).

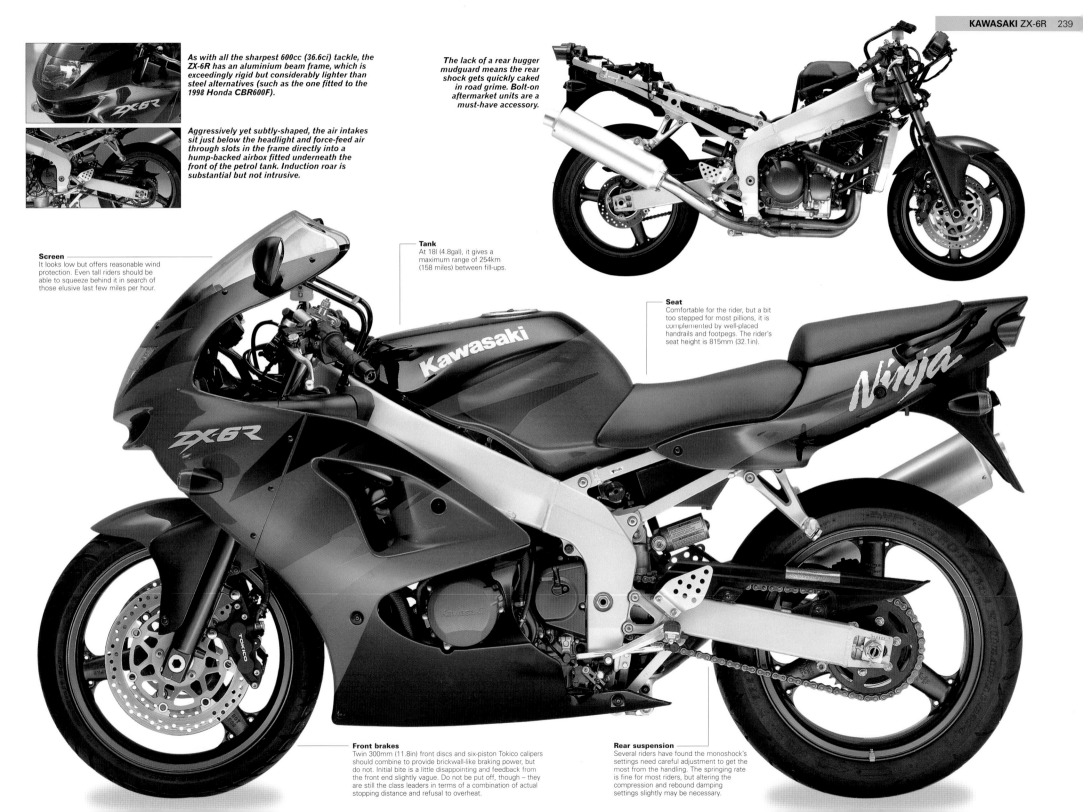

As with all the sharpest 600cc (36.6ci) tackle, the *ZX-6R* has an aluminium beam frame, which is exceedingly rigid but considerably lighter than steel alternatives (such as the one fitted to the 1998 Honda CBR600F).

Aggressively yet subtly-shaped, the air intakes sit just below the headlight and force-feed air through slots in the frame directly into a hump-backed airbox fitted underneath the front of the petrol tank. Induction roar is substantial but not intrusive.

The lack of a rear hugger mudguard means the rear shock gets quickly caked in road grime. Bolt-on aftermarket units are a must-have accessory.

**Screen**
It looks low but offers reasonable wind protection. Even tall riders should be able to squeeze behind it in search of those elusive last few miles per hour.

**Tank**
At 18l (4.8gal), it gives a maximum range of 254km (158 miles) between fill-ups.

**Seat**
Comfortable for the rider, but a bit too stepped for most pillions, it is complemented by well-placed handrails and footpegs. The rider's seat height is 815mm (32.1in).

**Front brakes**
Twin 300mm (11.8in) front discs and six-piston Tokico calipers should combine to provide brickwall-like braking power, but do not. Initial bite is a little disappointing and feedback from the front end slightly vague. Do not be put off, though – they are still the class leaders in terms of a combination of actual stopping distance and refusal to overheat.

**Rear suspension**
Several riders have found the monoshock's settings need careful adjustment to get the most from the handling. The springing rate is fine for most riders, but altering the compression and rebound damping settings slightly may be necessary.

# Kawasaki | *ZX-6R NINJA*

# Specifications

**The Kawasaki ZX-6R was** the middleweight to beat in 1998 – and it is not ready to give up the fight just yet. An impressive list of specifications helped initially to put it at the top of the pile, and it continues to remain competitive. Despite a few changes to the latest model, there is nothing radical in the bike's design – just a blend of time and track-proven components, dimensions and geometry.

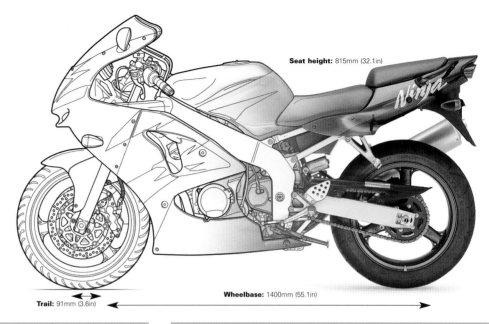

Seat height: 815mm (32.1in)

Width: 715mm (28.2in)

Trail: 91mm (3.6in)

Wheelbase: 1400mm (55.1in)

## ENGINE

| | |
|---|---|
| Type | 4-stroke |
| Layout | in-line four |
| Total displacement | 599cc (36.5in) |
| Bore | 66mm (2.6in) |
| Stroke | 43.8mm (1.7in) |
| Compression ratio | 11.8:1 |
| Valves | 4 per cylinder |
| Fuel system | 4 x 36mm (1.4in) Mikuni BDSR36R carburettors |
| Ignition | digital |
| Cooling | liquid |
| Maximum power | 78.5kW (105.3bhp) @ 12,168rpm |
| Maximum torque | 6.5kg-m (47lb-ft) @ 9911rpm |

## TORQUE

## POWER

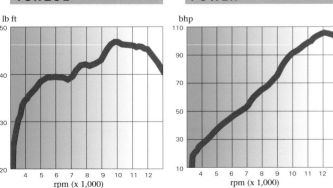

**Independent test measurements (above) differ from the manufacturer's claimed maximum power and maximum torque figures.**

## TRANSMISSION

| | |
|---|---|
| Primary drive | gear |
| Clutch | wet multiplate |
| Gearbox | 6-speed |
| Final drive | sealed chain |

## WEIGHTS & CAPACITIES

| | |
|---|---|
| Tank capacity | 18l (4.8gal) |
| Dry weight | 176kg (387.2 lb) |
| Weight distribution | |
| — front | N/A |
| — rear | N/A |
| Wheelbase | 1400mm (55.1in) |
| Overall length | 2025mm (79.72in) [2055mm (80.9in) in Germany, Sweden, Norway, Finland, Greece and Switzerland] |
| Overall width | 715mm (28.2in) |
| Overall height | 1160mm (45.7in) |
| Seat height | 815mm (32.1in) |

## CYCLE PARTS

| | |
|---|---|
| Frame | pressed aluminium perimeter |
| Rake/trail | 23.5°/91mm (3.6in) |
| Front suspension | 46mm (1.8in) telescopic forks |
| Travel | 120mm (4.7in) |
| Adjustment | spring preload, plus rebound (12-way) and compression (10-way) damping |
| Rear suspension | monoshock |
| Travel | 135mm (5.3in) |
| Adjustment | spring preload, plus rebound (20-way) and compression (20-way) damping |
| Tyres | |
| — make | Dunlop |
| — front | 120/60 x ZR17 |
| — rear | 170/60 x ZR17 |
| Brakes | |
| — make | Tokico |
| — front | 2 x semi-floating 300mm (11.8in) discs, 6-piston calipers |
| — rear | single 220mm (8.7in) disc, 1-piston caliper |

# Kawasaki ZZR600

This 599cc (36.5in), 16-valve, DOHC, in-line four engine design may be a decade old, but is still powerful enough to help the ZZ-R600 to a top speed of 256.4km/h (159.3mph) – within spitting distance of ultra-modern tackle. The motor has a bore and stroke of 64 x 46.6mm (2.5 x 1.8in) and a compression ratio of 12.0:1.

**Fairing screen**
Stretched shape tends to distort the actual view somewhat. Our test riders found it made oncoming vehicles appear to be further away than they actually are.

Instruments are fairly well specified thanks to a speedo, tacho, twin resettable trip meters, fuel gauge, coolant temperature gauge and the usual range of warning lights.

**Gearbox**
Six-speed box has the following ratios:
1st, 3.166:1;
2nd, 2.125:1;
3rd, 1.666:1;
4th, 1.380:1;
5th, 1.217:1;
6th, 1.083:1.
In practice, this well-balanced set-up gives theoretical max speeds of:
93km/h (57.8mph) in 1st,
138km/h (85.8mph) in 2nd,
175km/h (108.7mph) in 3rd,
209km/h (130.1mph) in 4th,
236km/h (146.6mph) in 5th and
256km/h (159.3mph) in 6th.

**Footpegs**
Spirited riding soon decks the pegs out, but there are no nasty surprises, only an unwillingness to lean further.

**Rear brake**
240mm (9.5in) disc and single piston caliper operating on a pin-slide.

**Tyres**
Standard 120/60 ZR17 front and 160/60 ZR17 rear fitments means plenty of rubber choice for the discerning owner.

*ZZ-R600*

***Launched in 1990,*** *Kawasaki's ZZ-R600 has seen a fair few updates and is still around to show the 'youngsters' of today what a real machine can do. It is certainly not a bike to be written off – it has the power, the comfort and the performance to prove it. Just look at its top speed of 256.4km/h (159.3mph) and compare that to the more modern 600s.*

**41mm (1.6in) forks feature**
*preload and four-way rebound
damping adjustment.
Maximum travel is 120mm
(4.7in). They feel soft and
slightly vague in comparison
to modern setups.*

*Kawasaki has gone for a four-into-one-
into-two arrangement, utilizing balanced
header pipes for maximum performance
and efficiency.*

*Pressed aluminium perimeter
frame combines well with the
engine's mounting position,
wheelbase of 1430mm (56.3in)
and 195kg (429lb) dry weight
to give a relaxed, very much
non-nervous ride.*

**Alarm/immobilizer**
Now fitted as standard at the
factory for many markets.

**Fuel tank**
With the full 18l (4.8gal) on board,
riders can expect typical riding to
return around 280km (175miles)
before it empties.

**Front brakes**
Dual semi-floating 300mm (11.8in) discs and four-
piston calipers work well, especially considering the
degree of fork bounce and judder encountered in
emergency situations. Stopping from a true 160km/h
(100mph) takes 99.4m (326ft) and there is little fade
unless hard braking is repeated several times.

**Rear suspension**
Uni-Trak system with gas-charged
shock features three-way
rebound damping adjustment and
a maximum 130mm (5.1in) of
wheel travel. The swingarm is
made of aluminium.

# Kawasaki ZZR600

# Specifications

*Still quick and reasonably* nimble, the ZZ-R600 was once a legitimate challenger to the middleweight sportster crown. Evolution of its rivals, together with a high new price, now relegates it to the second division. But do not be put off by that; it is still a good bike and can set the pulse racing, even if its styling looks a bit dated.

**Wheelbase:** 1430mm (56.3in)

## ENGINE

| | |
|---|---|
| Type | 4-stroke |
| Layout | in-line four |
| Total displacement | 599cc (36.5in) |
| Bore | 64mm (2.5in) |
| Stroke | 46.6mm (1.8in) |
| Compression ratio | 12:1 |
| Valves | 4 per cylinder |
| Fuel system | 4 x 36mm (1.4in) Keihin carburettors |
| Ignition | digital |
| Cooling | liquid |
| Maximum power | 66.7kW (89.5bhp) @ 11,500rpm |
| Maximum torque | 6kg-m (43.4 lb-ft) @ 8800rpm |

## TRANSMISSION

| | |
|---|---|
| Primary drive | gear |
| Clutch | wet multiplate |
| Gearbox | 6-speed |
| Final drive | chain |

## WEIGHTS & CAPACITIES

| | |
|---|---|
| Tank capacity | 18l (4.8gal) |
| Dry weight | 195kg (492 lb) |
| Weight distribution | |
| — front | not available |
| — rear | not available |
| Wheelbase | 1430mm (56.3in) |
| Overall length | 2070mm (81.5in) |
| Overall width | 695mm (27.4in) |
| Overall height | 1175mm (46.3in) |
| Seat height | 780mm (30. 7in) |

## CYCLE PARTS

| | |
|---|---|
| Frame | aluminium perimeter |
| Rake/trail | N/ A |
| Front suspension | 41mm (1.6in) telescopic forks |
| Travel | 120mm (4.7in) |
| Adjustment | preload, plus 4-way rebound damping |
| Rear suspension | Uni-Trak, gas-charged shock |
| Travel | 130mm (5.1in) |
| Adjustment | preload, plus 3-way rebound damping |
| Tyres | |
| — make | varies |
| — front | 120/60 x 17 |
| — rear | 150/60 x 17 |
| Brakes | |
| — make | Tokico |
| — front | 2 x 300mm (11.8in) semi-floating discs, 4-piston callipers |
| — rear | 240mm (9.5in) disc, single caliper |

# Kawasaki *W650*

*The electronic ignition computer (called K-TRIC – Kawa Throttle Response Ignition Control) lies beneath the seat, controlling the dual CVK 34mm (1.3in) carbs.*

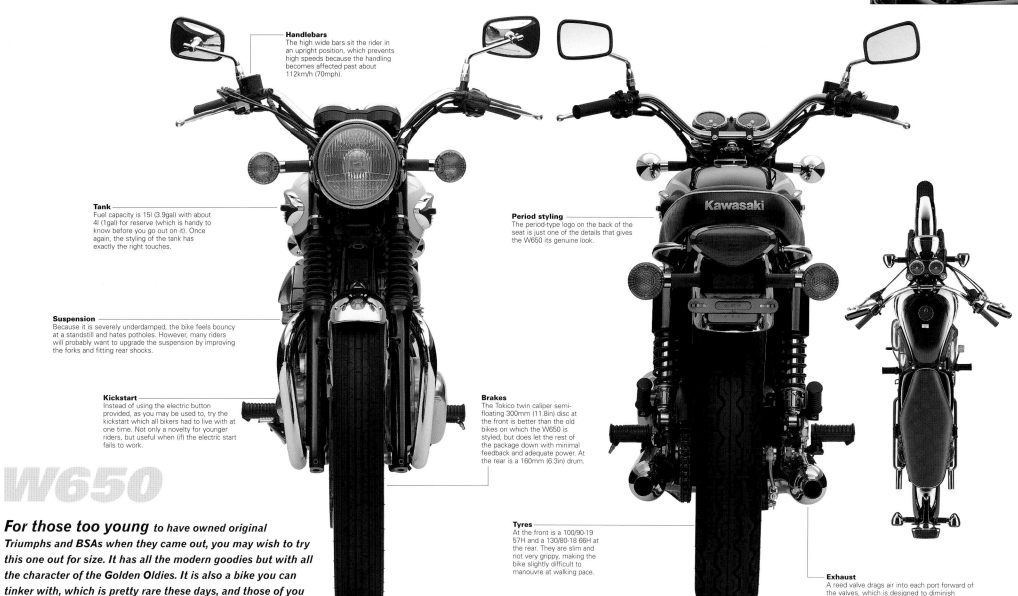

**Handlebars**
The high wide bars sit the rider in an upright position, which prevents high speeds because the handling becomes affected past about 112km/h (70mph).

**Tank**
Fuel capacity is 15l (3.9gal) with about 4l (1gal) for reserve (which is handy to know before you go out on it). Once again, the styling of the tank has exactly the right touches.

**Suspension**
Because it is severely underdamped, the bike feels bouncy at a standstill and hates potholes. However, many riders will probably want to upgrade the suspension by improving the forks and fitting rear shocks.

**Kickstart**
Instead of using the electric button provided, as you may be used to, try the kickstart which all bikers had to live with at one time. Not only a novelty for younger riders, but useful when (if) the electric start fails to work.

**Period styling**
The period-type logo on the back of the seat is just one of the details that gives the W650 its genuine look.

**Brakes**
The Tokico twin caliper semi-floating 300mm (11.8in) disc at the front is better than the old bikes on which the W650 is styled, but does let the rest of the package down with minimal feedback and adequate power. At the rear is a 160mm (6.3in) drum.

**Tyres**
At the front is a 100/90-19 57H and a 130/80-18 66H at the rear. They are slim and not very grippy, making the bike slightly difficult to manouvre at walking pace.

**Exhaust**
A reed valve drags air into each port forward of the valves, which is designed to diminish pollution. A vaccuum-operated valve shuts off the air to avoid backfires (in theory, at least).

*W650*

**For those too young** to have owned original Triumphs and BSAs when they came out, you may wish to try this one out for size. It has all the modern goodies but with all the character of the Golden Oldies. It is also a bike you can tinker with, which is pretty rare these days, and those of you who have never played around with an engine, can now find out what you have been missing.

*The fuel tank styling is so convincing it could almost have come directly from Triumph with its big chromed badge.*

*The chassis is pretty good with light and fairly accurate steering and stiff swingarm, but it is let down by the underdamped suspension.*

*The frame is difficult to complain about for a bike of this kind. All-steel double cradle with twin shocks linked to a box section swingarm. Does the job it sets out to do.*

**Seat**
With a seat height of 800mm (31.5in), the W650 just makes it for shorter riders. It has a nice look to it also, with the white beading around the edge.

**Forks**
The 49mm (1.9in) forks are fitted with sliders finished in black paint to add to the styling and rubber gaiters.

**Engine**
The 676cc air-cooled parallel twin sohc is probably more torquey than you would expect and has a very grunty mid-range. Sounds good too.

# Kawasaki ZR-7

**Mirrors**
Simple, unadorned and offer a decent amount of visibility, though their effectiveness is greatly reduced in the wet.

**Colour palette**
Three different hues are currently offered on the ZR-7 – Candy Lightning Blue (pictured), Candy Wine Red and Champagne Metallic Gold – quite exotic for what is, after all, a no-frills machine.

**Front suspension**
41mm (1.6in) telescopic forks with 130mm (5.1in) wheel travel and no adjustment. But they do feature plastic guards to protect the legs from flying stones...

**Luggage hooks**
Nifty and well positioned, they make loading and unloading easy – an added plus when touring.

**Transmission**
More of the same – wet multiplate clutch and a five speed, indirect constant mesh gearbox with just one novelty in Kawasaki's excellent positive stop neutral finder. Push the lever up from first when you are stationary, and a centrifugal stop mechanism makes it impossible to move through neutral to second.

**Rear suspension**
Not so retro that you have to manage with twin shocks. Instead, the ZR-7 is fitted with Kawasaki's Uni-Trak rising rate monoshock design, and includes 7-way adjustable spring preload and 4-way rebound damping adjustment. Swingarm is square section steel.

## ZR-7

### It is billed as 'The Naked Truth',

*but what that exactly entails is anyone's guess. Make no mistake, the ZR-7 is a budget bike, costing less than a number of 600s, and while some elements are uninspiring – notably the brakes and engine – a number of thoughtful touches enhance its appeal and elevate it above other budget bikes.*

The fuel tank holds a very generous 22l (5.8gal), endowing the bike with a range of 322km (200 miles).

The twin 300mm (11.8in) discs with floating two-piston calipers confirm the budget nature of the bike. They do their job, and no more.

*Like the motor, the chassis is by modern standards old hat, being a double cradle tubular steel affair – familiar on machines from the 1980s. It is still reasonably stiff, however.*

**Clocks**
Neat and easy to read. White faces and chrome bezels are a nice touch and add class.

**Bodywork**
Fairly low seat at 800mm (31.5in) suits medium height riders if not shorties, while fuel tank and tail section are sleekly styled.

**Frame**
Traditional double cradle tubular steel frame, although modern design and materials have made it much stiffer for no weight penalty compared with similar older versions, which means that handling does not suffer. Note, for example, the large diameter tubes.

**Engine**
Unexciting, perhaps, but a mainstay of Kawasaki's range for two decades. 738cc (45ci), four cylinders, air cooling, four carburettors and eight valves, plus a handful of changes on the ZR-7's version to deal with the latest noise and exhaust emissions legislation. Unfortunately, these rather dull the throttle response, despite K-TRIC, which alters ignition timing according to throttle position.

# Kawasaki *ZR-7*

# Specifications

*Kawasaki's ZR-7 is a machine* which was constructed with economy of build as an absolute priority. Its creation was achieved through the use of parts already in production. The engine, for example, is essentially identical to the four cylinder motor that made its debut in the Z750 during the early 1980s. The same also applies to the ZR-7's suspension – which is based almost entirely on the Z750 too.

*As a contemporary machine, it is antiquated, but when you add price and running costs into the equation, the ZR-7 is not so bad.*

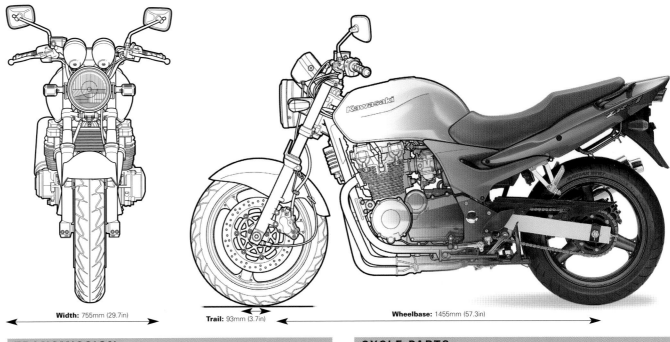

Width: 755mm (29.7in)　　Trail: 93mm (3.7in)　　Wheelbase: 1455mm (57.3in)

## ENGINE

| | |
|---|---|
| Type | 4-stroke |
| Layout | inline four |
| Total displacement | 738cc (45ci) |
| Bore | 66mm (2.6in) |
| Stroke | 54mm (2.1in) |
| Compression ratio | 9.5:1 |
| Valves | 2 per cylinder |
| Fuel system | 4 x 32mm (1.3in) carburettors with K-TRIC |
| Ignition | digital with electric starting |
| Cooling | air |
| Maximum power | 56kW (75bhp) @ 9500rpm |
| Maximum torque | 5.6kg-m (40.4 lb-ft) @ 7500rpm |

## TRANSMISSION

| | |
|---|---|
| Primary drive | gear |
| Clutch | wet multiplate |
| Gearbox | 5-speed with Positive Neutral Finder |
| Final drive | chain |

## WEIGHTS & CAPACITIES

| | |
|---|---|
| Tank capacity | 22l (4.8gal) |
| Dry weight | 202kg (444.4 lb) |
| Weight distribution | |
| — front | N/A |
| — rear | N/A |
| Wheelbase | 1455mm (57.3in) |
| Overall length | 2105mm (82.9in) |
| Overall width | 755mm (29.7in) |
| Overall height | 1075mm (42.3in) |
| Seat height | N/A |

## CYCLE PARTS

| | |
|---|---|
| Frame | double cradle |
| Rake/trail | 25.5°/ 93mm (3.7in) |
| Front suspension | 41mm (1.6in) telescopic forks |
| Travel | 130mm (5.1in) |
| Adjustment | non-adjustable |
| Rear suspension | Uni-Trak rising rate |
| Travel | N/A |
| Adjustment | N/A |
| Tyres | |
| — make | Bridgestone BT57s |
| — front | Tubeless 120/70 x ZR17 58W |
| — rear | 160/60 x ZR17 69W |
| Brakes | |
| — make | Tokico |
| — front | 300mm (11.8in) dual discs operated by 2-piston calipers |
| — rear | 240mm (9.4in) disc with 2-piston caliper |

# Kawasaki ZX-7R NINJA

*The noise the bike makes as it accelerates hard has got to be heard to be believed. A throaty growl, which builds to an aggressive roar, can be heard for miles. The noise is actually induction roar, courtesy of a huge airbox and the two wide-open channels (on either side of the headlamps) which ram cool air into the ZX-7R's bank of Keihin carburettors.*

**Headlamps**
The ZX-7R can be distinguished in an instant from its other family members – the ZX-6R and ZX-9R – courtesy of its aggressively-shaped twin headlights (the others have single lenses). The glass is fractionally rounded to ensure it follows the aerodynamic pattern set out by the fairing, while the twin beam is actually quite good at night.

**Forks**
43mm (1.7in) thick, inverted and fully adjustable for preload, plus compression and rebound damping, the ZX-7R's suspenders are some of the silkiest you will come across. Their feel both on the road and track is superlative, inspiring masses of confidence and always letting the rider know exactly what is going on.

## ZX-7R

**Introduced in 1996,** *Kawasaki's ZX-7R Ninja may well join other bikes in the history books – not for its outstanding sales, but for its outstanding handling. It has to be one of the best around in that department, as those who have ridden one will testify. Unfortunately, due more to its size and weight than anything else, it is not a bike you see often.*

**Mirrors**
Similar in style to items used as far back as 1989, when Kawasaki released its KR-1 (a two-stroke racer for the road), they are reasonably well-placed to allow a good view of what is going on behind, and are not prone to vibration. Stiff pivots mean they will not flop inward at high speed, although they can be manually retracted.

**Footpegs**
Pivot-mounted to allow them to retract if decked out through corners, they are placed fairly high up and rearwards, forcing riders into a semi-racing position.

**Tyres**
Dunlop Sportmax IIs are fitted as standard, while the racing version ZX-7RR gets stickier Michelin Hi-Sports. Whatever the rubber choice, Kawasaki recommends a 120/70-ZR17 front and 190/50-ZR17 rear be fitted. The ZX-7R has a healthy appetite for rears, but a voracious one for fronts if the bike is constantly cornered heavily.

**Instruments**
The cockpit houses a 180mph (260km/h) speedo in 10mph (16km/h) increments, an odometer, a trip gauge, a 15,000rpm tachometer with a 12,500rpm redline, an analogue temperature gauge, a sidestand warning switch, an indicator light, a headlamp indicator and a lights-on beam. The rev counter and temperature gauge are mounted in a brushed alloy plate, which can be quickly removed using an Allen key.

**Sidestand**
Simple to operate when on the bike, it will not retract automatically when the bike is lifted upright at rest. The ZX-7R has no mainstand.

*Twin Tokico six-piston front calipers provide awesome initial bite while not being the most powerful around. While Suzuki's lighter GSX-R750 could be brought to a standstill in under 80m (262ft) from 160km/h (100mph), the ZX-7R's best distance under identical test conditions was 101.2m (332ft).*

**Pillion accommodation**
The stepped rear seat immediately puts passengers' heads above the rider's. The footpegs are fractionally too far forward to make the ride a particularly comfortable one. Many passengers do not like the grab handles, which are placed either side of the seat rather than behind as conventional design dicates.

The ballistic liquid-cooled, four-cylinder, four-stroke engine produces more brake horsepower and torque than the benchmark Honda RC45, but fails to topple the mighty Suzuki GSX-R750. However, the ZX-7R can cover 400m (1312ft), from a standing start, in just 11.11 seconds, managing a terminal speed of 198.6km/h (123.4mph).

The twin spar frame looks beefy and is incredibly strong, but the pay-off is extra weight. It is just one of the component parts that makes the ZX-7R a comparatively heavy bike.

**Fuel tank**
With a capacity of 18l (4.8gal) and an mpg average of 31.5, the ZX-7R manages just 199km (124 miles) on a tankful. Careful riding could see this extend to just over 232km (144 miles). Of the 18l (4.8gal) total capacity, a whopping 5l (1.3gal) are allocated to reserve, giving riders plenty of warning before they run out.

**Sitting pretty**
The relationship between seat, footpegs and handlebars immediately puts the rider into a "racing crouch", although discomfort, particularly leg cramp and wrist ache, are less evident on this machine than on some of its rivals.

**Fairing**
At first glance, it is wide and the screen does not look tall enough to offer much wind protection. But riders will find that, in most cases, the longish stretch to the handlebars and plenty of onboard room allows them to get their head down low and tucked into the pocket of still air above the fuel tank.

**Wheels**
Three-spoke 43.2cm (17in) wheels offer the correct rim sizes for a wide tyre choice. However, like the frame, they are not particularly light and therefore hinder the ZX-7R's turning ability (and acceleration potential) to a degree.

**Swingarm**
The angular, conventionally double-sided swingarm is exceedingly heavy, weighing in at around 3kg (6.6 lbs) more than the same item used on the bike's forerunner, the ZXR750. It has about 26mm (1in) of adjustment built in for correct tensioning of the chain.

**Exhaust**
The standard black end can looks stylish and is placed just high enough to make grinding it out, when cornering fast, hard work.

# Kawasaki | *ZX-7R NINJA*

# Specifications

**The ZX-7R may be** almost an entirely new machine with most of its components making an appearance for the first time, but it is still very much a development of the previous ZXR750. It is a heavy bike but nonetheless goes like a missile. It will pull 0–240 km/h (0–150mph) in only 20.5 seconds compared with the 23.6 seconds of Honda's very expensive RC45 – awesome. Unfortunately for the Ninja, the GSX-R750 is around, providing fierce competition.

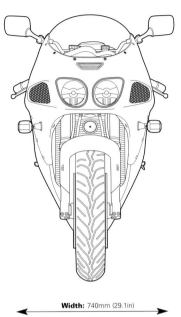

**Seat height:** 790mm (29.1in)

**Width:** 740mm (29.1in)

**Trail:** 99mm (3.9in)

**Wheelbase:** 1435mm (56.5in)

## ENGINE

| | |
|---|---|
| Type | 4-stroke |
| Layout | in-line four |
| Total displacement | 748cc (45.6ci) |
| Bore | 73mm (2.9in) |
| Stroke | 44.7mm (1.8in) |
| Compression ratio | 11.5:1 |
| Valves | 4 per cylinder |
| Fuel system | 4 x Keihin CVK-D38 carburettors |
| Ignition | CDI |
| Cooling | liquid |
| Maximum power | 94kW (126.1bhp) @ 11,199rpm |
| Maximum torque | 8.6kg-m (62.22lb-ft) @ 8890rpm |

## TRANSMISSION

| | |
|---|---|
| Primary drive | gear |
| Clutch | wet, multiplate |
| Gearbox | 6-speed |
| Final drive | chain |

## CYCLE PARTS

| | |
|---|---|
| Frame | aluminium beam |
| Rake/trail | 25°/99mm (3.9in) |
| Front suspension | 43mm (1.7in) inverted telescopic forks |
| Travel | 120mm (4.7in) |
| Adjustment | preload, plus compression and rebound damping |
| Rear suspension | Uni-Trak (monoshock) |
| Travel | 130mm (5.1in) |
| Adjustment | preload, plus compression and rebound damping |
| Tyres | |
| — make | Dunlop D204/ Bridgestone Battlax BT50 |
| — front | 120/70 x ZR17 |
| — rear | 190/50 x ZR17 |
| Brakes | |
| — make | Tokico |
| — front | 2 x 293mm (11.5in) discs, opposed 6-piston calipers |
| — rear | single 197mm (7.8in) disc, 1-piston caliper |

## WEIGHTS & CAPACITIES

| | |
|---|---|
| Tank capacity | 18l (4.8gal) |
| Dry weight | 203kg (446.6 lb) |
| Weight distribution | |
| — front | N/A |
| — rear | N/A |
| Wheelbase | 1435mm (56.5in) |
| Overall length | 2090mm (82.3in) |
| Overall width | 740mm (29.1in) |
| Overall height | 1130mm (44.5in) |
| Seat height | 790mm (31.1in) |

## TORQUE

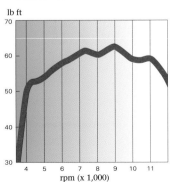

## POWER

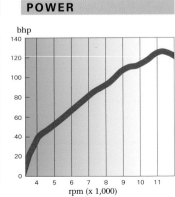

**Independent test measurements (above) differ from the manufacturer's claimed maximum power and maximum torque figures.**

# Kawasaki | ZX-9R NINJA

**The clutch is of wet multiplate design and generally a clean, strong performer.**

**Timing**
Electronically-advanced ignition timing shifts between 10° BTDC at 1100rpm and 32.5° at 5000rpm. Spark is supplied by either NGK CR9EK or ND U27ETR plugs. The firing order is 1-2-4-3 (as viewed from the left).

**Gearbox**
The constant mesh box sports six reasonably close ratio gears in the form of
1st, 2.571 (36/14);
2nd, 1.941 (33/17);
3rd, 1.556 (28/18);
4th, 1.333 (28/21);
5th, 1.200 (24/20);
6th, 1.095 (23/21).

**Rear lights**
Twin bulb design outputs 5 watts power for the tail light and 21 watts when braking.

**Rear suspension**
Fully-adjustable Uni-Trak monoshock design has a maximum 130mm (5.1in) of wheel travel.

**Tyres**
In keeping with current trends and demands, the ZX-9R sports 120/70 and 180/55 sized 43.2cm (17in) tyres bearing a ZR rating – 240+km/h (150+mph).

**Weight**
Following a complete model update in 1998, the ZX-9R lost 32kg (70.5 lb) of weight. The dry weight is now 183kg (402.6 lb).

## ZX-9R

**KAWASAKI launched its impressive ZX-9R in 1994. This competent sports bike offered high build quality, expert handling and great performance – reaching 0–96km/h (0–60mph) in just 2.87 seconds. But with Yamaha's R1 and Honda's FireBlade on the scene, the ZX-9R is often overlooked, despite being more than capable of matching both its rivals.**

**Four-stroke, DOHC** four-cylinder engine is liquid-cooled, runs a compression ratio of 11.5:1, displaces 899cc and has a bore and stroke of 75 x 50.9mm (2.9 x 2in).

Out goes fashionable braced rear ends and in comes a plainer, but lighter and equally strong, conventional double-sided box-section unit.

*In redesigning the ZX-9R and inventing the C1 model, Kawasaki has trimmed masses of weight from the engine and its associated components. New crankcases, crankshafts, transmission, generator, top end, exhaust and clutch, generator and chain covers have shaved almost 10kg (22 lb) off the previous model's weight.*

**Turning Lock**
The ZX-9R's minimum turning radius is 3.2m (10.5ft).

**Pillion seat**
Markedly stepped (making sitting on board feel a bit precarious at first), but surprisingly roomy and comfortable. Though the footpegs are placed highly, using them does not require quite the same levels of contortion as on most race replicas.

**Forks**
Conventional design front suspension offers full adjustment and has 120mm (4.7in) of wheel travel.

**Front brakes**
As strong as the twin six-piston Tokico set-up looks, actual braking performance is surprisingly average due, it seems, to the combination of the bike's low centre of gravity, fork action and rubber, as well as the braking system itself. Our test riders managed a best stop from 160km/h (100mph) of 103.4m (339ft)– poor compared with other big-bore sportsters.

# Kawasaki    *ZX-9R NINJA*

# Specifications

**To own a Kawasaki** *means owning a bike with a lot more potential than it has ever been given credit for. It has to be one of the most underrated bikes of all time. There are many reasons for this, not the least the fact that Yamaha's amazing R1 was launched at the same time as Kawasaki released its updated ZX-9R. But look at the facts – a top speed of 269km/h (167mph), 0–160km/h (0–100mph) in 6.54 seconds and a standing start 400m (1312ft) of 10.76 seconds at 219km/h (136.2mph). Facts you cannot argue with – this is a remarkable machine.*

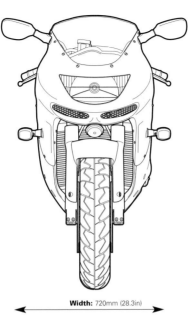

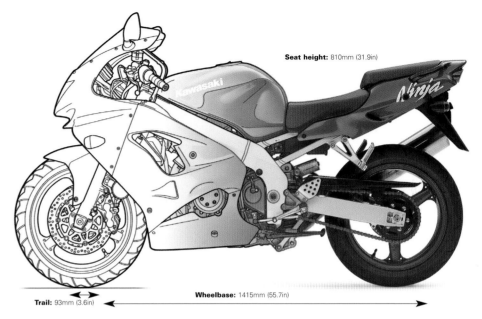

**Width:** 720mm (28.3in)

**Seat height:** 810mm (31.9in)

**Trail:** 93mm (3.6in)

**Wheelbase:** 1415mm (55.7in)

## ENGINE

| | |
|---|---|
| Type | 4-stroke |
| Layout | DOHC in-line four |
| Total displacement | 899cc (54.9ci) |
| Bore | 75.0mm (2.9in) |
| Stroke | 50.9mm (2in) |
| Compression ratio | 11.5:1 |
| Valves | 4 per cylinder |
| Fuel system | 4 x Keihin CVKD40 carburettors |
| Ignition | digital electronic |
| Cooling | liquid |
| Maximum power | 104kW (139.8bhp) @ 11,254rpm |
| Maximum torque | 10kg-m (72.35lb-ft) @ 9260rpm |

## TRANSMISSION

| | |
|---|---|
| Primary drive | gear |
| Clutch | wet multiplate |
| Gearbox | 6-speed |
| Final drive | chain |

## WEIGHTS & CAPACITIES

| | |
|---|---|
| Tank capacity | 19l (4.18gal) |
| Dry weight | 183kg (402.6lb) |
| Weight distribution | |
| — front | N/A |
| — rear | N/A |
| Wheelbase | 1415mm (55.7in) |
| Overall length | 2050mm (80.7in) |
| Overall width | 720mm (28.3in) |
| Overall height | 1155mm (45.5in) |
| Seat height | 810mm (31.9in) |

## CYCLE PARTS

| | |
|---|---|
| Frame | twin spar |
| Rake/trail | 24°/93mm (3.6in) |
| Front suspension | 46mm (1.8in) telescopic fork |
| Travel | 120mm (4.7in) |
| Adjustment | preload, plus compression and rebound damping |
| Rear suspension | monoshock |
| Travel | 130mm (5.1in) |
| Adjustment | fully adjustable rising rate |
| Tyres | |
| — make | varies |
| — front | 120/70 x ZR17 |
| — rear | 180/55 x ZR17 |
| Brakes | |
| — make | Tokico |
| — front | 2 x 296mm (11.7in) discs, opposed 6-piston calipers |
| — rear | single 220mm (8.7in) disc, 1-piston caliper |

## TORQUE

lb ft

rpm (x 1,000)

## POWER

bhp

rpm (x 1,000)

Independent test measurements (above) differ from the manufacturer's claimed maximum power and maximum torque figures.

# Kawasaki ZX-9R NINJA

*Rear subframe is lighter than before and now completely detachable too.*

**Instruments**
Analogue tachometer is paired with a lightweight digital LCD speedometer, and also includes engine temperature and a clock as well as the usual information.

**Bodywork**
New upper fairing features aggressive twin headlights with similar look to stablemates the ZX-6R and ZX-12. Wind protection is better than most bikes in the class.

**Front Forks**
46mm (1.8in) diameter forks are fully adjustable for spring preload, compression and rebound damping and provide a fine ride quality with good wheel control.

**Front brakes**
Six-piston Tokico calipers have differential piston sizes to provide even pad pressure. Loads of stopping power with good feedback to the rider. Discs are 310mm (12.2in) diameter.

**Tyres**
The front is still 120/70, but the rear is meatier than before, now 190/50.

**Rear suspension**
Kawasaki's Uni-Trak monoshock suspension is revised to give a fully linear suspension action. On earlier models, a rising rate system was used.

***ZX-9R***

***Boasting a number of** improvements, Kawasaki hoped the 2000 model of the ZX-9R would be more evenly matched against the likes of the 'Blade and Yamaha R1. Braking and handling are better than before and along with the bike's core strengths – good build quality, flexible engine and compliant ride – make it more attractive than ever.*

At the rear, the 2000 ZX-9R still features distinctive twin ovoid tail light lenses.

Still a box-section unit, the swingarm is even lighter and stronger than before.

*Twin spar aluminium frame has a 1415mm wheelbase, 97mm (3.8in) trail and 24° rake for a good combination of stability with agility.*

**Steering**
Geometry has been altered with an increase in trail from 93mm (3.7in) to 97mm (3.8in). Rake remains unchanged.

**Seat**
Fits well and is more comfortable and secure than many race replicas. Pillion comfort is not too bad, either.

**Ram Air**
Reshaped ducts below the headlights help improve breathing efficiency over the previous ZX-9R.

**Engine**
All new from the crankcase up for 2000, with electroplated ceramic liners to reduce weight, improve heat transfer and decreases piston clearances. 899cc (54.9ci) unit is liquid-cooled with double overhead cams and four carburettors. Immense top end power with loads of low and mid-range torque.

# Kawasaki ZX-9R NINJA

# Specifications

*This is a lot more* than just an updated model: changes to the brakes, wheels, bodywork, front and rear suspension, plus a new frame and swingarm, means there is little of the old bike left. The bike's bodywork has also been redesigned to freshen up the machine, and other changes include a lightweight and more compact stepper motor speedometer, with an *LCD* display in its face (which reads total and trip mileage as well as the time), and the clutc-free play adjuster is changed to the click type from the old screw adjuster.

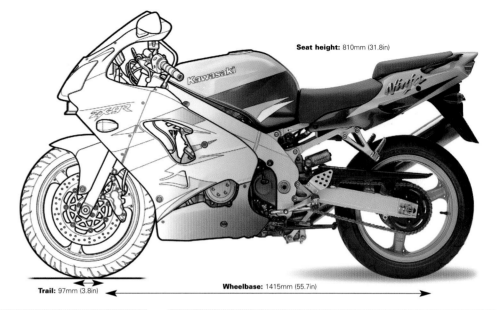

Seat height: 810mm (31.8in)

Width: 730mm (28.7in)

Trail: 97mm (3.8in)

Wheelbase: 1415mm (55.7in)

## ENGINE

| | |
|---|---|
| Type | 4 stroke |
| Layout | inline four |
| Total displacement | 899cc (54.9ci) |
| Bore | 75mm (2.9in) |
| Stroke | 50.9mm (2in) |
| Compression ratio | 12.2:1 |
| Valves | 4 per cylinder |
| Fuel system | 4 x 40mm Keihin carburettors |
| Ignition | digital |
| Cooling | liquid |
| Maximum power | 93.2kW (125bhp) @ 10,000rpm |
| Maximum torque | 9.7kg-m (69.9lb-ft) @ 8900rpm |

## TRANSMISSION

| | |
|---|---|
| Primary drive | gear |
| Clutch | wet, multi-disc |
| Gearbox | 6-speed |
| Final drive | chain |

## WEIGHTS & CAPACITIES

| | |
|---|---|
| Tank capacity | 19l (5gal) |
| Dry weight | 183kg (403lb) |
| Weight distribution | |
| — front | N/A |
| — rear | N/A |
| Wheelbase | 1415mm (55.7in) |
| Overall length | 2050mm (80.7in) |
| Overall width | 730mm (28.7in) |
| Overall height | 1155mm (45.5in) |
| Seat height | 810mm (31.8in) |

## CYCLE PARTS

| | |
|---|---|
| Frame | tubular, diamond |
| Rake/trail | 24°/97mm (3.8in) |
| Front suspension | 46mm (1.8in) telescopic forks |
| Travel | 120mm (4.7in) |
| Adjustment | preload, plus compression and rebound damping |
| Rear suspension | twin shock |
| Travel | 135mm (5.3in) |
| Adjustment | spring preload, plus compression and rebound damping, ride height |
| Tyres | |
| — make | Varies |
| — front | 120/70 x 17 |
| — rear | 190/50 x 17 |
| Brakes | |
| — make | N/A |
| — front | dual 310mm (12.2in) semi-floating discs, dual 6-piston caliper |
| — rear | 220mm (8.7in) disc, single bore pin-slide caliper |

## TORQUE

## POWER

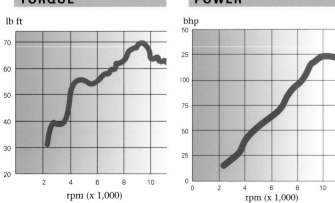

**Independent test measurements (above) differ from the manufacturer's claimed maximum power and maximum torque figures.**

# Kawasaki ZX10R

*This cutaway view gives an excellent view inside the ZX-10R's engine, showing the light forged pistons and titanium exhaust valves. Despite a conventional inline-four 16-valve design, the 998cc (60.9ci) motor provides phenomenal performance. The dual-valve fuel injection system and exhaust butterfly valve can also be seen here.*

**Indicators**
Flush-mounted with the fairing, these neat traffic signals reduce turbulence at speed and add a clean styling edge to the front section of the bodywork.

**Headlights**
Two large reflector headlights give brilliant illumination, with two small position lamps in the centre. Only one main bulb is lit on low beam.

**Air intake**
The large, centrally located engine air intake supplies the airbox with dense, cool, high pressure air at high speed, increasing power output. It passes directly through the steering head section of the frame.

*ZX-10R*

***Launched in 2003 to** critical acclaim, Kawasaki's incredible ZX-10R Ninja provides superlative, class-leading performance, both on the road and at the racetrack. Its engine produces 135kw (181bhp), while the bike weighs in at just 170kg (375lb). The Ninja's high-tech design includes advanced fuel injection, cutting-edge frame layout and distinctive MotoGP styling. It is a true flagship sports model, which put Kawasaki back on top in the ultimate superbike class.*

**Indicators**
Special small turn signals are tucked in below the tail unit.

**Tail light**
A light, reliable LED tail light replaces conventional incandescent bulbs. This saves weight, maintenance and electrical power, and the brake light also illuminates faster, improving safety in traffic.

**Rear tyre**
The ZX-10R is fitted with a very wide, sticky 190/50ZR 17 tyre, on a cast aluminium thin-spoked wheel. Standard tyre fitments were Dunlop D218 or the Bridgestone BT-014 model shown here.

**Silencer**
The exhaust end can is very high mounted and well tucked-in, to improve ground clearance during hard cornering.

**Seat**
The riders seat has large cutouts either side to allow the rider space to move around during high-speed manoeuvring and direction changes.

**Bodywork**
This overhead view shows the smooth, aerodynamic curves of the ZX-10R's bodywork.

*The ZX-10R was the first production machine to use petal-type shaped brake discs. These wavy-edged discs are lighter than standard round discs, and are more resistant to overheating and warping. The radial-mounted Tokico four-piston calipers use four individual brake pads for superb performance.*

*An unconventional frame design passes up and over the engine, to allow a narrower overall width, improving aerodynamics. The frame itself is made from cast and pressed aluminium sections, welded together in a stiff, lightweight construction.*

**Fairing cutouts**
Large holes in the fairing sidepanels allow hot air from the radiator to escape, and improves air flow through and past the ZX-10R. This reduces drag at high speeds.

**Pillion seat**
Like most modern sports bikes, the ZX-10R has rather limited passenger-carrying ability. All but the smallest pillions will suffer on the small seat and high-mounted footpegs.

**Exhaust system**
The sinuous header pipes are made from tough, light titanium, as is the oval silencer. A butterfly valve in the main collector pipe opens and closes at various enginerpm to adjust exhaust characteristics to engine needs, improving midrange power.

**Front forks**
The 43mm (1.7in) upside-down forks are fully adjustable for damping and spring preload. The inner stanchion tubes have a special black carbon coating that reduces static friction, allowing more compliant operation.

**Swingarm**
The ZX-10R has an extra-long swingarm to improve rear tyre grip and stability under acceleration. Extensive bracing and aluminium construction makes it extremely stiff and very light.

# Kawasaki *GPZ1100*

*The mirrors have a distinctive design and are both wide enough and free of vibration to be considered useful at any speed.*

*The fairing takes knocks and even low speed crashes well, provides all-enclosing protection for the bike and makes a fair job of keeping rider's legs dry too.*

**Fairing screen**
Does the job 90 per cent of the time, though touring owners often fit a raised replacement for ultimate comfort.

**Steering geometry**
With a rake of 27° and trail of 110mm (4.33in), the GPZ1100 is clearly intended to perform more as a roadster than a sports bike. Though generally stable under most conditions, a handful of riders have reported front end oscillation and shimmying if they remove their hands from the bars.

**Footpegs**
Touch down easily on roundabouts and through tighter bends.

**Gearbox**
The six-speed unit behaves well under all conditions, engages positively and rarely jumps out of gear. Its ratios are: 6th 1.035:1; 5th 1.153:1; 4th 1.333:1; 3rd 1.59:1; 2nd 2.055:1; 1st 2.8:1. The clutch is of wet, multiplate design and final drive is by chain.

**Rear brake**
Works reasonably well, but lacks feel.

## GPZ1100

**Something of a cult bike** *in its home country the GPZ was brought out as almost a 'budget bike' here. It does everything well and nothing superbly well – but must be satisfying to those who own them because there are rarely secondhand 1100s for sale. More of a tourer than a sports bike, the GPZ is a reliable machine.*

**Tyres**
Now considered almost skinny by current big bike standards, thanks to a 170/60 x ZR17 rear and 120/70 x ZR17 front fitment.

*Despite their beefy appearance, the GPZ's front brakes are not an inspired choice. Our riders have previously taken them to their limits on the road (and fried them under testing), to the point where fade became a worrying problem. This has occurred on at least three GPZ1100s, indicating that it is not isolated to one rogue machine. An ABS option was introduced in 1996.*

*High tensile steel double backbone frame with the almost legendary ZZR1100 engine (downtuned for mid-range) at its heart.*

**Dry weight**
At 242 kg (532.4 lb), the GPZ refuses to turn like a sportster, yet is more nimble than the weight suggests.

**Fuel tank**
Holds 22l (5.8gal).

**Seat height**
Average at 790mm (31.1in).

**Headlamp**
Reasonably small but effective at night.

**Turning circle**
Average to good on a bike of its type at 120mm (4.7in).

**Engine**
Traditional four-stroke DOHC design sports 16 valves and four cylinders. Total capacity is 1052cc (64.2ci), with a compression ratio of 11.0:1 and bore and stroke measuring 76 x 58mm (2.9 x 2.3in). A bank of four 34mm (1.3in) Keihin carburettors meters the fuel and air, while semi-cool-running NGK CR9EK (and sometimes ND U27ETR) plugs provide the spark.

**Ground clearance**
The minimum space needed to complete a U-turn is exactly 3m (9.8ft).

# Kawasaki | *GPZ1100*

# Specifications

**The GPZ1100 has always** *been in the ZZ-R1100's*
*shadow, which is not really surprising, as its engine is a detuned*
*ZZ-R's. But while the latter was designed for flat-out sports riding,*
*the GPZ was aimed at those who wanted that, plus style, plus*
*touring ability. It has its good points, but is also poor in a few*
*areas, including the brakes. On a bike such as this, you would*
*expect better stopping ability, which Kawasaki has shown it can*
*provide. But the engine is strong and reliable and is a good choice*
*for those who like the ZZ-R but want more of an all-rounder.*

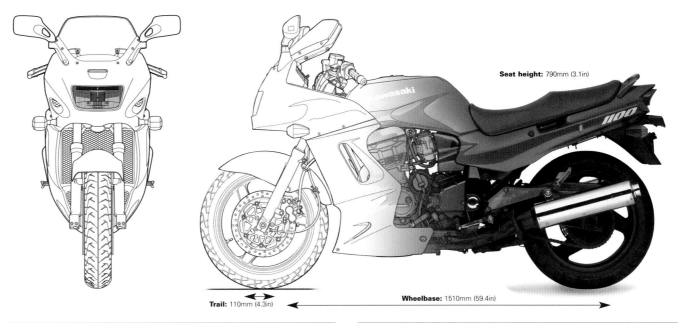

Seat height: 790mm (3.1in)

Trail: 110mm (4.3in)

Wheelbase: 1510mm (59.4in)

## ENGINE

| | |
|---|---|
| Type | 4 stroke |
| Layout | in-line four |
| Total displacement | 1052cc (64.2ci) |
| Bore | 76mm (2.9in) |
| Stroke | 58mm (2.3in) |
| Compression ratio | 11.0:1 |
| Valves | 4 per cylinder |
| Fuel system | 4x 34mm (1.3in) carburettors |
| Ignition | digital electronic |
| Cooling | liquid |
| Maximum power | 86kW (115.4bhp) @ 11,500rpm |
| Maximum torque | 9.9kg-m (72.3lb-ft) @ 7,900rpm |

## TRANSMISSION

| | |
|---|---|
| Primary drive | gear |
| Clutch | wet, multiplate |
| Gearbox | 6-speed |
| Final drive | chain |

## WEIGHTS & CAPACITIES

| | |
|---|---|
| Tank capacity | 22l (5.8gal) |
| Dry weight | 242kg (534lb) |
| Weight distribution | |
| — front | N/A |
| — rear | N/A |
| Wheelbase | 1510mm (59.4in) |
| Overall length | N/A |
| Overall width | N/A |
| Overall height | N/A |
| Seat height | 790mm (3.1in) |

## CYCLE PARTS

| | |
|---|---|
| Frame | steel double backbone |
| Rake/trail | 27°/110mm (4.3in) |
| Front suspension | 41mm (1.6in) telescopic forks |
| Travel | N/A |
| Adjustment | preload, plus rebound damping |
| Rear suspension | Uni-Trak |
| Travel | N/A |
| Adjustment | preload, plus rebound damping |
| Tyres | |
| — make | N/A |
| — front | 120/70 x 17 |
| — rear | 170/60 x 17 |
| Brakes | |
| — make | N/A |
| — front | twin discs |
| — rear | single disc |

## TORQUE

lb ft

rpm (x 1,000)

## POWER

bhp

rpm (x 1,000)

Independent test measurements (above) differ from the manufacturer's claimed maximum
power and maximum torque figures.

# Kawasaki ZZR1100

**ZZR1100**

*The 43mm (1.7in) tescopic forks are adjustable only for spring preload, as well as rebound damping, but that is enough.*

*All the information is at hand in the fairly effiicient cockpit. Bars are positioned well for comfortable riding.*

**Mirrors**
Decent size, good position, and thankfully free of intrusive, distorting vibes, these work well.

**Engine**
The 1052cc (64.2ci) inline four engine was probably the best powerhouse in the business until Suzuki's Hayabusa arrived, as even Honda's Super Blackbird could not beat the old Zed motor for usability. Depending on who dynos the bike, it is not unreasonable to expect around 100kW (135bhp) at the rear wheel of a good ZZR1100, which potentially translates to almost 112kW (150bhp) taking into account account the ram-air effect from the pressurized air-box.

**Rear suspension**
The single shock with rising-rate linkage offers nothing new, but does do the job of controlling 233kg (514lb) and 112kW (150bhp) quite well. Set on the soft side for comfort, the bike will wallow with over-enthusiastic use of the throttle coming out of bends.

**Ground clearance**
More than enough in sports-touring mode, but don your Eddie Lawson hat and the pegs can drag, quickly followed by a silencer. This is only really a problem on tracks, though, and they are hardly the ZZ-R1100's natural domain.

**Tyres**
The original 180/55 x 17 rear tyre was worthy of show when the ZZ-R1100 first came out. Indeed, owners used to shorten the rear mudguard just to show the massive hoop off. Nowadays, it is less impressive as 190-section tyres begin to appear. The 120/70 x 17 front allows a wide choice of replacements.

**Front suspension**
The lack of compression damping adjustment is unimportant as the bike fulfills a sports-touring rather than race replica role. The springing is soft as standard, soaking up bumps well, but allowing the front to dive quite markedly under braking.

*The ZZR1100 has been around a while, but it still holds its own with the best of them. It has been updated over the years to maintain the high standard set by Kawasaki.*

*The exhaust system is now KLEEN (Kawasaki Low Exhaust Emission) in some countries. The system consists of a catalytic converter in the muffler, a clean air system which injects fresh air into the exhaust ports and a pre-catalyst located in the pipes just upstream of the muffler.*

*Now old and heavy by comparison to modern tackle, the twin spar alloy frame certainly is not the lightest or stiffest in its class any more. Still, it has served well enough for many years!*

**Fuel tank**
Holds an impressive 24l (6.3gal) yet does not feel ponderously large. Expect to get 257–306km (160–190 miles) between fill-ups.

**Pillion comforts**
Passengers are well catered for. The wide seat, good grab-rail and low-placed foot pegs mean pillions should not find high speed, long distance work overbearing.

**Ram-air**
The huge inlets underneath the headlamp draw air into the airbox, where it is then pressurized. This helps to feed a more condensed charge into the combustion chambers, which leads to better and more complete firing – and, hence, more power.

**Seat**
Surprisingly low at 780mm (30.7in), it enables shorter riders to feel at ease with the ZZR1100. And it is also comfortable, reinforcing the bike's distance-chomping design intentions.

**Front brakes**
Dual 320mm (12.6in) semi-floating discs, and opposed four-piston Tokico calipers manage well enough considering the bike's enormous potential top speed, but fade noticeably after two successive flat-out runs. That's more to do with the big 233kg (512.6lb) dry weight than any shortcomings in the components, though.

**Main stand**
Something of a rarity these days, but essential for maintenance on something this big and heavy. Being able to get the rear wheel out without having to stretch to the added cost of a paddock stand is a bonus.

# Kawasaki | *ZZR1100*

# Specifications

*Motorcycling has come a long* way in the last two decades. In 1990, when the ZZR1100 was launched – to public acclaim from most and concern from others about its speed – who could have envisaged the Yamaha YZF-R1 with its 0–96km/h (0–60mph) in 2.5 seconds or the Hayabusa with its top speed of almost 322km/h (200mph)?
*Even so, the ZZR1100 has been keeping up with these new kids on the block. A bike that was way, way ahead of its time, it can still take on all-comers.*

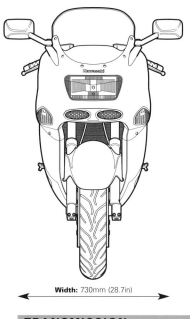

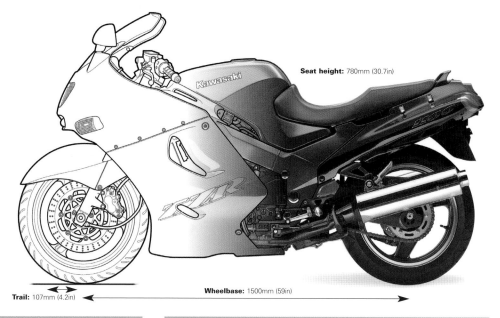

**Seat height:** 780mm (30.7in)

**Width:** 730mm (28.7in)

**Trail:** 107mm (4.2in)

**Wheelbase:** 1500mm (59in)

## ENGINE

| | |
|---|---|
| Type | 4-stroke |
| Layout | inline four |
| Total displacement | 1052cc (64.2ci) |
| Bore | 76mm (2.9in) |
| Stroke | 58mm (2.3in) |
| Compression ratio | 11:1 |
| Valves | 4 per cylinder |
| Fuel system | Ram-Air induction, 4 x 40mm carburettors |
| Ignition | digital electronic |
| Cooling | liquid |
| Maximum power | 93.9kw (125.9bhp) @ 10,200rpm |
| Maximum torque | 10kg-m (72.5lb-ft) @ 8500rpm |

## TRANSMISSION

| | |
|---|---|
| Primary drive | gear |
| Clutch | wet, multiplate |
| Gearbox | 6-speed |
| Final drive | chain |

## WEIGHTS & CAPACITIES

| | |
|---|---|
| Tank capacity | 24l (5.28gal) |
| Dry weight | 233kg (512.6lb) |
| Weight distribution | |
| — front | N/A |
| — rear | N/A |
| Wheelbase | 1500mm (59in) |
| Overall length | 2165mm (85.2in) |
| Overall width | 730mm (28.7in) |
| Overall height | 1205mm (47.4in) |
| Seat height | 780mm (30.7in) |

## CYCLE PARTS

| | |
|---|---|
| Frame | aluminium perimeter |
| Rake/trail | 26.5°/107mm (4.2in) |
| Front suspension | 43mm (1.7in) telescopic forks |
| Travel | 120mm (4.7in) |
| Adjustment | preload, plus rebound damping |
| Rear suspension | Uni-Trak, aluminium swingarm |
| Travel | 112mm (4.4in) |
| Adjustment | preload, plus rebound damping |
| Tyres | |
| — make | Dunlop D204, but varies |
| — front | 120/70 x ZR17 |
| — rear | 180/55 x ZR17 |
| Brakes | |
| — make | Tokico |
| — front | dual 320mm (12.6in) semi-floating discs, opposed 4-piston calipers |
| — rear | 250mm (9.8in) disc, single caliper |

## TORQUE

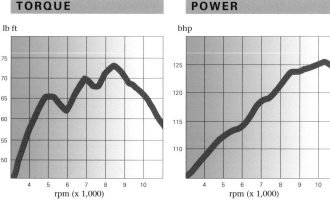

lb ft

rpm (x 1,000)

## POWER

bhp

rpm (x 1,000)

Independent test measurements (above) differ from the manufacturer's claimed maximum power and maximum torque figures.

# Kawasaki ZRX1100

*Brakes are Tokico calipers, in keeping with the Kawasaki range. The front system, which is derived from the ZX-7RR Ninja, features twin six-piston calipers and semi-floating 310mm (12.2in) stainless steel discs, while the single rear uses a 250mm (9.8in) disc.*

*Fuel is provided by a bank of four 36mm (1.4in) semi-flat slide constant velocity Keihin carburettors.*

**Handlebars**
Neutrally placed which, together with neutral footpegs, ensures a relaxed riding position. Maximum turning lock is a useful 38°, which means no more five-point U-turns on tight roads!

**Fairing**
The 'C-type' ZRX1100 gets a bikini fairing, the 'D-type' does not. Wind blast is reduced, although not substantially, when one is fitted. Purists argue the bike looks more authentic in its naked state.

**Rear suspension**
Twin 'piggyback' shocks boost the ZRX's muscular retro looks and feature preload, as well as four-way compression and rebound damping adjustment.

**ZRX1100**

**This bike is a peculiar mix** with looks harking back to long ago but performance which is pure 1990s. This will not appeal to all, of course, but purists should approve. The engine is not covered up by loads of plastic and its handling is not to be sniffed at. In fact, nothing on this bike can be faulted in any major way. Kawasaki has produced a very desirable 1100cc (67ci) machine.

**Wheels**
Three-spoke wheels measure x 8.9 x 43.2cm (3.5 x 17in) front and 1.27 x 43.2 cm (5 x 17in) rear. Standard rubber is Bridgestone BT57s in 120/70 and 170/60 sizes.

**Exhaust**
Looks, at first glance, like an 'old school' four-into-one system, but is actually a four-into-two-into-one, which boosts midrange torque without busting stringent worldwide noise regulations. The semi-upswept end can is made of aluminium.

Now unusual on modern bikes, the truss-type (underbraced) set-up mimics classic 1980s style without sacrificing handling capabilities or stability. Weight is kept low by the use of aluminium, while alumite surface treatment helps protect the metal from road salt and grime. Eccentric chain adjusters reduce tensioning time and ensure accuracy.

Double-cradle steel frame helps ensure maximum exposure for the good-looking engine and works well in the handling department too.

**Fuel tank**
Sculpted to give an illusion of being smaller than its 20l (4.5gal) capacity, it meets with an equally narrow front seat area to ensure maximum comfort during long distance rides.

**Seat**
The seat height of 800mm (31.2in) is fairly average. No help to shorties.

**Front suspension**
43mm (1.7in) forks are derived from Kawasaki's Ninja race replica stable and feature 10-way compression and rebound damping adjustment.

**Engine**
Derived from the 1990's version of the GPZ1100 (which itself partly came from the ZZ-R1100 powerplant), the 1052cc (64.2ci) in-line four motor features liquid-cooling, a 76 x 58mm (2.9 x 2.3in) bore and stroke, 10.1:1 compression ratio, four valves per cylinder and double overhead camshafts. The gearbox has five ratios. Ignition is digital and the alloy cylinder head boasts extra fins to give the bike a classic, but dummy, air-cooled retro look.

# Kawasaki ZRX1100

# Specifications

**Because of its retro** *styling, many make the mistake of thinking the ZRX is 'past it' even though it appeared only in 1997.But only the inexperienced or uninformed would let the styling fool them. It may look like a retro, but the ZRX1100 handles as well as any of today's superbikes, due to the very stable chassis, brakes which certainly do the trick and a top speed of 225km/h (139.6mph). You can take a ride out with your mates on the most up-to-date of machines and the ZRX will be in amongst the pack. It deceives with its slightly old-fashioned look, but the technology used to create this machine is state of the art. Ride it and you will see what we mean.*

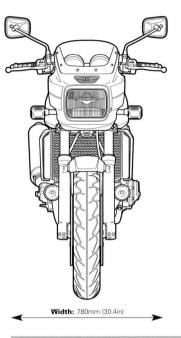

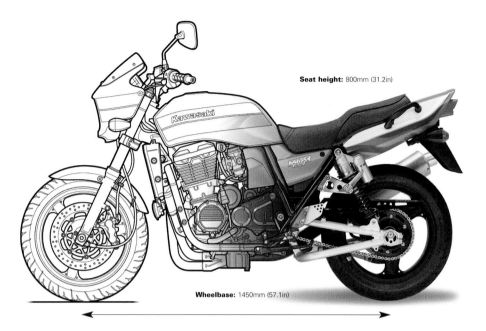

**Seat height:** 800mm (31.2in)

**Wheelbase:** 1450mm (57.1in)

**Width:** 780mm (30.4in)

## ENGINE

| | |
|---|---|
| **Type** | 4 stroke |
| **Layout** | inline four |
| **Total displacement** | 1052cc (64.2ci) |
| **Bore** | 76mm (2.9in) |
| **Stroke** | 58mm (2.3in) |
| **Compression ratio** | 10.1:1 |
| **Valves** | 4 per cylinder |
| **Fuel system** carburettors | 4 x 36mm (1.4in) Keihin |
| **Ignition** | digital |
| **Cooling** | liquid |
| **Maximum power** | 71.5kW (95.9bhp) @ 8600rpm |
| **Maximum torque** | 9.8kg-m (71.2lb-ft) @ 10,350rpm |

## TORQUE

lb ft

rpm (x 1,000)

## POWER

bhp

rpm (x 1,000)

Independent test measurements (above) differ from the manufacturer's claimed maximum power and maximum torque figures.

## TRANSMISSION

| | |
|---|---|
| **Primary drive** | gear |
| **Clutch** | wet, multiplate |
| **Gearbox** | 5-speed |
| **Final drive** | chain |

## WEIGHTS & CAPACITIES

| | |
|---|---|
| **Tank capacity** | 20l (4.5gal) |
| **Dry weight** | 222kg (488.4lb) |
| **Weight distribution** | |
| — front | N/A |
| — rear | N/A |
| **Wheelbase** | 1450mm (57.1in) |
| **Overall length** | 2120mm (82.6in) |
| **Overall width** | 780mm (30.4in) |
| **Overall height** | 1150mm (44.8) |
| **Seat height** | 800mm (31.2in) |

## CYCLE PARTS

| | |
|---|---|
| **Frame** | double cradle |
| **Rake/trail** | N/A |
| **Front suspension** | 43mm (1.7in) telescopic forks |
| **Travel** | 120mm (4.7in) |
| **Adjustment** | compression and rebound damping |
| **Rear suspension** | twin shock |
| **Travel** | 112mm (4.4in) |
| **Adjustment** | spring preload, plus compression and rebound damping |
| **Tyres** | |
| — make | Bridgestone |
| — front | 120/70 x 17 |
| — rear | 170/60 x 17 |
| **Brakes** | |
| — make | Tokico |
| — front | twin disc, 6-piston calipers |
| — rear | disc, single caliper |

# Kawasaki DRIFTER 1500

**Brakes**
The brakes use twin-piston calipers front and rear, and are rather marginal in terms of stopping power, particularly the single front disc.

**Air filter**
The round, chrome, 'pancake'- style air-filter case hides a modern airbox design.

**Fuel injection**
The electronic fuel injection system uses twin 36mm (1.4in) throttle bodies.

**Wheels**
The Drifter 's wire-spoked wheels with chromed rims wear wide, cruiser-style tyres.

*DRIFTER 1500*

*Taking retro design fashion to new levels, Kawasaki went back to the 1940s for inspiration for the Drifter, which is styled like the Indian motorcycle from America. The flared mudguards, wide handlebars and long exhaust pipe, which all look so strange today, are based on the extravagant Indian design cues. On the road, the Drifter provides the typical cruising machine experience: plenty of low-rpm pulling power, but with minimal top-end power. The engine has been tuned for torque, which allows relaxing progress with few gearchanges – the rider can essentially stay in top gear for most of the time.*

*Below the unusual design, the Drifter is mostly comprised of standard cruiser parts taken from Kawasaki's VN1500 range. With the fuel tank and seat removed, there is little of the Drifter to see, apart from the huge V-twin engine and skinny steel frame tubes.*

**Ignition**
The ignition switch is located below the fuel tank.

**Seat**
The rider's seat is extremely low, allowing even the shortest rider to put both feet firmly on the floor. The passenger sits higher and has a large grabrail to hang on to. The broad seat and wide handlebars are comfortable, but the riding position is less so, particularly at higher speeds.

**Rear mudguard**
The rear mudguard is mounted to the swingarm to ensure constant clearance between tyre and fender, and give the necessary vintage styling.

**Engine**
The engine is the venerable SOHC 1470cc (90ci), eight-valve V-twin first used in the 1988 VN1500. Despite its age, this engine is comparatively high-tech, with twin spark plugs per cylinder head, electronic fuel injection and water-cooling. The huge engine's considerable torque is transmitted to the wide rear tyre by a five-speed gearbox and an efficient, maintenance-free shaft drive.

# KTM LC4

**Brakes**
A floating two-piston Brembo caliper at the front grabs a single stainless steel 320mm (12.6in) disc solidly mounted to the front wheel hub, while at the back a lightweight 220mm (8.7in) fixed disc is used.

**Body**
Designed for offroad racing, the high-quality suspension and and brakes of the LC4 is a devastating package in the hands of an experienced rider.

**Rear suspension**
The WP shock absorber is operated through KTM's own rising rate monoshock linkage system, which provides an impressive 300mm (11.8in) of wheel travel. Adjustability includes rebound and compression damping as well as spring preload and rear ride height.

**Forks**
43mm (1.7in) inverted telescopic units from Dutch company WP (formerly White Power), with full adjustment facility and providing a lengthy 270mm (10.6in) of wheel travel.

## LC4

***The LC4 is different from most off-road** style bikes – it really is designed to go off road! The technology comes directly from KTM's competition machines, which have been enormously successful over the years in enduro and rally racing, including the toughest event of the lot, the Paris-Dakar.*

*The injection moulded plastic fuel tank with impregnated colouring holds a cavernous 30l (7.9gal), giving the bike an enormous 480+km (300+ mile) on-road range. Just make sure that you do not use a magnetic tank bag.*

*A twin cradle frame constructed from chrome molybdenum steel and designed to combine reasonably light weight with the exceptional toughness needed for hard off-road use. The rear subframe is bolted on for easy repairs.*

**Wheels**
If you thought spoked wheels were old fashioned, think again. These feature light-weight aluminium rims with high-tech, M4.5, double-thick chrome-plated steel spokes and a tough powder-coated hub. Front diameter is 53.3cm (21in) with 45.7cm (18in) at the back.

**Engine**
A single-cylinder unit with liquid-cooling and dry sump lubrication to minimize the height of the motor and enhance ground clearance. The 35.8kw (48bhp) unit revs to around 8000rpm and features four valves, a central spark plug and a peripheral squish band for efficient combustion.

# Specifications

**KTM realized the value** of a reliable four stroke off-roader when they saw Honda's XR400 becoming more and more outdated but still outselling the newer and more sporty 2-stroke models. **B**etter still, the French invented something called Supermotard, designed to separate the men from the boys by riding on tarmac and dirt at high speed. **T**hus a whole new class of motorcycle was born, and it suited **KTM** down to the ground. The LC range of six models include two supermoto's, one commuter, one dual sport, one desert rally and an all-out enduro.

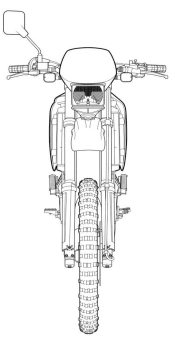

**Seat height:** 940mm (37in)

**Wheelbase:** 1510mm (59.4in)

## ENGINE

| | |
|---|---|
| Type | 4-stroke |
| Layout | transverse single |
| Total displacement | 625cc (38.1ci) |
| Bore | 101mm (3.9in) |
| Stroke | 75mm (2.9in) |
| Compression ratio | 10.4:1 |
| Valves | 4 |
| Fuel system | 40mm Mikuni |
| Ignition | kick start |
| Cooling | liquid |
| Maximum power | 35.8kW (48bhp) @ 9000rpm |
| Maximum torque | N/A |

## TRANSMISSION

| | |
|---|---|
| Primary drive | gear |
| Clutch | wet multiplate |
| Gearbox | 5 speed |
| Final drive | chain |

## WEIGHTS & CAPACITIES

| | |
|---|---|
| Tank capacity | 30l (7.9gal) |
| Dry weight | 122kg (269lb) |
| Weight distribution | |
| — front | N/A |
| — rear | N/A |
| Wheelbase | 1510mm (59.4in) |
| Overall length | N/A |
| Overall width | N/A |
| Overall height | N/A |
| Seat height | 940mm |

## CYCLE PARTS

| | |
|---|---|
| Frame | Molybdenum twin cradle |
| Rake/trail | N/A |
| Front suspension | 43mm (1.7in) WP inverted telescopic |
| Travel | 270mm (10.6in) |
| Adjustment | full |
| Rear suspension | WP monoshock |
| Travel | 300mm (11.8in) |
| Adjustment | spring preload, compression damping, rebound and rear ride |
| Tyres | |
| — make | N/A |
| — front | 90/90 x 21 |
| — rear | 140/80 x 18 |
| Brakes | |
| — make | Brembo |
| — front | 320mm (12.6in) disc, 2-piston caliper |
| — rear | 220mm (8.7in) disc |

# KTM DUKE 620

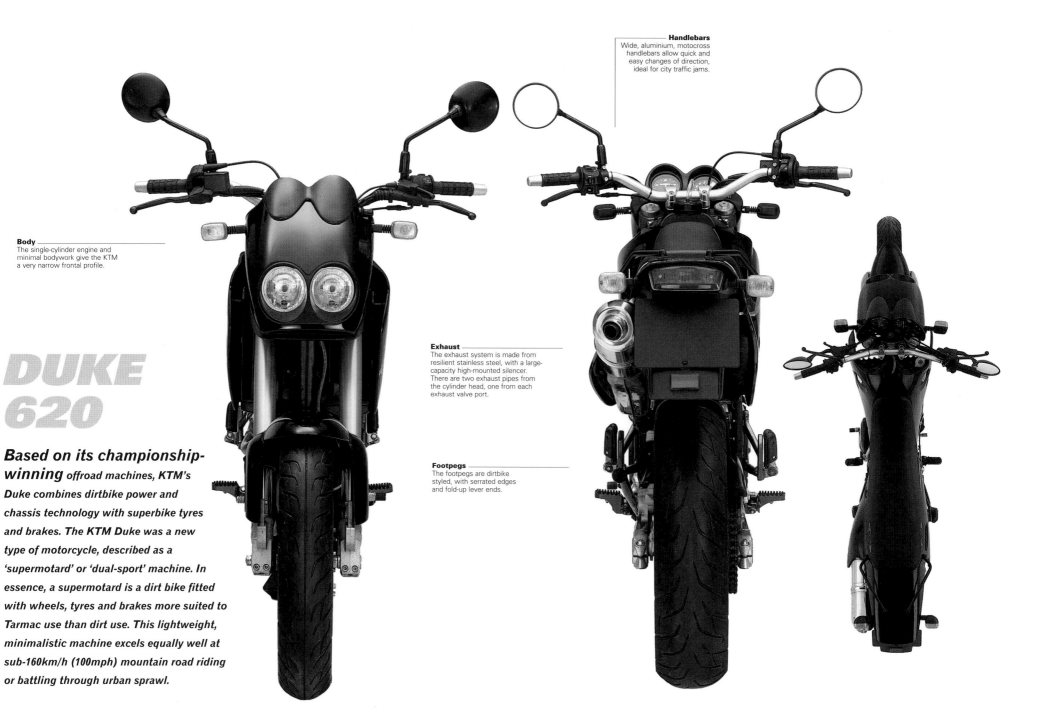

**Handlebars**
Wide, aluminium, motocross
handlebars allow quick and
easy changes of direction,
ideal for city traffic jams.

**Body**
The single-cylinder engine and
minimal bodywork give the KTM
a very narrow frontal profile.

**Exhaust**
The exhaust system is made from
resilient stainless steel, with a large-
capacity high-mounted silencer.
There are two exhaust pipes from
the cylinder head, one from each
exhaust valve port.

**Footpegs**
The footpegs are dirtbike
styled, with serrated edges
and fold-up lever ends.

## DUKE 620

**Based on its championship-winning** offroad machines, KTM's Duke combines dirtbike power and chassis technology with superbike tyres and brakes. The KTM Duke was a new type of motorcycle, described as a 'supermotard' or 'dual-sport' machine. In essence, a supermotard is a dirt bike fitted with wheels, tyres and brakes more suited to Tarmac use than dirt use. This lightweight, minimalistic machine excels equally well at sub-160km/h (100mph) mountain road riding or battling through urban sprawl.

*Under the tank and body panels, the KTM's dirtbike-type cradle frame exposes a tough design that remains acceptably light and stiff. The high-specification chassis components let the rider get the absolute best from the engine's 41kw (55bhp). Like most other supermotards, the Duke is an excellent stunt machine – the light weight, strong brakes and grunty engine allowing wheelies and stoppies at the drop of a hat.*

**Fuel tank**
The Duke is not a very practical machine. The fuel range is around 145km (90 miles), and the seat is thin and hard.

**Rear mudguard**
A close-fitting rear 'hugger' mudguard protects the rear shock and engine from splashes from the rear tyre.

**Engine**
The Duke is built around KTM's single-cylinder, water-cooled, four-stroke, 609cc (37ci) engine. The single-cylinder engine has four valves and a single overhead camshaft. The valves are operated by roller bearing rocker arms. Carburation is by a 40mm (1.5in) Dell'Orto carburettor, and a single balancer shaft reduces vibration.

# 750S

Clocks are well placed, easy to read and look the part with white faces and orange needles, matching the exterior graphics.

**Front end**
The half-faired version of the 750S (a full-faired model is also available) features a sculpted sports fairing with piercing twin round headlamps so typical of Italian superbikes.

**Paintscheme**
First available in metallic black only, this colour scheme lends itself to the distinct Italian Laverda styling.

**Front suspension**
Nico-Bakker designed chassis features high-quality upside-down Paioli 41mm (1.6in) USD front forks with 120mm (4.7in) of wheel travel and both compression and preload adjustment.

**Exhaust**
As if the overall effect of the Laverda 750S was not inspiring enough, the Italian factory added twin Termignoni silencers for the ultimate in unadulterated power delivery.

**Brakes**
Easily one of the most outstanding features on the 750S are the Brembo Goldline brakes with triple discs – dual 320mm (12.6in) discs on the front and a single 245mm (9.6in) disc at the rear – giving the sort of stopping power rivalled only by a brick wall.

**Rear suspension**
At the back is a top-quality oil-filled Paioli monoshock with adjustable preload and compression.

## 750S

## This was the first truly new

machine to come out of the Italian factory since it was taken over by Italian industrialist Francesco Tognon in 1993. The 750's predecessor, the 668, had served to keep the Laverda name alive, but the new bike was a markedly improved machine, with a punchy engine, fine handling and truly outstanding braking ability.

These days, the twin circular headlights are almost unusual and succeed in giving the 750S a distinct and dramatic look.

The chassis is largely unchanged from that found in the Laverda 668, which preceded the 750S. The aluminium twin spar frame suspended on high-quality Paioli forks and rear shock offers a truly awe-inspiring handling package.

**Tank**
Average fuel economy of the 18l (4.8gal) tank falls in the region of 43mpg, although the desperately pessimistic fuel light is known for its tendency to flash as the fuel in the underseat tank surges even when there is at least 128km (80 miles) of fuel still left to go.

**Seat**
The two-piece race style seat is (not unexpectedly) more suited to short journeys. The pillion has a comfortable ride, however.

**Engine**
An air-cooled 748cc (45.6ci) in-line twin cylinder engine with 83 x 69mm (3.3 x 2.7in) bore and stroke, four valves per cylinder, six-speed sequential gearbox and Marelli fuel injection. Its maximum power is almost as laudable as the Ducati 748 whilst rivalling many a Japanese superbike.

**Wheelbase**
A stubby 1375mm (54in) wheelbase offers an astonishing level of agility, with viciously fast cornering speeds balanced by the bike's relatively slow but natural steering.

# Specifications

**The Laverda 750S was** first introduced in June 1997 as a half-faired model only and it was only in November of that same year that the full-faired version became available. The two bikes are very much the same, especially as regards the chassis, so below we have given the figures for the half-faired version. Since its introduction it has gained quite a following, particularly on the European continent. It has exceptional handling, and it would be hard to find another bike whose brakes are as sharp. An excellent bike which sells less well than it should.

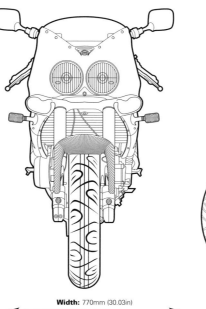

**Width:** 770mm (30.03in)

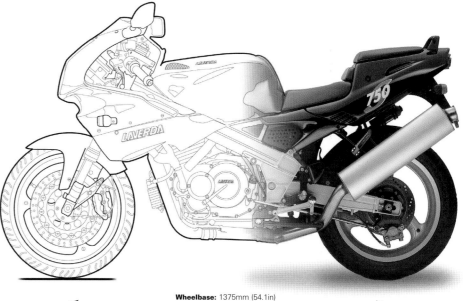

**Wheelbase:** 1375mm (54.1in)

## ENGINE

| | |
|---|---|
| Type | 4-stroke |
| Layout | parallel twin |
| Total displacement | 747cc (45.6ci) |
| Bore | 83mm (3.3in) |
| Stroke | 69mm (2.7in) |
| Compression ratio | 11.5:1 |
| Valves | 4 per cylinder |
| Fuel system | electronic fuel injection |
| Ignition | electronic |
| Cooling | liquid |
| Maximum power | 77.9bhp @ 8700rpm |
| Maximum torque | 50.9lb-ft @ 8400rpm |

## TRANSMISSION

| | |
|---|---|
| Primary drive | gear |
| Clutch | wet, multiplate |
| Gearbox | 6-speed |
| Final drive | chain |

## WEIGHTS & CAPACITIES

| | |
|---|---|
| Tank capacity | 19l (5gal) |
| Dry weight | 190kg |
| Weight distribution | |
| — front | N/A |
| — rear | N/A |
| Wheelbase | 1375mm (54.1in) |
| Overall length | 2000mm (78in) |
| Overall width | 770mm (30.03in) |
| Overall height | N/A |
| Seat height | N/A |

## CYCLE PARTS

| | |
|---|---|
| Frame | aluminium twin spar |
| Rake/trail | N/A |
| Front suspension | inverted 42mm (1.7in) forks |
| Travel | N/A |
| Adjustment | preload, plus compression and rebound damping |
| Rear suspension | monoshock |
| Travel | N/A |
| Adjustment | preload, plus compression and rebound damping |
| Tyres | |
| — make | varies |
| — front | 120/60 x 17 or 120/70 x 17 |
| — rear | 160/60 x 17 or 170/60 x 17 |
| Brakes | |
| — make | N/A |
| — front | dual 320mm (12.6in) floating discs, opposed 4-piston calipers |
| — rear | 245mm (9.6in) disc, single caliper |

## TORQUE

## POWER

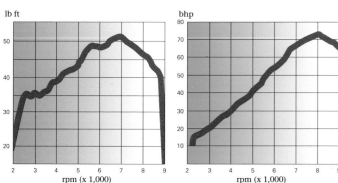

Independent test measurements (above) differ from the manufacturer's claimed maximum power and maximum torque figures.

# LAVERDA

# 750S FORMULA

One of the 750's best attributes is the chassis. It is near faultless, ultra-stiff, and looks spectacular. The aluminium perimeter beam assembly is polished and lacquered, which boosts its appeal.

*Twin downpipes meet high-quality Termignoni carbon end cans which look the part, afford good ground clearance, but could be louder to fully appreciate the boom the parallel twin is capable of making. Surprise, surprise: Laverda offers competition end cans for racing.*

**Clocks**
White-faced clocks feature a 260km/h (162mph) speedo, analogue trip and odometers, 11,000rpm speedo with the redline at 9200rpm (coincides with peak horsepower delivery), and an analogue temperature gauge. The carbon-look instrument panel accommodates the usual array of idiot lights.

**Headlamps**
Distinctly 1980s styling (think old Yamaha FZRs and the like), but instantly recognizable as a Laverda. They would probably sell many more by bringing the plastics up to date.

**Front suspension**
Top-name inverted 41mm (1.6in) Paioli forks deliver 24 compression damping and 30 rebound damping settings, adjustable spring preload, and wheel travel of 120mm (4.7in). Behaviour on most surfaces at fast road-riding speeds is very good, although Laverda offers replacement WP units for racing application at extra cost.

## 750S FORMULA

*Cheaper than Ducati's 748, which is probably the Laverda's main rival, it unfortunately fails to attract the punters. Some do not even know it exists! But this is probably down to low-key marketing. Those who do give it a go, find the motor disappointing. Very good handling only makes the engine's poor performance more marked.*

**Footpegs**
Ergal rearsets not only look the business but are adjustable too.

**Wheels**
Another top name, this time Marchesini, and this time in a lightweight five-spoke design. Standard sizes are 8.9 x 43.2cm (3.5 x 17in) front and 12.7 x 43.2cm (5 x 17in) rear, which allows 120/70 and 170/60 profile tyres to be fittted respectively. Most bikes are supplied on Pirellis.

**Dimensions:**
Overall length is 2000mm (78.7in); wheelbase 1375mm (54.1in); overall width 770mm (30.3in); weight 195kg (429lb) wet (claimed); 189kg (415.8lb) dry (claimed and including battery).

Top braking performance from the twin front *Brembo* four-potters and floating 320mm (12.6in) discs. To the rear is a single *Brembo* caliper and 245mm (9.6in) disc. Overall stopping distance from 160km/h (100mph) is recorded as a creditable 96.7m (317ft), although there is room for improvement, as *Laverda* knows, for it will fit a racing master cylinder up front, as an optional extra.

Four-stroke parallel twin has a 747cc (45.6ci) capacity, four valves per cylinder, compression ratio of 11.5:1, and a bore and stroke of 83 x 69mm (3.3 x 2.7in). Fuel is delivered through a *Weber Marelli* injection system which uses 44mm (1.7in) throttle bodies and can be considered glitch-free. Maximum horsepower is actually delivered on the redline – at 9200rpm.

**Mirrors**
Nothing good to say about these, thanks to mounts which work loose, allowing the pods to fold in on themselves at speed. Only useful if you need to check your forearms from time to time; some riders resort to gluing the mounts in place.

**Rear suspension**
Paioli again, this time with 16 compression and 19 rebound damping adjustments, plus provision to alter spring preload. Setup firm as standard.

**Clutch and gearbox**
Both the clutch and gearbox selector have been uprated over previous Laverda twins to improve longevity and feel. Neutral is easier to hook too. The 750S uses a six-speed box.

*It is an option that* is often overlooked by sports bike buyers, but the specs are high and the handling remarkably good. The engine's lack of ultimate power is arguably the weak link, but the 750 *S* Formula is a surprise all round. It is lighter than Ducati's 748, and in the performance stakes there is not a lot to choose between the two – but enough, it seems, to put people off buying the Laverda.
Either that, or they just do not know enough about it.

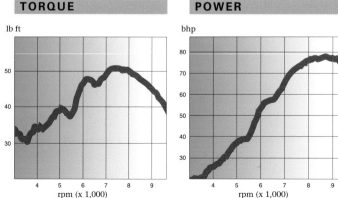

**Seat height:** 770mm (30.3in)

**Width:** 770mm (30.3in)

**Wheelbase:** 1375mm (53.6in)

## ENGINE

| | |
|---|---|
| **Type** | 4-stroke |
| **Layout** | parallel twin |
| **Total displacement** | 747cc (45.6ci) |
| **Bore** | 83mm (3.3in) |
| **Stroke** | 69mm (2.7in) |
| **Compression ratio** | 11.5:1 |
| **Valves** | 4 per cylinder |
| **Fuel system** | Weber Marelli electronic fuel injection, 44mm (1.7in) throttle bodies |
| **Ignition** | Weber Marelli |
| **Cooling** | liquid |
| **Maximum power** | 58kW (77.9bhp) @ 8700rpm |
| **Maximum torque** | 7kg-m (50.9lb-ft) @ 8400rpm |

### TORQUE

lb ft

rpm (x 1,000)

### POWER

bhp

rpm (x 1,000)

**Independent test measurements (above) differ from the manufacturer's claimed maximum power and maximum torque figures.**

## TRANSMISSION

| | |
|---|---|
| **Primary drive** | gear |
| **Clutch** | wet, multiplate |
| **Gearbox** | 6-speed |
| **Final drive** | chain |

## WEIGHTS & CAPACITIES

| | |
|---|---|
| **Tank capacity** | 19l (5gal) |
| **Dry weight** | 187kg (411.4lb) |
| **Weight distribution** | |
| — front | N/A |
| — rear | N/A |
| **Wheelbase** | 1375mm (54.1in) |
| **Overall length** | 2000mm (78.7in) |
| **Overall Width** | 770mm (30.3in) |
| **Overall height** | 1120mm (43.6in) |
| **Seat height** | 770mm (30.3in) |

## CYCLE PARTS

| | |
|---|---|
| **Frame** | aluminium twin-spar |
| **Rake/trail** | N/A |
| **Front suspension** | 41mm (1.6in) inverted telescopic forks |
| **Travel** | 120mm (4.7in) |
| **Adjustment** | preload, plus compression and rebound damping |
| **Rear suspension** | rising rate monoshock |
| **Travel** | 120mm (4.7in) |
| **Adjustment** | preload, plus compression and rebound damping |
| **Tyres** | |
| — make | varies |
| — front | 120/60 x 17 (120/70 in some markets) |
| — rear | 160/60 x 17 (170/60 in some markets) |
| **Brakes** | |
| — make | Brembo |
| — front | 2 x 320mm (12.6in) discs, opposed 4-piston calipers |
| — rear | 245mm (9.6in) disc, 2-piston caliper |

# CALIFORNIA SPECIAL

*The sidestand is seriously raked for solid support, but the protracting lug can be difficult to reach thanks to its close proximity to the footpeg. A mainstand comess standard too.*

**Mirrors**
Placed on handlebars as wide as an oil-tanker, you will never have problems checking out what is behind you – except for the vibration, that is.

**Clocks**
Equally sized and spaced speedo and tacho provide a fresh appearance, thanks to white clocks in chrome surrounds. The usual array of idiot lights is well laid out and easy to read.

**Headlight**
Larger than the EV's but still not brilliant

**Steering damper**
Fitted as standard and needed on bumpy roads at high speed – a scenario where the softly sprung Special can wobble and weave on occasion.

**Front suspension**
The 45mm (1.8in) Marzocchi forks are heavily raked in keeping with cruiser style and are 17-way adjustable for compression and rebound damping. Maximum travel is 140mm (5.5in).

**Fuel tank**
Holds 19l (5gal), of which around 4l (1gal) are for reserve.

**Rear mudguard**
So-called 'Eagle's Beak' shape helps distinguish the Special from the California EV when viewed from behind, as does a new number plate holder and light design.

**Wheels**
Spoked with tubeless rims, the front measures 2.5 x 18in, the rear 8.9 x 43.2cm (3.5 x 17in). Standard fitment tyres are often Pirelli Match and are V-rated in 110/90 front and 140/80 rear sizes.

*Californias have been around* a while, and now we have the *California Special. Fairly closely based on the EV of 1997, it nonetheless has an identity of its own. More 'cruiser' than ever, Moto Guzzi is hoping it will appeal to those who like a laid-back ride but have no wish to ride Harleys.*

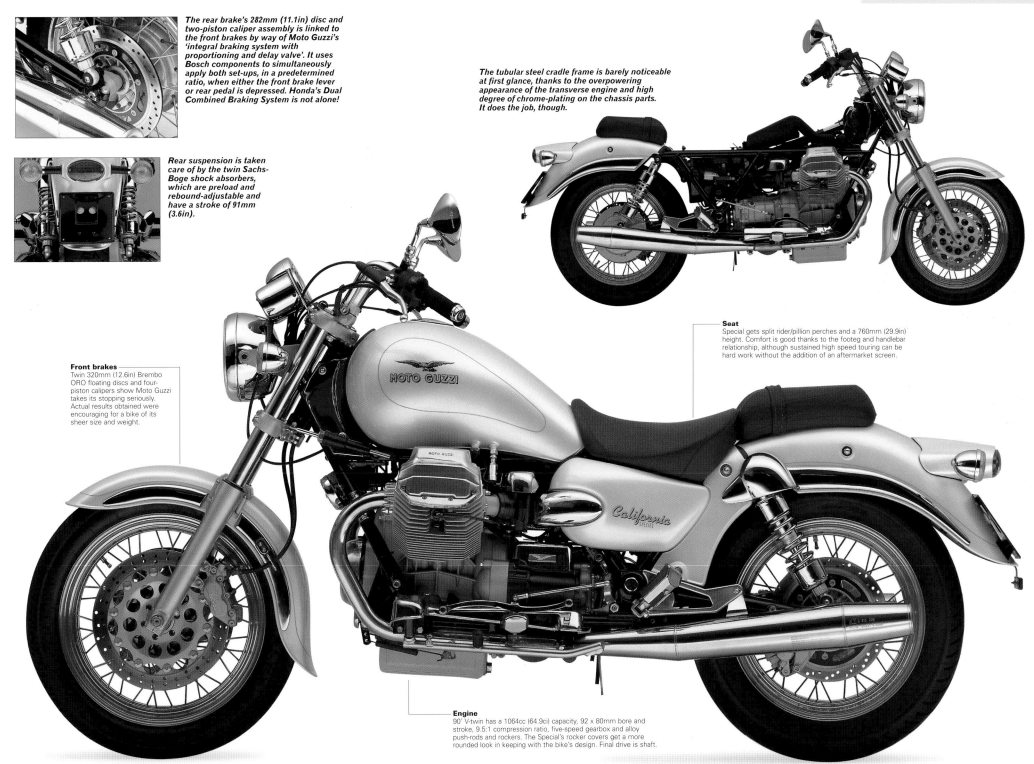

The rear brake's 282mm (11.1in) disc and two-piston caliper assembly is linked to the front brakes by way of Moto Guzzi's 'integral braking system with proportioning and delay valve'. It uses Bosch components to simultaneously apply both set-ups, in a predetermined ratio, when either the front brake lever or rear pedal is depressed. Honda's Dual Combined Braking System is not alone!

Rear suspension is taken care of by the twin Sachs-Boge shock absorbers, which are preload and rebound-adjustable and have a stroke of 91mm (3.6in).

The tubular steel cradle frame is barely noticeable at first glance, thanks to the overpowering appearance of the transverse engine and high degree of chrome-plating on the chassis parts. It does the job, though.

**Front brakes**
Twin 320mm (12.6in) Brembo ORO floating discs and four-piston calipers show Moto Guzzi takes its stopping seriously. Actual results obtained were encouraging for a bike of its sheer size and weight.

**Seat**
Special gets split rider/pillion perches and a 760mm (29.9in) height. Comfort is good thanks to the footeg and handlebar relationship, although sustained high speed touring can be hard work without the addition of an aftermarket screen.

**Engine**
90° V-twin has a 1064cc (64.9ci) capacity, 92 x 80mm bore and stroke, 9.5:1 compression ratio, five-speed gearbox and alloy push-rods and rockers. The Special's rocker covers get a more rounded look in keeping with the bike's design. Final drive is shaft.

# Specifications

**One of the most tastefully** put-together cruisers on the market, the Moto Guzzi California Special conforms almost religiously to the standard Moto Guzzi tradition of engineering.

The engine layout of a transverse cylinder, air-cooled 90° V-twin with dry clutch and shaft drive has been the factory's staple diet since the 1960s and the California itself has been around for more than 30 years. The Special is thus living proof of the old adage that if something ain't broke, then don't fix it.

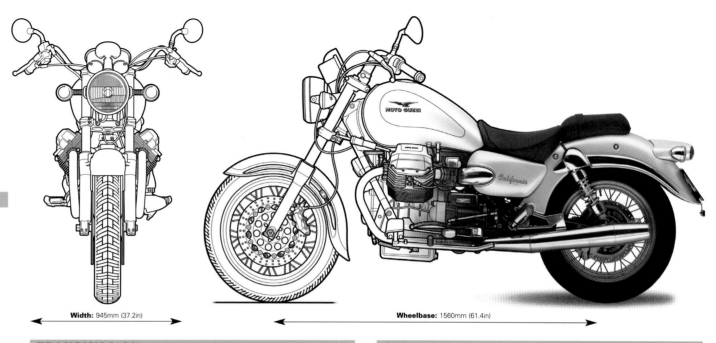

Width: 945mm (37.2in)

Wheelbase: 1560mm (61.4in)

## ENGINE

| | |
|---|---|
| **Type** | 4-stroke |
| **Layout** | 90° transverse V-twin |
| **Total displacement** | 1064cc 64.9ci) |
| **Bore** | 92mm (3.6in) |
| **Stroke** | 80mm (3.1in) |
| **Compression ratio** | 9.5:1 |
| **Valves** | 2 per cylinder |
| **Fuel system** | Weber Marelli indirect sequential fuelinjection with 40mm (1.6in) throttle bodies |
| **Ignition** | electronic digital ignition with inductive spark |
| **Cooling** | air |
| **Maximum power** | 48.5kW (65bhp) @ 6500rpm |
| **Maximum torque** | 8.5kg-m (61.8lb-ft) @ 5200rpm |

## TORQUE

## POWER

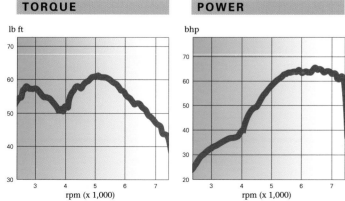

Independent test measurements (above) differ from the manufacturer's claimed maximum power and maximum torque figures.

## TRANSMISSION

| | |
|---|---|
| **Primary drive** | helical gears |
| **Clutch** | double disc, dry, mechanically operated |
| **Gearbox** | 5-speed |
| **Final drive** | chain |

## WEIGHTS & CAPACITIES

| | |
|---|---|
| **Tank capacity** | 19l (5gal) |
| **Dry weight** | 251kg (552.2lb) |
| **Weight distribution** | |
| — front | N/A |
| — rear | N/A |
| **Wheelbase** | 1560mm (61.4in) |
| **Overall length** | 2380mm (93.7in) |
| **Overall width** | 945mm (37.2in) |
| **Overall height** | 1150mm (45.3in) |
| **Seat height** | |

## CYCLE PARTS

| | |
|---|---|
| **Frame** | detachable tubular duplex steel cradle |
| **Rake/trail** | N/A |
| **Front suspension** | 45mm (1.8in) hydraulic telescopic fork |
| **Travel** | 140mm (5.5in) |
| **Adjustment** | adjustable for compression and rebound |
| **Rear suspension** | twin shocks |
| **Travel** | 114mm (4.5in) |
| **Adjustment** | preload and rebound damping |
| **Tyres** | |
| — make | Metzeler, Pirelli |
| — front | 110/90 VB18 |
| — rear | 140/80 VB17 |
| **Brakes** | |
| — make | Brembo |
| — front | twin stainless steel 320mm (12.6in) floating front discs with 4-piston calipers |
| — rear | single rear stainless steel 282mm (11.1in) fixed disc with parallel 2-piston caliper |

**Mirrors**
Forget about them or find
yourself an aftermarket
pair which will not vibrate
as much. These eventually
work themselves loose
and, although they do not
come off, they do spin
around.

**Weight**
At 251kg (553lb) dry weight, the Guzzi is
not as heavy as you might expect from
looking at it, and would certainly suit
almost everyone as far as being able to
manoeuvre and climb aboard goes.

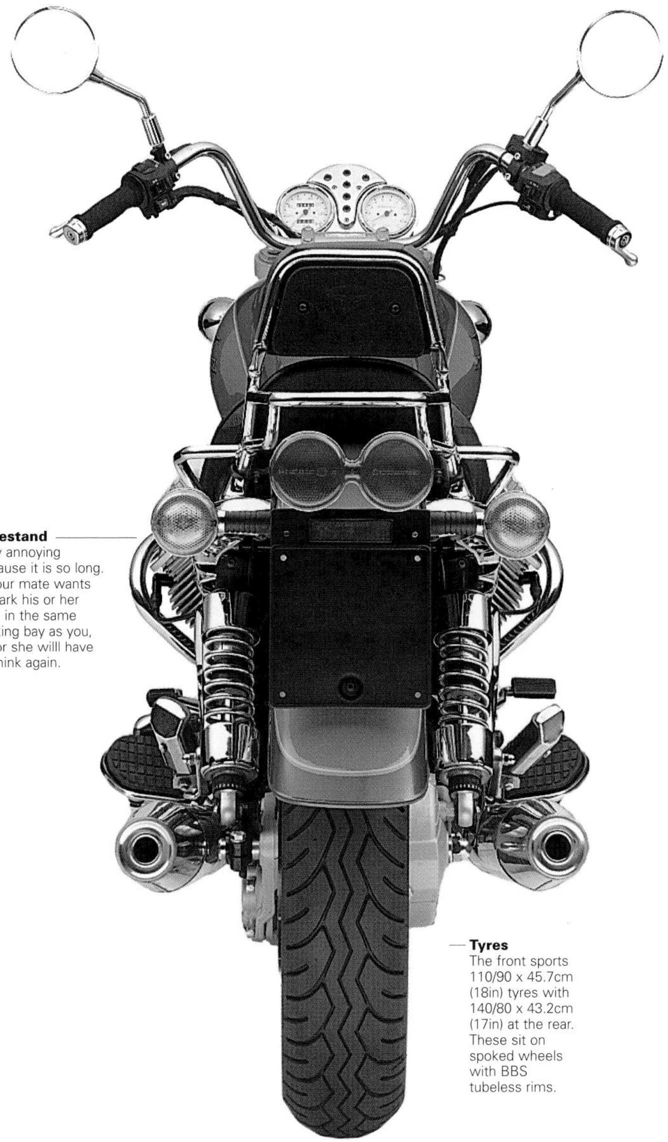

**Sidestand**
Very annoying
because it is so long.
If your mate wants
to park his or her
bike in the same
parking bay as you,
he or she willl have
to think again.

**Tyres**
The front sports
110/90 x 45.7cm
(18in) tyres with
140/80 x 43.2cm
(17in) at the rear.
These sit on
spoked wheels
with BBS
tubeless rims.

## CALIFORNIA
## EV

**The MOTO GUZZI California EV was**
launched in July of 1997 and three years down the line
seems to have retained its appeal for Guzzi fans. But there
is nothing special enough about it to attract new followers
to the fold. It looks good enough and performs very well,
but today there are so many other similar bikes which are
real crowd pullers that a newcomer to the world of cruisers
is likely to go for something which looks more exciting.
However, the California has always had its fair share of
fans and there will be many who will have switched to this
upgraded version with its many improvements. This is an
excellent cruiser and newcomers to this laid-back world are
bound to enjoy the California EV.

*The original California (simply named the California 1100) was discontinued just after the launch of the EV, which is basically an updated version of the former bike.*

**Seat height**
It does not sound high at 775mm (30.5in), but when you climb aboard the Guzzi you do get the impression that it is a tall bike. This could be due to its slim aspect.

**Chassis**
Nothing special here, with a detachable tubular steel duplex cradle frame which does the job but looks incredibly flimsy when this big bike is stripped down.

**Brakes**
The front is equipped with twin 320mm (12.6in) Brembo floating discs and integral braking – the front brake lever operates the right caliper only while the brake pedal operates the rear and left front calipers. These work extremely well.

**Forks**
Marzocchi 45mm (1.8in) hydraulic telescopic forks with a separate adjustment on each leg top does not appeal to everybody, but handles well. The left leg handles compression damping while the right sees to the rebound.

**Engine**
The 1064cc (64.9ci) engine is a four stroke, water-cooled 90° V-twin with a bore and stroke of 92 x 90 mm (3.6 x 3.2in). It has two overhead valves with pushrods and rockers.

# MZ MASTIFF

*A fairly low seat height (830mm/32.7in) means shorter riders will have no problem getting on the Mastiff. Good padding makes longer trips pleasurable.*

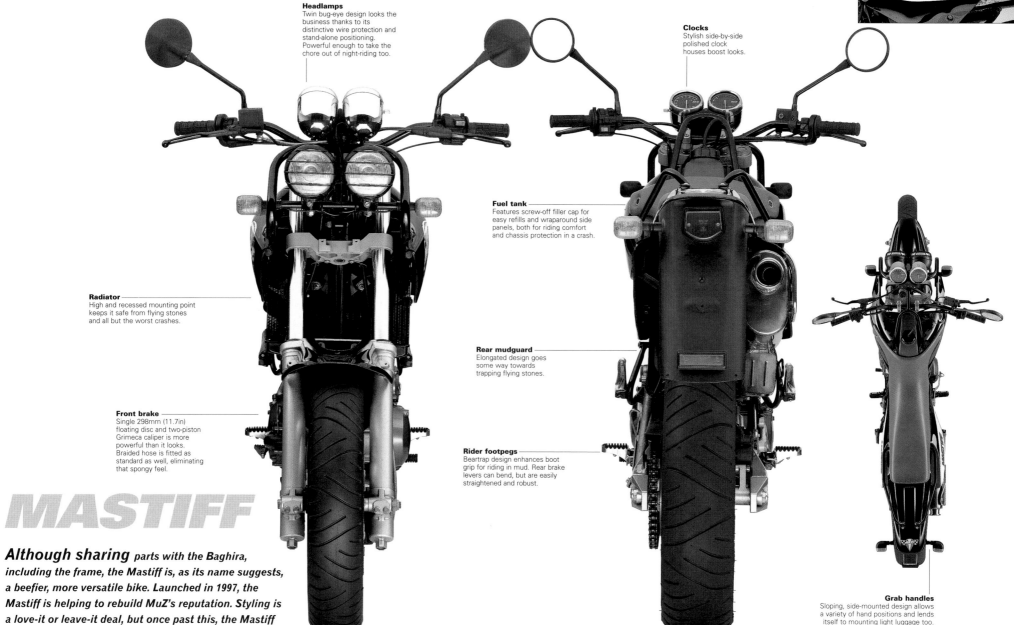

**Headlamps**
Twin bug-eye design looks the business thanks to its distinctive wire protection and stand-alone positioning. Powerful enough to take the chore out of night-riding too.

**Clocks**
Stylish side-by-side polished clock houses boost looks.

**Radiator**
High and recessed mounting point keeps it safe from flying stones and all but the worst crashes.

**Front brake**
Single 298mm (11.7in) floating disc and two-piston Grimeca caliper is more powerful than it looks. Braided hose is fitted as standard as well, eliminating that spongy feel.

**Fuel tank**
Features screw-off filler cap for easy refills and wraparound side panels, both for riding comfort and chassis protection in a crash.

**Rear mudguard**
Elongated design goes some way towards trapping flying stones.

**Rider footpegs**
Beartrap design enhances boot grip for riding in mud. Rear brake levers can bend, but are easily straightened and robust.

**Grab handles**
Sloping, side-mounted design allows a variety of hand positions and lends itself to mounting light luggage too.

# MASTIFF

**Although sharing** parts with the Baghira, including the frame, the Mastiff is, as its name suggests, a beefier, more versatile bike. Launched in 1997, the Mastiff is helping to rebuild MuZ's reputation. Styling is a love-it or leave-it deal, but once past this, the Mastiff is a machine of considerable merit and extremely fun to ride, both on and off the Tarmac.

Power comes courtesy of Yamaha's 660cc (40.3ci) four-stroke single as fitted to the XTZ660. This alone means the Mastiff has one major advantage over previous MuZs – reliablity – and will ensure that images of broken MuZ trailbikes in back yards are all but a distant memory.

In the modern world, emissions and noise standards are a fact of life, hence the Mastiff is fitted with a massive silencer and single end pipe.

Unlike the Baghira, the more road-oriented Mastiff features twin bug-eye headlights, providing better illumination at night – just one indication that it is a more civilized machine. It is also good value.

**Seat**
Not overly tall for a trailie at 830mm (32.7in), while its narrow design helps shorties too. Padding is ample and its integration with the tank is welcome over longer journeys on trick ground.

**Frame**
Tubular steel cradle is powder-coated in white for a distinctive appearance and copes with the engine's power output easily. Box-section swingarm is also strong and flex-free.

**Engine**
Single cylinder 660cc (40.3ci) four-stroke motor is basically a rebadged Yamaha Tenere unit. MuZ claims 37.3kW (50bhp) from it, while Yamaha reckons on 35.8kW (48bhp) in the Tenere. The difference may be due to a free-breathing exhaust. A 25.6kW (33bhp) restricted version is available too.

**Wheels**
Polished rims take 120/60 x 17 front and 150/60 x 17 rear tyres, opening up a decent choice. Sticky Metzelers are usually provided when new.

**MZ** MASTIFF

# Specifications

**The Mastiff engine is not** new to MuZ. Sourced from Yamaha's XTZ660 trail bike, it was originally used in the Baghira. Sticking with the same engine has enabled MuZ to minimize their production costs – it also shares the Baghira's chassis. The only distinctive feature to this rather conventional engine is the use of two carburettors on that single cylinder, allowing the engine to suck in enough air at high engine revs to maintain the power.

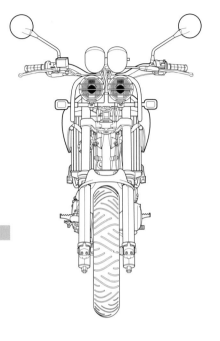

**Seat height:** 830mm (32.7in)

**Wheelbase:** 1465mm (57.7in)

## ENGINE

| | |
|---|---|
| Type | 4-stroke |
| Layout | single |
| Total displacement | 660cc (40.3ci) |
| Bore | 100mm (3.9in) |
| Stroke | 84mm |
| Compression ratio | 9.2:1 |
| Valves | 5 |
| Fuel system | CDI |
| Ignition | electric |
| Cooling | liquid |
| Maximum power | 34.7kW (46.6bhp @ 6200rpm |
| Maximum torque | 5.8kg-m (41.8lb-ft) @ 5200rpm |

## TRANSMISSION

| | |
|---|---|
| Primary drive | chain |
| Clutch | multiplate |
| Gearbox | 5-speed |
| Final drive | chain |

## WEIGHTS & CAPACITIES

| | |
|---|---|
| Tank capacity | 12.5l (33gal) |
| Dry weight | 162kg (357lb) |
| Weight distribution | |
| — front | N/A |
| — rear | N/A |
| Wheelbase | 1465mm (57.7in) |
| Overall length | N/A |
| Overall width | N/A |
| Overall height | N/A |
| Seat height | 830mm (32.7in) |

## CYCLE PARTS

| | |
|---|---|
| Frame | tubular steel |
| Rake | 26° |
| Front suspension | 45mm (1.8in) telescopic fork |
| Travel | N/A |
| Adjustment | none |
| Rear suspension | Monoshock |
| Travel | N/A |
| Adjustment | preload, plus compression and rebound damping |
| Tyres | |
| — make | N/A |
| — front | 120/60 x 17 |
| — rear | 150/60 x 17 |
| Brakes | |
| — make | N/A |
| — front | 298mm (11.7in) floating disc 2-piston calipers |
| — rear | 245mm (9.6in) disc, 1-piston caliper |

## TORQUE

## POWER

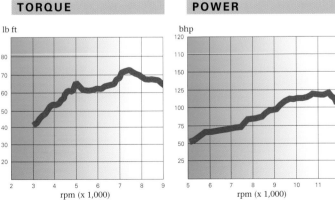

Independent test measurements (above) differ from the manufacturer's claimed maximum power and maximum torque figures.

# MZ BAGHIRA

*Shorter riders may have some trouble actually climbing on board the 930mm (3.7in) seat but, once there, the soft suspension compresses enough to allow most users to get at least one foot firmly on the ground to stop. Rider comfort is excellent, even over 320–480km (200-300 miles).*

# BAGHIRA

**When the Baghira was** launched in November 1997, it was already facing an up-hill struggle to impress many riders because of MuZ's poor reputation. But thanks partly to its Yamaha-derived engine, the Baghira has proved to be a good off-road machine, which is more than capable of handling road riding too, and which is slowly but surely bringing riders to the MuZ marque.

**Pillion perch**
Once the rider is aboard and compressing the suspension, average-height passengers should be able to mount the tall Baghira without too much hardship. The grab handles are generally given a massive thumbs-up by all who experience them, although the seat could be a little wider and the pillion pegs a fraction lower to maximize comfort if distances involving more than half a tank of petrol are to be regularly endured.

**Engine**
The Baghira and its road-styled brother, the Mastiff, both use the same Japanese-sourced engine rather than one built 'in-house'. The motor – basically Yamaha's XTZ660 Tenere powerplant – arrives pre-badged and already assembled for fitting into either chassis at the MuZ factory. The single-cylinder unit displaces just shy of 660cc (40.3ci), has a 100 x 84mm (3.9 x 3.3in) bore and stroke, a five-valve head and is water-cooled. The gearbox is five-speed.

**Guard**
Front-end plumbing is neat and has a small, four point-mounted guard fitted just below the carburettor to protect the rider's leg from burns.

**Wheels**
Rebuildable 53.3cm (21in) front and 45.7cm (18in) rear hoops are strong enough for most off-road riding. The 90/90-section front and 120/80 rear tyres are the limiting factor, however, offering a compromised stance between on and off-road riding without excelling particularly in either field.

**Bodywork**
Minimalist and made of a very strong but bendy plastic/Nylon material, which helps ensure repair bills are lower after a spill. It tends to tear and scuff rather than shatter upon impact.

Tall, straight bars with a single brace are ideally designed and placed for three important Baghira applications – seated road work; tricky, standing off-road manoeuvres; and, of course, obligatory wheelies.

Much less effective in terms of actual power than the Mastiff's twin bug-eye arrangement, the headlamp is still okay for relaxed night work. Oncoming drivers often flash in dismay as the beam rises and falls markedly thanks to the Baghira's long-travel forks.

Though somewhat crude and uninspiring to look at, the tubular steel cradle frame is actually well up to the job and remains flex-free at all times. The box-section swingarm is unremarkable in appearance but competent too. The bike's balanced feel and predictable motor make it an ideal machine for learning wheelies on.

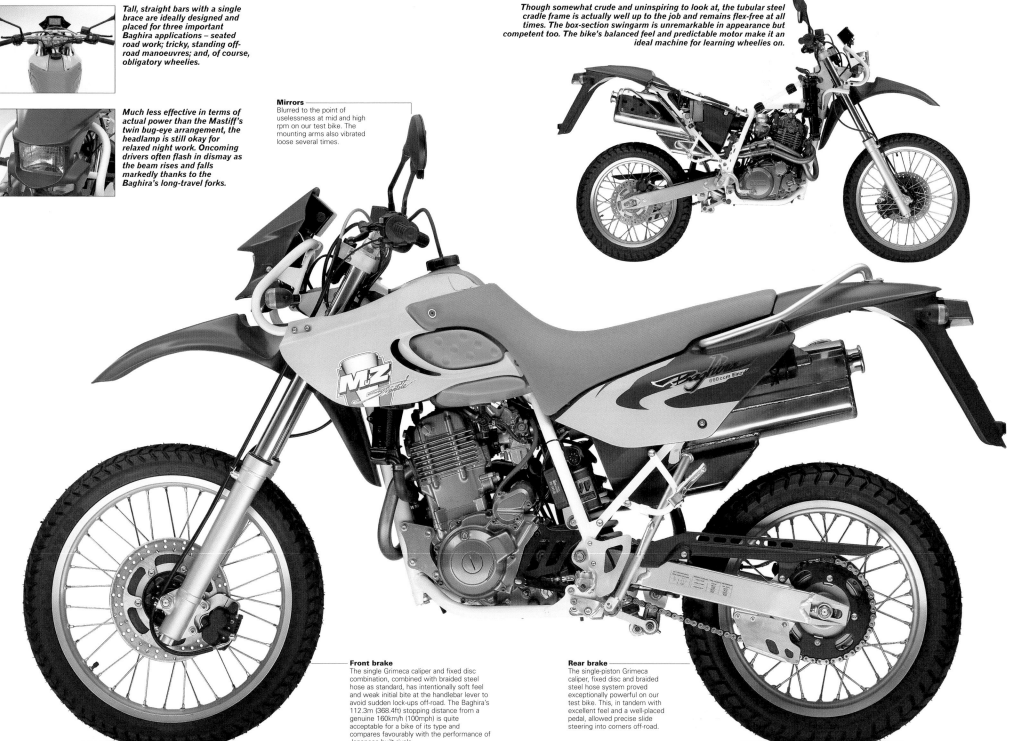

**Mirrors**
Blurred to the point of uselessness at mid and high rpm on our test bike. The mounting arms also vibrated loose several times.

**Front brake**
The single Grimeca caliper and fixed disc combination, combined with braided steel hose as standard, has intentionally soft feel and weak initial bite at the handlebar lever to avoid sudden lock-ups off-road. The Baghira's 112.3m (368.4ft) stopping distance from a genuine 160km/h (100mph) is quite acceptable for a bike of its type and compares favourably with the performance of Japanese-built rivals.

**Rear brake**
The single-piston Grimeca caliper, fixed disc and braided steel hose system proved exceptionally powerful on our test bike. This, in tandem with excellent feel and a well-placed pedal, allowed precise slide steering into corners off-road.

# M/Z BAGHIRA

# Specifications

*Still trying to rid* itself of the old MZ reputation, MuZ has done a respectable job with the Baghira, which would probably sell better in Britain with a different badge. In Europe, New Zealand and Australia, this 'dual-purpose' bike sells well: it looks good and is, surprisingly, very comfortable. And, of course, it is reliable with the well-proven Yamaha XTZ Tenere at its heart.

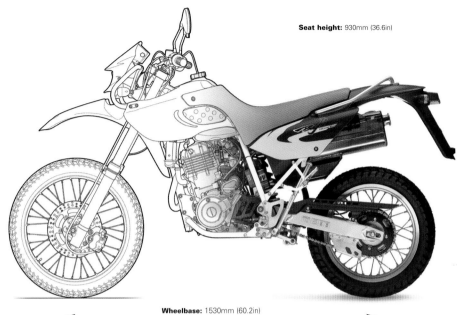

**Seat height:** 930mm (36.6in)

**Width:** 930mm (36.6in)

**Wheelbase:** 1530mm (60.2in)

## ENGINE

| | |
|---|---|
| **Type** | 4-stroke |
| **Layout** | five valve single cylinder |
| **Total displacement** | 660cc (40.3ci) |
| **Bore** | 100mm (3.9in) |
| **Stroke** | 84mm (3.3in) |
| **Compression ratio** | 9.2:1 |
| **Valves** | 5 per cylinder |
| **Fuel system** | CDI |
| **Ignition** | electric |
| **Cooling** | water |
| **Maximum power** | 32.8kW (43.97bhp) @ 6100rpm |
| **Maximum torque** | 7.5kg-m (53.98lb-ft) @ 5600rpm |

## TRANSMISSION

| | |
|---|---|
| **Primary drive** | chain |
| **Clutch** | multiplate |
| **Gearbox** | 5-speed |
| **Final drive** | chain |

## CYCLE PARTS

| | |
|---|---|
| **Frame** | tubular double cradle |
| **Rake/trail** | 6.2°/94mm (3.7in) |
| **Front suspension** | telescopic forks |
| **Travel** | N/A |
| **Adjustment** | none |
| **Rear suspension** | monoshock |
| **Travel** | N/A |
| **Adjustment** | preload |
| **Tyres** | |
| — make | N/A |
| — front | 90/90 x 17 |
| — rear | 120/80 x 17 |
| **Brakes** | |
| — make | Grimeca |
| — front | fixed disc, single piston caliper |
| — rear | fixed disc, single piston caliper |

## WEIGHTS & CAPACITIES

| | |
|---|---|
| **Tank capacity** | 12.5l (3.3gal) |
| **Dry weight** | 180kg (397lb) |
| **Weight distribution** | |
| — front | N/A |
| — rear | N/A |
| **Wheelbase** | 1530mm (60.2in) |
| **Overall length** | N/A |
| **Overall width** | N/A |
| **Overall height** | N/A) |
| **Seat height** | 930mm (36.6in) |

## TORQUE

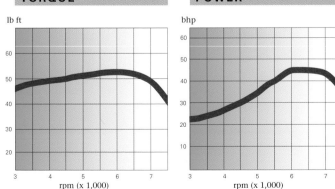

lb ft

## POWER

bhp

rpm (x 1,000)

rpm (x 1,000)

Independent test measurements (above) differ from the manufacturer's claimed maximum power and maximum torque figures.

# Norton

# 850 COMMANDO

*Even for its era, the Norton Commando 850's clocks were impressive, providing almost all the information the rider should need.*

**Ignition**
Unlike its 750 predecessor, late versions of the 850 Commando were fitted with an electric start which was, unfortunately, not very reliable.

**Gearbox**
A four-speed gearbox on all models with primary and secondary drive by chain through a diaphragm multi-plate dry clutch.

**Engine**
The air-cooled 828cc (50.5ci) overhead valve vertical twin had a bore and stroke of 77 x 89mm (3 x 3.5 in) with a claimed 48.5kW (65bhp) @ 7000rpm and a claimed top speed of 193km/h (120mph).

**Rubber mounting**
The engine and transmission, plus the swingarm, were isolated from the rest of the engine by a sophisticated form of rubber mounting which was named 'Isolastic'.

**Brakes**
The front wheel was fitted with a with a 272mm (10.7in) disc while the back sported a 178mm (7in) drum at the rear which was later changed to a disc.

# Commando 850

***One of the greatest names*** *in motorcycling, Norton did themselves proud with the Commando 850 (and the 750 which preceded it). It may have had a few problems, but its production figure of 55,000 speaks for itself. A great name and a great bike.*

Unlike the very popular 'Fastback' model which sported a flatter tank, the 850 had the 'rounded' model which held about 23l (6gal). The side panel boasted the electric starter fitted (which, considering its poor performance, was not the best of ideas).

The Norton Commando's engine boasted air-cooled parallel twin cylinders with two pushrod-operated valves per cylinder.

The tubular steel twin cradle welded frame incorporated rubber (Isolastic)mountings for engine and gearbox assembly.

**Seat**
With a seat height of 813mm (32in), the Commando was not for shorties. However, its riding position and handling made it available to most.

**Front end**
Unlike the 750 which could be a little vague at the front, the handling on the 850 was very good providing the Isolastics were correctly shimmed.

**Wheelbase**
The Norton boasted a wheelbase of 1447.8mm (57in) and had a ground clearance of 152.4mm (6in).

# ⚡ SUZUKI *RGV250*

*Braking is a great feature of the RGV: it is balanced and powerful, and needs to be. Four piston front calipers do the job efficiently and the rear-end stopping power feels comfortably capable of stopping the bike from full flow.*

## RGV 250

*Since being introduced in 1989, this blast of a bike has captured the hearts of many bikers. Sadly no longer available, you may be able to get your hands on a secondhand model – and you should certainly try to. The 249cc (15.2ci) V-twin thrills with its racing heritage, and there is probably nothing better out on the open road.*

**Suspension**
Also in lightweight metal, the seat-carrying subframe is easily removed to facilitate maintenance. A rigid, inverted telescopic fork with stout outer tubes aids precise steering, and full traction is gained by using link-type monoshock rear suspension.

**Gearbox**
The gearbox coupled with a poorish clutch is not the best piece of engineering on this bike. The middle gears are nice and close; first is short enough to lend interest at traffic lights and sixth struggles in headwinds. The shifts themselves are horribly slow and give a nasty thunk when used with gusto. Suzuki sets great store by its 'coaxially mounted' gear lever – but why is just not clear.

**Seat**
The wide seat places you comfortably on the bike, the high rear rests tipping you forward onto wide bars, which seem to be in direct touch with the front wheel. There is no stretching or neck strain and plenty of room even for tall riders. The short screen leaves your head exposed, lifts weight off the wrist at high speeds, and somehow still works at 160km/h (100mph).

*The upswept exhaust pipes feature 'stinger' cans on the starboard side of the Suzuki and reflect the sports racing look that categorize this as a genuine performance machine. Noted for a very slim power band between 10,000rpm and 12,000rpm, the wail of the exhausts is not for the faint-hearted.*

*Bristling with racetrack features, the featherlight chassis is designed to make rapid changes of direction, ride smoothly over bumps or ripples and stop abruptly. The main frame is an aluminium twin-spar type that has double cradle tubes to support the engine.*

**Engine**
A wide-angled V layout places one cylinder almost upright and the second pointing forwards and slightly downwards. For lightness, strength and efficient heat loss, the cylinder bores are plated with a hard alloy – but these are impossible to re-bore, and the Suzuki has a reputation for dropping valves.

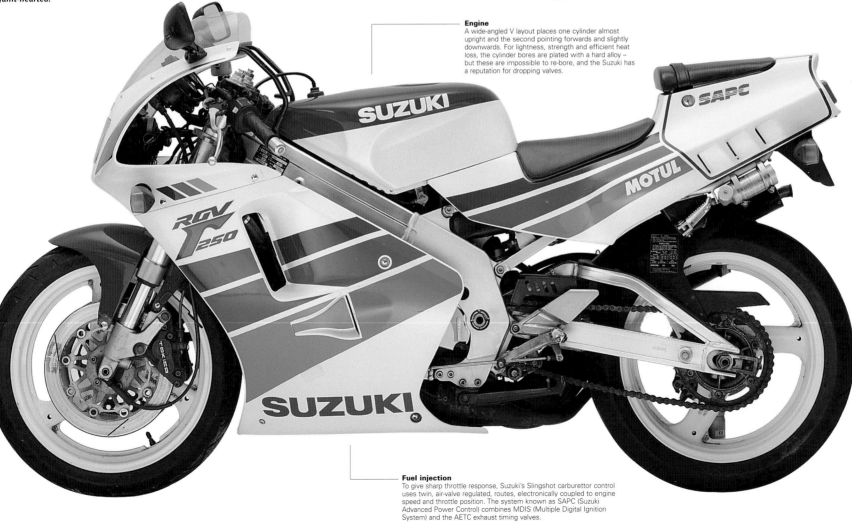

**Fuel injection**
To give sharp throttle response, Suzuki's Slingshot carburettor control uses twin, air-valve regulated, routes, electronically coupled to engine speed and throttle position. The system known as SAPC (Suzuki Advanced Power Control) combines MDIS (Multiple Digital Ignition System) and the AETC exhaust timing valves.

# Specifications

**The RGV250 was introduced** by Suzuki to combat the competition they perceived to be coming from the Yamaha **TZ** range. It was a move which put the small, two-stroke sports bike on the map again after ten years in the wilderness, as Yamaha's **TZR**s had never been very mainstream, despite selling well to the racing fraternity. What Suzuki managed to do was supply a high-performance machine with the reliability of a four-stroke, and it appealed to a wide cross-section of the public.

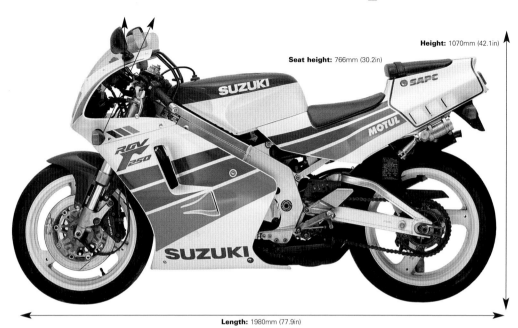

**Height:** 1070mm (42.1in)

**Seat height:** 766mm (30.2in)

**Length:** 1980mm (77.9in)

## ENGINE

| | |
|---|---|
| Type | 2-stroke |
| Layout | 90° V-twin |
| Total displacement | 249cc (15.2ci) |
| Bore | 56mm (2.2in) |
| Stroke | 50.6mm (1.9in) |
| Compression ratio | 7.3:1 |
| Valves | – |
| Fuel system | 2 x 34mm (1.3in) slingshot |
| Ignition | SAPC |
| Cooling | liquid |
| Maximum power | 41kW (55bhp) @ 10,750rpm |
| Maximum torque | 4kg-m (29lb-ft) @ 10,500rpm |

## TRANSMISSION

| | |
|---|---|
| Primary drive | gear |
| Clutch | wet multiplate |
| Gearbox | 6-speed |
| Final drive | chain |

## WEIGHTS & CAPACITIES

| | |
|---|---|
| Tank capacity | 16l (4.2gal) |
| Dry weight | 139kg (306lb) |
| Weight distribution | |
| — front | N/A |
| — rear | N/A |
| Wheelbase | 1380mm |
| Overall length | 1980mm (77.9in) |
| Overall width | 690mm (27.2in) |
| Overall height | 1070mm (42.1in) |
| Seat height | 766mm (30.2in) |

## CYCLE PARTS

| | |
|---|---|
| Frame | aluminium twin spar |
| Rake/trail | N/A |
| Front suspension | Inverted telescopic |
| Travel | 130mm (5.1in) |
| Adjustment | spring 5-way adjustable |
| Rear suspension | Full floating monoshock |
| Travel | 135mm (6.5in) |
| Adjustment | spring preload fully adjustable |
| Tyres | |
| — front | 110/70 x 17 |
| — rear | 150/70 x 17 |
| Brakes | |
| — front | 2 x 300mm (11.8in) discs, 4-piston calipers |
| — rear | 1 disc, 2-piston calipers |

# SUZUKI *RG500*

## *RG500*

*It is unlikely that you will* **see** *many of these around today, as they were in production for only four years. So here is a rare chance to have a close-up look at this stunner. Suzuki's race replica is as raw as they come with a brilliant combination of stunning beauty and great power.*

**Bodywork**
Beautiful. It was perfect for its era and still stands out today. The blue and white paint job replicated the factory race bikes.

**Front wheel**
The front sports a 40.6cm (16in) wheel which, although not popular with everyone at the time, did look the part.

**Fairing**
This comes right around to the back, adding to the bike's racey looks.

**Engine**
The 495cc (30.2ci) water-cooled rotary disc-valve, two-stroke, square four engine which powers the RG500 was impressive in its day.

*The two beautifully-concealed exhaust pipes tucked away under the tail look just the job.*

*The **GP**-style engine is mounted into a then-radical race replica chassis. The frame is constructed of square-section alumnium tubing in a cradle arrangement, making it very stiff and light.*

**Seat**
The riding position proved just right for high speed riding, with a natural racer's crouch induced by the positioning of seat, pegs and bars.

**Front end**
The RG500 is equipped with an anti-dive fork system which was popular at the time of its launch. The front brake has never been that good on the RG500.

**Oil tank**
This sits under the seat, a practice usual for two-strokes.

**Gearbox**
This rather lets the side down, as first gear is tall and tends to clunk into second. In fact, it is clunky between all gears.

# Specifications

*With its two-stroke,* water cooled engine, the RG500 was an authentic race replica of the Suzuki 1980s road racer, right down to the paint job. Today it has become a cult classic – not surprising because once ridden, it is never forgotten.

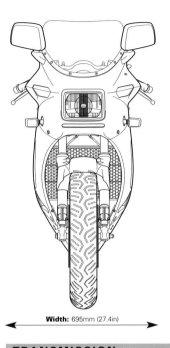

**Width:** 695mm (27.4in)

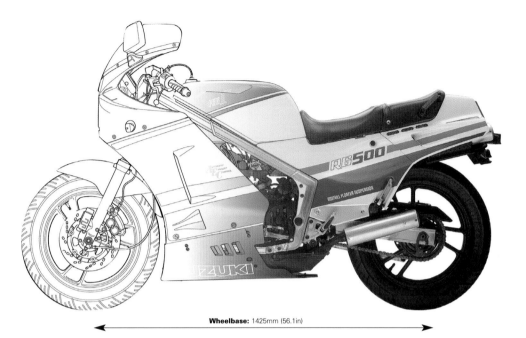

**Wheelbase:** 1425mm (56.1in)

## ENGINE

| | |
|---|---|
| Type | 2-stroke |
| Layout | square-4 |
| Total displacement | 495cc (30.2ci) |
| Bore | 56mm (2.2in) |
| Stroke | 50.6mm (1.9in) |
| Compression ratio | 7.0:1 |
| Fuel system | 4 Mikuni 28mm (1.1in) flat slide |
| Ignition | electronic |
| Cooling | water |
| Maximum power | 70.8kW (95bhp) @ 9500rpm |
| Maximum torque | N/A |

## POWER

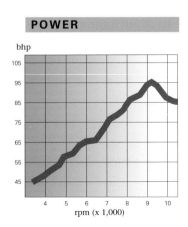

bhp

(graph axes: vertical 45, 55, 65, 75, 85, 95, 105; horizontal 4, 5, 6, 7, 8, 9, 10)

rpm (x 1,000)

## TRANSMISSION

| | |
|---|---|
| Primary drive | helical gear |
| Clutch | wet multiplate |
| Gearbox | 5-speed |
| Final drive | chain |

## WEIGHTS & CAPACITIES

| | |
|---|---|
| Tank capacity | 16l (4.2gal) |
| Dry weight | 154kg (339.5lb) |
| Weight distribution | |
| — front | N/A |
| — rear | N/A |
| Wheelbase | 1425mm (56.1in) |
| Overall length | 2100mm (82.7in) |
| Overall width | 695mm (27.4in) |
| Overall height | 1185mm (46.7in) |
| Seat height | 820mm (32.2in) |

## CYCLE PARTS

| | |
|---|---|
| Frame | twin duplex aluminum |
| Rake/trail | N/A |
| Front suspension | 40mm (1.6in) telescopic forks |
| Travel | N/A |
| Adjustment | none |
| Rear suspension | Full floater single shock |
| Travel | N/A |
| Adjustment | spring preload |
| Tyres | |
| — make | N/A |
| — front | 110/90 V16 |
| — rear | 120/90 V17 |
| Brakes | |
| — make | N/A |
| — front | 260mm (10.2in) disc, four pot caliper |
| — rear | 220mm (8.7in) disc, twin pot caliper |

**Independent test measurements (above) differ from the manufacturer's claimed maximum power and maximum torque figures.**

# SUZUKI *GSF600 BANDIT*

**GSF600**

**Square vision**
Half-faired Bandit has a square headlamp; unfaired version gets a classier round light. Both are adequate.

**Familiar forks**
The softly sprung front suspension was also used on the RF600. Weedy by superbike standards, the Bandit can still corner safely at speed, but hard braking can cause it to bottom out.

**Stand delivers**
The centrestand was a welcome addition to the 600S and makes wheel removal and chain lubing a doddle.

**When Suzuki launched its GSF600**
*Bandit in January 1995, it cornered a part of the market other manufacturers are only now beginning to fill. Here was a lightweight, reliable and nippy middleweight with good looks and a modest price tag. It was exactly the sort of bike thousands of riders had been looking for – uncomplicated to work on, well made, and powerful enough to nudge 193km/h (120mph). The first Bandit was completely naked. There was no fairing, so the rider had to put up with wind-blast and aching neck muscles every time he approached the ton. But it sold exceptionally well. Exactly one year later, Suzuki released a half-faired version. While perhaps not as attractive as the original version, the GSF600S with its small but effective fairing made riding to work far more bearable and flat-out speeding much more fun. If anything, it proved 600cc (36.6ci) fours can be practical and exciting at the same time.*

*The four-into-one exhaust contributes to the engine's sweet sound, but the downpipes are prone to rust.*

*Clear and simple dials suit the Bandit's overall minimalist look.*

*The Bandit's all-new double-cradle steel frame was developed specially and copes well with the bike's awesome power.*

**Tasty tank**
The 19l (5gal) petrol tank gives a range of up to 314km (195 miles). But it is easily scratched by jacket zips and buckles, making a protective tank pad a must.

**Pillion friendly**
Comfy but not overly-padded seat, average height rear footpegs and useful grab handles make the Bandit acceptable for long distance two-up work.

**Grab on**
The 600S has pillion grab handles. Passengers on earlier versions of the naked model have to do without.

**Middleweight motor**
Bandit's reliable engine, from the GSX600, makes a claimed 58.9kW (79bhp) from 599cc (36.5in). It uses oil and air-cooling and an in-line four-cylinder configuration.

# SUZUKI GSX600F

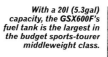

**With a 20l (5.3gal) capacity, the GSX600F's fuel tank is the largest in the budget sports-tourer middleweight class.**

**Headlamps**
Distinctive, soft-edged twin bug eyes are a little outdated now, but work well enough at night.

*Dual 290mm (11.4in) discs and two-piston calipers feel weedy, offer only average feedback and were accompanied by poor test results. Braided hose would help them.*

**Fuel system**
The GSX600F uses a bank of four moderately sized 32mm (1.3in) carburettors.

**Mudguard**
Huge mudguards express once again Suzuki's unique rich tapestry of aerodynamics.

**Footpegs**
Rubber-covered to deaden mechanical vibration.

## GSX600F

**Suzuki's GSX600F is virtually** indistinguishable from its 750cc (45.8ci) bigger brother to the untrained eye, and that's exactly the intention. The GSXF range is designed to provide the best of both worlds; touring bike comfort with sports bike handling and performance. Unfortunately in our experience the feeble brakes and vague suspension setup stifle any of the chassis' latent sportiness.

**Tyres**
Front is a fairly standard 120/70 x 17 fitment, while the rear harks back to the early 1990s with a narrow design of just 150/50 x 43.2cm (17in).

**Exhaust**
Stainless steel, so it is unlikely to rot, the exhaust system is of a four-into-one design and features a chamfered silencer to boost ground clearance.

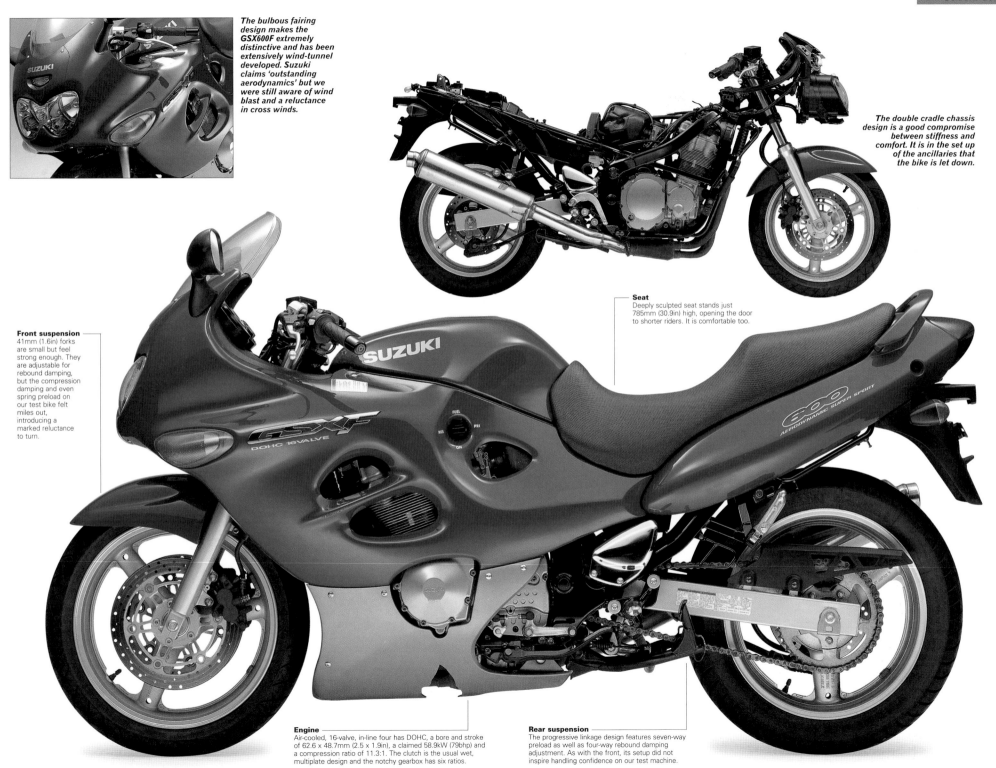

The bulbous fairing design makes the **GSX600F** extremely distinctive and has been extensively wind-tunnel developed. Suzuki claims 'outstanding aerodynamics' but we were still aware of wind blast and a reluctance in cross winds.

The double cradle chassis design is a good compromise between stiffness and comfort. It is in the set up of the ancillaries that the bike is let down.

**Seat**
Deeply sculpted seat stands just 785mm (30.9in) high, opening the door to shorter riders. It is comfortable too.

**Front suspension**
41mm (1.6in) forks are small but feel strong enough. They are adjustable for rebound damping, but the compression damping and even spring preload on our test bike felt miles out, introducing a marked reluctance to turn.

**Engine**
Air-cooled, 16-valve, in-line four has DOHC, a bore and stroke of 62.6 x 48.7mm (2.5 x 1.9in), a claimed 58.9kW (79bhp) and a compression ratio of 11.3:1. The clutch is the usual wet, multiplate design and the notchy gearbox has six ratios.

**Rear suspension**
The progressive linkage design features seven-way preload as well as four-way rebound damping adjustment. As with the front, its setup did not inspire handling confidence on our test machine.

**SUZUKI** *GSX600F*

# Specifications

**The GSX600F is a good** multi-purpose bike, great for touring, commuting and even a bit of sports riding! Although it has been around for over a decade it has had only minor technical changes during that time, but it still manages to hold its own against the more modern water-cooled engines.

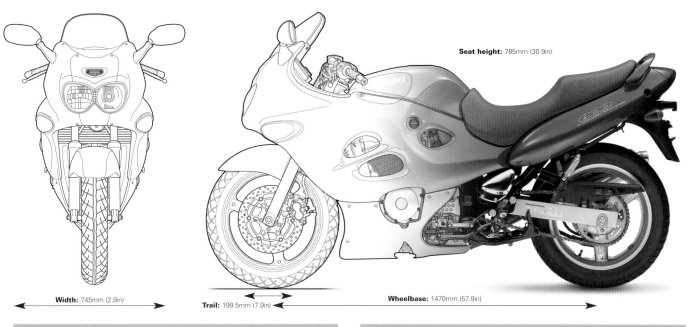

**Seat height:** 785mm (30.9in)

**Width:** 745mm (2.9in)

**Trail:** 199.5mm (7.9in)

**Wheelbase:** 1470mm (57.9in)

## ENGINE

| | |
|---|---|
| Type | 4-stroke |
| Layout | in-line 4 |
| Total displacement | 599.6cc |
| Bore | 62.6mm (2.5in) |
| Stroke | 48.7mm (1.9in) |
| Compression ratio | 11.3:1 |
| Valves | 4 per cylinder |
| Fuel system | Mukuni Carburettors |
| Ignition | Digital electronic |
| Cooling | air/oil |
| Maximum power | 76.7bhp @ 10,850rpm |
| Maximum torque | 41lb-ft @ 9,400rpm |

## TORQUE

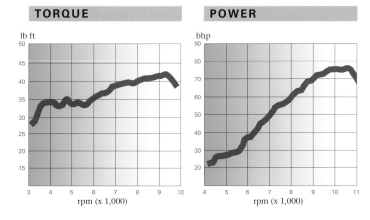

lb ft
rpm (x 1,000)

## POWER

bhp
rpm (x 1,000)

## TRANSMISSION

| | |
|---|---|
| Primary drive | gear |
| Clutch | wet multiplate |
| Gearbox | 6-speed |
| Final drive | chain |

## WEIGHTS & CAPACITIES

| | |
|---|---|
| Tank capacity | 20l (5.3gal) |
| Dry weight | 200kg (440lb) |
| Weight distribution | |
| — front | N/A |
| — rear | N/A |
| Wheelbase | 1470mm (57.9in) |
| Overall length | 2135mm (84.1in) |
| Overall width | 745mm (2.9in) |
| Overall height | 1195mm (47in) |
| Seat height | 785mm (30.9in) |

## CYCLE PARTS

| | |
|---|---|
| Frame | steel double cradle |
| Rake | 25.3° |
| Front suspension | 41mm (1.6in) telescopic fork |
| Travel | N/A |
| Adjustment | preload, compression and rebound damping |
| Rear suspension | Monoshock |
| Travel | N/A |
| Adjustment | 7-way preload, plus 4-way compression and rebound damping |
| Tyres | |
| — make | N/A |
| — front | 120/70 x 17 |
| — rear | 150/70 x 17 |
| Brakes | |
| — make | N/A |
| — front | twin 290mm (11.4in) discs 2-piston calipers |
| — rear | single disc and caliper |

**Independent test measurements (above) differ from the manufacturer's claimed maximum power and maximum torque figures.**

# SUZUKI **GSX-R600**

*The seat hump is thankfully (as far as styling goes) smaller than the monstrosities fitted to the TL1000R and Hayabusa, and is easily removed for carrying pillions who may find they are perched quite high up. Nor does the lack of standard grab rail or tall passenger pegs help.*

**Screen**
Bigger from 1998 to aid comfort and reduce wind blast at high speed.

**Fairing**
Wide compared with others in its class, which makes tucking in an easy task for most riders. Just do not expect it to save you in a rainstorm.

**Clutch**
No surprises here. The wet, multiplate assembly can take heaps of abuse under hard use and has a positive, light and pleasant manner. Repeated misbehaviour eventually takes its toll, though.

**Forks**
Conventional 45mm (1.7in) forks are fully adjustable for compression and rebound damping, and offer a full 15mm (0.6in) of spring preload too.

**Bungee hooks**
Unbelievably handy addition, making the black art of luggage attachment a much more simple task. Suzuki has thoughtfully fitted four under the pillion seat.

**Footpegs**
Rider's offerings are placed high and this, combined with low handlebars, means a true racer's crouch for all. Fun on short runs, a pain when there are still 480km (300 miles) to go.

**Wheels**
Lightweight three-spoke rims are sized to take popular rubber choices. Owners have a theoretical choice of around a dozen top tyres to experiment with in 120/70 ZR17 front and 180/55 ZR17 rear fitments.

**Paintwork**
Attractive and aggressively styled, although some owners feel it is not of great quality and is also a bit thin.

*GSX-R600*

***It first appeared in 1996** and since then has been taken to the heart of many a would-be racer. This is a ballistically fast machine with superb agility and fantastic braking power. It may not be for you if you prefer touring, but if you just want a super-fast bike with great performance, then this is one of the few really quick 600s around which will suit you.*

*Suzuki Ram Air Direct (SRAD) is a pressurized air induction system which feeds huge charges of cold air from giant fairing scoops through to the bank of Mikuni BDSR36 carburettors. The theory is that the faster you go, the more air you flow, and hence the better the combustion in the engine's chambers. This, in turn, equals more power.*

*Headlamps twin setup is aerodynamically designed, which not only improves looks from the front, but aids acceleration and ultimate top speed too. For night riding, the beam is perfectly acceptable.*

*As with any Japanese multi worth its salt these days, the GSX-R600 gets a twin spar aluminium frame and detachable subframe.*

**Fuel tank**
An average capacity at 18l (4.8gal) and by no means intrusive to the rider, thanks to carefully sculpted rear sides.

**Seat**
Reasonably comfortable for all but the very biggest riders, although long distances can be hard work, it stands 830mm (32.7in) from the ground.

**Rake/trail**
Racey looks and potential demand racey geometry, and the GSX-R600 has got it with 24° of rake and 96mm (37.8in) trail. Wheelbase is a short 1385mm (54.5in), which means a bit of head-waggling can often be the order of the day on poorly surfaced, fast roads.

**Engine**
Suzuki's interpretation of the typical four-stroke, four cylinder, DOHC, four valves per cylinder middleweight engine is a fairly peaking offering. There is little midrange power, virtually nothing at low revs, but super-strong delivery once the 600cc (36.6ci) engine comes on song. Its characteristics fully match the bike's image.

**Rear shock**
Progressive linkage, monoshock design is fully adjustable for compression and rebound damping, and offers a 10mm (0.4in) range of spring preload settings. Damping quality seems to degenerate quickly in a short space of time.

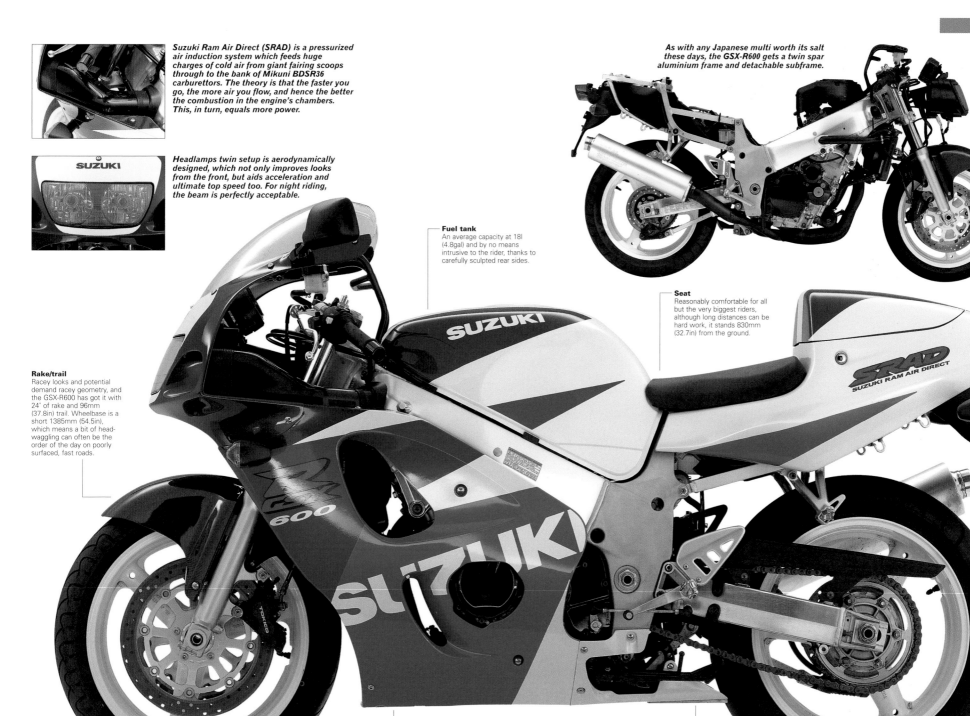

# Specifications

*Suzuki's GSX-R600 has stood out from the other 600 sportsters since it was launched in December 1996, thanks mainly to its track-focused design.*
*In fact, its only challenge came when Yamaha launched the YZF-R6. However, the GSX-R remains the most peaky in its class, one of the heaviest and also the least powerful.*

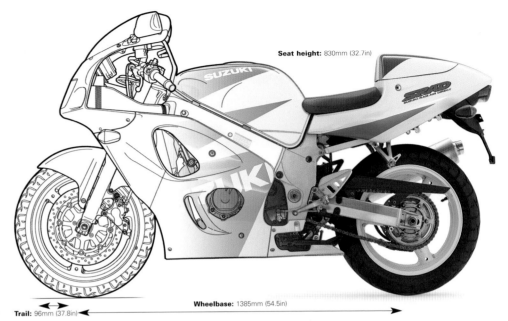

Seat height: 830mm (32.7in)

Width: 720mm (28.4in)

Trail: 96mm (37.8in)

Wheelbase: 1385mm (54.5in)

## ENGINE

| | |
|---|---|
| Type | 4 stroke |
| Layout | DOHC in-line four |
| Total displacement | 600cc (36.6ci) |
| Bore | 65.5mm (2.6in) |
| Stroke | 44.5mm (1.8in) |
| Compression ratio | 12.0:1 |
| Valves | 4 per cylinder |
| Fuel system | 4 x Mikuni BDSR36 carburettors |
| Ignition | CDI |
| Cooling | liquid |
| Maximum power | 76kW (102bhp) @ 11,847rpm |
| Maximum torque | 6.7kg-m (48.5lb-ft) @ 9583rpm |

## TRANSMISSION

| | |
|---|---|
| Primary drive | gear |
| Clutch | wet multiplate |
| Gearbox | 6-speed |
| Final drive | chain |

## WEIGHTS & CAPACITIES

| | |
|---|---|
| Tank capacity | 18l (4.8gal) |
| Dry weight | 174 kg (382.8lb) |
| Weight distribution | |
| — front | N/A |
| — rear | N/A |
| Wheelbase | 1385mm (54.5in) |
| Overall length | 2065mm (81.3in) |
| Overall width | 720mm (28.4in) |
| Overall height | 1165mm (45.9in) |
| Seat height | 830mm (32.7in) |

## CYCLE PARTS

| | |
|---|---|
| Frame | aluminium twin spar |
| Rake/trail | 24°/96mm (37.8in) |
| Front suspension | 45mm (1.8in) telescopic forks |
| Travel | N/A |
| Adjustment | 15mm (0.6in) preload, plus compression and rebound damping |
| Rear suspension | progressive linkage, monoshock |
| Travel | N/A |
| Adjustment | 10mm (0.4in) preload, plus compression and rebound damping |
| Tyres | |
| — make | varies |
| — front | 120/70 x ZR17 |
| — rear | 180/55 x ZR17 |
| Brakes | |
| — make | Tokico |
| — front | 2 x 320mm (12.6in) discs, opposed 4-piston calipers |
| — rear | 220mm (8.7in) disc, 2-piston caliper |

## TORQUE

## POWER

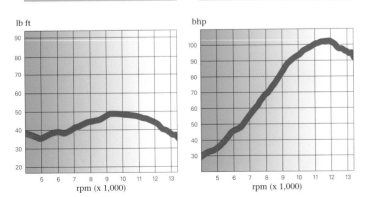

Independent test measurements (above) differ from the manufacturer's claimed maximum power and maximum torque figures.

# ![Suzuki logo] **SUZUKI** *SV650*

*Suzuki engineers built the engine and chassis into a simple, light and compact integrated unit.*

**Brakes**
Twin 290mm (11.4in) disc and two-piston Tokico front brake assembly helps the SV650 to stop in 94.3m (309.4ft) from 160km/h (100mph). This figure compares favourably with expensive set-ups on 750cc (45.8ci) middleweight race replicas, but lags behind out-and-out sports 600s.

**Fairing**
Two SV derivatives are available; one is naked to enhance the urban streetfighter look while the other comes with a neat half fairing.

**Front suspension**
41mm (1.6in) conventional forks are, sadly, unadjustable, but are set up as standard to cope with most conditions.

**Rear suspension**
Rising-rate monoshock is firm as standard and offers seven-way adjustable preload settings. Keeping the front and rear suspension simple also helps lower the price – essential when the SV is aimed very much at the bargain market.

**Wheels**
Lightweight three-spoke wheels look surprisingly upmarket for such a budget machine and take standard 43.2cm (17in) rubber in 120/60 front and 160/60 rear sizes. UK bikes are usually supplied on Metzeler MEZ4 tyres.

**Exhaust**
Two-into-one system exits on the right-hand side and features a chamfered silencer to boost ground clearance. Although the finish looks reasonable, expect it to last for no more than a few years.

## SV650

**Bikers the world over** *fell in love with Suzuki's SV650, and is it any wonder? Just look at it. A sporty V-twin with good handling, performance and comfort. Just as importantly, the SV650 is a fun bike. You will want to ride it everywhere. Commuting to work will be a different experience on this bike. Try it!*

*The rear end features a dual-bulb tail lamp and a handy but small compartment underneath the passenger seat, which can only carry items such as a **U**-shaped lock and any other small items.*

*The half-fairing on the SV650S includes dual integrated headlamps, a fairing-mounted instrument panel, side-mount mirrors and clip-on bars.*

*Aluminium trellis frame mimics heavy-duty versions of both Honda's VTR FireStorm and the Suzuki TL1000S, and is finished with a hard-wearing anodized paint to ensure it keeps its looks.*

**Tank**
Holds 16l (4.2 gal) and is hinged for access to the air filter and rear cylinder spark plug.

**Engine**
645cc (39.4ci), 90° V-twin is water-cooled, features a six-speed gearbox, uses a pair of 39mm (1.5in) Mikuni carburettors and makes a claimed 52.2kW (70bhp) at 8800rpm. This is more likely to translate to a real world 49.2kW (66bhp).

**Wheelbase**
1420mm (55.9in) wheelbase offers a good mix between agility and stability, which further enhances the design philosophy that the SV650 must be easy to ride for experienced and novice owners alike.

**SUZUKI** *SV650*

# Specifications

*There is not a lot* of difference between the SV650 and the SV650S, and in the engine none at all. For some reason, the SV is sometimes underrated, which is a pity, because this Suzuki is a fun bike. The throttle response is instant and it has a good spread of power from low rpm. It handles well and some consider it to be very stylish. It will do the trick not only for commuting, but also for weekend fun and even touring (as long as you do not expect too much from what is not, after all, a tourer).

**Seat height:** 805mm (31.7in)

**Width** 760mm (29.1in)   **Trail:** 100mm (3.9in)   **Wheelbase:** 1415mm (55.7in)

## ENGINE

| | |
|---|---|
| Type | 4-stroke |
| Layout | 90° V-twin |
| Total displacement | 645cc (394ci) |
| Bore | 81mm (3.2in) |
| Stroke | 62.6mm (2.5in) |
| Compression ratio | 11.5:1 |
| Valves | 4 per cylinder |
| Fuel system | 2 x BDSR39 carburettors |
| Ignition | digital electronic |
| Cooling | liquid |
| Maximum power | 51kw (68.8bhp) @ 9390rpm |
| Maximum torque | 61.4kg-m (44.4lb-ft) @ 7420rpm |

## TRANSMISSION

| | |
|---|---|
| Primary drive | gear |
| Clutch | constant mesh |
| Gearbox | 6-speed |
| Final drive | chain |

## WEIGHTS & CAPACITIES

| | |
|---|---|
| Tank capacity | 16l (4.2gal) |
| Dry weight | 165kg (364lb) |
| Weight distribution | |
| — front | N/A |
| — rear | N/A |
| Wheelbase | 1415mm (55.7in) |
| Overall length | 2045mm (80.5in) |
| Overall width | 760mm (29.1in) |
| Overall height | 1070mm (42.1in) |
| Seat height | 805mm (31.7in) |

## CYCLE PARTS

| | |
|---|---|
| Frame | aluminium alloy truss |
| Rake/trail | 24.8°/100mm (3.9in) |
| Front suspension | 41mm (1.6in) telescopic forks |
| Travel | 130mm (5.1in) |
| Adjustment | none |
| Rear suspension | swingarm, progressive linkage |
| Travel | 125mm (4.9in) |
| Adjustment | 7-step spring preload |
| Tyres | |
| — make | N/A |
| — front | 120/70 x 17 |
| — rear | 160/60 x 17 |
| Brakes | |
| — make | N/A |
| — front | 290mm (1.1in) dual discs, 2-piston calipers |
| — rear | 240mm (9.4in) disc, 2-piston caliper |

## TORQUE

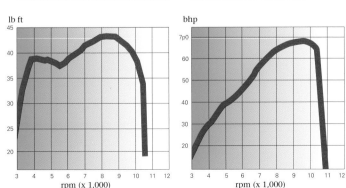

lb ft

rpm (x 1,000)

## POWER

bhp

rpm (x 1,000)

**Independent test measurements (above) differ from the manufacturer's claimed maximum power and maximum torque figures.**

# SUZUKI **GSX-R750**

*New in 1998 is electronic fuel injection using 46mm (1.8in) throttle bodies. Fuel injection offers improvements in both performance and fuel consumption.*

**Mirrors**
Wide enough to provide a decent rear view when not completely filled with elbows. They do not vibrate excessively at less than 160km/h (100mph), either.

**Hi-tech**
On-board computer monitors throttle postion, air intake pressure, revs, and engine and air temperature to deliver maximum performance.

*Igniton is via piggy-back coils sitting directly on top of each spark plug. This system was introduced on the GSX-R600 in 1997 – Suzuki says it reduces weight.*

**Clocks**
Speedometer and tachometer are rotary dials with digital odometer and water temperature displays. Nothing very much out of the ordinary, but well positioned.

**Headlamps**
Twin headlamps, on the endurance racing theme, work well and look the biz. Holes on each side are ram air intakes, which boost top end power at higher speeds.

**Forks**
43mm (1.7in) upside-down, telescopic forks are made by Showa. Because of their stiffness, upside-down (or inverted) forks have become increasingly common on modern sports bikes.

**Rear suspension**
Adjustable for compression and rebound damping, as well as preload, the rising rate monoshock now features a push-rod which works together with needle valves to compensate for the oil thinning as it heats up. This ensures consistent handling performance at the back end.

**Gearbox**
Six-speed sequential gearbox with revised fifth and sixth gear ratios. They are closer than ever before to help keep the bike in its powerband at high speed.

**Seat**
Wide, comfortable and reasonably padded, but at 83mm (32.7in) off the ground, it is a fair stretch for shorter riders.

## GSX-R750

*Suzuki's* **GSX-R750** *has been steadily evolving since its introduction in 1985, becoming faster and offering better handling along the wa. The 1998 machine, shown here, had improvements in both performance and comfort, while still remaining a bike that is happiest when being pushed to its limits. No surprise, then, that this bike is the street racer's favourite.*

*A change at the rear is the addition of reinforcing plates. This improves the stiffness of the rear suspension linkage mountings.*

*Hole in frame, behind headstock is where ram air duct goes through to the airbox. A radiator hose also goes through the frame.*

**Steering damper**
Standard steering damper does a good job at preventing headshake on bumpy surfaces, but can be hard work around town.

*The '98 GSX-R has the same twin spar aluminium frame as earlier models, but for this year it has been fitted with a steering damper. Although some may feel it problematic at times, this makes for a more stable, secure feeling and tames the misbehaving front end.*

**Engine**
749cc in-line four with four valves per cylinder, whopping 46mm injector throttle bodies, a redesigned crankshaft and cams, and 11.8:1 compression.

**Chassis**
Latest frame is almost identical to last year's. Wheelbase is 5mm (0.2in) shorter to quicken steering.

**Seat hump**
Suzuki says this improves aerodynamics. However, when it was introduced, there was a 'love it or hate it' debate – a controversy long since forgotten.

**Front brakes**
Two Tokico six-piston calipers, combined with modified, thicker, semi-floating steel discs, provide awesome stopping power.

**Tyres**
Original equipment Michelin Hi-Sports on 43.2cm (17in) wheels are very grippy. Rear tyre is a massive 190 section.

**Fairing**
Paintwork and graphics need redesigning to make the GSX-R750 look its best. Bodywork is so thin and slim that it is prone to disintegrating in even low speed tumbles.

# Specifications

**The main change to** this year's model is the use of fuel injection rather than carbs, although there are other small changes, mainly to the engine.

It is faster, more civilised and the powerband has gone – an improvement. It may feel as though the engine is making less power; actually, what is happening is that it is smoother.

It is a pity, though, that Suzuki did not redesign the bodywork to give it a new identity to match its new character.

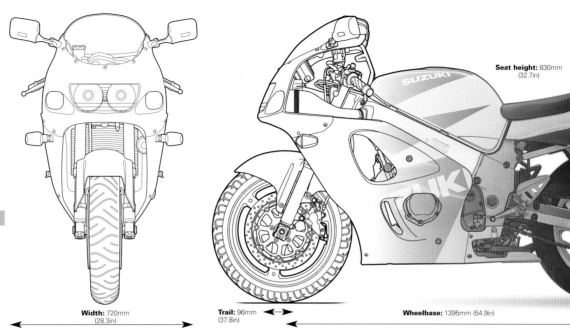

Seat height: 830mm (32.7in)

Width: 720mm (28.3in)

Trail: 96mm (37.8in)

Wheelbase: 1395mm (54.9in)

## ENGINE

| | |
|---|---|
| Type | 4-stroke |
| Layout | transverse four |
| Total displacement | 749cc (45.7ci) |
| Bore | 72mm (2.8in) |
| Stroke | 46mm (1.8in) |
| Compression ratio | 11.8:1 |
| Valves | 4 per cylinder |
| Fuel system | indirect, 46mm throttle bodies |
| Ignition | digital electronic |
| Cooling | liquid |
| Maximum power | 91.7kW (123bhp) @ 12,000rpm |
| Maximum torque | 7.9kg-m (57lb-ft) @ 10,000rpm |

## TORQUE

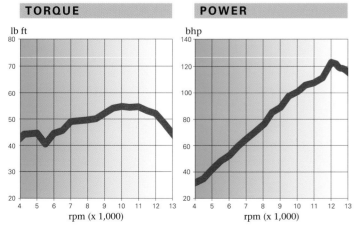

## POWER

lb ft

bhp

rpm (x 1,000)

rpm (x 1,000)

Independent test measurements (above) differ from the manufacturer's claimed maximum power and maximum torque figures.

## TRANSMISSION

| | |
|---|---|
| Primary drive | straight-cut gears |
| Clutch | wet multiplate |
| Gearbox | 6-speed |
| Final drive | 106 link chain |

## WEIGHTS & CAPACITIES

| | |
|---|---|
| Tank capacity | 18l (3.96 gal) |
| Dry weight | 179kg (393.8lb) |
| Weight distribution | |
| — front | 51% |
| — rear | 49% |
| Wheelbase | 1395mm (54.9in) |
| Overall length | 2065mm (81.3in) |
| Overall width | 720mm (28.3in) |
| Overall height | 1165mm (45.9in) |
| Seat height | 830mm (32.7in) |

## CYCLE PARTS

| | |
|---|---|
| Frame | aluminium twin spar |
| Rake/trail | 24°/96mm (37.8in) |
| Front suspension | 43mm (1.7in) Showa inverted telescopic forks |
| Travel | 120mm (4.7in) |
| Adjustment | spring preload, plus rebound and compression damping |
| Rear suspension | gas/oil-damped monoshock, piggyback reservoir |
| Travel | 120mm (4.7in) |
| Adjustment | spring preload, plus rebound and compression damping |
| Tyres | |
| — make | Michelin Hi-Sport II |
| — front | 120/70 x 17 |
| — rear | 190/50 x 17 |
| Brakes | |
| — make | Tokico |
| — front | 2 x 320mm (12.6in) steel semi-floating discs, opposed six-piston calipers |
| — rear | 220mm (8.7in) steel disc, opposed two-piston caliper |

# SUZUKI GT750

**Headlights**
Fitted with the, typical for its time, single round headlamp, the GT750 looked big and imposing front on.

**Fuelling**
The engine is piston-ported and fed (in later versions) by three 40mm (1.6in) CV carbs.

**Crash bars**
The wide crash bars and radiator at the front went towards giving the GT750 its nickname of the 'water kettle'

**Engine**
Sitting at the heart of this huge machine is a 738cc (45ci), liquid-coole,d three-cylinder two-stroke engine.

**Brakes**
At the front, later versions of the GT750 were equipped with twin discs while at the rear sat a drum on all models.

**Ground clearance**
Ground clearance was poor on the GT750. It did not take much to scrape the pipes.

**Exhaust**
The chrome three-into-four exhaust system aided the imposing look of the big engine.

# GT750

***The big 'water kettle'** as the GT750 became known was unique in the world of motorcycling as both the first and last of the big two-strokes. It still has a loyal following, due mainly to its styling plus its renowned reliability and capability of covering huge distances with no problems at all. Just as importantly, the triple was smooth, quick and braked well.*

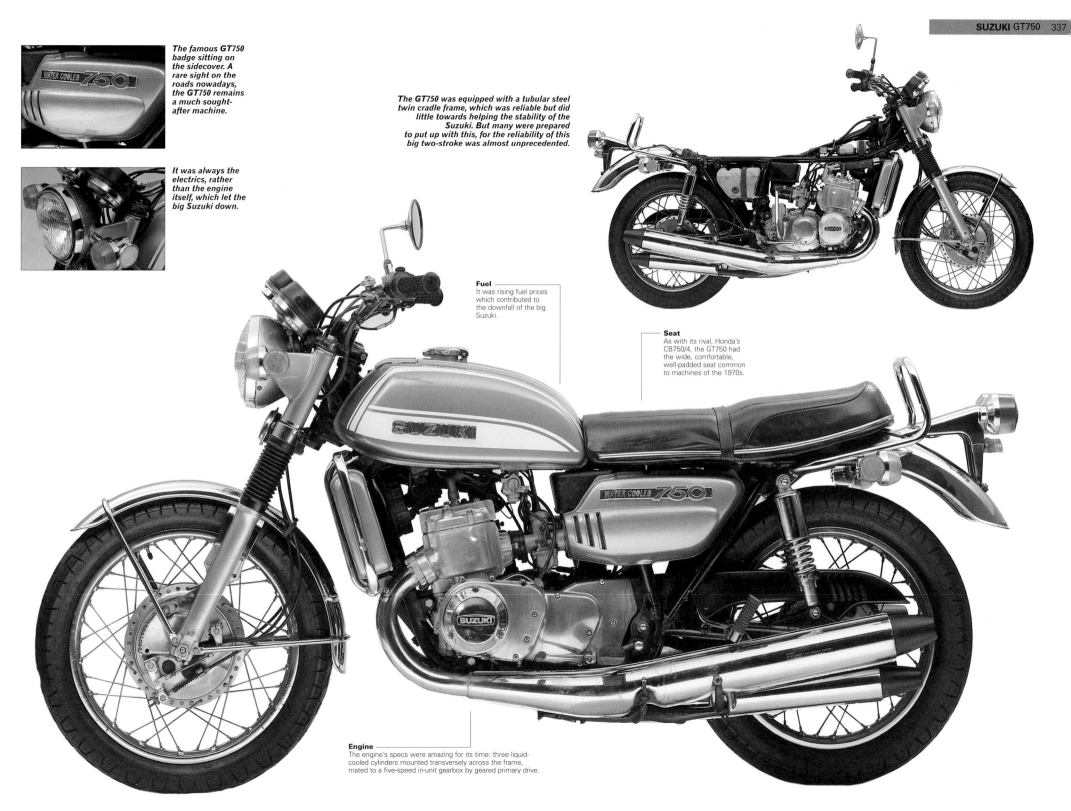

The famous GT750 badge sitting on the sidecover. A rare sight on the roads nowadays, the GT750 remains a much sought-after machine.

It was always the electrics, rather than the engine itself, which let the big Suzuki down.

The GT750 was equipped with a tubular steel twin cradle frame, which was reliable but did little towards helping the stability of the Suzuki. But many were prepared to put up with this, for the reliability of this big two-stroke was almost unprecedented.

**Fuel**
It was rising fuel prices which contributed to the downfall of the big Suzuki.

**Seat**
As with its rival, Honda's CB750/4, the GT750 had the wide, comfortable, well-padded seat common to machines of the 1970s.

**Engine**
The engine's specs were amazing for its time: three liquid-cooled cylinders mounted transversely across the frame, mated to a five-speed in-unit gearbox by geared primary drive.

# SUZUKI RF900R

The bank of 36mm (1.5in) Mikuni carburettors is positively miniscule by latest standards, but helps the RF return acceptable consumption figures without encroaching on performance excessively.

**Fairing**
Part of the reason the RF900 never really caught on, offering louvred panels more akin to an 1980s sports tourer than a 1990's sports-focused machine.

**Headlamp**
Sculpted glass precisely follows the fairing's retracting lines. It is adequate for night-riding and no more.

**Front suspension**
Conventional telescopic forks are adjustable for spring preload, plus compression and rebound damping.

**Engine**
Massively underrated liquid-cooled, four-cylinder, 16-valver features a bore and stroke of 73 x 56mm (2.9 x 2.2in), 11.3:1 compression ratio, five-speed gearbox and 937cc (57.2ci) displacement and makes a claimed 91.8kw (123bhp) @ 10,000rpm

**Footpegs**
A minor concession to touring, thanks to rubber mounts to isolate what little vibration there is. More focused tackle usually uses bare alloy.

**Grab rail**
Massive, to accommodate even the biggest hands. The paint finish is not all it should be, however. Premature wear can occur on the rear bodywork and fuel tank coatings too.

**Exhaust**
The silencer can be quickly and easily unbolted thanks to three prominent and substantial exhaust bolts as well as one used to secure it to the chassis. Finish is adequate, but some owners do complain over time.

## RF900R

## This is a massively underrated bike.
*It has pieces taken from various GSX-R models, which should give an idea of its performance. Unfortunately, many consider that it looks dated. Unfortunate for them too, as this means that they are missing out on a good machine from a top manufacturer.*

The radiator is widely exposed behind the short-reach front mudguard. Expect to pick stones from it frequently.

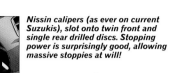

Nissin calipers (as ever on current Suzukis), slot onto twin front and single rear drilled discs. Stopping power is surprisingly good, allowing massive stoppies at will!

The substantial beam frame has withstood many a crash and survived to tell the tale. The subframe assembly often bears up well too.

**Fuel tank**
Large at 21l (5.5gal), but feels even bigger on the bike. The RF is definitely one machine which feels a touch top heavy with a tankful.

**Seat**
Plush, reasonably wide and comfortable for most journeys. Many have toured for hundreds of miles at a time and never felt cause to complain. It has an 805mm (31.7in) height.

**Wheels**
Modern-looking but actually bearing rim widths more common six years ago. The bike wears 120/70 x 17 front and 170/60 x 17 tyres as a result. Dunlops are usually supplied on UK-specification bikes.

**Rear suspension**
Link-type monoshock assembly has spring preload, as well as seven-way rebound and four-way compression damping adjustment.

**SUZUKI** *RF900R*

# Specifications

*This is not just* an updated RF600 – it has been claimed by many to be a brilliant bike for its class and price. So who are we to argue?
The chassis is stiffer than the 600's pressed steel frame; it is lighter than the ZX-9R and the VFR750, and is stable and well-planted. The supple suspension keeps up with the performance, too. This may not be a perfect bike, but it will do what supposedly better bikes will do, and do it with ease. Realistically priced, too.

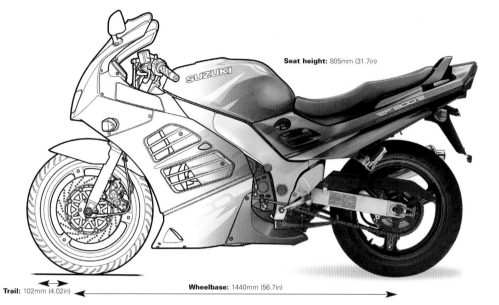

**Seat height:** 805mm (31.7in)

**Width:** 730mm (28.7in)   **Trail:** 102mm (4.02in)   **Wheelbase:** 1440mm (56.7in)

## ENGINE

| | |
|---|---|
| Type | 4-stroke |
| Layout | in-line four |
| Total displacement | 937cc (57.2ci) |
| Bore | 73mm (2.9in) |
| Stroke | 56mm (2.2in) |
| Compression ratio | 11.3:1 |
| Valves | 4 per cylinder |
| Fuel system | 4 x Mikuni BDST36 carbs |
| Ignition | digital electronic |
| Cooling | liquid |
| Maximum power | 87.8kW (117.8bhp) @ 9800rpm |
| Maximum torque | 9.3kg-m (67.5lb-ft) @ 8300rpm |

## TRANSMISSION

| | |
|---|---|
| Primary drive | gear |
| Clutch | wet, multi-plate |
| Gearbox | 5-speed |
| Final drive | chain |

## WEIGHTS & CAPACITIES

| | |
|---|---|
| Tank capacity | 21l (5.5gal) |
| Dry weight | 203kg (446.6lb) |
| Weight distribution | |
| — front | N/A |
| — rear | N/A |
| Wheelbase | 1440mm (56.7in) |
| Overall length | 2130mm (83.9in) |
| Overall width | 730mm (28.7in) |
| Overall height | 1165mm (45.9in) |
| Seat height | 805mm (31.7in) |

## CYCLE PARTS

| | |
|---|---|
| Frame | perimeter beam |
| Rake/trail | 24.5°/102mm (4.02in) |
| Front suspension | telescopic forks |
| Travel | N/A |
| Adjustment | spring preload, plus rebound damping |
| Rear suspension | link monoshock |
| Travel | N/A |
| Adjustment | spring preload, plus rebound damping |
| Tyres | |
| — make | Dunlop |
| — front | 120/70 x 17 |
| — rear | 170/60 x 17 |
| Brakes | |
| — make | Nissin |
| — front | 2 x 320mm (12.6in) discs, opposed 4-piston calipers |
| — rear | single disc and caliper |

## TORQUE

## POWER

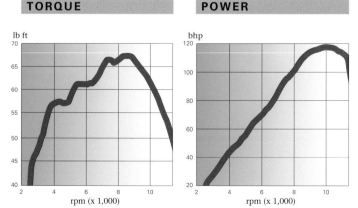

**Independent test measurements (above) differ from the manufacturer's claimed maximum power and maximum torque figures.**

# SUZUKI *TL1000R*

ELECTRONIC FUEL INJECTION

**Mirrors**
Styling is at odds with the rest of the bike, but at least they are placed wide enough to give a rearward view of more than your shoulders.

**Steering damper**
While the TL1000S had to be recalled to have a damper fitted to soften its lively front end, the TL1000R gets one as standard. Some owners have made the mistake of fitting another, aftermarket unit at the same time – a move that upsets the bike's low-speed handling.

**Headlamps**
Single, sculpted lens holds powerful twin headlamps which work well enough for swift night-time riding

**Engine**
A claimed 99.2kW (133bhp) makes this the most powerful V-twin Suzuki has ever built. Peak power from the 996cc (60.8ci), liquid-cooled, four-stroke, 90° configuration is delivered at 10,000 rpm. The bike also features the ubiquitous six-speed gearbox, together with fuel injection and a compression ratio of 11.7:1.

**Front suspension**
Suzuki has gone for inverted 43mm (1.7in) forks, which are fully compression and rebound damping-adjustable, and also feature 15mm (5.9in) of spring preload adjustment.

**Exhausts**
Twin exhausts exit one either side and feature quickly removed silencers, which are often junked in favour of noisier, better-looking and freer-breathing race end cans.

**Swingarm**
Aluminium swingarm features heavy under-bracing, which not only increases rigidity but looks ace too.

# TL1000R

*Every indication is that the TL1000R is proving to be a very popular machine indeed. And for those who think it is just an updated TL1000S, it is time they had a ride on one and discovered just how mistaken they are. This is a good all-rounder and most will be very happy with its performance. That said, there is nothing really special about this particular Suzuki.*

**Tyres**
The exact brand used can vary according to the country, but is always sticky. Standard sizes are 120/70 front and a massive 190/50 rear.

**Rear suspension**
Though the idea had a tough time from many journalists when it was introduced on the TL1000S, Suzuki has decided to push on with an unconventional rotary damper unit on the R. It is adjustable for rebound and compression damping and has a 6mm (0.2in) spring preload range.

*Just like the GSX13000R Hayabusa, the R gets an aerodynamic and removable seat hump that is visually over the top. No chance of you sliding off backwards pulling a monster wheelie, though.*

*Twin six-piston calipers have been drafted in to help slow the awesomely quick beast. Feel, feedback and outright power are all excellent. 320mm (12.6in) semi-floating drilled discs are used.*

*A new twin-spar aluminium frame supersedes the lattice offering on the R's stablemate, the TL1000S.*

**Fuel tank**
Perhaps looks bigger than its holding capacity suggests, but still manages to accommodate a useful 17l (4.5gal).

**Seat**
Seat is medium-high at 815mm (32.1in), although the seat's sheer width and the rear suspension's firm feel can make it seem taller. Comfort is good at all times.

**Airscoops**
Massive, front fairing-mounted scoops deliver a cool charge through the frame and into a voluminous airbox. The grunty induction roar is excellent.

**Rear brake**
A single two-piston, under-slung caliper and 220mm (8.7in) fixed, drilled disc.

**Ground clearance**
At just 130mm (5.1in) off the deck, the R's fairing bellypan gives it 10mm (3.9in) less clearance than the naked S.

**Wheelbase**
At 1405mm (55.3in), it is a full 10mm (3.9in) shorter than the TL1000S's.

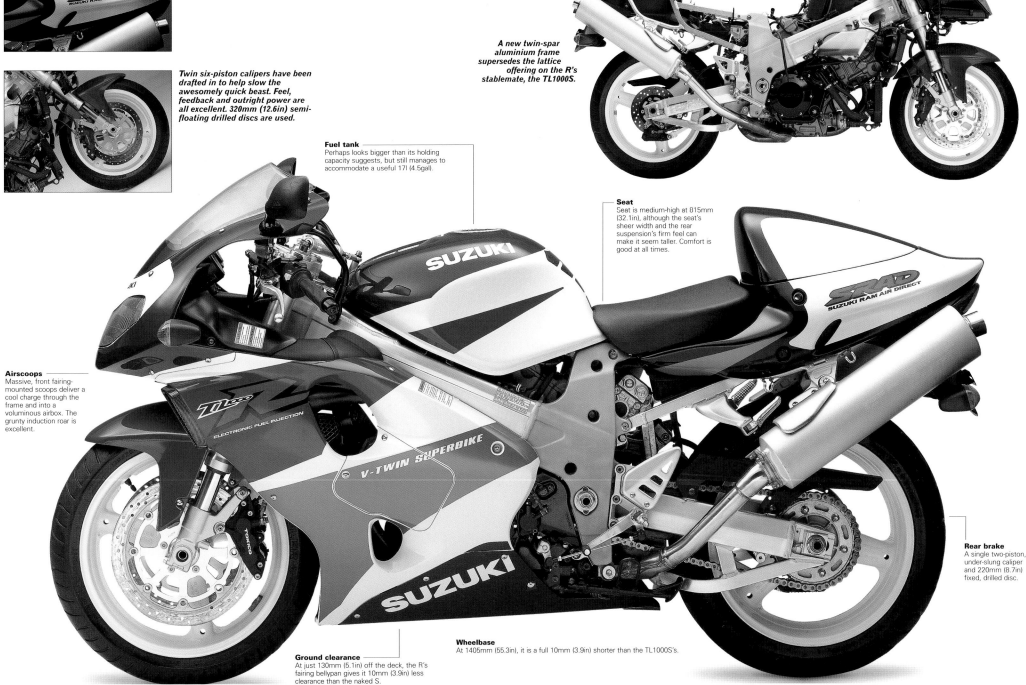

# Specifications

*This is a bike to* respect in every way. Suzuki is proud of its aerodynamics, which it describes as 'ground-breaking', allowing the bike and the rider to always feel the edge. Included in these are lift-reducing front fender, turbulence-reducing tail section, hot air exhaust ducts and silencers tucked up to reduce drag.
The colour schemes for 2000 were black (mean and fast), yellow (fast and stylish) and blue and white (GSX-R lookalike which is perhaps a bit overdone now). Well worth taking a ride on this one.

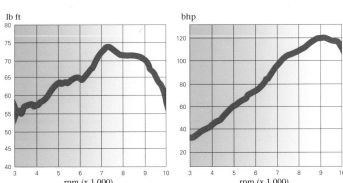

**Seat height:** 815mm (32.1in)

**Width:** 740mm (29.1in)

**Wheelbase:** 1406mm (55.3in)

## ENGINE

| | |
|---|---|
| Type | 4-stroke |
| Layout | 90° V-twin |
| Total displacement | 996cc (60.8ci) |
| Bore | 98mm (3.9in) |
| Stroke | 66mm (2.6in) |
| Compression ratio | 11.7:1 |
| Valves | 4 per cylinder |
| Fuel system | electronic fuel injection, individually mapped |
| Ignition | electronic |
| Cooling | liquid |
| Maximum power | 89.7kW (120.3bhp) @ 9200rpm |
| Maximum torque | 10.1kg-m (73.3lb-ft) @ 7250rpm |

## TORQUE

lb ft

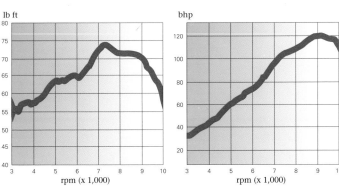

rpm (x 1,000)

## POWER

bhp

rpm (x 1,000)

**Independent test measurements (above) differ from the manufacturer's claimed maximum power and maximum torque figures.**

## TRANSMISSION

| | |
|---|---|
| Primary drive | gear |
| Clutch | wet, multiplate |
| Gearbox | 6-speed |
| Final drive | chain |

## WEIGHTS & CAPACITIES

| | |
|---|---|
| Tank capacity | 17l (4.5gal) |
| Dry weight | 197kg (434.3lb) |
| Weight distribution | |
| — front | N/A |
| — rear | N/A |
| Wheelbase | 1406mm (55.3in) |
| Overall length | 2100mm (82.7in) |
| Overall width | 740mm (29.1in) |
| Overall height | 1120mm (44.1in) |
| Seat height | 815mm (32.1in) |

## CYCLE PARTS

| | |
|---|---|
| Frame | aluminium alloy twin spar |
| Rake/trail | N/A |
| Front suspension | inverted telescopic forks |
| Travel | N/A |
| Adjustment | preload, rebound and compression damping |
| Rear suspension | rotary damper |
| Travel | N/A |
| Adjustment | preload, rebound and compression damping |
| Tyres | |
| — make | varies |
| — front | 120/70 x 17 |
| — rear | 190/50 x 17 |
| Brakes | |
| — make | Tokico |
| — front | twin 320mm (12.6in) discs. six-piston calipers |
| — rear | single 220mm (8.7in) disc, two-piston caliper |

# **SUZUKI** *TL1000S*

*The bodywork looks the business but quality and finish, like many Suzukis, is not of the highest standard.*

**Steering**
Early models were notoriously poor handlers, but Suzuki later reduced the problem by fitting a non-adjustable damper as standard.

**Fairing**
The half fairing is designed to show off the engine and frame, but offers good protection with little turbulence.

**Forks**
Inverted Kayaba front forks measure 43mm (1.7in) in diameter and feature internal cartridge dampers.

**Clutch**
It is extra compact and has special dogs, which help reduce rear wheel lock up on the overrun.

**Front brakes**
Four-piston Tokico calipers provide excellent power with good feedback.

**Wheels**
Alloy three spokes are hollow to save weight.

**Rear suspension**
The controversial rotary damper unit is sited just behind the engine – it is blamed by some for occasional wayward handling problems. The rear spring is sited separately on the right side of the engine. Each has its own linkage system.

## *TL1000S*

***Many things have been said** about the TL1000S, but 'boring' is not one of them. The bike has suffered from recalls and controversy about its 'wayward' handling but has overcome all criticisms and matured into a fine sports bike with a character and punch that some can only dream of. Not bad value, either.*

*Carbon fibre clock surround looks the part. Speedo features a black face whilst tachometer has a sporty looking white one.*

*Like the distinctive trellis frame, the swingarm is made from aluminium and is quite a costly and labour intensive affair.*

*The only aluminium trellis frame used on a production motorcycle. It was chosen for its unique style, but is still stiff enough to provide reasonably good handling.*

**Fuel tank**
It gives the TL1000S a range of 258km (160 miles) between fill-ups and the shape enables the rider to tuck in at high speed.

**Seat**
Perches the rider quite high on the bike, but comfort is good enough for long distance riding.

**Bodywork**
The small fairing gives the TL that distinctive streetfighter look. The V-twin legend is bound to make some take a second look.

**Engine**
The TL1000S's strongest feature, the fuel-injected, liquid-cooled 996cc (60.8ci) V-twin has plenty of torque matched to lots of top end power. The clever cam drive system mixes chains with gears to reduce the size of the cylinder heads.

**SUZUKI** *TL1000S*

# Specifications

*Suzuki's TL1000S has now* outgrown the 'bad boy' image it had just a couple of years ago, mainly due to its handling, which was described by some as 'uncontrollable' and others as 'exciting'. This could be put down to the (slightly odd) reason that early models came out without a steering damper, although Suzuki did send complete kits out to customers later.

Along with Suzuki's *GSF1200*, it is a favourite among stunt riders, who obviously have no fears about its handling. Basically, this is a good, reliable, powerful and fairly stylish machine, which many owners are only too pleased to stick with.

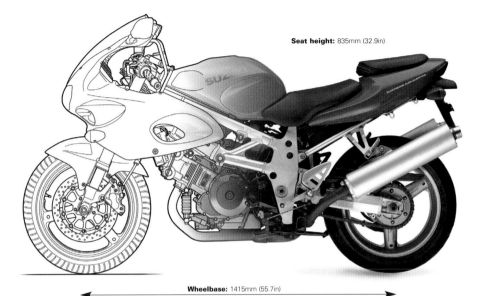

**Seat height:** 835mm (32.9in)

**Width:** 735mm (28.9in)

**Wheelbase:** 1415mm (55.7in)

## ENGINE

| | |
|---|---|
| Type | 4-stroke |
| Layout | 90° V-twin |
| Total displacement | 996cc (60.8ci) |
| Bore | 98mm (3.9in) |
| Stroke | 66mm (2.6in) |
| Compression ratio | 11.2:1 |
| Valves | 4 per cylinder |
| Fuel system | two-stage electronic injection |
| Ignition | digital transistorized |
| Cooling | liquid |
| Maximum power | 83.6kw (112.1bhp) @ 8950rpm |
| Maximum torque | 10.1kg-m (73.2lb-ft) @ 6750rpm |

## TRANSMISSION

| | |
|---|---|
| Primary drive | gear |
| Clutch | wet, multiplate |
| Gearbox | 6-speed |
| Final drive | chain |

## WEIGHTS & CAPACITIES

| | |
|---|---|
| Tank capacity | 17l |
| Dry weight | 191kg |
| Weight distribution | |
| — front | N/A |
| — rear | N/A |
| Wheelbase | 1415mm (55.7in) |
| Overall length | 2050mm (80.7in) |
| Overall width | 735mm (28.9in) |
| Overall height | 1150mm (42.3in) |
| Seat height | 835mm (32.9in) |

## CYCLE PARTS

| | |
|---|---|
| Frame | aluminium truss |
| Rake/trail | N/A |
| Front suspension | 43mm (1.7in) inverted telescopic |
| Travel | N/A |
| Adjustment | fully adjustable |
| Rear suspension | link-type |
| Travel | N/A |
| Adjustment | fully adjustable |
| Tyres | |
| — make | N/A |
| — front | 120/70 x 17 |
| — rear | 190/50 x 17 |
| Brakes | |
| — make | N/A |
| — front | dual discs |
| — rear | single disc |

## TORQUE

## POWER

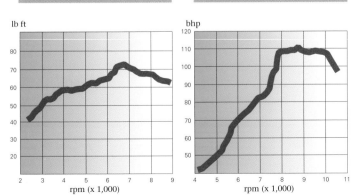

**Independent test measurements (above) differ from the manufacturer's claimed maximum power and maximum torque figures.**

# SUZUKI GSF1200 BANDIT

*Taken from Suzuki's GSX-R1100 and returned for extra mid-range torque, it makes a claimed 74.6kW (100bhp) in standard guise. Plenty of top end tuning work can be carried out to increase performance, although the bike's main restriction is in its exhaust. It is air and oil-cooled, has four valves per cylinder, a capacity of 1157cc (70.6ci) and a compression ratio of 9.5:1.*

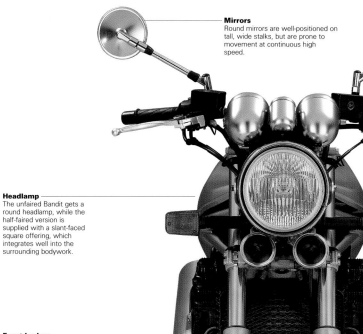

**Mirrors**
Round mirrors are well-positioned on tall, wide stalks, but are prone to movement at continuous high speed.

**Headlamp**
The unfaired Bandit gets a round headlamp, while the half-faired version is supplied with a slant-faced square offering, which integrates well into the surrounding bodywork.

**Front brakes**
Twin 310mm (12.2in) discs and four-piston calipers work as well as some dedicated sports bike components, offering good stopping power and feedback at the lever. There is, though, some fade under repeated hard application.

**Carburettors**
The four 36mm (1.4in) Mikunis are considered small today, but are a good size compared with the ones gracing many race replicas of the late 1980s and early 1990s – the era the engine was originally derived from. They are easily removed for maintenance and are often fitted with an aftermarket Dynojet kit and K&N air filters.

**Footpegs**
Rubber-covered footpegs absorb vibration well.

**Silencer**
One of the most commonly junked standard parts. Many GSF1200s sport aftermarket, illegal and noisy race cans.

**Front wheel**
The 43.2cm (17in) three-spoke hoop is immensely strong and manages to put up with repeated hard landings from 160km/h (100mph) by stunt riders such as British star Craig Jones.

## GSF1200 BANDIT

***The launch of the 1200 Bandit** in 1996 was the answer to many a punter's prayer. You can take almost anything you want from this bike – be totally mad on it or completely relaxed. Your choice. It will do almost anything you ask of it, is fun and is priced reasonably. Too good to be true? See what you think.*

**Retro-styled chrome clock surrounds house dull faces which display speed in 10mph (16km/h) increments to 170mph (274km/h), revs in 1000rpm increments to 12,000rpm and a conventional analogue fuel gauge.**

**The rake and trail are 25° and 107mm (4.2in).**

**Made of tubular steel and distinctly low-tech, it is surprisingly stiff for its size and helps the bike handle better than expected. It has a dry weight of 214kg (470.8lb) and is the lightest machine in its musclebike class.**

**Grab handles**
Both versions of the Bandit feature side-mounted pillion handles, which are arguably not as a good as a rear-mounted grab rail.

**Seat**
At a height of 835mm (32.9in), it is a fraction taller than most other bikes and is wide enough to make long distance work comfortable.

**Front suspension**
No-frills 43mm (1.7in) telescopic forks are adjustable for spring preload only, but are reasonably well-damped as standard.

**Wheelbase**
At 1435mm (56.5in), it is long enough to significantly aid stability, but still short enough to allow rewarding riding on twisty roads.

**Rear suspension**
Monoshock is adjustable for spring preload and rebound damping, and feels basic yet better than the bike's price would suggest.

# Specifications

*It has been around only* a few years, yet the Bandit 1200 has not only surprised Suzuki by its success but has proved a hit with bikers of all types.

*Labelled as a bit of a 'hooligan's machine' by those who bought it purely because of its ability to wheelie easily, it has also been taken up by those intent on touring and those who just wanted a cheap, everyday 'workhorse'.*

*The latter group were not disappointed but were probably more than a little surprised at its all-round performance. And it is great value for money too.*

**Width:** 790mm (31.1in)

**Seat height:** 835mm (32.9in)

**Trail:** 107mm (4.2in)

**Wheelbase:** 1435mm (56.5in)

## ENGINE

| | |
|---|---|
| Type | 4-stroke |
| Layout | inline four |
| Total displacement | 1157cc (70.6ci0 |
| Bore | 79mm (3.1in) |
| Stroke | 59mm (2.3in) |
| Compression ratio | N/A |
| Valves | 4 per cylinder |
| Fuel system | 4 x Mikuni BST36 carburettors |
| Ignition | CDI |
| Cooling | air/oil |
| Maximum power | 86.4kW (115.9bhp) @ 8997rpm |
| Maximum torque | 10.9kg-m (78.8lb-ft) @ 6105rpm |

## TRANSMISSION

| | |
|---|---|
| Primary drive | gear |
| Clutch | wet, multiplate |
| Gearbox | 5-speed |
| Final drive | chain |

## WEIGHTS & CAPACITIES

| | |
|---|---|
| Tank capacity | 19l (5gal) |
| Dry weight | 211kg (464.2lb) unfaired, 214kg (470.8lb) faired |
| Weight distribution | |
| — front | N/A |
| — rear | N/A |
| Wheelbase | 1435mm (56.5in) |
| Overall length | 2095mm (82.5in) |
| Overall width | 790mm (31.1in) |
| Overall height | 1100mm (43.3in) |
| Seat height | 835mm (32.9in) |

## CYCLE PARTS

| | |
|---|---|
| Frame | steel cradle |
| Rake/trail | 25˚, 36'/107mm (4.2in) |
| Front suspension | telescopic fork |
| Travel | N/A |
| Adjustment | preload |
| Rear suspension | link-type monoshock |
| Travel | N/A |
| Adjustment | 7-way preload, 4-way damping |
| Tyres | |
| — make | often Michelin, but varies |
| — front | 120/70 x ZR17 |
| — rear | 180/50 x ZR17 |
| Brakes | |
| — make | Nissin |
| — front | 2 x 310mm (12.2in) discs, opposed 4-piston calipers |
| — rear | 240mm (9.5in) disc, single caliper |

## TORQUE

## POWER

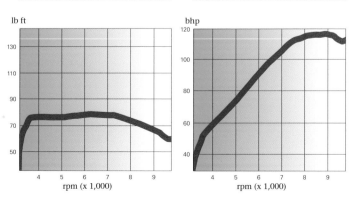

**Independent test measurements (above) differ from the manufacturer's claimed maximum power and maximum torque figures.**

# SUZUKI *GSX1300R HAYABUSA*

*Carbon-look dash contains almost everything you will need for your warp factor nine journey up the speedo and into the land of an indicated 194+km/h (210+mph).*

**Headlamp**
Looks odd, but works very well, allowing fast night riding, although not at the speeds the engine is capable of. Keeping it narrow also let Suzuki place the SRAD (Suzuki Ram-Air Direct) air-scoops into a central position inside the fairing, boosting airflow.

**Paint**
Colours are up for debate and finish is merely good rather than excellent. Minimal garish graphics can only be a good thing.

**Styling**
Ugly as sin, but not because Suzuki's designers were drunk in charge of a drawing board and computer screen. The reason is down to aerodynamic efficiency – it had to look like this to ensure low drag through the air!

**Mudguard**
Huge and droopy, it is shaped this way so that aerodynamics can again come into play, diverting the bulk of the airflow around the outer fairing bodywork.

## GSX1300R

***In 1999, the Hayabusa** hit the market as one of the fastest racers around. At the time, there were few other bikes to match it for speed, and it was tested close to 320km/h (200mph). It is not the most beautiful piece of machinery around, but then it is in a different world to most other bikes.*

**Tyres**
Specifically designed Bridgestone BT56 rubber grips strongly, but will break away if you seriously abuse the throttle. In short supply at the moment, so order in advance of needing them if you do not want to spend time looking at your Hayabusa in its garage.

**Exhausts**
Twin exhausts are remarkably sleek given the bike's power. The standard of finish is good, but they will not last for ever. Silencers can be unbolted in seconds to fit race end cans instead. Internal catalysts in the exhaust pipes help reduce emissions.

Six-piston Tokico calipers work amazingly well given the weight of the bike, helping the Hayabusa stop in just 98.3m (322.5ft) from a true 160km/h (100mph) – sports bike territory.

The seat hump is huge and ugly, but apparently needed to maximize aerodynamic efficiency, even though we still got exactly the same top speed with or without it.

The huge beam frame is part of the reason the Hayabusa will never be flickable but it is certainly stable when riding at the edge. Suzuki reckons that is around a sixth stiffer than GSX-R750 components too.

**Airbox**
Huge box works brilliantly, thanks to a computer-controlled 'flapper' valve that adjusts the rate of flow according to the engine revs and rate of acceleration.

**Seat**
Very comfortable and, at 80.5cm (31.7in), spot-on for most riders too. Trips of several hundred miles posed no problems.

**Pillion comforts:**
Removable grab-rail is just the job when passengers climb aboard, thanks to its perfect positioning. Although the footpegs look like they are placed high up, they actually encourage the passenger's body into a slight forward lean – of benefit on a bike with a 0160km/h (0-100mph) time of just 5.6 seconds.

**Engine**
Manages 400m (1312ft) in just over 10 seconds, propels the Hayabusa to 312km/h (194mph) in ideal conditions, and is so unstressed while doing it the components should last forever. Tuning work can liberate stacks more power, but why bother when the 1298cc (79.2ci) in-line four puts out a claimed 126+kW (170+bhp) as standard?

# Specifications

*We are all familiar with* the hype surrounding the *Hayabusa by now, but does it really have what it takes to live up to that hype?*
*Yes. You may not get the claimed 322km/h (200mph) on it (although you will by reading the indicator,) but you can see around 305km/h (190mph) – and surely that is enough.*
*This bike's lineage goes back to the GSX-R1100, and that was brutal enough. It has good brakes, behaves very well and is reasonably comfortable.*

**Seat height:** 805mm (31.7in)

**Width:** 740mm (29.1in)

**Trail:** 97mm (3.8in)

**Wheelbase:** 1485mm (58.5in)

## ENGINE

| | |
|---|---|
| **Type** | 4-stroke |
| **Layout** | in-line four |
| **Total displacement** | 1298cc (79.2ci) |
| **Bore** | 81mm (3.2in) |
| **Stroke** | 63mm (2.5in) |
| **Compression ratio** | 11.0:1 |
| **Valves** | 4 per cylinder |
| **Fuel system** | fuel injection, 46mm (1.8in) throttle bodies |
| **Ignition** | digital electronic |
| **Cooling** | liquid |
| **Maximum power** | 116.5kW (156.2bhp) @ 9300rpm |
| **Maximum torque** | 13.5kg-m (97.7lb-ft) @ 7600rpm |

## TORQUE

## POWER

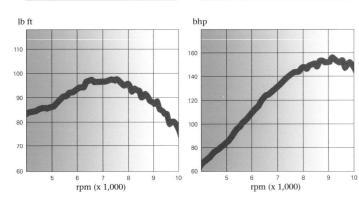

**Independent test measurements (above) differ from the manufacturer's claimed maximum power and maximum torque figures.**

## TRANSMISSION

| | |
|---|---|
| **Primary drive** | gear |
| **Clutch** | wet, multiplate |
| **Gearbox** | 6-speed |
| **Final drive** | chain |

## WEIGHTS & CAPACITIES

| | |
|---|---|
| **Tank capacity** | 22l (4.8 gall) |
| **Dry weight** | 215kg (473lb) |
| **Weight distribution** | |
| — front | N/A |
| — rear | N/A |
| **Wheelbase** | 1485mm (58.5in) |
| **Overall length** | 2140mm (84.3in) |
| **Overall width** | 740mm (29.1in) |
| **Overall height** | 1165mm (45.9in) |
| **Seat height** | 805mm (31.7in) |

## CYCLE PARTS

| | |
|---|---|
| **Frame** | aluminium twin-spar |
| **Rake/trail** | 24.2°/97mm (3.8in) |
| **Front suspension** forks | 43mm (1.7in) inverted telescopic |
| **Travel** | N/A |
| **Adjustment** | preload, plus compression and rebound damping |
| **Rear suspension** | monoshock |
| **Travel** | N/A |
| **Adjustment** | preload, plus compression and rebound damping |
| **Tyres** | |
| — make | Bridgestone |
| — front | 120/70 x 17 |
| — rear | 190/50 x 17 |
| **Brakes** | |
| — make | Tokico |
| — front | twin 320mm (12.6in) discs, opposed 6-piston calipers |
| — rear | 240mm (9.4in) disc, opposed 2-piston caliper |

# SUZUKI VL1500 INTRUDER

**Handlebars**
Splayed wide, but when raked back, they ensure a comfortable, upright riding position at low to moderate speeds.

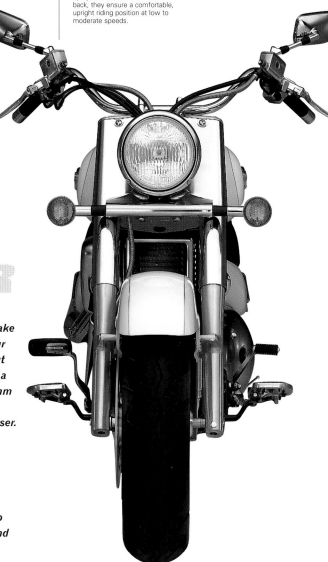

**IF size really does matter,** then make your way to yor nearest bike dealer to get your hands on this! Of course, it is not just size, but weight and everything that goes with it. With a dry weight of 292kg and a wheelbase of 1520mm (59.8in), the Suzuki could never be deemed either light or short. Not untypical of any cruiser. Looks the part, but the question is, Will it perform the way you expect a good cruiser to perform? The SOHC V-twin has been around only since 1998 so it does not draw on a long heritage, but it does draw on the many years' experience of Suzuki in the custom market, so we can expect it to do everything it should, and perhaps a little bit more.

**Fuel system**
Nothing surprising here – just a pair of comparatively small 36mm (1.4in) Mikuni carbs.

**Exhausts**
Twin, chromed exhausts exit on the bike's right hand side, further adding to the traditional and authentic American cruiser image.

**Wheels**
Huge, semi-solid rims look like they are from a car but match traditional cruiser design well. Tyre sizes are a huge 150/80 x 16 front and 180/70 x 15 rear.

When the throttle is opened, the clutch plates are squeezed harder together, so less surface area is needed and the clutch is more compact than an equivalent conventional one. On the overrun, the pressure is reduced and plates can slip to a limited extent, which helps prevent the rear wheel from locking up due to the considerable engine braking typical of a big capacity V-twin.

With a rake figure of an ultra-relaxed 32°, 138mm (5.4in) of trail and a whopping 1700mm (66.9in) wheelbase, the Intruder is as stable as anything we have ever tested over bumps, crests and rises, but changes direction extremely slowly through bends.

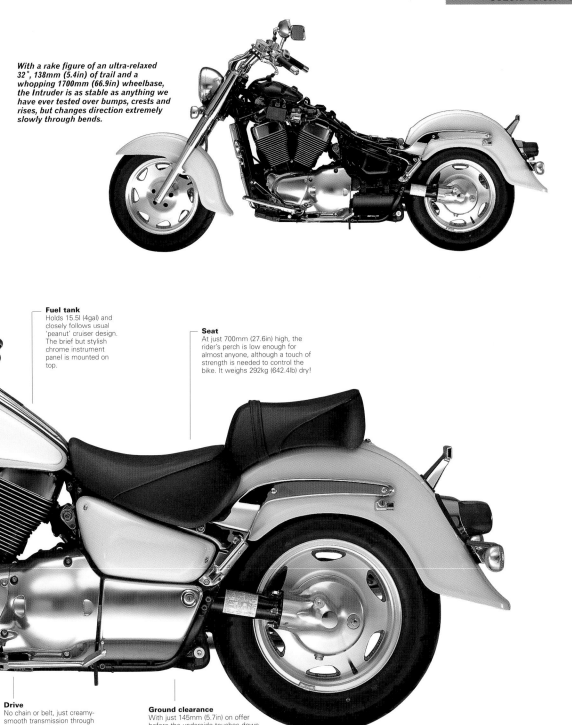

**Fuel tank**
Holds 15.5l (4gal) and closely follows usual 'peanut' cruiser design. The brief but stylish chrome instrument panel is mounted on top.

**Seat**
At just 700mm (27.6in) high, the rider's perch is low enough for almost anyone, although a touch of strength is needed to control the bike. It weighs 292kg (642.4lb) dry!

**Engine**
Massive 45° V-twin lump looks, at first glance, like something from the Harley stable, although the air-filter cover shape quickly gives the game away.

**Drive**
No chain or belt, just creamy-smooth transmission through a monster shaft drive to the back wheel. Maintenance is almost zero.

**Ground clearance**
With just 145mm (5.7in) on offer before the underside touches down, kerb-laden shortcuts to garages and parking spaces are not an option.

# SUZUKI VL1500 INTRUDER

# Specifications

**After their American visit**, the Intruder 1500LC design team came back with three key words for their concept: long, low and massive, which the enormous 1700mm (66.9in) wheelbase shows they took to heart (compare that with a Harley Fat Boy at 1590mm (62.6in), Kawasaki VN1500 Classic at 1665mm (65.6in) and even the giant V-four Yamaha Royal Star, pipped by the Intruder at 695mm (66.7in). The bike seems to extend almost as far in the other direction, with its arm-stretching 845mm (33.3in) wide handlebars.

In keeping with the 'massive' description, many components on the Intruder are made of pressed steel where they would normally be made of plastic – this is to increase the perception of quality, although in practice plastic is usually preferable.

The frame is a full double cradle design, similar to the VS1400's but with thicker tubing, which not only serves to enhance that massive look, but which also happens to be a considerable 70 per cent stiffer, thereby offering a substantial handling advantage.

Wheelbase: 1520mm (59.8in)

## ENGINE

| | |
|---|---|
| Type | 4-stroke |
| Layout | V-twin |
| Total displacement | 1462cc (89.2ci) |
| Stroke | 101mm (3.9in) |
| Fuel system | 2 x 36mm (1.4in) CV carbs |
| Ignition | computer controlled |
| Cooling | air |
| Maximum power | 49.9kW (67bhp) @ 2300rpm (claimed) |
| Maximum torque | 15.7kg-m (113.8lb-ft) @ 2300rpm (claimed) |

## WEIGHTS & CAPACITIES

| | |
|---|---|
| Tank capacity | 15l (4gal) |
| Dry weight | 299kg (659lb) |
| Weight distribution | |
| – front | N/A |
| – rear | N/A |
| Wheelbase | 1700mm (66.9in) |
| Overall length | 2525mm (99.4in) |
| Overall width | 965mm (38in) |
| Overall height | 1165mm (46in) |
| Seat height | 700mm (27.6in) |

## CYCLE PARTS

| | |
|---|---|
| Frame | double cradle |
| Front suspension | 41mm (1.6in) telescopic forks |
| Travel | 140mm (5.5in) |
| Wheels | 1520mm (59.8in) |
| – front | 40.6cm (16in) |
| – rear | 38.1cm (15in) |
| Tyres | |
| – make | varies |
| – front | 150/80 x 16 |
| – rear | 180/70 x 15 |
| Brakes | |
| – front | 320mm (12.6in) floating disc, opposed 2-piston caliper |
| – rear | 275mm (10.8in) disc |

## TRANSMISSION

| | |
|---|---|
| Primary drive | gear |
| Clutch | wet multiplate |
| Gearbox | 6-speed |
| Final drive | sealed O-ring chain |

# TRIUMPH TT600

**Display**
Instrumentation includes an array of measuring equipment, including an analogue tacho, digital speedo, warning lights, digital trip metres, odometer and temperature display, surrounded by a lightweight aluminium cockpit arrangement.

**Fairing**
The sculpted fairing features the forced air induction inlets slightly below the headlamp, one per side. This does not prevent the aerodynamics from having one of the lowest drag coefficients in its class. The overall effect is one of purposeful intent.

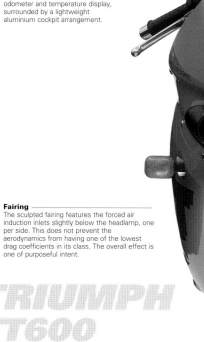

*Triumph's TT600 is a* superb piece of engineering that represents a bold move into the ultra-competitive 600cc (36.6ci) 4-cylinder sports bike arena. During the past two years, the Triumph has managed to take on the Japanese at their own and has won many friends and new admirers. This is a machine packed full of detailing and designed with the utmost care and attention.

**Front suspension**
The front end consists of Kayaba 43mm (1.7in) cartridge forks - specifically designed in conjunction with Triumph and features adjustable preload, compression and rebound damping. Twin 310mm (12.1in) floating discs with four-piston calipers supplies braking.

**Rear suspension**
The rear suspension is a monoshock with adjustable preload, compression and rebound damping. The brake is a single 220mm (8.7in) disc with a single piston caliper. The front and rear wheels are very light cast aluminium, helping to reduce unsprung weight.

**Frame**

The frame is nothing remarkable in itself, featuring a de rigeur lightweight perimeter beam frame of aluminium that weighs in at a highly commendable 12.6kg (27.8lb). The main frame uses the engine as an intergral stressed member.

**EMS**

The engine management system is sublime. A Sagem MC1000 electronic ems features automatic cold start compensation and has a self-diagnostic facility - this initially proved to be a bugbear, but now the glitches have been fixed. Highly sophisticated, highly effective.

**Engine**

The engine features very light alloy cylinders that have been Nikasil coated to improve heat transfer and facilitate enhanced durability. This treatment also helps to lower internal engine friction. The engine crankcases are high pressure die-cast for greater consistency of expansion and distortion levels.

# LEGEND

*Retro styling really looks the part and harks back to the great Bonnevilles of the 1960s. The Legend is offered in three different colour schemes from the factory: Imperial Green, Cardinal Red (shown) or Obsidan Black In each case as a solid colour or two-tone with silver inserts.*

**Handlebars**
The bars on the Legend are pulled subtly back so that even the shortest of arms can reach them, making it the ideal entry-level Triumph.

**Suspension**
At the rear is a rising rate monoshock rear suspension with preload-only adjustment, whilst at the front are 43mm (1.7in) telescopic front forks with triple rate springs.

**Exhaust system**
Chrome reverse megaphone silencers give the Legend's retro styling that vital touch of authenticity, with a bright chrome finish for added durability and good looks.

**Wheels**
The oh-so-retro traditional wire-spoked wheels on the Legend, again based on those of the Thunderbird, feature 43.2cm (17in) chromed rims and lower-than-normal profile tyres, which aids the bike's accessibility to shorter riders.

## LEGEND

**Introduced in 1998,** *the Legend is mechanically identical to the Thunderbird, which means you get entry-level Hinckley progeny in a gentle rider-friendly state of tune. With the rev-happy, yet torquey 885cc (53.9ci) triple engine combined with a lowered rear subframe and narrow seat, buying a Legend is the ideal first stab at owning a classically styled Triumph.*

*The simple-looking clocks feature chrome bezels, which are far more accurate and easier to read at night than those on the old Triumphs.*

*Here we have the same setup as on many other Triumphs, with a single big Nissin disc at the front and a smaller one at the rear. Both are more than up to coping with what is still rather a heavy bike.*

*The Legend features a lightweight, powder-coated steel spine frame, which uses the engine as a structural member, and an anodized oval section aluminium alloy swingarm.*

**Tank**
Sumptuously styled, curvaceous teardrop fuel tank is another of the Legend's features that have been borrowed from its older brother, the Thunderbird. With a 15l (3.9gal) capacity, expect to get between 46 and 58 mpg.

**Seat height**
The Legend is a favourite among vertically challenged classic motorcycle fans, thanks to its low 72.4cm (28.5in) seat height and narrow profile which makes it easy to manoeuvre at low speeds.

**Engine**
Borrowed from Triumph's own Thunderbird, the liquid-cooled 885cc (54ci) three-cylinder engine is tuned for the same powerful torque and crisp throttle response which made it a hit in other models. The satin black powder coating adds a tasteful edge to the bike's classic styling.

# Specifications

*Launched in 1998, with* retro 1960s looks derived from the successful Triumph Thunderbird, the Legend is an attempt to match classic styling with real-world practicality and performance, at a premium price. The eye-catching retro styling incorporated a curvaceous 15l (3.9gal) tear drop fuel tank, wire spoked wheels and classic reverse cone silencers. Power comes from Triumph distinctive **DOHC** triple, tuned for abundant low rev torque for effortless acceleration.

**Height:** 1340mm (52.8in)

**Seat height:** 675mm (26.6in)

**Length:** 2320mm (91.3in)

## ENGINE

| | |
|---|---|
| Type | 4- stroke |
| Layout | DOHC in line 3 |
| Total displacement | 885cc (54ci) |
| Bore | 76mm (2.9in) |
| Stroke | 65mm (2.6in) |
| Compression ratio | 10:1 |
| Fuel system | 3 x 36mm (1.4in) flat slide CV |
| Ignition | Digital-inductive type |
| Cooling | liquid |
| Maximum power | 51.5kW (69bhp) @ 8000rpm |
| Maximum torque | 7.3kg-m (53lb-ft) @ 4800rpm |

## TRANSMISSION

| | |
|---|---|
| Primary drive | gear |
| Clutch | wet multiplate |
| Gearbox | 5-speed |
| Final drive | chain |

## WEIGHTS & CAPACITIES

| | |
|---|---|
| Tank capacity | 15l (3.9gal) |
| Dry weight | 215kg (474lb) |
| Weight distribution | |
| — front | not available |
| — rear | not available |
| Wheelbase | 1580mm (62.2in) |
| Overall length | 2320mm (91.3in) |
| Overall width | 870mm (34.3in) |
| Overall height | 1340mm (52.8in) |
| Seat height | 675mm (26.6in) |

## CYCLE PARTS

| | |
|---|---|
| Frame | high tensile tubular steel |
| Rake/trail | 27 /106mm (4.2in) |
| Front suspension | 43mm (1.7in) telescopic |
| Travel | 106mm (4.2in) |
| Adjustment | none |
| Rear suspension | rising rate monoshock |
| Travel | 110mm (4.3in) |
| Adjustment | spring preload |
| Tyres | |
| — make | N/A |
| — front | 120/70 x 17 |
| — rear | 160/60 x 17 |
| Brakes | |
| — make | Nissin |
| — front | 320mm (12.6in) discs, 2-piston caliper |
| — rear | 285mm (11.2in) , 2-piston caliper |

# TRIUMPH
# THUNDERBIRD SPORT

As befits a styled-up 1960s refugee, the classic Triumph logo sits proud on each side of the tank. No cheap transfers or dodgy paint here.

**Clocks**
More fashion than function – they look like a bit of an afterthought. The dials are simple to read, but there is little more on offer apart from that. The 'idiot' lights are hard to see clearly too.

**Fuel tank**
15l (3.9gal), and no more.

**Steering**
Here is one area which definitely deserves the 'Sport' tag. The rake and trail dimensions offer excellent stability, but they also allow the bike to turn as fast as any modern day plastic torpedo. Very little effort is needed to get the bike on its side, and the first time you ride it , this can catch you out – yes, it is that fast.

**Pillion position**
The only person you would want to take on the back is someone you hate, not love! The seat is too small for the average-sized pair of buttocks, there is nothing in easy reach to hold on to and the footpegs are way too high..

**Rear suspension**
The back is much the same as the front – a little too soft. Fine for riding that suits the bike, but just remember the Sport tag does not make it a racer.

**Exhaust**
No doubt cool looking and in keeping with the sport's retro image, but also prone to rotting if not carefully looked after.

# THUNDERBIRD
# SPORT

*The Thunderbird Sport is a* fine attempt by *Triumph at creating a retro-style bike. The looks ape its 1970s predecessors and the three-cylinder engine follows the layout of earlier machines. The Sport tag is justified by its exciting handling, but the brakes, sadly, fail to live up to the billing. Pillion comfort is also below par. However, retro bikes are about image, and in this respect the Thunderbird Sport excels.*

*The front brake's stopping performance is not bad, although some owners complain that feel at the lever is below par. The twin 310mm (12.2in) discs are met by two-piston Triumph calipers.*

*The forks do a good job if the bike is ridden within the spirit of the machine, although hard braking uses up all the travel in a second, leaving the front end feeling wooden and vague.*

*The frame is best described as basic but functional. It is neither the latest nor the best design, but it does do the job well and the basic geometry helps the bike handle well.*

**Wheels**
Wire wheels are very nice, but a single bad winter will leave them looking the worse for wear. The rims should hold up quite well, but the spokes tend to be the first things to go – both in terms of finish and tension. Modern and sensible 43.2cm (17in) rims allow a wide range of 120/70 front and 160/60 rear aftermarket rubber to be used.

**Engine**
Staying true to Triumph's modular concept, the Thunderbird Sport has the famous three-cylinder engine sitting between the frame rails. Designed with more of a sports focus compared to the standard Thunderbird, it is lively, offers decent acceleration and more than adequate top speed.

**Rear brake**
Triumph may have taken the retro styling a little too far by offering a setup which feels similar to a 1960s BSA. The 285mm (11.2in) disc is bitten by another two-piston Triumph-made caliper.

# THUNDERBIRD SPORT

# Specifications

*With Triumph, you can* always rely on getting a test ride from your local dealer, so put aside any preconceptions you may have about the T'Bird Sport and go!
*You will find that this is most definitely a sports bike, with plenty of torque, excellent handling and stability, and pretty good brakes. The acceleration is good and the grunty midrange allows plenty of fun to be had with other bikes off the motorway. But do not even bother to compare it to the Thunderbird (as some have mistakenly done) because it is had too many changes and is a far more aggressive bike.*

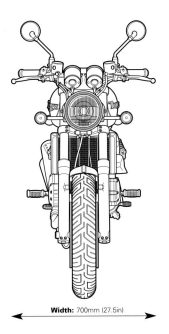
**Width:** 700mm (27.5in)

**Seat height:** 790mm (31.1in)
**Wheelbase:** 1580mm (62.2in)

## ENGINE

| | |
|---|---|
| Type | 4-stroke |
| Layout | in-line three cylinder |
| Total displacement | 885cc (54ci) |
| Bore | 76mm (2.9in) |
| Stroke | 65mm (2.6in) |
| Compression ratio | 10:1 |
| Valves | 4 per cylinder |
| Fuel system | 3 x 36mm (1.4in) flat side CV carbs |
| Ignition | digital, inductive type |
| Cooling | liquid |
| Maximum power | 56.2kW (75.3bhp) @ 8275rpm |
| Maximum torque | 7.7kg-m (55.8lb-ft) @ 6450rpm |

## TORQUE

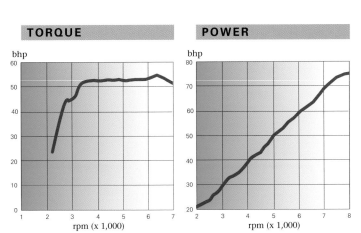

## POWER

## TRANSMISSION

| | |
|---|---|
| Primary drive | gear |
| Clutch | wet, multi-plate |
| Gearbox | 6-speed |
| Final drive | chain |

## WEIGHTS & CAPACITIES

| | |
|---|---|
| Tank capacity | 15l (3.9gal) |
| Dry weight | 224kg (628lb) |
| Weight distribution | |
| — front | N/A |
| — rear | N/A |
| Wheelbase | 1580mm (62.2in) |
| Overall length | 2250mm (88.6in) |
| Overall width | 700mm (27.5in) |
| Overall height | 1105mm (43.5in) |
| Seat height | 790mm (31.1in) |

## CYCLE PARTS

| | |
|---|---|
| Frame | Micro alloyed high tensile steel |
| Rake/trail | N/A |
| Front suspension | 43mm (1.7in) telescopic forks |
| Travel | N/A |
| Adjustment | compression, rebound damping and spring preload |
| Rear suspension | monoshock |
| Travel | N/A |
| Adjustment | compression, rebound damping and spring preload |
| Tyres | |
| — make | Avon & others |
| — front | 120/70 x R17 |
| — rear | 160/70 x R17 |
| Brakes | |
| — make | Triumph |
| — front | 310mm (12.1in) dual discs |
| — rear | 285mm (11.2in) disc |

**Independent test measurements (above) differ from the manufacturer's claimed maximum power and maximum torque figures.**

# TRIUMPH
## TIGER 900

**Protection**
Plastic hand guards and metal sump guard offer some hope that the Tiger can be used off road. It can, up to a point.

**Engine**
The 1999 unit was a retuned version of the one powering the outgoing T509 Speed Triple and makes 1.5kw (2bhp) and 0.27kg-m (2lb-ft) of torque more than the old Tiger, according to Triumph. It has an 885cc (54ci) capacity, liquid cooling, three cylinders, double overhead cams and 12 valves (bucket and shim adjustment).

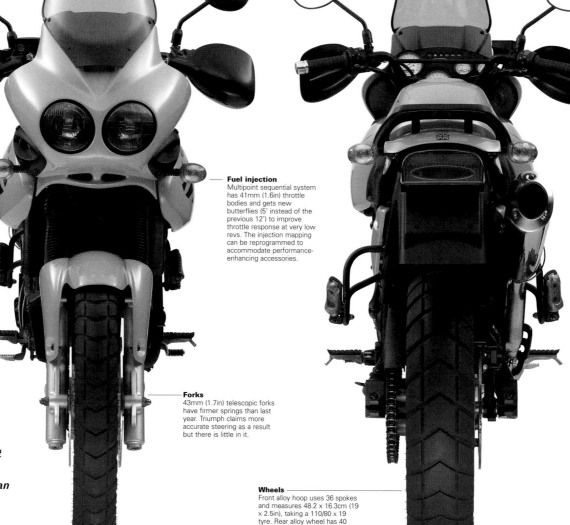

**Fuel injection**
Multipoint sequential system has 41mm (1.6in) throttle bodies and gets new butterflies (5° instead of the previous 12°) to improve throttle response at very low revs. The injection mapping can be reprogrammed to accommodate performance-enhancing accessories.

**Forks**
43mm (1.7in) telescopic forks have firmer springs than last year. Triumph claims more accurate steering as a result but there is little in it.

**Wheels**
Front alloy hoop uses 36 spokes and measures 48.2 x 16.3cm (19 x 2.5in), taking a 110/80 x 19 tyre. Rear alloy wheel has 40 spokes, measures 43.2 x 10.8cm (17 x 4.25in) and takes a 150/80 x 17 tyre.

**Exhaust**
Headers are made of stainless steel, which should ensure longevity. A closed-loop catalytic convertor is fitted where the bike is sold in some emissions-tough markets.

## TIGER 900

*Triumph's Tiger may not meet the standards of others in its class in the off-road or comfort stakes, but it beats them in others. Great acceleration and braking make this a bike to seriously consider if you appreciate a bike that can be ridden hard on twisty, uneven roads. Be adventurous – try one on for size.*

*Cam, clutch, water pump and outlet covers are all made from magnesium to reduce weight. The sprocket cover is made of a light plastic polymer, and the clutch is cable-operated for more of the same (plus, it is cheaper to make).*

*Twin headlamp unit is frame-mounted to ensure better stability at speed than handlebar-fixed alternatives. Night vision is good.*

*New tubular steel perimeter frame uses the engine as a stressed component, is lighter than previous offerings, and offers scope for seat height adjustment. The engine's position is lower than before, bringing the centre of gravity nearer ground level. Low speed balance is noticeably improved as a result.*

**Fuel tank**
Lightweight plastic and holds a whopping 24l (6.3gal), but is mounted high, so full loads can be clearly felt when cornering.

**Seat**
Tall but slightly adjustable, allowing settings of between 840mm (33.1in) and 860mm (33.9in). Shorties will struggle.

**Front brakes**
Twin new-design calipers meet 310mm (12.2in) discs. Last year's bike had 276mm (10.9in) items. Brake lines are braided steel as standard.

**Rear suspension**
Rising-rate monoshock features preload as well as rebound damping and copes well on any road surfaces, soaking up bumps remarkably competently, even two-up.

# TRIUMPH

## TIGER 900

# Specifications

**Triumph gave the Tiger** *a major reworking in 1999 and the result is a seriously improved bike. Among the changes were a new engine (the 855cc/52.2ci motor from the departing Speed Triple, now with sequential multi-point fuel injection) and a new tubular steel chassis incorporating the engine as a stressed member, which results in greater stiffness, a lower centre of gravity and consequently better handling. The brakes have been uprated too, with bigger discs (310mm/12.1in versus 276mm/10.9in on the 1998 model). As big dual purpose bikes go, the new Tiger is one of the best.*

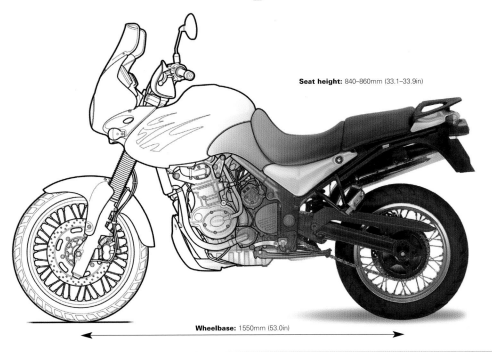

**Seat height:** 840–860mm (33.1–33.9in)

**Width:** 860mm (33.9in)

**Wheelbase:** 1550mm (53.0in)

## ENGINE

| | |
|---|---|
| **Type** | 4-stroke |
| **Layout** | in-line triple |
| **Total displacement** | 855cc (52.2ci) |
| **Bore** | 76mm (2.9in) |
| **Stroke** | 65mm (2.6in) |
| **Compression ratio** | 11.2:1 |
| **Valves** | 4 per cylinder |
| **Fuel system** | fuel injection |
| **Ignition** | digital electronic |
| **Cooling** | liquid |
| **Maximum power** | 58.6kW (78.6bhp) @ 8200rpm |
| **Maximum torque** | 7.7kg-m (55.8lb-ft) @ 6600rpm |

## TRANSMISSION

| | |
|---|---|
| **Primary drive** | gear |
| **Clutch** | wet, multi-plate |
| **Gearbox** | 6-speed |
| **Final drive** | chain |

## CYCLE PARTS

| | |
|---|---|
| **Frame** | tubular steel perimeter |
| **Rake/trail** | N/A |
| **Front suspension** | 43mm (1.7in) telescopic forks |
| **Travel** | N/A |
| **Adjustment** | none |
| **Rear suspension** | rising rate monoshock |
| **Travel** | N/A |
| **Adjustment** | spring preload, plus rebound damping |
| **Tyres** | |
| — make | varies |
| — front | 110/80 x 19 |
| — rear | 150/80 x 17 |
| **Brakes** | |
| — make | Triumph |
| — front | 2 x 310mm (12.2in) discs, 2-piston calipers |
| — rear | 285mm (11.2in) disc, 2-piston caliper |

## TORQUE

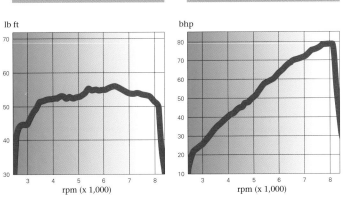

lb ft

rpm (x 1,000)

## POWER

bhp

rpm (x 1,000)

## WEIGHTS & CAPACITIES

| | |
|---|---|
| **Tank capacity** | 24l (6.3 gal) |
| **Dry weight** | 215kg (473lb) |
| **Weight distribution** | |
| — front | N/A |
| — rear | N/A |
| **Wheelbase** | 1550mm (61in) |
| **Overall length** | 2175mm (85.6in) |
| **Overall width** | 860mm (33.9in) |
| **Overall height** | 1345mm (53in) |
| **Seat height** | 840–860mm (33.1–33.9in) |

**Independent test measurements (above) differ from the manufacturer's claimed maximum power and maximum torque figures.**

# TROPHY 900

TROPHY
900

### Triumph's Trophy 900 was

*launched way back in the spring of 1991 and is still around today – and doing very nicely, thank you – having undergone several changes in almost a decade. The most notable was in 1995, when the bodywork was restyled. But there were technical changes also, and it was this model which really brought the Trophy to the prospective bike buyer's attention. The quality of the paintwork alone is worthy of mention and it is good to see Triumph paying such attention to detail. The bike, however, will really only appeal to those interested in a tourer, for that is clearly what it is. In 1995, for the first time, Triumph designed the bodywork of the Trophy 900 so that it has an integrated luggage system. Everything about the 900 is slick and designed for ease of use. The six-speed gearbox is smooth, the handling good and sharp, albeit slightly heavy, the riding position could hardly be bettered and the clocks are easy to read. Even the headlamps are excellent.*

**Handlebars**
Nicely placed, the one-piece bars are higher and pulled back more than on earlier models.

**Screen**
Although Triumph offers a taller screen, this is unnecessary, as the standard one protects tal rdiers from windblast and unnecessary noise.

**Suspension**
At the rear, the suspension is fully adjustable and is of a rising rate monoshock design. It does the trick, and you can get off the bike after a couple of hours riding feeling no pain at all.

**Clocks**
The Trophy 900 is equipped with a four-clock console and warning lights which are all easy to read.

*Triumph is now justifiably proud of its well-proven tubular steel spine frame, which sports an aluminium swingarm.*

**Seat**
At 790mm (31.1in), it is lower than you might expect, but every bit as comfortable as it looks. It is more sculpted than the earlier editions and with more effective padding.

**Luggage**
Now fully integrated into the bodywork. Looks okay, fits well and is, of course, colour-coded.

**Engine**
The 885cc (54ci) liquid-cooled, in-line three cylinder engine is smooth, strong and reliable. It has a bore and stroke of 76 x 65mm (2.9 x 2.6in) and a compression ratio of 10.6:1.

# TRIUMPH DAYTONA 955i

*The exhaust got a practical rather than style update for 1999 in the form of re-routed header pipes to improve ground clearance.*

**Injection mapping system**
Reprogrammable to ensure optimum performance when aftermarket Triumph accessories are fitted.

**Engine and peripherals**
The next generation from the part-Lotus-designed T595 motor sees the introduction of a modified exhaust camshaft to boost mid-range power, revised 41mm (1.6in) throttle bodies (5° instead of 12° butterflies improve low rpm running), a new stepper motor in the air bypass system (better tickover) and a remapped engine management system (to blend these other alterations and improve fuel consumption). The familiar 12-valve, liquid-cooled, DOHC 955cc (58.3ci) triple-cylinder design remains.

**Clutch**
Wet, multiplate assembly takes quite serious abuse. Adjustment is cable rather than hydraulic in an apparent bid to further reduce weight.

**Rear shock**
The Showa monoshock unit has a firmer spring (up from 13kg/mm to 14kg/mm) than the T595's, and revised compression and rebound damping characteristics too. In theory, this makes high speed riding more precise and increases feedback to the rider.

**Forks**
Inverted 45mm (1.8in) Showa forks use dual-rate springs to improve handling and are adjustable for preload as well as compression and rebound damping.

**Rear brake**
220mm (8.7in) fixed disc, two-piston caliper.

*DAYTONA 955i*

**The Daytona 955i** *was the follow-up to the T595, Triumph's first attempt at a cutting-edge sports bike. The individuality of the three-cylinder motor has been maintained, but major developments were made to improve the ground clearance, mid-range power and suspension, making the 955i more than capable of going up against the best the world has to offer.*

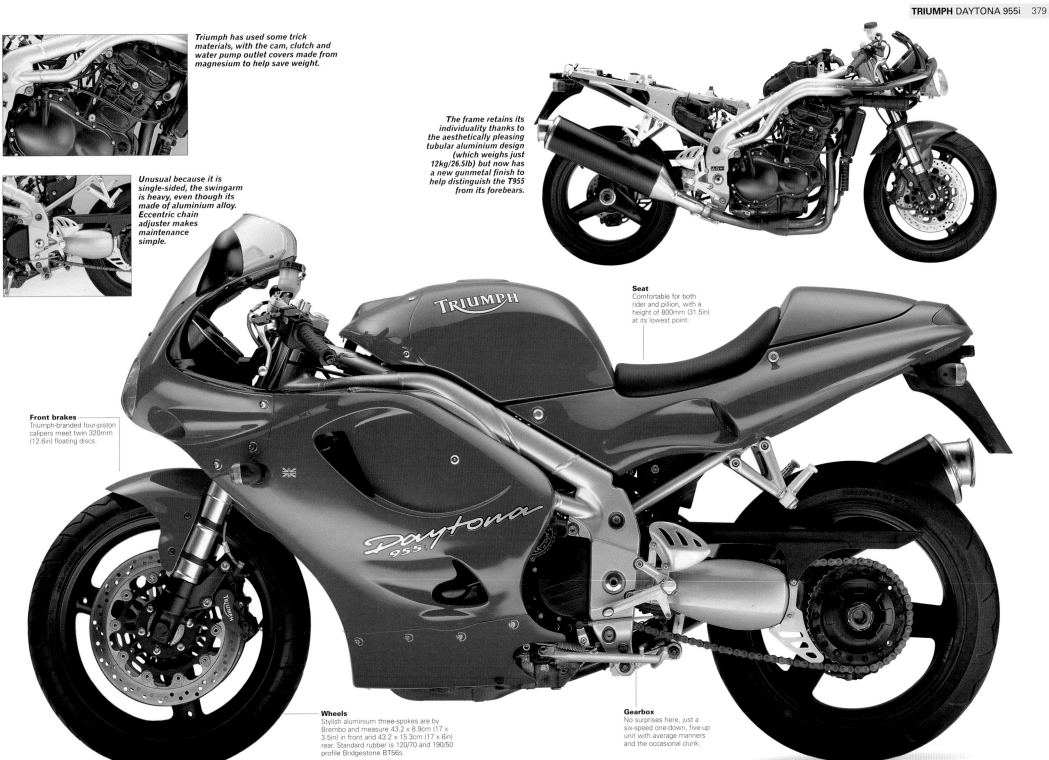

Triumph has used some trick materials, with the cam, clutch and water pump outlet covers made from magnesium to help save weight.

Unusual because it is single-sided, the swingarm is heavy, even though its made of aluminium alloy. Eccentric chain adjuster makes maintenance simple.

The frame retains its individuality thanks to the aesthetically pleasing tubular aluminium design (which weighs just 12kg/26.5lb) but now has a new gunmetal finish to help distinguish the T955 from its forebears.

**Seat**
Comfortable for both rider and pillion, with a height of 800mm (31.5in) at its lowest point.

**Front brakes**
Triumph-branded four-piston calipers meet twin 320mm (12.6in) floating discs.

**Wheels**
Stylish aluminium three-spokes are by Brembo and measure 43.2 x 8.9cm (17 x 3.5in) in front and 43.2 x 15.3cm (17 x 6in) rear. Standard rubber is 120/70 and 190/50 profile Bridgestone BT56s.

**Gearbox**
No surprises here, just a six-speed one-down, five-up unit with average manners and the occasional clunk.

# DAYTONA 955i

# Specifications

**The Daytona is basically** a renamed T595 with a few modifications; modifications which, however, have improved it noticeably.

It looks much the same, but a lot of attention has been paid to the engine such as slightly modifying the exhaust camshaft, revising the throttle bodies, adding a new airbox, new header pipes and updated electrics.

But apart from the resulting refinement in power delivery, the bike is more or less the same machine as the earlier T595.

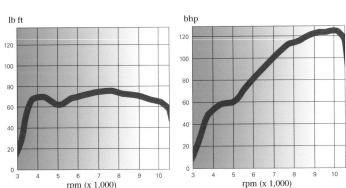

**Seat height:** 800mm (31.5in)

**Width:** 720mm (28.3in)

**Trail:** 86mm (3.4in)

**Wheelbase:** 1440mm (56.7in)

## ENGINE

| | |
|---|---|
| Type | 4-stroke |
| Layout | in-line triple |
| Total displacement | 955cc (58.3ci) |
| Bore | 79mm (3.1in) |
| Stroke | 65mm (2.6in) |
| Compression ratio | 11.2:1 |
| Valves | 4 per cylinder |
| Fuel system | 41mm (1.6in) throttle bodies, multipoint sequential EFI |
| Ignition | digital electronic |
| Cooling | liquid |
| Maximum power | 93.4kW (125.2bhp) @ 10,095rpm |
| Maximum torque | 10.4kg-m (75lb-ft) @ 7550rpm |

## TORQUE

lb ft

rpm (x 1,000)

## POWER

bhp

rpm (x 1,000)

**Independent test measurements (above) differ from the manufacturer's claimed maximum power and maximum torque figures.**

## TRANSMISSION

| | |
|---|---|
| Primary drive | gear |
| Clutch | wet, multiplate |
| Gearbox | 6-speed |
| Final drive | chain |

## WEIGHTS & CAPACITIES

| | |
|---|---|
| Tank capacity | 18l (4.8gal) |
| Dry weight | 198kg (435.6lb) |
| Weight distribution | |
| — front | N/A |
| — rear | N/A |
| Wheelbase | 1440mm (56.7in) |
| Overall length | 2115mm (83.3in) |
| Overall width | 720mm (28.3in) |
| Overall height | 1170mm (46.1in) |
| Seat height | 800mm (31.5in) |

## CYCLE PARTS

| | |
|---|---|
| Frame | aluminium tubular perimeter |
| Rake/trail | 24°/86mm (3.4in) |
| Front suspension | inverted 45mm (1.8in) Showa telescopic forks |
| Travel | N/A |
| Adjustment | spring preload, plus compression and rebound damping |
| Rear suspension | Showa rising-rate monoshock |
| Travel | N/A |
| Adjustment | spring preload, plus compression and rebound damping |
| Tyres | |
| — make | Bridgestone BT56 |
| — front | 120/70 x 17 |
| — rear | 190/50 x 17 |
| Brakes | |
| — make | Triumph |
| — front | 2 x 320mm (12.6in) floating discs, opposed 4-piston calipers |
| — rear | 220mm (8.7in) disc, 2-piston caliper |

# TRIUMPH SPEED TRIPLE

*The 45mm (1.8in) inverted Showa forks feature dual rate springs and full preload as well as compression and rebound damping adjustment – just like the 955 Daytona.*

**Tank**
Carries 18l (4.8gal).

**Clutch**
Simple cable-operated mechanism, which might require more maintenance over time, but helps to reduce weight.

**Engine**
The 1999 model year saw the proven 885cc (54ci) lump abandoned in favour of a unit derived from the successful 955 Daytona. Peak output increased by around 1.5kW (2bhp) as a result, but with it came a stronger, broader spread of torque. Now the in-line triple engine has a 955cc (58.3ci) capacity, 79 x 65mm (3.1 x 2.6in) bore and stroke, 11.2:1 compression ratio, liquid-cooling and electronic fuel injection aided by 41mm (1.6in) throttle bodies.

**Rear suspension**
Again the same components used in the 955 Daytona, courtesy of a rising rate Showa monoshock assembly that has adjustments for preload, compression and rebound damping.

## SPEED TRIPLE

***Triumph fans everywhere** are bound to be surprised by the look of this beauty. Or should we say beast? Its mean, streetfighting, 'Don't mess with me' look is not the old Triumph style. And that is a good thing for the Speed Triple. Its powerful performance does not belie its looks either – this is one Triumph everyone is going to want to try.*

**Brakes**
More components which share their lineage with the 955 Daytona. The Triumph-branded four-piston calipers bite on twin 320mm (12.6in) floating discs, while the rear gets a single 220mm (8.7in) disc and two-piston caliper.

**Wheels**
Brembo three-spokes not only look the business but are claimed to be lightweight too, helping the bike to turn more easily into corners. Bridgestone BT56s are the rubber of choice and come in 120/70 x 17 and 190/50 x 17 front and rear sizes.

The new engine demanded changes to help it breathe better. These include throttle bodies with 5° as opposed to the old model's 12° butterflies, a new stepper motor in the air bypass system, new exhaust header pipes and a redesigned airbox.

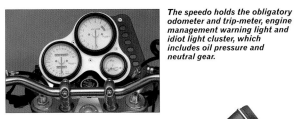

The speedo holds the obligatory odometer and trip-meter, engine management warning light and idiot light cluster, which includes oil pressure and neutral gear.

A handful of weak frames in the model's early days prompted factory action and a design overhaul. All new models are now equipped with a sturdier example of the bike's traditional aluminium alloy tubular perimeter chassis. A new gunmetal finish boosts looks.

**Seat height**
At 800mm (31.5in), the Speed Triple's perch is the same height as the 955 Daytona's.

**Options**
Triumph offers a stylish carbon fibre mudguard as an optional extra. Other aftermarket parts include a solo seat cowl, colour-co-ordinated flyscreens, low bar conversion, rear hugger, tankbag, mudguard extension kits, a fork protector kit and a cast aluminium grab-rail.

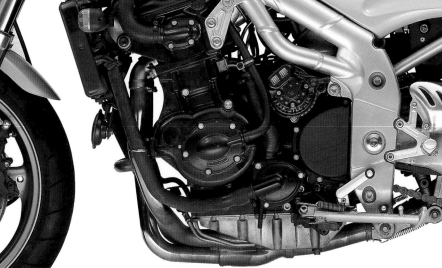

**Engine changes**
Though based on the 955's unit, actual differences occur in the cylinder liners, which are steel instead of coated ceramic; pistons matched to the liners; camshafts bearing revised lift and timing for a midrange power boost; remapped electronic fuel ignition to suit the new characteristics; and a larger capacity but slimmer radiator.

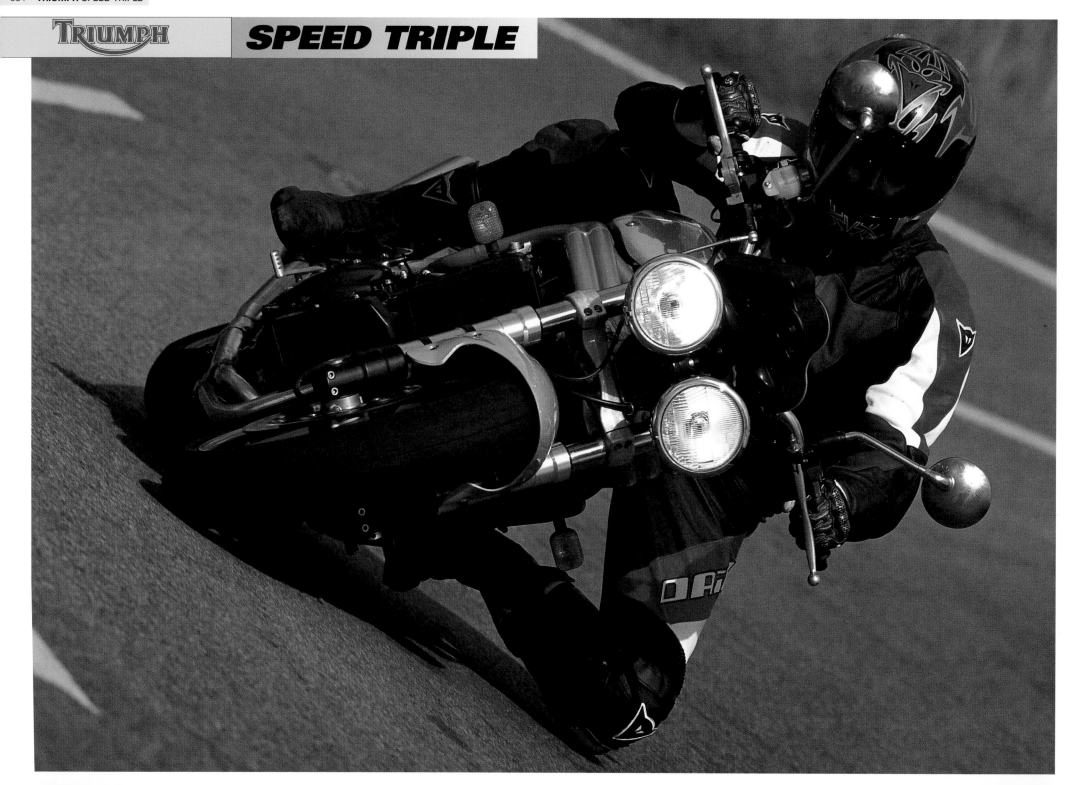

# Specifications

**Once known as the** T509, now simply called the Speed Triple, this stunning Triumph gained an extra 70cc (4.3ci), 1.5kW (2bhp) and a broader spread of torque in 1999. It remains a sought-after alternative to other roadsters due to its uncompromisingly brutal looks and surprisingly nimble handling. In fact, the whole package gels. The engine has ample power and the combination of four-piston caliper front discs and the 220mm (8.7in) rear disc, two caliper set-up offers tremendous stopping power with plenty of feedback to the rider.

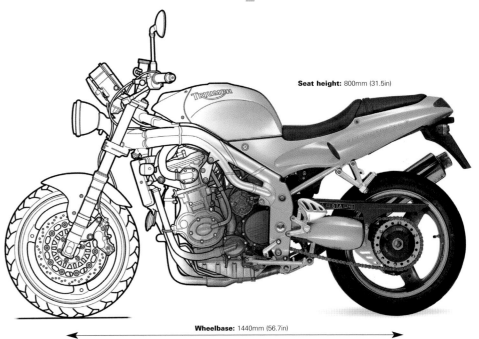

Seat height: 800mm (31.5in)

Width: 720mm (28.4in)

Wheelbase: 1440mm (56.7in)

## ENGINE

| | |
|---|---|
| Type | 4-stroke |
| Layout | in-line triple |
| Total displacement | 955cc (58.3ci) |
| Bore | 79mm (3.1in) |
| Stroke | 65mm (2.6in) |
| Compression ratio | 11.2:1 |
| Valves | 4 per cylinder |
| Fuel system | multipoint sequential EFI |
| Ignition | digital inductive |
| Cooling | liquid |
| Maximum power | 75.9kW (101.8bhp) @ 9400rpm |
| Maximum torque | 8.7kg-m (63.1lb-ft) @ 5500rpm |

## TRANSMISSION

| | |
|---|---|
| Primary drive | gear |
| Clutch | wet, multiplate |
| Gearbox | 6-speed |
| Final drive | chain |

## WEIGHTS & CAPACITIES

| | |
|---|---|
| Tank capacity | 18l (4.8gal) |
| Dry weight | 196kg (431.2lb) |
| Weight distribution | |
| — front | N/A |
| — rear | N/A |
| Wheelbase | 1440mm (56.7in) |
| Overall length | 2115mm (83.3in) |
| Overall width | 720mm (28.4in) |
| Overall height | 1230mm (48.4in) |
| Seat height | 800mm (31.5in) |

## CYCLE PARTS

| | |
|---|---|
| Frame | tubular aluminium alloy perimeter |
| Rake/trail | N/A |
| Front suspension | 45mm (1.8in) inverted Showa forks |
| Travel | N/A |
| Adjustment | preload, plus compression and rebound damping |
| Rear suspension | Showa rising-rate monoshock |
| Travel | N/A |
| Adjustment | preload, plus compression and rebound damping |
| Tyres | |
| — make | Bridgestone BT56 |
| — front | 120/70 x 17 |
| — rear | 190/50 x 17 |
| Brakes | |
| — make | Triumph |
| — front | 2 x 320mm (12.6in) floating discs, 4-piston calipers |
| — rear | 220mm (8.7in) disc, 2-piston caliper |

## TORQUE

## POWER

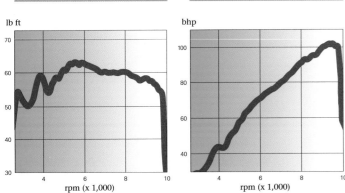

**Independent test measurements (above) differ from the manufacturer's claimed maximum power and maximum torque figures.**

# TRIUMPH

# SPRINT RS

*The Daytona-based motor features a noise suppression block at the back of the crankcase to quell engine noise.*

**Fairing**
Made from injection moulded plastic by an Italian company – the same material and methods are more or less universal in motorcycling. Paint schemes are single colours only, as preferred by the more mature riders likely to buy the Sprint RS.

**Mirrors**
Fairly big and vibration free, they offer the rider decent rearward vision and are easy to adjust, even on the move.

**Intakes**
Twin inlet tracts, which feed into the airbox, feature specially curved ducting to reduce intake roar.

**Cooling**
An ingenious secondary cooling circuit enables a quicker warm-up time and also helps prolong engine life.

**Front brakes**
Another feature taken directly from the supersports 955i, although on the Sprint RS their fearsome power is tamed a little by having to haul up more weight. Nissin four-piston calipers are used.

**Exhaust**
The silencer can be adjusted between two positions, the higher to improve ground clearance while the lower one allows the fitment of panniers.

## SPRINT RS

**Though it obviously** *shares bloodlines with the ST and Daytona, the Sprint RS has been blessed with enough changes to give it a distinct personality from its stablemates. It is equally happy carving up a twisty back road, or alternatively cruising down the motorway, and comes at an attractive price.*

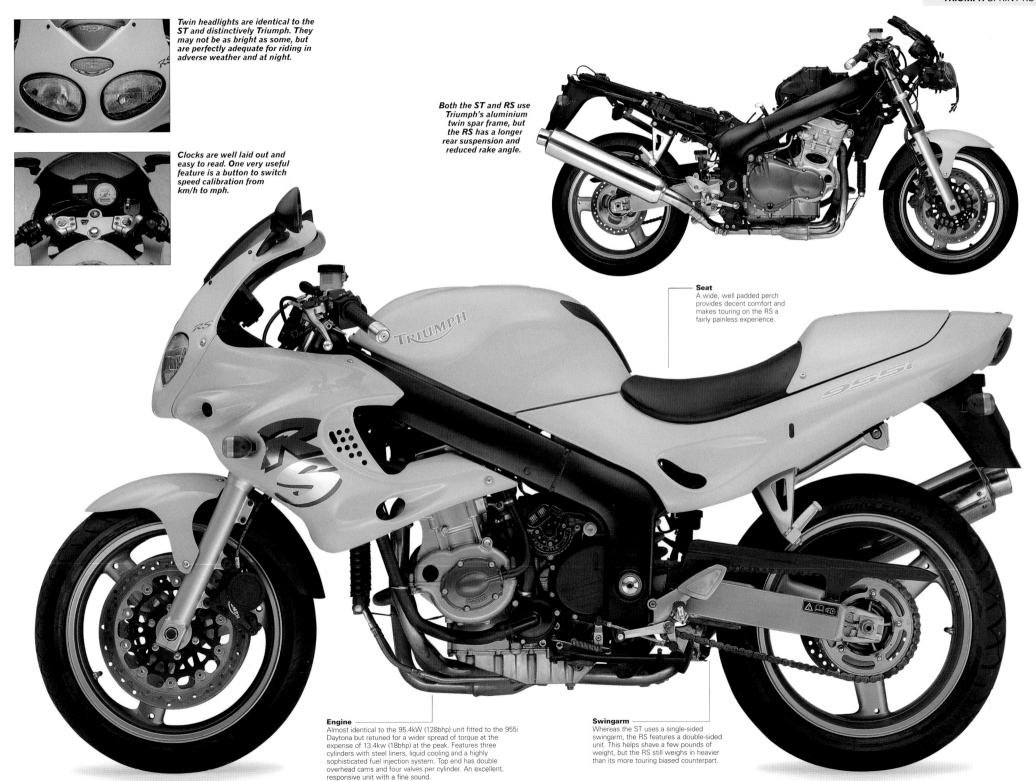

*Twin headlights are identical to the ST and distinctively Triumph. They may not be as bright as some, but are perfectly adequate for riding in adverse weather and at night.*

*Clocks are well laid out and easy to read. One very useful feature is a button to switch speed calibration from km/h to mph.*

*Both the ST and RS use Triumph's aluminium twin spar frame, but the RS has a longer rear suspension and reduced rake angle.*

**Seat**
A wide, well padded perch provides decent comfort and makes touring on the RS a fairly painless experience.

**Engine**
Almost identical to the 95.4kW (128bhp) unit fitted to the 955i Daytona but retuned for a wider spread of torque at the expense of 13.4kw (18bhp) at the peak. Features three cylinders with steel liners, liquid cooling and a highly sophisticated fuel injection system. Top end has double overhead cams and four valves per cylinder. An excellent, responsive unit with a fine sound.

**Swingarm**
Whereas the ST uses a single-sided swingarm, the RS features a double-sided unit. This helps shave a few pounds of weight, but the RS still weighs in heavier than its more touring biased counterpart.

# Specifications

The **RS** shares its four stroke, in-line three engine with its big brother, the **ST**, which means that there should no surprises in store. The ride is as smooth as you would expect, but slight modifications in the chassis give the **RS** a fresh sporty feel, while upgrades to the front end make even the most challenging roads fun. Add the comfort factor and fuel consumption and you have got yourselves a great tourer. Mix in the price and you are on to a real winner!

Seat height: 805mm (31.7in)

Length: 2120mm (83.5in)

## ENGINE

| | |
|---|---|
| Type | 4-stroke |
| Layout | in-line 3 |
| Total displacement | 955cc (58.3ci) |
| Bore | 79mm (3.1in) |
| Stroke | 65mm (2.6in) |
| Compression ratio | 11.2:1 |
| Valves | 4 per cylinder |
| Ignition | Digital inductive |
| Cooling | liquid |
| Maximum power | 80.5kW (108bhp) @ 9200rpm |
| Maximum torque | 9.9kg-m (72lb-ft) @ 6200rpm |

## TRANSMISSION

| | |
|---|---|
| Primary drive | gear |
| Clutch | wet multiplate |
| Gearbox | 6-speed |
| Final drive | X-ring chain |

## WEIGHTS & CAPACITIES

| | |
|---|---|
| Tank capacity | 21l (5.5gal) |
| Dry weight | 198kg (437lb) |
| Weight distribution | |
| — front | N/A |
| — rear | N/A |
| Wheelbase | 1470mm (57.9in) |
| Overall length | 2120mm (83.5in) |
| Overall width | 745mm (29.3in) |
| Overall height | 1170mm (46in) |
| Seat height | 805mm (31.7in) |

## CYCLE PARTS

| | |
|---|---|
| Frame | Aluminium twin spar |
| Rake | 25° |
| Front suspension | 43mm (1.7in) Cartride forks |
| Travel | N/A |
| Adjustment | preload |
| Rear suspension | Monoshock |
| Travel | N/A |
| Adjustment | preload and rebound damping |
| Tyres | |
| — front | 120/70 ZR17 |
| — rear | 180/55 ZR17 |
| Brakes | |
| — make | N/A |
| — front | 320mm (12.6in) floating duel discs |
| — rear | 255mm (10in) single disc |

# SPRINT ST

SPRINT ST

*The instrument panel features a 180 mph (290km/h) analogue clock marked clearly in 10mph (16km) increments and a rev counter with a red dial and redline at 9500rpm. There are also engine management, fuel, neutral, headlamp, oil and indicator warning lights, and an analogue fuel gauge, digital mileometer and clock, and a temperature gauge.*

**Screen**
One of the best available in terms of rider protection, our performance testing revealed that tucking in behind it at absolutely maximum speed removed all wind buffeting to the head, shoulders and chest.

**Headlamps**
The twin 'bug eye' design is immediately recognizable as being from Triumph and provides enough illumination for swift night riding. They are not the most powerful, but not bad either.

**Fairing**
Part of the designers' brief was to make the bike look instantly recognizable as a Triumph and the chosen plastics certainly help them fulfil their task. But this is not just a styling exercise – it is well made, easily fitted and removed, and wide enough to offer decent weather protection without being bulky.

**Handlebars**
The raised clip-on design immediately puts most riders into a comfortable position for long distance travelling. The left bar features a dip/main beam light switch, hazard light switch, indicators button and a cable-operated clutch lever. The right bar has the lights on/off switch, electric start button, engine kill switch and four-way span adjustable front brake lever.

**Mirrors**
Not the highest build quality ever seen, but big and spaced wide enough to ensure a good view behind. Vibration was absent during our tests and they were easy to adjust on the move.

**Exhaust**
The stainless steel headers use a balancer which has been designed to maximize mid-range performance. The aluminium silencer features a chrome end cap.

**Tyres**
Bridgestone BT57s are fitted as standard and come in 120/70 x ZR17 front and 180/55 x ZR17 rear sizes.

**Storage**
A small tray underneath the easily removed seat provides token storage capacity.

**The Sprint ST** *has borrowed its engine from the Daytona 955i and combined it with an all-new aluminium perimeter beam frame to make what some say is the best bike Triumph ever built. It looks attractive and appears to be a fascinating blend of sports bike and tourer, handling both nimbly and precisely. Time will tell what the punters think of it.*

The Sprint ST uses an updated airbox system initially designed for the 955i and multipoint sequential electronic fuel injection. The engine is fed by three 41mm (1.6in) throttle bodies, which use newly designed butterflies. A new air bypass system enhances low rev control. Throttle response is instantaneous at almost any revs.

Triumph has opted for twin four-piston calipers and 320mm (12.6in) floating discs. The combination worked outstandingly well during our performance testing, stopping the bike in 102.9m (338ft) from 160km/h (100mph).

Triumph has used its new aluminium perimeter beam frame in the quest for light weight and stable handling. It uses the engine as a structural member too. The 955cc (58.3ci), four-stroke, DOHC triple is closely based on the motor powering Triumph's Daytona 955i but has been retuned to offer extra mid-range grunt. It has a 79mm (3.1in) bore, 65mm (2.6in) stroke and a compression ratio of 11.2:1, together with four valves per cylinder.

**Fuel tank**
Big enough to hold 21l (5.5gal) and give a theoretical tank range of fractionally more than 322km (200 miles), it is deep rather than wide and so does not intrude into the rider's space.

**Weight saving**
The cam, clutch and water pump covers are all made from magnesium, while the coils are now integrated into the suppressor caps. The combined effect shaves vital weight off the total package.

**Grab rail**
Made of cast aluminium and big enough for even the largest hands, it is clear proof that Triumph takes heed of passengers' needs.

**Front Suspension**
The 43mm (1.7in) inverted Showa telescopic forks are adjustable for preload only.

**Gearbox**
The six-speed box proved slick and clunk-free during our performance testing, although it sometimes hesitated to change up quickly during standing start 400m (13112ft) runs.

**Rear wheel**
The cast aluminium hoop differs from almost all designs as it features three markedly-curved spokes. They fall to the wheel's right side, allowing the rear disc, unusually, to be fitted in-line with the sprocket on the left side.

# Specifications

*Triumph set itself some* tough goals in designing the Sprint ST. It had to be both torquey and powerful, provide superior weather protection to a race replica, look slimline and attractive, and, equally importantly, adopt the famously recognizable Triumph appearance. In achieving this, it was necessary for the engine, chassis and styling departments to work closely together. Here, we examine the specifications of such a superbly capable all-round machine.

**Seat height:** 800mm (31.2in)

**Width:** 750mm (29.5in)

**Trail:** 92mm (3.6in)

**Wheelbase:** 1470mm (57.9in)

## ENGINE

| | |
|---|---|
| Type | 4-stroke |
| Layout | DOHC in-line triple |
| Total displacement | 955cc (58.3ci) |
| Bore | 79mm (3.1in) |
| Stroke | 65mm (2.6in) |
| Compression ratio | 11.2:1 |
| Valves | 4 per cylinder |
| Fuel system | multipoint sequential electronic fuel injection, 41mm (1.6in) throttle bodies |
| Ignition | CDI |
| Cooling | liquid |
| Maximum power | 82.5kW (110.7bhp) @ 9290rpm |
| Maximum torque | 9.9kg-m (71.63lb-ft) @ 5167rpm |

## TRANSMISSION

| | |
|---|---|
| Primary drive | gear |
| Clutch | wet multiplate |
| Gearbox | 6-speed |
| Final drive | sealed O-ring chain |

## WEIGHTS & CAPACITIES

| | |
|---|---|
| Tank capacity | 21l (5.5gal) |
| Dry weight | 207kg (455.4lb) |
| Weight distribution | |
| — front | 49 per cent |
| — rear | 51 per cent |
| Wheelbase | 1470mm (57.9in) |
| Overall length | 2160mm (85in) |
| Overall width | 750mm (29.5in) |
| Overall height | 1220mm (48in) |
| Seat height | 800mm (31.5in) |

## CYCLE PARTS

| | |
|---|---|
| Frame | aluminium perimeter beam |
| Rake/trail | 25°/92mm (3.6in) |
| Front suspension | 43mm (1.7in) inverted Showa telescopic forks |
| Travel | 120mm (4.7in) |
| Adjustment | preload |
| Rear suspension | Showa rising rate monoshock |
| Travel | 120mm (4.7in) |
| Adjustment | preload, plus rebound damping |
| Tyres | |
| — make | Bridgestone BT57 |
| — front | 120/70 x ZR17 |
| — rear | 180/55 x ZR17 |
| Brakes | |
| — make | Nissin |
| — front | twin 4-piston calipers, 320mm (12.6in) floating discs |
| — rear | single 2-piston caliper, 255mm (10in) disc |

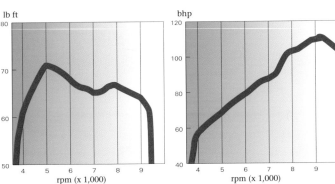

## TORQUE

lb ft

rpm (x 1,000)

## POWER

bhp

rpm (x 1,000)

**Independent test measurements (above) differ from the manufacturer's claimed maximum power and maximum torque figures.**

# TROPHY 1200

*Quick-detach panniers have a total capacity of 72l (4394ci) and the pannier brackets remain hidden when the luggage is removed to ensure the bike's lines are unspoilt.*

**Instruments**
Include speedometer, odometer, trip meter, tacho, fuel gauge, analogue clock, warning lights for indicators, main beam, oil pressure, engine temperature and neutral gear.

**Handlebars**
Aluminium handlebars reposition the rider slightly over previous versions to enhance touring comfort and also shave a substantial 2kg (4.4lb) off older model weight.

**Headlights**
Feature remote-adjusters, making beam co-ordination easier when taking a pillion on board.

**Fairing**
The fairing upper, together with the screen, has been redesigned to reduce wind noise and buffeting. Weather protection remains unaltered and exceptional.

**Rear shock**
Well-sprung but continuing to offer a plush ride, the monoshock features remote, stepless preload and 10-way adjustable rebound damping.

**Swingarm**
Aluminium alloy swingarm uses eccentric chain adjusters.

**Wheels**
Alloy three-spokes are both 43.2cm (17in) and come in 8.9cm (3.5in) front and 13.9cm (5.5in) rear sizes, allowing popular rubber of 120/70 and 170/60 to be used.

TROPHY 1200

***Mile-munching*** *is what this bike does best, coming high on anyone's list of machines for covering long distances. The dependable engine has plenty of torque but is heavy and has a high fuel consumption, which makes it look old-fashioned compared to newer designs. That said, the Trophy 1200 is still a serious and enjoyable touring machine.*

Dual Triumph-branded front stoppers use 310mm (12.2in) discs, opposed four-piston calipers, and come with braided steel hose as standard.

Liquid-cooled, **DOHC** motor uses four in-line cylinders each of 295cc (18ci). The Trophy 900 shares the same cylinders, but uses only three. Both bikes have a bore and stroke of 76 x 65mm (2.9 x 2.6in) and a compression ratio of 10.6:1.

The high tensile tubular steel frame is of the single spine type. This is seen as an old design, but considering the success of the Trophy, who can argue with Triumph's decision to stick with it?

**Fuel tank**
25l (6.6gal) tank allows a whopping maximum range of 362km (225 miles) under normal touring circumstances.

**Chrome**
Classy, if a little large, headlight surrounds make the Trophy stand out from the crowd.

**Front suspension**
43mm (1.7in) telescopic forks use triple-rate springs to enhance ride quality and feature 150mm (5.9in) of travel. They are unadjustable.

**Sidestand**
After listening to owner feedback, Triumph has changed the sidestand design, lengthening it slightly to reduce the effort needed to pull the bike upright at rest.

TRIUMPH

# TROPHY 1200

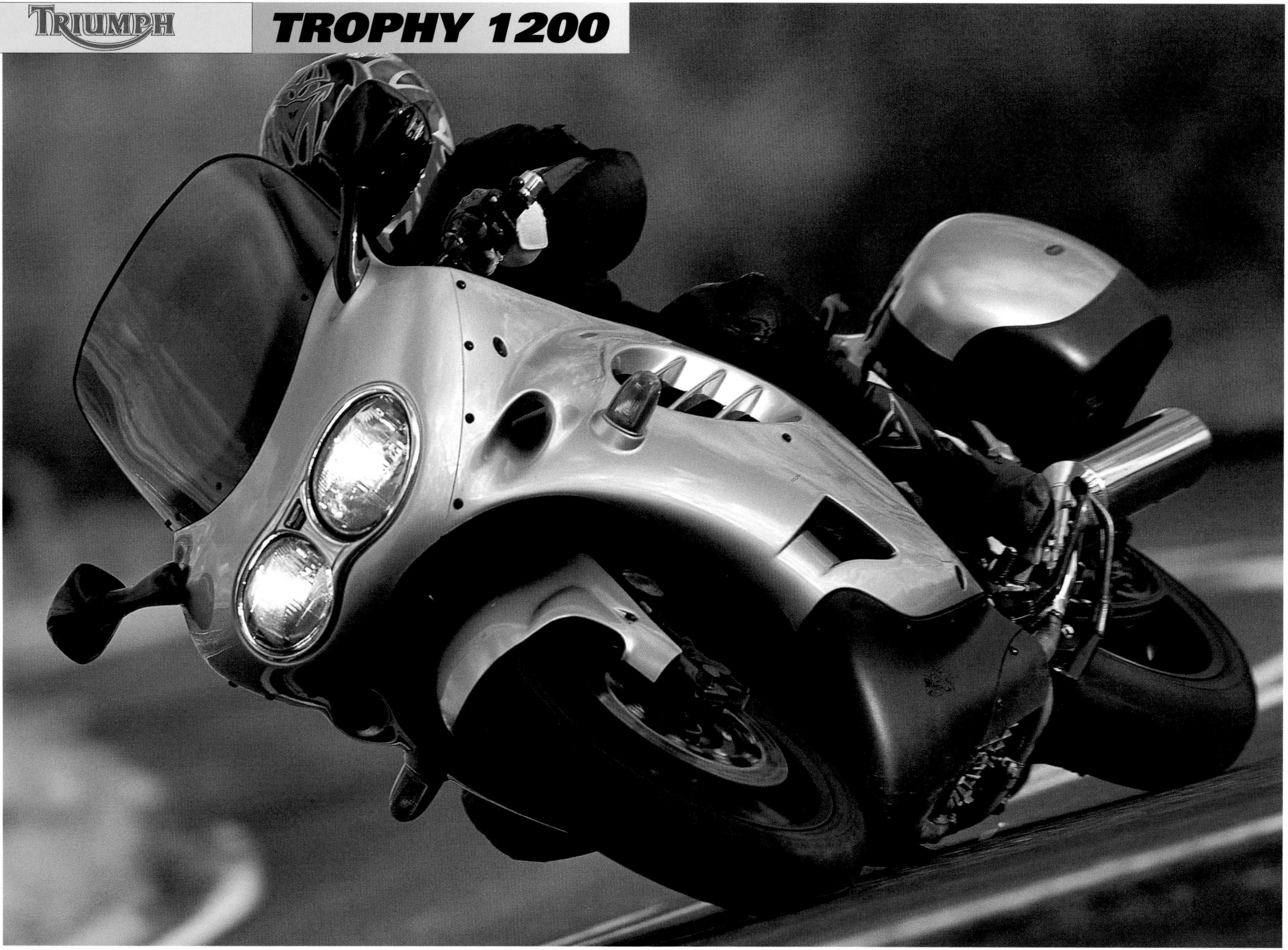

# Specifications

**As far as big** tourers go, the Triumph Trophy 1200 pretty much has it all. It has been a great machine over the last decade, but is now even better.
This is thanks to the 1999 version getting a redesigned and windblast-beating fairing and screen; more comfortable handlebars; revised gearing which improves fuel consumption by around 10 per cent; a taller sidestand; and new carburettors for improved throttle response. Long-serving it may be, but there is plenty of life in it yet.

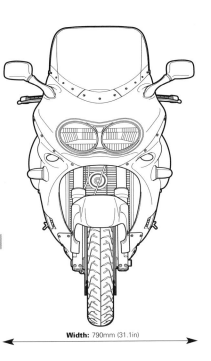

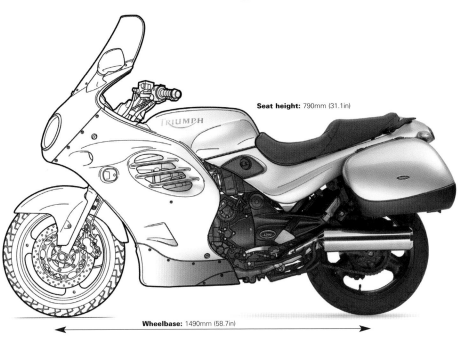

**Seat height:** 790mm (31.1in)

**Width:** 790mm (31.1in)

**Wheelbase:** 1490mm (58.7in)

## ENGINE

| | |
|---|---|
| Type | 4-stroke |
| Layout | DOHC in-line four |
| Total displacement | 1180cc (72ci) |
| Bore | 76mm (2.9in) |
| Stroke | 65mm (2.6in) |
| Compression ratio | 10.6:1 |
| Valves | 4 per cylinder |
| Fuel system | 4 x 36mm (1.4in) flat slide CV carburettors |
| Ignition | digital-inductive |
| Cooling | liquid |
| Maximum power | 72.1kW (96.7bhp) @ 8700rpm |
| Maximum torque | 8.9kg-m (64.4lb-ft) @ 6500rpm |

## TORQUE

## POWER

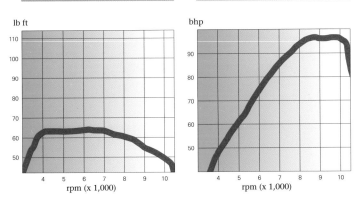

## TRANSMISSION

| | |
|---|---|
| Primary drive | gear |
| Clutch | wet multiplate |
| Gearbox | 6-speed |
| Final drive | chain |

## WEIGHTS & CAPACITIES

| | |
|---|---|
| Type | 4-stroke |
| Layout | DOHC in-line four |
| Total displacement | 1180cc (72ci) |
| Bore | 76mm (2.9in) |
| Stroke | 65mm (2.6in) |
| Compression ratio | 10.6:1 |
| Valves | 4 per cylinder |
| Fuel system | 4 x 36mm (1.4in) flat slide CV carburettors |
| Ignition | digital-inductive |
| Cooling | liquid |
| Maximum power | 96.7bhp @ 8700rpm |
| Maximum torque | 64.4lb-ft @ 6500rpm |

## CYCLE PARTS

| | |
|---|---|
| Frame | high-tensile tubular steel |
| Rake/trail | N/A |
| Front suspension | 43mm (1.7in) telescopic forks, triple-rate springs |
| Travel | 150mm (5.9in) |
| Adjustment | none |
| Rear suspension | rising rate monoshock |
| Travel | 126mm (4.9in) |
| Adjustment | preload, plus 10-way rebound damping |
| Tyres | |
| — make | varies |
| — front | 120/70 x ZR17 |
| — rear | 170/60 x ZR17 |
| Brakes | |
| — make | Triumph |
| — front | 2 x 310mm (12.1in) discs, opposed 4-piston calipers |
| — rear | 255mm (10in) disc, 2-piston caliper |

**Independent test measurements (above) differ from the manufacturer's claimed maximum power and maximum torque figures.**

# YZF-R6

**Fairing**
Sporting similar headlamps to the YZF-R1, the diminutive fairing is both light and effective in the wind tunnel, although the screen is too small for most riders to fit properly behind. A wide range of aftermarket screens are available.

*As with too many bikes nowadays, this has only a sidestand. The lack of mainstand can be a pain when it comes to chain lubrication and rear-end maintenance.*

**YZF-R6**

**JUST** *when you thought* machines *could not get much better, the R6 arrived. This new Yamaha is exciting and wild and the kind of machine that is at its very best going full speed – breaking all the limits. It has astounded journalists, bikers and its competitors – not least Honda's* **CBR600.**

**Forced air induction**
A recess underneath the headlamp provides an opening for a charge of cool air to ram its way into the engine at speed, helping the bike to burn more fuel more efficiently at the same time, thus boosting outputted power. Although Yamaha reckons on around 78–80kW (105–108bhp) from the engine on a static dyno, it claims this climbs to 89kW (120bhp) at high speed when the forced air induction system is working at peak efficiency. The engine breathes through a bank of four 37mm (1.5in) Keihin carburettors.

**Forks**
At the limit on the track, the conventional 43mm (1.7in) telescopic forks may feel fractionally soft and could benefit from stiffer springs. This will never be a problem on the road and should manifest itself to highly experienced trackday riders only once the bike has covered several thousand miles.

**Tyres**
As is fast becoming the class standard, the R6 wears a mighty 180-section rear tyre and 120 front. The standard Dunlops offer decent grip.

**Subframe**
As is now the norm with sports bikes, the rear subframe can be simply unbolted and replaced if damaged. Older designs sometimes forced owners to scrap the entire frame following a crash that caused only rear end damage.

Unlike the R6's big brother, the YZF-R1, the engine gets four valves per cylinder instead of five. The reason is simply that the top end is so diminutive and the head area so small that there is not enough room to make the greater number perform effectively. The 599cc (36.5in) four-stroke engine has a bore and stroke of 65.5mm x 44.5mm (2.6 x 1.8in), a compression ratio of 12.4:1 and a shade over a true 74.6kW (100bhp) output at the rear wheel.

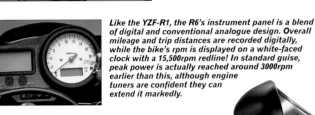

Like the YZF-R1, the R6's instrument panel is a blend of digital and conventional analogue design. Overall mileage and trip distances are recorded digitally, while the bike's rpm is displayed on a white-faced clock with a 15,500rpm redline! In standard guise, peak power is actually reached around 3000rpm earlier than this, although engine tuners are confident they can extend it markedly.

The aluminium twin spar design is the latest incarnation of Yamaha's famed Deltabox chassis design and has been made ultra-compact to aid handling. Its overall shortness (made possible by the compact engine) goes a long way to explaining the tiny 1380mm (54.3in) wheelbase, which is a full 15mm (0.59in) shorter than the 1999 Honda CBR600F's and a whopping 35mm (1.38in) less than Yamaha's old 600cc (36.6ci) sports competitor – the Thundercat.

**Seat height**
At 820mm (32.28in), it comes in slap bang in the middle of the class. The narrow design goes a long way to helping shorter riders cope, though.

**Tank**
Holds 17l (4.5gal), making it the smallest in its class.

**Gearbox**
As with the R1, Yamaha has seen fit to stack the gearbox's shafts on top of each other rather than side by side. The effect is to help shorten the engine's length. First to second gear change is a little notchy although the 'box is smooth into third and beyond. The clutch is much improved over previous designs and suffers less with shudder during fast launches from a standstill.

**Brakes**
The twin Sumitomo front calipers are of an opposed four-piston design and bite on twin 295mm (11.61in) discs. Combined with the light weight of the bike and its compliant suspension and tyres, braking efficiency is very impressive indeed.

**Swingarm**
As with GP bikes, the R6's swingarm is artificially longer than it might otherwise need to be because the engine has been made so compact. In the simplest terms, the overall effect of this engineering design is to push more weight over the bike's front end, aiding handling and reducing the likelihood of progress-sapping wheelies.

# Specifications

**The R6's engine is** *really a smaller version of its big brother's – the amazing R1 – and shares many of its features, although it does get four valves instead of five. The aluminium twin spar frame is ultra-compact to aid handling and its overall shortness goes a long way to explaining the tiny wheelbase of 1380mm (54.3in). What you really need to know is that the R1 is a bike designed to be ridden as quickly as the rider can manage. It may not be the perfect commuter, but that is not why you will be buying one.*

Seat height: 820mm (32.3in)

Width: 690mm (27.2in)

Trail: 81mm (3.2in)

Wheelbase: 1380mm (54.3in)

## ENGINE

| | |
|---|---|
| Type | 4-stroke |
| Layout | DOHC in-line four |
| Total displacement | 599cc (36.5in) |
| Bore | 65.5mm (2.6in) |
| Stroke | 44.5mm (1.8in) |
| Compression ratio | 12.4:1 |
| Valves | 4 per cylinder |
| Fuel system | 4 x 37mm (1.5in) Keihin carburettors |
| Ignition | CDI |
| Cooling | liquid |
| Maximum power | 72.3kW (96.9bhp) @ 12,480rpm |
| Maximum torque | 5.9kg-m (43lb-ft) @ 10,800rpm |

## TRANSMISSION

| | |
|---|---|
| Primary drive | straight-cut gear |
| Clutch | wet multiplate |
| Gearbox | 6-speed |
| Final drive | sealed O-ring chain |

## WEIGHTS & CAPACITIES

| | |
|---|---|
| Tank capacity | 17l (4.5gal) |
| Dry weight | 169kg (371.8lb) |
| Weight distribution | |
| — front | N/A |
| — rear | N/A |
| Wheelbase | 1380mm (54.3in) |
| Overall length | 2025mm (79.7in) |
| Overall width | 690mm (27.2n) |
| Overall height | 1105mm (43.5in) |
| Seat height | 820mm (32.3in) |

## CYCLE PARTS

| | |
|---|---|
| Frame | aluminium twin spar Deltabox II |
| Rake/trail | 24°/81mm (3.2in) |
| Front suspension | 43mm (1.7in) telescopic fork |
| Travel | 130mm (5.1in) |
| Adjustment | rebound and compression damping, plus preload |
| Rear suspension | monoshock |
| Travel | 120mm (4.7in) |
| Adjustment | rebound and compression damping, plus preload |
| Tyres | |
| — make | Dunlop |
| — front | 120/60 x 17 |
| — rear | 180/55 x 17 |
| Brakes | |
| — make | Sumitomo |
| — front | 2 x 295mm (11.6in) discs, opposed four-piston calipers |
| — rear | 1 x 220mm (8.7in)disc, single-piston caliper |

## TORQUE

## POWER

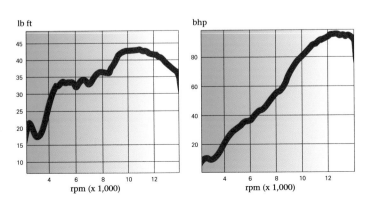

Independent test measurements (above) differ from the manufacturer's claimed maximum power and maximum torque figures.

# YZF600R THUNDERCAT

**Good protection**
The wide, tallish screen affords excellent wind and adequate rain protection to the rider.

**Mirrors**
Little vibration and good positioning make them a useful asset, although some riders will find their shoulders making a guest appearance in the view.

**Cat's eye**
The large headlamp is quite powerful, but tends to point at the sky under hard acceleration if a heavy rider/standard suspension settings combination is present. Firming up the rear and adjusting the beam height is almost mandatory straight from the crate.

**Seat**
It is 797.56mm (31.4in) tall and very comfortable for both rider and pillion.

**Pegs**
Once the Cat's suspension is set up properly for hard riding, the hero blobs underneath the pegs will quickly wear away. Really hard cornering can eat into the pegs themselves.

*YZF600R THUNDERCAT*

**Tyres**
43.2cm (17in) rims take a 120/60 tyre front and 160/60 rear, although some rubber manufacturers recommend a 170-section back hoop as an aftermarket fitment.

**Rear suspension**
Like the front, the rear suspension is too soft and wallowy on factory settings. Although the spring is up to the job, the level of compression and rebound damping afforded by the adjustable setup is not. This becomes particularly apparent under fast riding conditions on bumpy roads. Riders around 13 stone in leathers could do worse than set the spring to position four and experiment with the final eight positions on both the compression and rebound damping. Once sorted, this transforms the bike.

**It is one of the best 600s** on the market, so it is a pity the Thundercat has always been overshadowed by Honda's *CBR600F*. Put it up against most bikes in its class, however, and it will happily show them its rear end. A superb all-rounder, it offers the rider everything they are ever likely to need in terms of performance.

Unlike many bikes, the silencer cannot simply be unbolted and replaced with an aftermarket unit. The design, where four downpipes join to one rear tube which is integrated to the silencer, means a complete end can/rear pipework swop is needed. It is slightly fiddly to fit, but not a lot more expensive than a straightforward can to buy. Hard riding can deck the end of the standard silencer out on the road or track.

Big, wide and bulky in comparison to other 600s, the rider soon gets used to it and can enjoy superior wet weather protection when it rains. Some think it looks a little slabby and too angular.

The Thundercat excels in the 4000–8000rpm bracket where its competitors lag behind. This is all thanks to a strong 599cc (36.5in), in-line four-cylinder, double overhead cam engine, with a strong torque curve which peaks at 9500rpm. Maximum power, just under 74.6kW (100bhp), comes in at 11,500rpm. The engine is liquid-cooled and has six gears and a compression ratio of 12.1:1.

**Fuel tank**
Holds a useful 19l (5gal).

**Dated**
The twin spar Deltabox chassis is undeniably strong but, since the introduction of the aluminium-framed 1999 Honda CBR600F, makes the Thundercat now the only Japanese-built 600cc (36.6ci) sportster to use steel. The disadvantage is increased weight.

**Front suspension**
Too soft on standard settings, the average weight rider will need to wind the preload fully in and experiment with compression and rebound settings between two and six clicks off the max to get the most from the bike.

**Stylish**
Good-fitting, elongated front mudguard looks the business.

**Front brakes**
Twin four-piston Sumitomo calipers and 298mm (11.7in) discs provide plenty of initial bite, feel and excellent stopping power. Outright stopping performance is good, although the bike's overall weight is the limiting factor here.

**Wheelbase**
At 1415mm (55.7in), it is the longest in its class, although the steering does not feel particularly slow, merely a fraction lazy instead.

**Rear brake**
Single, two-piston Sumitomo caliper and 245mm (9.6in) disc.

# Specifications

*Make no comparison to* any other bike and you will find the *Thundercat is superb. The slant block, liquid-cooled, four-cylinder engine is the most powerful 600 Yamaha has ever built for the road. The Cat has a super-stiff Deltabox chassis, which is directly descended from the design used on Yamaha's factory bikes. According to Yamaha, this will run straight as an arrow while you sit comfortably. Sounds good. And the superbike racer-style cockpit design features a compact, easy to read instrument console.*

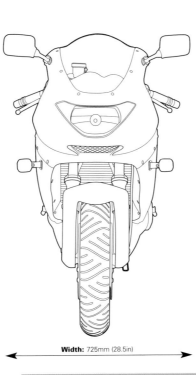

Width: 725mm (28.5in)

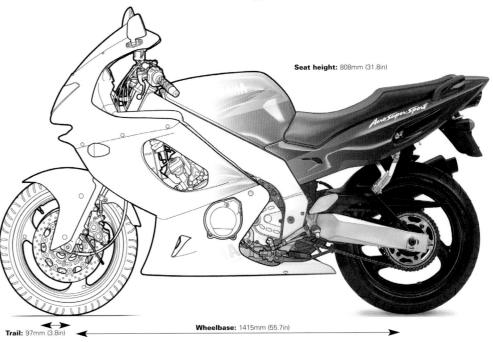

Seat height: 808mm (31.8in)

Trail: 97mm (3.8in)

Wheelbase: 1415mm (55.7in)

## ENGINE

| | |
|---|---|
| Type | 4-stroke |
| Layout | transverse four |
| Total displacement | 599cc (36.5in) |
| Bore | 62mm (2.4in) |
| Stroke | 49.6mm (1.9in) |
| Compression ratio | 12.0:1 |
| Valves | 4 per cylinder |
| Fuel system | 4 x 36mm (1.4in) CV Mikuni carburettors |
| Ignition | CDI |
| Cooling | liquid |
| Maximum power | 70.8kW (95bhp) @ 11,500rpm |
| Maximum torque | 7.3kg-m (53lb-ft) @ 8500rpm |

## TRANSMISSION

| | |
|---|---|
| Primary drive | straight-cut gears |
| Clutch | wet multiplate |
| Gearbox | 6-speed |
| Final drive | chain |

## WEIGHTS & CAPACITIES

| | |
|---|---|
| Tank capacity | 19l (5gal) |
| Dry weight | 187kg (411.4lb) |
| Weight distribution | |
| — front | N/A |
| — rear | N/A |
| Wheelbase | 1415mm (55.7in) |
| Overall length | 2060mm (81.1in) |
| Overall width | 725mm (28.5in) |
| Overall height | 1190mm (46.9in) |
| Seat height | 808mm (31.8in) |

## CYCLE PARTS

| | |
|---|---|
| Frame | steel twin spar |
| Rake/trail | 25°/97mm (3.8in) |
| Front suspension | 41mm (1.6in) telescopic forks |
| Travel | 130mm (5.1in) |
| Adjustment | spring preload, plus compression and rebound damping |
| Rear suspension | rising rate monoshock |
| Travel | 120mm (4.7in) |
| Adjustment | spring preload, plus compression and rebound damping |
| Tyres | |
| — make | Dunlop D207 |
| — front | 120/60-ZR17 |
| — rear | 160/60-ZR17 |
| Brakes | |
| — make | Sumitomo |
| — front | 2 x 298mm (11.7in) discs, 4-piston calipers |
| — rear | 1 x 245mm (9.6in) disc, 2-piston caliper |

## TORQUE

## POWER

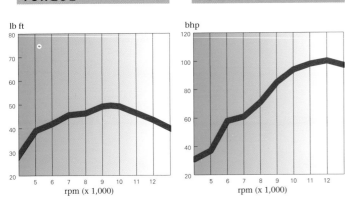

**Independent test measurements (above) differ from the manufacturer's claimed maximum power and maximum torque figures.**

# YAMAHA XVS650 DRAG STAR

*Yamaha has chosen shaft drive over both chain and toothed belt to ensure maintenance is kept to a minimum.*

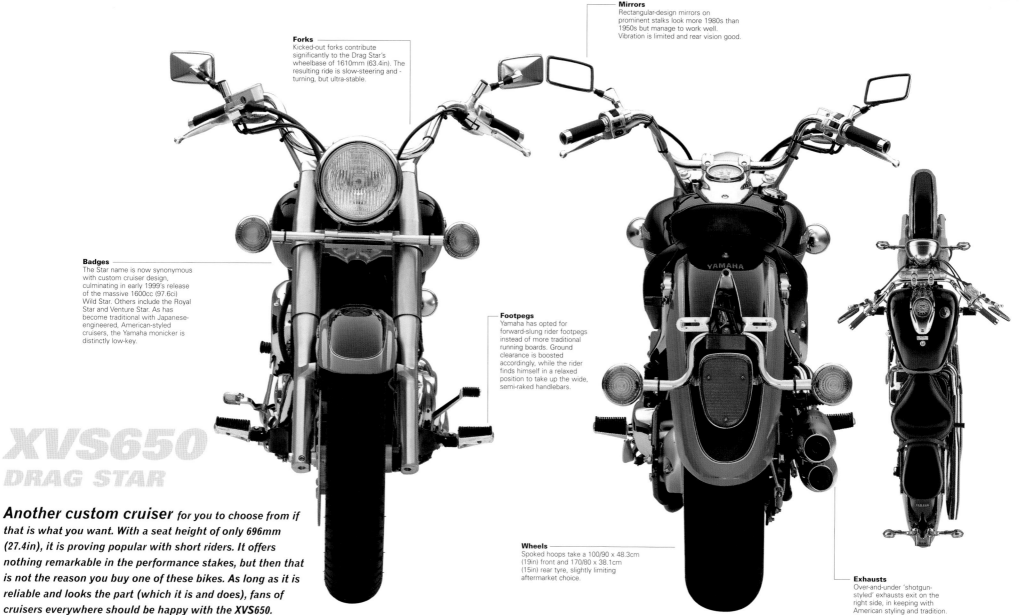

**Forks**
Kicked-out forks contribute significantly to the Drag Star's wheelbase of 1610mm (63.4in). The resulting ride is slow-steering and -turning, but ultra-stable.

**Mirrors**
Rectangular-design mirrors on prominent stalks look more 1980s than 1950s but manage to work well. Vibration is limited and rear vision good.

**Badges**
The Star name is now synonymous with custom cruiser design, culminating in early 1999's release of the massive 1600cc (97.6ci) Wild Star. Others include the Royal Star and Venture Star. As has become traditional with Japanese-engineered, American-styled cruisers, the Yamaha monicker is distinctly low-key.

**Footpegs**
Yamaha has opted for forward-slung rider footpegs instead of more traditional running boards. Ground clearance is boosted accordingly, while the rider finds himself in a relaxed position to take up the wide, semi-raked handlebars.

**XVS650 DRAG STAR**

**Wheels**
Spoked hoops take a 100/90 x 48.3cm (19in) front and 170/80 x 38.1cm (15in) rear tyre, slightly limiting aftermarket choice.

**Exhausts**
Over-and-under 'shotgun-styled' exhausts exit on the right side, in keeping with American styling and tradition. Chrome-plating boosts looks and should ensure longevity.

***Another custom cruiser*** *for you to choose from if that is what you want. With a seat height of only 696mm (27.4in), it is proving popular with short riders. It offers nothing remarkable in the performance stakes, but then that is not the reason you buy one of these bikes. As long as it is reliable and looks the part (which it is and does), fans of cruisers everywhere should be happy with the XVS650.*

*A drilled 298mm (11.7in) disc and single twin-pot caliper are all that is needed to keep the Drag Star under control. The disc's styling varies on the limited edition Drag Star Classic.*

*A double cradle frame with a long wheelbase of 1610mm (63.4in) holds this baby cruiser together.*

*The engine derives from Yamaha's popular XV535 Virago with some changes and an increase in bore and stroke.*

**Instruments**
The tank houses a large-faced speedo, which also boasts an odometer and tripmeter - traditional cruiser layout.

**Headlamp**
Small and showy but has limited power for fast night riding. Could be improved.

**Fuel tank**
The teardrop design holds 16l (4.2gal), of which 3l (0.8gal) are reserve.

**Seat**
At just 695mm (27.4in) tall, the Drag Star's seat height is proving popular with shorter riders. Comfort is good over middle distances and pillions should find they also have plenty of room.

**Air filter cover**
Round filter cover mounted midway between both engine blocks on the right-hand side looks every inch a part of the cruiser scene.

**Engine**
Air-cooled, 75°, four-stroke, middleweight engine features a single overhead cam (SOHC), 649cc (39.6ci) capacity, 81 x 63mm (3.2 x 2.5in) bore and stroke, and a compression ratio of 9:1. Yamaha claims 29.8kW (40bhp) at 6500rpm. Fuelling is by a pair of 28mm (1.1in) Mikuni carburettors and the gearbox is five-speed.

# Specifications

*An air-cooled 649cc (39.6ci) V-twin, the Drag Star is derived from the XV535 Virago but with a few updates and an increase in the bore and stroke.*

*One look at it and you could be forgiven for thinking that this is yet another Harley clone – and as far as looks go, you would not be far off the mark. But start it up and you can feel the difference. It revs quickly and easily, it does not shudder, it brakes reasonably well and even corners well (although definitely no scratcher). It is quick and capable – just not individual.*

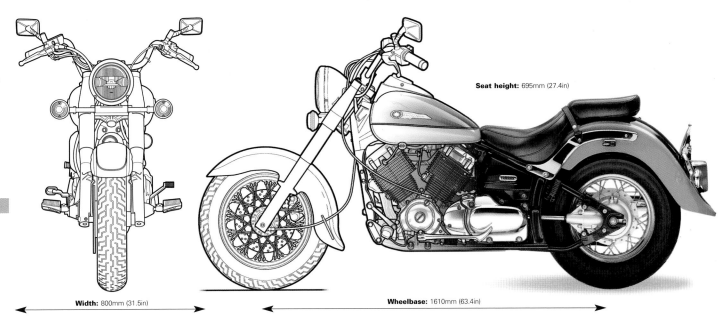

**Seat height:** 695mm (27.4in)

**Width:** 800mm (31.5in)

**Wheelbase:** 1610mm (63.4in)

## ENGINE

| | |
|---|---|
| **Type** | 4-stroke |
| **Layout** | V-twin |
| **Total displacement** | 649cc (39.6ci) |
| **Bore** | 81mm (3.2in) |
| **Stroke** | 63mm (2.5in) |
| **Compression ratio** | 9:1 |
| **Valves** | 2 per cylinder |
| **Fuel system** | 2 x Mikuni BDS28 |
| **Ignition** | CDI |
| **Cooling** | air |
| **Maximum power** | 24.8kW (33.2bhp) @ 6400rpm |
| **Maximum torque** | 4.3kg-m (30.9lb-ft) @ 3100rpm |

## TRANSMISSION

| | |
|---|---|
| **Primary drive** | gear |
| **Clutch** | wet, multiplate |
| **Gearbox** | 5-speed |
| **Final drive** | shaft |

## WEIGHTS & CAPACITIES

| | |
|---|---|
| **Tank capacity** | 16l (4.2gal) |
| **Dry weight** | 214kg (470.8lb) |
| **Weight distribution** | |
| — front | N/A |
| — rear | N/A |
| **Wheelbase** | 1610mm (63.4in) |
| **Overall length** | 2340mm (92.1in) |
| **Overall width** | 800mm (31.5in) |
| **Overall height** | 1065mm (41.9in) |
| **Seat height** | 695mm (27.4in) |

## CYCLE PARTS

| | |
|---|---|
| **Frame** | steel spine |
| **Rake/trail** | N/A |
| **Front suspension** | telescopic forks |
| **Travel** | N/A |
| **Adjustment** | none |
| **Rear suspension** | swinging arm |
| **Travel** | N/A |
| **Adjustment** | preload |
| | |
| **Tyres** | |
| — make | varies |
| — front | 100/90 x 19 |
| — rear | 170/80 x 15 |
| **Brakes** | |
| — make | Yamaha |
| — front | 298mm (11.7in) single disc |
| — rear | drum |

## TORQUE

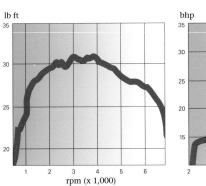

lb ft / rpm (x 1,000)

## POWER

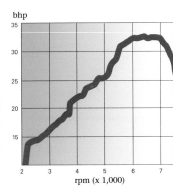

bhp / rpm (x 1,000)

**Independent test measurements (above) differ from the manufacturer's claimed maximum power and maximum torque figures.**

# YAMAHA YZF-R7

**Styling**
Almost makes the R1 look dated. This is most definitely a bike for the track.

**Forks**
The Ohlins inverted, flex-resistant 43mm (1.7in) forks have a special coating to enable smooth compression and rebound action over bumps.

**Valves**
The three intake and two exhaust valves are made from titanium – reducing weight even further.

**Clutch**
For the road, the R7 has a wet clutch. It also has a back torque limiter, so if the rider downchanges too early with the revs still too high, the clutch automatically slips, preventing the back wheel from locking up.

## YZF-R7

***What you are looking at here** is little more than a full-on, factory-built race bike with headlights and indicators. It is the result of the need for Yamaha to build a small number of machines for public sale in order to qualify its racers for the World Superbike championship. The R7 is expensive, exclusive and packed with cutting edge technology.*

The tail light and rear indicators look like afterthoughts simply stuck on, which is exactly what they are – necessary for the road but not the track.

Clocks are strictly business with analogue rev counter and liquid crystal displays for everything else.

The Deltabox II frame is of a lightweight, rigid design, in which the engine acts as a stressed member, something we now expect from this family of bikes.

**Fuel injection**
Two injectors per cylinder controlled by a multi-functional Electronic Control Unit (ECU), which is responsible for ensuring top performance throughout the engine's rev range. It controls ignition timing, injection timing and the amount of fuel that is injected into the motor.

**Engine**
The 749cc (45.7ci), liquid cooled, 20-valve four is slanted forward, helping air flow from the airbox into the fuel-injection system as well as throwing some weight over the front end for better balance and grip. It is also a stressed member of the frame.

**Swingarm**
As on the R1, the swingarm is longer than usual, the idea behind this being that a long swingarm and a short chassis brings the swingarm pivot closer to the bike's middle point, thus reducing rear-end weight and helping to improve balance at the front.

# Specifications

*The biking world waited* to see the R7 with probably the most eager anticipation since news of the R1 leaked out – nobody was disappointed. Marketed purely to be eligible for superbike racing, the R7 is produced in limited numbers with a price-tag that limits it further! But this is the bike for committed road racers and is the only road bike around today which has such pure race specs. It has the most powerful engine Yamaha has ever made available to the public and a chassis based on the GP bikes. The YZF-R7 is one of the most mouth-watering bikes in the world – no exaggeration.

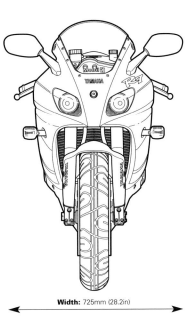

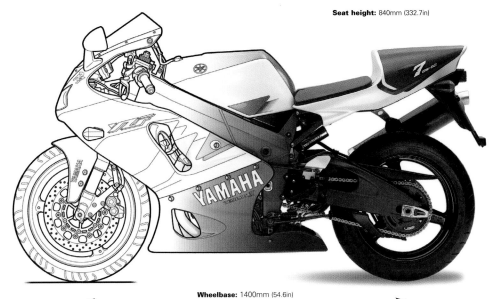

**Seat height:** 840mm (332.7in)

**Width:** 725mm (28.2in)

**Wheelbase:** 1400mm (54.6in)

## ENGINE

| | |
|---|---|
| Type | 4-stroke |
| Layout | in-line four |
| Total displacement | 749cc (45.7ci) |
| Bore | 72mm |
| Stroke | 46mm (1.8in) |
| Compression ratio | N/A |
| Valves | 5 per cylinder |
| Fuel system | dual electronic fuel injection |
| Ignition | electric |
| Cooling | liquid |
| Maximum power | 76.4kW (102.4bhp) @ 10,950rpm |
| Maximum torque | 6kg-m (44.1lb-ft) @ 9000rpm |

## TRANSMISSION

| | |
|---|---|
| Primary drive | gear |
| Clutch | racing type |
| Gearbox | 6-speed |
| Final drive | chain |

## WEIGHTS & CAPACITIES

| | |
|---|---|
| Tank capacity | 24l (6.3gal) |
| Dry weight | 176kg (388lb) |
| Weight distribution | |
| — front | N/A |
| — rear | N/A |
| Wheelbase | 1400mm (54.6in) |
| Overall length | 2060mm (80.3in) |
| Overall width | 725mm (28.2in) |
| Overall height | 1190mm (46.4in) |
| Seat height | 840mm (32.7in) |

## CYCLE PARTS

| | |
|---|---|
| Frame | GP-type aluminium |
| Rake/trail | N/A |
| Front suspension | Ohlins upside-down forks |
| Travel | N/A |
| Adjustment | preload, rebound and compression damping |
| Rear suspension | Ohlins shock |
| Travel | N/A |
| Adjustment | preload, rebound and compression damping |
| Tyres | |
| — make | Metzeler |
| — front | 120/70 x 17 |
| — rear | 180/55 x 17 |
| Brakes | |
| — make | N/A |
| — front | 320mm (12.6in) dual discs one-piece caliper |
| — rear | single disc, single caliper |

## TORQUE

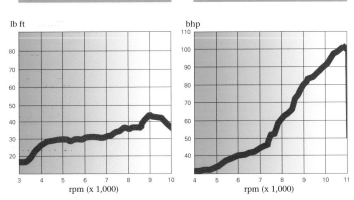

lb ft

rpm (x 1,000)

## POWER

bhp

rpm (x 1,000)

**Independent test measurements (above) differ from the manufacturer's claimed maximum power and maximum torque figures.**

# **YAMAHA** *TDM850*

*The plastic, carbon-look dash holds a speedometer which reads up to 225km/h (140mph); a temperature gauge; neutral, indicators and high beam lights; and a tacho with an 8000rpm redline. Our performance tests found that the rev limiter cuts in only when the engine is revving at 9300rpm – when the tacho needle is off the clock!*

**Steering lock**
Excellent and allows the bike to be turned very easily in tight situations.

**Handlebars**
Well-placed bars combine with decently located seat and footpegs to create a comfortable, mile-chomping riding position.

*The rear shock utilizes a 'dual spring' system, by which pulling a lever alters the preload tension to allow either a single rider or two-up progress. Gimmicky rather than good, the back end's handling can feel odd under cornering situations.*

**Choke switch**
This handy cable-operated switch is mounted on the top yoke.

**Switches**
Left handlebar switches are run-of-the-mill, including a headlamp flash button, off/dip/on light switch, high/low beam rocker switch, an indicator switch and horn button. The engine kill and electric start buttons are on the right handlebar.

**U-lock**
For the security conscious, the underside of the seat is pre-moulded to carry a hefty U-lock, while the wiring loom features a plug-in adaptor to take an alarm. Like all new Yamahas, the ignition switch has been hardened to deter thieves.

**Clutch**
The cable-operated clutch has no span adjusters, to allow for different-sized hands, at the lever.

**Forks**
Mushy and unresponsive on pre-1996 models, but reasonable from then on. Beware of soft lacquer on legs.

**Tyres**
Bridgestone BT54s are fitted in 110/80 ZR18 front and 150/70 ZR17 rear sizes.

**Bungee hooks**
Situated near the passenger grab handles, these useful hooks can be used to secure luggage to the back seat or rear mini-rack.

*TDM850*

**Since its launch in 1991,** Yamaha's *TDM850 has appeared in a couple of different guises. The first one was fairly uninspired and left owners complaining, but in 1996 Yamaha more or less re-invented the bike, making it a huge success.*

Fairly routine two-into-one-into-two system looks good, but the exhaust is often plagued by rust and is not cheap to replace. Huge collector box.

270° crank gives a staggered firing sequence and the 849cc (51.8ci) slant-block, liquid-cooled motor packs a fair punch. Fuel is supplied by two 38mm (1.5in) BDST Mikuni carburettors, there are five gears, and the compression ratio is 10.5:1.

A running light is located above the main headlamps. Unlike some bikes, it comes on only when the lights are activated. Headlamp power is no more than average.

**Fuel tank**
The 20l (5.3gal) tank on later TDMs gives a range of 233–298km (145–185 miles), depending on how the bike is ridden.

**Grab handles**
Passengers get to hold onto grab handles rather than a rail. Some like them, some do not, but these are quite well positioned.

**Screen**
Some taller riders complain the one fitted to the later TDM is too low, causing bad wind buffeting at high speed.

**Seat**
For a bike with on/off road pretensions, the TDM850 has a low seat at 795mm (31.3in).

**Mudguard**
This close-fitting front mudguard and rear hugger reveal the bike is not really intended for serious off-road duties. A muddy patch would jam both guards solid.

**Brakes**
Twin four-piston Sumitomo front calipers may not feel that strong, but they are, hauling the bike to a reasonably rapid standstill, as our road test data shows.

**No bashplate**
The lack of under-engine bashplate is another clue as to the TDM's limited off-road capability.

The overall design of *the TDM850 may look good for some serious back-lane scratching, but it does suffer because of the behaviour of its rear shock design.*
*However, the engine is strong, the frame and forks are decent and the brakes great.*
*It is certainly stylish and eye-catching, but it does have a few niggles. For example, the screen appears to be of no use at all to tall riders and the finishing is not all it could be.*
*Not ideal for a commuter but worth considering for touring.*

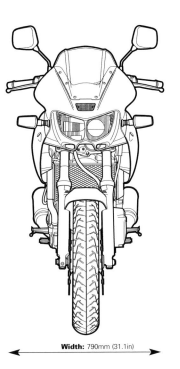

**Width:** 790mm (31.1in)

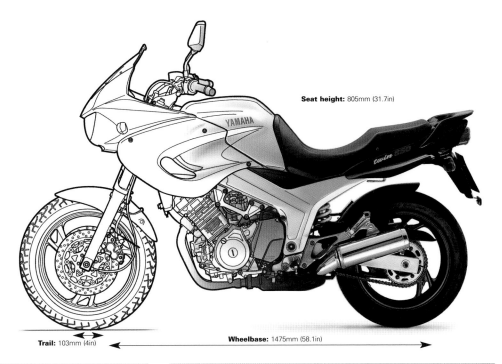

**Seat height:** 805mm (31.7in)

**Trail:** 103mm (4in)

**Wheelbase:** 1475mm (58.1in)

## ENGINE

| | |
|---|---|
| Type | 4-stroke |
| Layout | forward inclined parallel twin |
| Total displacement | 849cc (51.8ci) |
| Bore | 89.5mm (3.5in) |
| Stroke | 67.5mm (2.7in) |
| Compression ratio | 10.5:1 |
| Valves | 5 per cylinder |
| Fuel system | Mikuni BDST38 carburettors |
| Ignition | digital |
| Cooling | liquid |
| Maximum power | 5.9kW (80bhp) @ 7500rpm |
| Maximum torque | 8kg-m (58lb-ft) @ 6250rpm |

## TORQUE

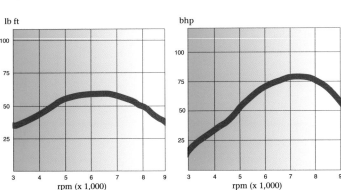

lb ft

rpm (x 1,000)

## POWER

bhp

rpm (x 1,000)

Independent test measurements (above) differ from the manufacturer's claimed maximum power and maximum torque figures.

## TRANSMISSION

| | |
|---|---|
| Primary drive | gear |
| Clutch | multiplate |
| Gearbox | 5-speed |
| Final drive | chain |

## WEIGHTS & CAPACITIES

| | |
|---|---|
| Tank capacity | 20l (5.3gal) |
| Dry weight | 198kg (435.6lb) |
| Weight distribution | |
| — front | N/A |
| — rear | N/A |
| Wheelbase | 1475mm (58.1in) |
| Overall length | 2165mm (85.2in) |
| Overall width | 790mm (31.1in) |
| Overall height | 1285mm (50.6in) |
| Seat height | 805mm (31.7in) |

## CYCLE PARTS

| | |
|---|---|
| Frame | steel twin spar |
| Rake/trail | 24.5°/103mm (4in) |
| Front suspension | telescopic fork |
| Travel | 149mm (41.3in) |
| Adjustment | spring preload, plus rebound damping |
| Rear suspension | monoshock with dual rate spring |
| Travel | N/A |
| Adjustment | spring preload |
| Tyres | |
| — make | Bridgestone/Pirelli/Michelin |
| — front | 110/80 ZR18 |
| — rear | 150/70 ZR17 |
| Brakes | |
| — make | Yamaha |
| — front | 2 x 298mm (11.7in) discs, opposed 4-piston calipers |
| — rear | 245mm (9.6in) disc, opposed 2-piston caliper |

# YAMAHA *TRX850*

*With a passenger perch inches above the rider's, firm padding, closely placed footpegs and a lack of grab-rail, there are no pillion comforts. Only for short spins.*

**Fairing**
Half-fairing helps save weight and does a good job, together with the moderately tall screen, of keeping wind blast off the rider. Staying dry is another matter, though.

**Engine**
Liquid-cooled, four-stroke parallel twin is inclined to shorten overall bike length, has an 849cc (51.8ci) capacity, bore and stroke of 89.5 x 67.5mm (3.5 x 2.7in), and a compression ratio of 10.5:1. Yamaha claims peak bhp is produced at just 7500rpm and maximum torque at 6000rpm. Our tests showed the bike reaches a maximum speed of 233km/h (145mph) – still in the ballpark of newer, more expensive middleweight twins.

**Riding position**
Quite good for covering long distances. The bars are wide and flat and the pegs allow the rider a relaxed crouch.

*Twin end cans exit high, sound remarkably quiet, and bear up well over several winters. Owners in search of more style and noise though, are more likely to be looking for a replacement item.*

*Twin end cans exit high, sound remarkably quiet, and bear up well over several winters. Owners in search of more style and noise though, are more likely to be looking for a replacement item.*

**Wheels**
Three-spoke design is nothing special, but has proven itself to be tough following repeated wheelies and hard landings. Standard tyre sizes are 120/60 ZR17 front and 160/60 ZR17 rear.

**Dimensions**
The overall length of the TRX is 2070mm (81.5in); overall width 700mm (27.6in); overall height 1155mm (45.5in); and wheelbase 1435mm (56.5in).

# *TRX850*

***Launched in Europe** in 1996 after proving a great success for Yamaha at home in Japan, the TRX offers a unique, affordable and, to wax lyrical, charming bike. It may be somewhat predictable, but why do we think of that as a 'bad' thing nowadays? Surely, having a predictably safe machine is half the fun. You may enjoy riding 'on the edge', but it is not necessarily a good thing to be surprised by how your bike handles on certain surfaces!*

*Twin 298mm (11.7in) front discs and single 245mm (9.6in) rear are not the biggest around. Combined with the average calipers, they are not the best either, as a 160–0km/h (100–0mph) stopping distance of a poor 118.1m (387.5ft) shows.*

*The lattice frame design is reminiscent of traditional Ducati styling, only not as trick. Keeps weight lower, however, even if the bike does tip the scales at a not inconsiderable 190kg (418lb) dry.*

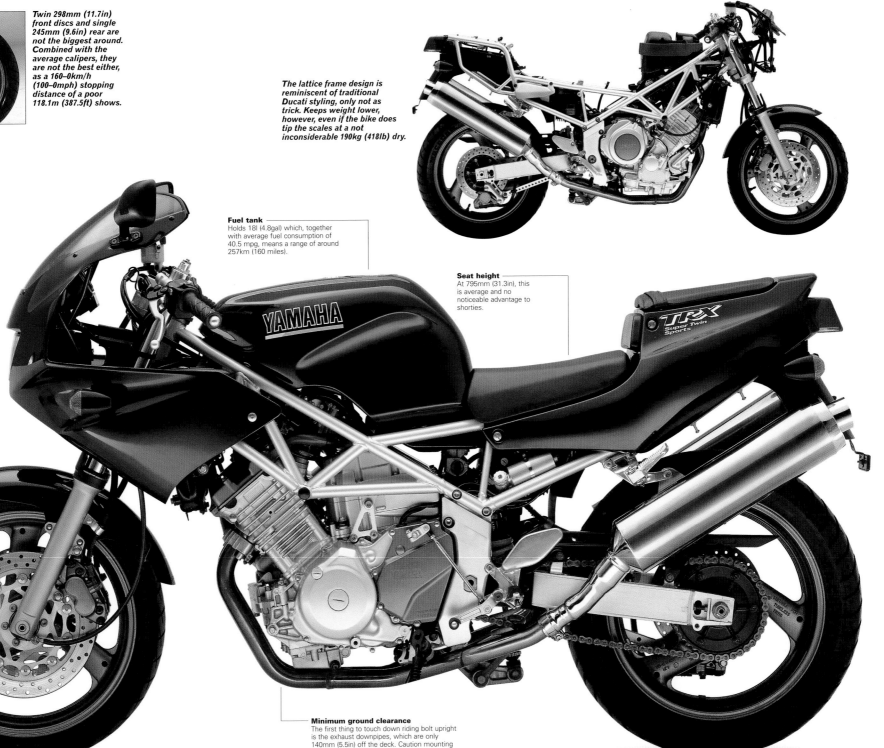

**Fuel tank**
Holds 18l (4.8gal) which, together with average fuel consumption of 40.5 mpg, means a range of around 257km (160 miles).

**Seat height**
At 795mm (31.3in), this is average and no noticeable advantage to shorties.

**Minimum ground clearance**
The first thing to touch down riding bolt upright is the exhaust downpipes, which are only 140mm (5.5in) off the deck. Caution mounting tall kerbs is advised.

# Specifications

*Introduced in January of 1996* with an engine uprated from the TDM850, the TRX850 has proved more popular than many expected, although it is difficult to see why when you consider that it is not particularly cheap and has little going for it in the styling department. While it handles well and is equipped with a strong, well-proven engine, the *TRX* is unfortunately let down by its looks. It has less appeal than many of its peers, and when you consider the *CBR600F* costs only slightly more, well... Still, it is quick and reliable - just unlikely to appeal to the sports bike fans.

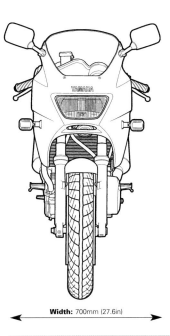
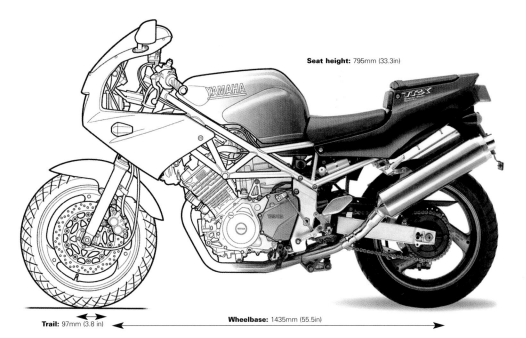

**Seat height:** 795mm (33.3in)

**Width:** 700mm (27.6in)

**Trail:** 97mm (3.8 in)

**Wheelbase:** 1435mm (55.5in)

## ENGINE

| | |
|---|---|
| Type | 4- stroke |
| Layout | parallel twin |
| Total displacement | 849cc (51.8ci) |
| Bore | 89.5mm (3.5in) |
| Stroke | 67.5mm (2.7in) |
| Compression ratio | N/A |
| Valves | 4 per cylinder |
| Fuel system | 2 X Mikuni BDST38 carburettors |
| Ignition | electronic |
| Cooling | liquid |
| Maximum power | 58.9kW (79bhp) @ 7251rpm |
| Maximum torque | 8.6kg-m (62.2lb-ft) @ 5840rpm |

## TRANSMISSION

| | |
|---|---|
| Primary drive | chain |
| Clutch | wet multiplate |
| Gearbox | 5-speed |
| Final drive | chain |

## WEIGHTS & CAPACITIES

| | |
|---|---|
| Tank capacity | 18l (4.8gal) |
| Dry weight | 190kg (419lb) |
| Weight distribution | |
| — front | not available |
| — rear | not available |
| Wheelbase | 1435mm (56.5in) |
| Overall length | N/A |
| Overall width | 700mm (27.6in) |
| Overall height | 1155mm (45.5in) |
| Seat height | |

## CYCLE PARTS

| | |
|---|---|
| Frame | tubular trellis |
| Rake/trail | 25°/97mm (3.8in) telescopic forks (3.8in) |
| Front suspension | 41mm (1.6in) telescopic forks |
| Travel | 120mm (4.7in) |
| Adjustment | preload, compression and rebound damping |
| Rear suspension | monoshock |
| Travel | 130mm (5.1in) |
| Adjustment | preload, plus compression and rebound damping |
| Tyres | |
| — make | N/A |
| — front | 120/60 x ZR17 |
| — rear | 160/60 x ZR17 |
| Brakes | |
| — make | N/A |
| — front | 2 x 298mm (11.7in) discs, opposed 4-piston calipers |
| — rear | 245mm (9.6in) disc, single 2-piston caliper |

## TORQUE

## POWER

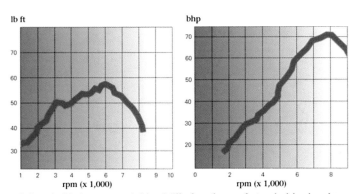

Independent test measurements (above) differ from the manufacturer's claimed maximum power and maximum torque figures.

# YAMAHA XJ900 DIVERSION

*The four-into-two system may not be the prettiest on the planet, but at least the chrome finish is of very good quality and the silencers are raised high enough to remain clear of the road under everyone but the most extreme riders.*

**Screen**
Plenty big enough to offer decent rain and excellent wind protection, a slot has been cut into its upper half to aid dynamic airflow, reducing wind buffeting.

**Mirrors**
Cheap, uninspiring square-shaped items, they do provide a good, vibration-free rear view, however.

**Handlebar switches**
Conventional design means the left bar houses a choke lever, main/dip beam switch, indicator switch, pass light button, horn button and a useful hazard warning lights switch. The right bar plays home to the engine kill switch, off/park/main lights switch, and the electric start button. Unlike the clutch lever, the brake lever is span-adjustable.

**Forks**
Adjustable for preload only and in need of better damping even when new, they let the bike down under hard cornering on uneven surfaces and during hard braking.

**Grab handles**
Pillions remain divided over the usefulness of grab handles. They appear to offer no advantage over a more conventional grab rail and can even make holding on under hard, emergency braking slightly difficult.

**Hooks**
The luggage hooks mounted on the seat midway between the rider and pillion are non-retractable and can rip waterproofs.

**Rear suspension**
The no-frills monoshock can overheat when covering long distances two-up. This results in further loss of its already limited damping qualities.

**Mainstand**
A handy addition that is easily operated.

**Rear Brake**
The single two-piston caliper and 267mm (10.5in) disc combine to offer a noticeable lack of feel.

**Tyres**
Yamaha has chosen budget Dunlop K505s, in sizes 150/70 rear and 120/70 front to fit its 43.2cm (17in) wheels. Grip is good for normal riding but not when the bike is being pushed hard.

## XJ900 DIVERSION

**The XJ900 Diversion** *has been around since the early 1990s which, in biking terms, means it is quite old – and it shows. It is very unlikely bikers will get into a frenzy over this bike. But for those who want a reliable commuter/tourer, this may well be the bike that fits the bill.*

The dash is very much bare bones with a 150mph (240km/h) speedo which ascends in 5mph (8km/h) increments, a rev counter which shows 11,000rpm although the ignition retards at 9500rpm, a digital clock, a woefully inaccurate fuel gauge, and a trip reset button. The idiot light cluster displays indicators, low fuel, neutral, main beam, and oil.

Twin two-piston calipers grip non-floating 320mm (12.6in) discs to give adequate but uninspiring brake performance.

The air-cooled, double overhead cam, forward-inclined, parallel, four-cylinder four-stroke engine produces a factory-claimed 66.4kW (89bhp) at 8250rpm. The reality is fairly smooth but flat delivery with moderate acceleration and a very poor top speed.

**Fuel tank**
Holds 24l (6.3gal), which is quite noticeable by making the bike feel top heavy when full.

**Seat**
This is 795mm (31.3 inches) tall, which means that many shorter riders find the bike a bit of a handful, particularly when turning round. The seat's exceptional width does nothing to counter this either, although at least the padding is plush and ultra-comfortable.

**Carburettors**
The bank of four 34mm (1.3in) Mikuni BDSR carbs does its best to flow fuel and air into the basic engine but is set-up fractionally rich by the factory. Misfires, however, are not a problem.

**Transmission**
The five-speed box performs merely averagely with a precise click of the foot needed to smoothly and swiftly engage the next gear. Occasional missed gears resulted in false neutrals during our road test.

**Shaft Drive**
The absence of a chain final drive means messy essential maintenance is reduced.

**YAMAHA** *XJ900 DIVERSION*

# Specifications

**Launched towards the end** *of 1994, just two years after its little brother's debut, the XJ900 is a fairly bland road bike with little to recommend it in the styling department.*
*It sells well enough, though, because it is reliable and will always get you to where you are going and do the job well – but no more. It has neither flair nor appeal, and, unfortunately for the XJ900, brilliant styling and exciting engines are what riders have come to expect from our road bikes.*

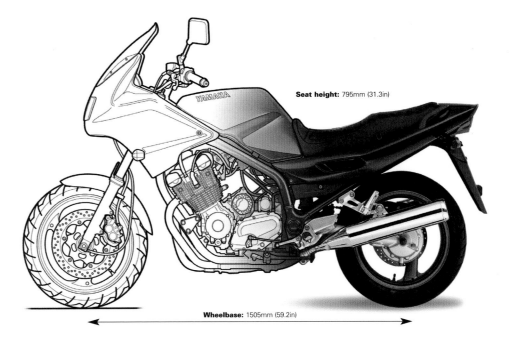

**Seat height:** 795mm (31.3in)

**Width:** 750mm (29.5in)

**Wheelbase:** 1505mm (59.2in)

## ENGINE

| | |
|---|---|
| Type | 4-stroke |
| Layout | in-line four |
| Total displacement | 892cc (54.4ci) |
| Bore | 68.5mm (2.7in) |
| Stroke | 60.5mm (2.4in) |
| Compression ratio | N/A |
| Valves | 2 per cylinder |
| Fuel system | 4 x Mikuni BDSR 34 |
| Ignition | electric |
| Cooling | air |
| Maximum power | 57.9kW (77.6bhp) @ 7950rpm |
| Maximum torque | 7.5kg-m (54.1lb-ft) @ 6950rpm |

## TRANSMISSION

| | |
|---|---|
| Primary drive | chain |
| Clutch | wet, multiplate |
| Gearbox | 5-speed |
| Final drive | shaft |

## WEIGHTS & CAPACITIES

| | |
|---|---|
| Tank capacity | 24l (6.3gal) |
| Dry weight | 239kg (526.9lb) |
| Weight distribution | |
| — front | N/A |
| — rear | N/A |
| Wheelbase | 1505mm (59.3) |
| Overall length | 2230mm (87.8in) |
| Overall width | 750mm (29.5in) |
| Overall height | 1300mm (51.2in) |
| Seat height | 795mm (31.3in) |

## CYCLE PARTS

| | |
|---|---|
| Frame | double cradle |
| Rake/trail | 27°/121mm (4.8in) |
| Front suspension | telescopic forks |
| Travel | N/A |
| Adjustment | none |
| Rear suspension | link monoshock |
| Travel | N/A |
| Adjustment | preload |
| Tyres | |
| — make | |
| — front | 120/70 x 17 |
| — rear | 150/70 x 17 |
| Brakes | |
| — make | |
| — front | 320mm (12.6in) dual discs, 2-piston calipers |
| — rear | 267mm (10.5in) disc and caliper |

## TORQUE

## POWER

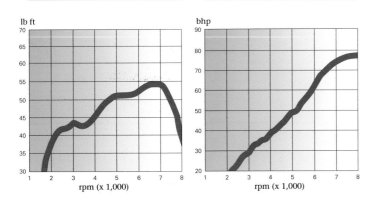

Independent test measurements (above) differ from the manufacturer's claimed maximum power and maximum torque figures.

# YAMAHA FZR1000

**Fairing**
The slant nose fairing seen here came into being on the 1991 model. In 1994 it was updated again, with Yamaha claiming there was now an aerodynamic advantage.

**Headlights**
The twin headlights changed from the squarish style to the more up-to-date fox-eye look in 1994. The ones shown here are the projector twin beam lamps introduced for 1992.

# FZR1000

*Now that the YZF-R1 in particular has pushed the FZR out of the limelight, there are probably younger riders who barely remember this bike. But those who have ever ridden one are unlikely to forget what an effortless, powerful and incredibly exciting bike the FZR1000 was – and remains today.*

**Forks**
Yamaha said the new forks (from 1994 onwards) had a new rubber bung inside the fork top to reduce the violence of the bang if the forks should bottom out. Most noticed no difference, however.

**Brakes**
The rear disc and twin front disc brakes were upgraded in 1994 – and if they were good before, they were now great, offering fantastic bite and power.

**End can**
This model sports the grey finish alloy sleeve on the end can which replaced the alloy finish in 1991.

*The Ohlins forks were uprated in 1994, but were so similar to the previous ones that few riders noticed the difference. Yamaha even told Ohlins to make the forks look exactly like the previous ones, which begs the question: why the change?*

*The graphics were new for 1992 with the FZR and EXUP on the side/bottom of the fairing.*

*The aluminium Deltabox frame used the forward inclined engine as a stressed member, and this 1992 model shows the frame with the 'A' shaped strut extending below the seat, which came into being in January of 1991 and remained with the FZR until it was discontinued in 1995.*

**Guard**
The guard shown here appeared first on the 1991 model and is equipped with stone deflectors for the forks.

**Engine**
The liquid-cooled, 20-valve, dohc transverse four powerplant was a legend in its own time with Yamaha claiming a peak of 110kW (147bhp) for derestricted EXUP motors.

# Specifications

This Yamaha utilizes a 20-valve engine that has been around in various guises for 13 years. The frame is taught and very much the norm for this breed of machine. Power figures are eclipsed by the much more modern Blade or R1 (or, now, GSX1100). This is a fast, race replica bike for the serious speed freak. Though range and comfort are not impressive, the fun factor is still there in abundance.

Rake: 26.25°

Height: 1170mm (46in)

Seat height: 775mm (30.5in)

Length: 2205mm (86.8in)

## ENGINE

| | |
|---|---|
| Type | 4-stroke |
| Layout | in-line 4 |
| Total displacement | 1002cc (61.1ci) |
| Bore | 75.5mm (2.9in) |
| Stroke | 56mm (2.2in) |
| Compression ratio | N/A |
| Valves | 5 per cylinder |
| Fuel system | 4 x 38mm (1.5in) Mikuni carbs |
| Ignition | electronic |
| Cooling | liquid |
| Maximum power | 108kW (145bhp) @ 10,000rpm |
| Maximum torque | N/A |

## TRANSMISSION

| | |
|---|---|
| Primary drive | gear |
| Clutch | wet multiplate |
| Gearbox | 5-speed |
| Final drive | chain |

## WEIGHTS & CAPACITIES

| | |
|---|---|
| Tank capacity | 19l (5gal) |
| Dry weight | 214kg |
| Weight distribution | |
| — front | N/A |
| — rear | N/A |
| Wheelbase | 1470mm (57.9in) |
| Overall length | 2205mm (86.8in) |
| Overall width | 745mm (2.9in) |
| Overall height | 1170mm (46in) |
| Seat height | 775mm (30.5in) |

## CYCLE PARTS

| | |
|---|---|
| Frame | aluminium Deltabox |
| Rake/trail | 26.25°/108mm |
| Front suspension | 41mm (1.6in) telescopic fork |
| Travel | 120mm (4.7in) |
| Adjustment | spring preload |
| Rear suspension | monoshock |
| Travel | 130mm (5.1in) |
| Adjustment | spring preload and rebound damping |
| Tyres | |
| — make | N/A |
| — front | 130/60 x 17 |
| — rear | 170/60 x 17 |
| Brakes | |
| — make | N/A |
| — front | 2 x 310mm (12.1in) floating discs, 4-piston caliper |
| — rear | 267mm (10.5in) disc, 2-piston caliper |

# YZF1000 THUNDERACE

*Twin four-piston Sumitomo calipers up front have tremendous bite and massive stopping power.*

**Mirrors**
The decent mirrors offer a good view of the road behind. Vibration can be a problem at some revs, though.

**Fairing**
It looks big, feels big – and is. Slabby and awkward-looking though it may be, there is no denying it offers superb weather protection, even at high speeds.

**Headlamp**
Powerful beam meets stylish enclosed looks.

**Engine**
1002cc (61.1ci) in-line four-cylinder engine churns out power, kicking through the rev range. The bike's large feel, hefty weight and wallowy suspension prevent you making the most of it, though. Bulbous torque at low revs means surging power wheelies are only a throttle-blip away.

**Suspension**
Rear monoshock and 43mm (1.7in) forks are both underdamped in comparison to cutting-edge sports bikes, instantly relegating the powerful Thunderace to the sports/tourer league. Replace, or professionally re-calibrate both, and you will transform the bike. Plenty of modified ones were raced at the punishing Isle of Man TT for years, until the Ace's successor, the YZF-R1, came along in 1998.

**Silencers**
Many owners replace their standard silencers with aftermarket units, which are generally not only lighter and better-looking, but often fruitier-sounding too.

*YZF1000*
*THUNDERACE*

**Since its introduction in 1996,** *Yamaha's Thunderace has undergone very few changes – why fix it if it ain't broke? Its aluminium twin spar frame is stylish while its engine is full of power and pull. Many may now go for the YZF-R1 instead of the Thunderace as the R1 is lighter and smaller.*

*Shorter riders (attracted by the seat height) may find their arms not long enough to comfortably reach the bars.*

*The aluminium twin spar is yet another variant of Yamaha's successful Deltabox chassis. It is stiff, stylish and remarkably resilient in a crash.*

**Fuel tank**
Takes 20l (5.3gal) from empty to full.

**Seat**
The seat height of just 31.3in (795mm) attracts some shorter riders.

**Mudguard**
Ace gets an extended, wheel-enclosing front mudguard just like its baby brother, the 600cc (36.6ci) Thunderace. It helps protect fork stanchions from grime, salt and chippings.

**Wheelbase**
With a whopping wheelbase of 1435mm (56.5in), the Thunderace is never going to excel at changing direction in a hurry.

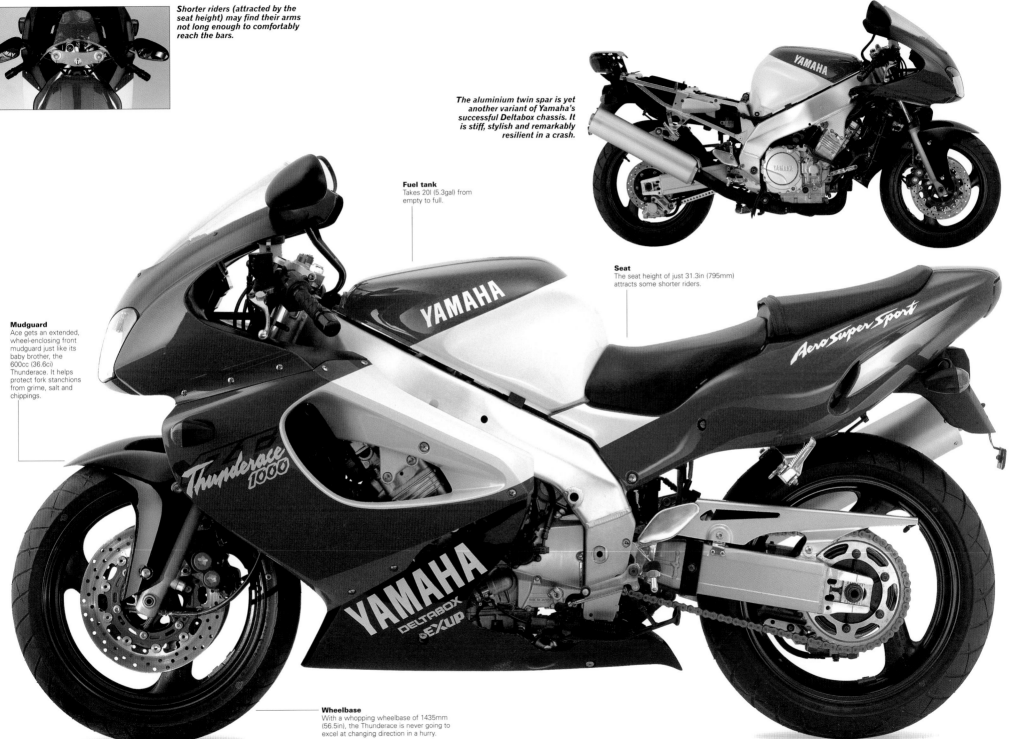

# Specifications

**Yamaha's 1002cc (61.2ci) Thunderace hit** *the ground at maximum revs when it was launched in 1996 and has since proved a very real challenge to Honda's closest rival, the CBR1100XX Super Blackbird. The slant block layout of the Thunderace's 5-valve liquid-cooled engine optimizes front/rear weight distribution and keeps the YZF1000R's centre of gravity low, while Yamaha's famous EXUP valve helps control back-pressure in the exhaust to maximize performance right across the rev range.*

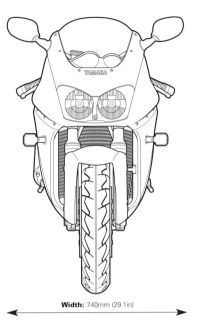

**Width:** 740mm (29.1in)

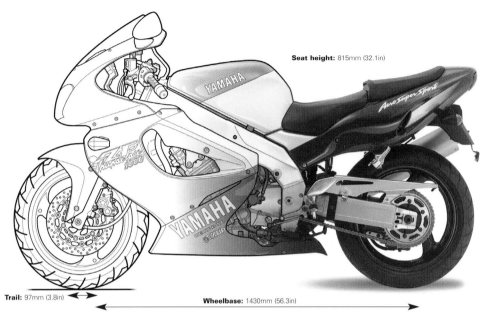

**Seat height:** 815mm (32.1in)

**Trail:** 97mm (3.8in)

**Wheelbase:** 1430mm (56.3in)

## ENGINE

| | |
|---|---|
| **Type** | 4-stroke |
| **Layout** | DOHC in-line four |
| **Total displacement** | 1002cc (61.2ci) |
| **Bore** | 75.5mm (2.9in) |
| **Stroke** | 56mm (2.2in) |
| **Compression ratio** | 11.5:1 |
| **Valves** | 5 per cylinder |
| **Fuel system** | 4 x 38mm (1.5in) Mikuni CV-type carburettors |
| **Ignition** | digital transistorized with Throttle Position Sensors |
| **Cooling** | liquid |
| **Maximum power** | 110kW (147.6bhp) @ 10,040rpm |
| **Maximum torque** | 11.6kg-m (83.9lb-ft) @ 8400rpm |

## TORQUE

## POWER

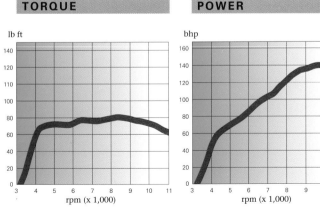

Independent test measurements (above) differ from the manufacturer's claimed maximum power and maximum torque figures.

## TRANSMISSION

| | |
|---|---|
| **Primary drive** | straight-cut gears |
| **Clutch** | wet, multiplate |
| **Gearbox** | 5-speed |
| **Final drive** | chain |

## WEIGHTS & CAPACITIES

| | |
|---|---|
| **Tank capacity** | 20l (5.3gal) |
| **Dry weight** | 224kg (494lb) |
| **Weight distribution** | |
| — front | N/A |
| — rear | N/A |
| **Wheelbase** | 1430mm (56.3in) |
| **Overall length** | 2085mm (82.1in) |
| **Overall width** | 740mm (29.1in) |
| **Overall height** | 1175mm (46.3in) |
| **Seat height** | 815mm (32.1in) |

## CYCLE PARTS

| | |
|---|---|
| **Frame** | aluminium Deltabox |
| **Rake/trail** | 24°, 97mm (3.8in) |
| **Front suspension** | 46mm (1.8in) telescopic forks |
| **Travel** | 120mm (4.7in) |
| **Adjustment** | spring preload, rebound and compression damping |
| **Rear suspension** | Bilstein-type monoshock |
| **Travel** | 120mm (4.7in) |
| **Adjustment** | spring preload and rebound damping |
| **Tyres** | |
| — make | Bridgestone BT50, Dunlop D204 |
| — front | 120/70 ZR17 |
| — rear | 180/55 ZR17 |
| **Brakes** | |
| — make | Yamaha |
| — front | 298mm (11.7in) twin discs with four-pot one-piece calipers |
| — rear | 245mm (9.6in) single disc with two pistons, opposed |

# ⊗ **YAMAHA**    **YZF-R1**

*The 245mm (9.6in) disc and twin piston caliper has been cleverly mounted under the swingarm. This saves having the weight of a separate torque arm.*

*Twin, single-cast Sumitomo four-piston calipers up front bite onto 298mm (11.7in) discs. This provides awesome, progressive stopping power.*

**Seating**
Relatively low seat height (800mm/31.5in) combines well with narrow seat and side panels to allow shorter riders to touch the floor with ease.

**Mirrors**
For such an agressive sports bike, the R1's mirrors work surprisingly well, not restricting the rider to little more than a view of his elbows, as on the Ducati 916.

**Bodywork**
Bodywork is minimalist – no clutter, no excess baggage and no waste.

**Storage**
The rear seat lifts off to reveal a small storage space. It is not as roomy or as useful as the Honda CBR900 FireBlade's, although it is big enough to carry a lock and chain.

**Footpegs**
Yamaha has designed the R1 to lean to a monster 56˚. You need to be near this point just to scrape the tiny footpegs' 'hero blobs'.

**Silencer**
The standard single silencer offers good ground clearance, but makes the exhaust note quite quiet.

**Chassis**
Twin spar Deltabox II chassis was developed from the preceeding YZF1000 Thunderace and FZR1000EXUP frames and is ultra-stiff but also light.

**Tyres**
Tyre choice is critical on the R1. Some owners have discovered the sticky Metzeler MEZ3 tyres may not be sticky enough but, with so much power on tap, finding something better is tricky.

# *YZF-R1*

***THE** sports bike of 1998, Yamaha's R1 is so potent it has made all other bikes instantly redundant. It is a 112kW (150bhp), 1000cc (61ci) mega-bike that towers over its peers. Smaller than most 600s and lighter than any production V-twin, the R1 is amazingly easy to ride, stunningly styled, beautifully built and reasonably priced.*

*The analogue rpm counter takes pride of place in the well thought-out dash. The digital speedo can be converted between mph and kph at the press of a button. The temperature gauge is digital too.*

*Take that classy fairing away and you could be looking at some bug-eyed machine from outer-space. But it still looks the business.*

**Exhaust**
The bike's EXUP (exhaust ultimate powervalve) system is the most advanced by Yamaha so far. As well as boosting engine response by altering the exhaust back-pressure according to the motor'srpm and throttle position, it adjusts itself by monitoring what the CDI (capacitor discharge ignition) system is up to.

**Fuel tank**
The sculpted fuel tank holds only 18l (4.8gal), but the R1 does boast a fuel trip meter – when the bike goes into reserve, the distance available from the remaining fuel counts down.

**Alarming**
With the R1 being, perhaps, the most desirable bike this year, it is a pity the factory has not seen fit to bolt on an alarm as standard. It could easily have been mounted inside the fairing or under the seat unit.

**Engine**
R1's 998cc (60.9ci) in-line four cylinder engine packs a claimed 112kW (150bhp) (a true 99–106kW/ 134-142bhp on most dynos). Coupled with a dry weight of just 177kg (389.4lb), it gives the monster Yamaha the best power-to-weight ratio ever on a production road bike.

**Wheelbase**
A tiny wheelbase of 1395mm (54.9in) would ordinarily make such a powerful bike almost too wheelie-prone. Although still a one-wheel monster, Yamaha has calmed it down by resorting to grand prix technology and making the swingarm longer than usual, boosting traction and ultimate stability.

# Specifications

*The radical new design* of Yamaha's YZF-R1 has been much talked about since its unveiling – and for good reason. Its all-new slant-block 998cc (60.9ci) in-line four cylinder engine forms an integral part of the chassis.
And even the chassis is new – named the *Deltabox II* by Yamaha, it is lighter, stiffer and slimmer than ever before with an ultra-short 1395mm (54.9in) wheelbase. Its key factor is the use of the one-piece cylinder block and upper crankcase, which means the lightweight structure is much more rigid than the conventional two-piece design. Yamaha really have excelled themselves.

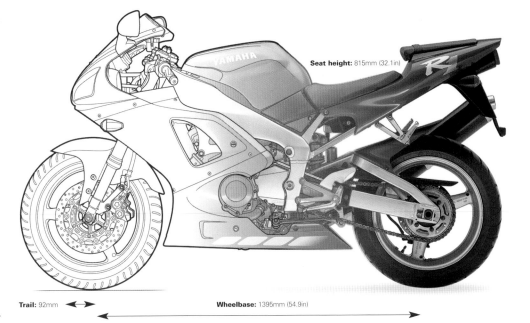

**Seat height:** 815mm (32.1in)

**Width:** 740mm (29.1in)  **Trail:** 92mm  **Wheelbase:** 1395mm (54.9in)

## ENGINE

| | |
|---|---|
| Type | 4-stroke |
| Layout | transverse four |
| Total displacement | 998cc (60.9ci) |
| Bore/stroke | 74 x 58mm (2.3in) |
| Compression ratio | 11.8:1 |
| Valves | 5 per cylinder |
| Valve gear | DOHC |
| Fuel system | 4 x 40mm (1.6in) Mikuni carburettors |
| Ignition | CDI |
| Cooling | liquid |
| Maximum power | 102kW (137bhp) @ 10,000rpm |
| Maximum torque | 10.6kg-m (77lb-ft) @ 7400rpm |

## TRANSMISSION

| | |
|---|---|
| Primary drive | straight-cut gears |
| Clutch | wet multiplate |
| Gearbox | 6-speed |
| Final drive | chain |

## WEIGHTS & CAPACITIES

| | |
|---|---|
| Tank capacity | 18l (4.8gal) |
| Dry weight | 177kg (390lb) |
| Weight distribution | |
| — front | 50% |
| — rear | 50% |
| Wheelbase | 1395mm (54.9in) |
| Overall length | 2035mm (80.1in) |
| Overall width | 740mm (29.1in) |
| Overall height | 1095mm (43.1in) |
| Seat height | 815mm (32.1in) |

## CYCLE PARTS

| | |
|---|---|
| Frame | aluminium twin spar |
| Rake/trail | 24°/ 92mm |
| Front suspension | 41mm (1.6in) inverted telescopic forks |
| Travel | 135mm |
| Adjustment | spring preload plus rebound and compression damping |
| Rear suspension | rising rate monoshock |
| Travel | 110mm (4.3in) |
| Adjustment | spring preload plus rebound and compression damping |
| Tyres | |
| — make | Metzeler ME-Z3 |
| — front | 120/70 x 17 |
| — rear | 190/50 x 17 |
| Brakes | |
| — make | Sumitomo |
| — front | 2 x 298mm (11.7in) discs, 4-piston calipers |
| — rear | single 245mm (9.6in) disc, 2-piston caliper |

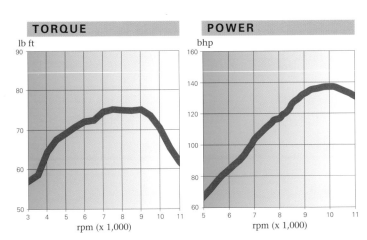

### TORQUE

lb ft

rpm (x 1,000)

### POWER

bhp

rpm (x 1,000)

Independent test measurements (above) differ from the manufacturer's claimed maximum power and maximum torque figures.

# YAMAHA VMX1200 V-MAX

*The white-faced speedo is centrally mounted and housed in a circular chrome-plated pod. The tachometer, temperature gauge and indicator light console sit on top of the fuel tank.*

**Forks**
Long and weedy-looking in the company of the rest of the bike, they dive under braking and flex under hard cornering,, quickly persuading the rider to go back to posing in a straight line.

**Brakes**
Dual 298mm (11.7in) drilled floating front disc gripped by lightweight differential bore 4-piston calipers. Many might find this inadequate when trying to stop this heavy lump.

**Seat height**
A seat height of just 762mm (30in) makes the V-Max an attractive proposition for shorter cruiser fans.

**Fuel tank**
The underseat tank holds only 15l (3.9gal) so you won't get far down the road before looking for a petrol station.

**Shocking**
Twin rear shocks may be moderately adjustable but they squat under acceleration anyway. They do not inspire much confidence.

**Small**
The five-spoke spun aluminium rear wheel is only 38.1cm (15in) tall. It takes a 150/90 V-rated tyre as standard.

**Silencers**
The four-into-two exhaust has stubby upswept silencers finished in extra-thick chrome plate. Some would say they are downright ugly, while for others the silencers are just a part of the V-Max appeal.

## VMX1200

***Introduced in 1991,*** *Yamaha's big 1198cc (73.1ci) V-four has no comparison in the way of looks – still. It may be about the oldest Japanese big-bore bike in production, but it can still cut it with modern muscle machines. It is uncompromising, unforgiving and intimidating – reasons enough to buy one.*

*The 1198cc (73.1ci) 16-valve V-four engine has double overhead cams, a five-speed gearbox and is liquid cooled. It is shaft driven and puts out up to 107kW (143bhp), depending on the dyno that measures it.*

*What a rear end! The four-into-two exhaust with its thick chrome-plated silencers should help you lay down heaps of torque. Many owners tend to opt for Avon Super Venoms for front and back rubber.*

*Oddball, mental, wild… call it what you will, bikers obviously like the V-Max with its radically weird styling. It is hard to know what to classify it as – some say custom cruiser, some raw street machine. If you own one, it would probably be the latter.*

**Eyecatching**
The huge airscoops are the first thing many people notice.

**Tyres**
Try using the power the V-Max has on offer, and you will quickly torture any rubber you lay your hands on into submission. Massive torque equals massive stress. The Avons mentioned overleaf are said to give both a more neutral feel and more feedback. More feedback cannot be bad.

**Passenger comforts**
The relationship between rear seat and footpegs puts pillions into a very upright position. It is fine for cruising, but a bit of a panic if the bike pulls one of its mega wheelies.

**Fat fender**
The rear mudguard looks unfinished to those used to more sporty bikes.

**Shaft drive**
What do you do with a bike like this? Yamaha decided that to handle the brutal torque output generated by its engine, the V-Max had to have a heavy-duty shaft drive.

**Wheelbase**
A monster 1590mm (62.6in) long, the V-Max is never going to steer quickly. But if you are going in a straight line, the V-Max can get off from a standstill like nothing else around. Still, unless you live in parts of Australia or some place like Texas, you are going to want to go around a corner some time!

**YAMAHA** *VMX1200 V-MAX*

# Specifications

*IT IS massively long, lives* with a huge wheelbase and lazy steering, does not go round corners properly and becomes a handful on the brakes.
Yet many thousands of owners still swear by them.
It just has to be the look of this massive beast, because it is a show-stopper whether you love it or hate it. If you do not like it, you will consider it ugly, and who is to say you are wrong? Only all those bikers who own a V-Max.

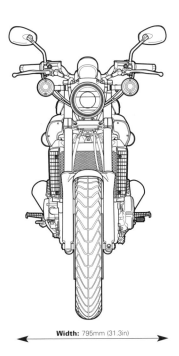

**Seat height:** 762mm (30in)

**Width:** 795mm (31.3in)

**Trail:** 119mm (4.7in)

**Wheelbase:** 1590mm (62.6in)

## ENGINE

| | |
|---|---|
| Type | 4-stroke |
| Layout | V-four |
| Total displacement | 1198cc (73ci) |
| Bore | 76mm (2.9in) |
| Stroke | 66mm (2.6in) |
| Compression ratio | 10.6:1 |
| Valves | 4 per cylinder |
| Fuel system | 4 x 35mm Mikuni carburettors, V-Boost |
| Ignition | CDI |
| Cooling | liquid |
| Maximum power | 86.5kW (116bhp) @ 8500rpm |
| Maximum torque | 11.8kg-m (85lb-ft) @ 6200rpm |

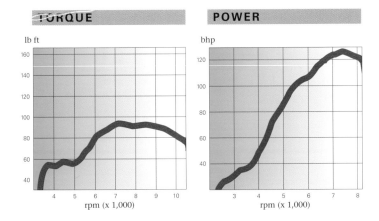

## TRANSMISSION

| | |
|---|---|
| Primary drive | gear |
| Clutch | wet multiplate |
| Gearbox | 5-speed |
| Final drive | shaft |

## WEIGHTS & CAPACITIES

| | |
|---|---|
| Tank capacity | 15l (3.9gal) |
| Dry weight | 262kg (576lb) |
| Weight distribution | |
| — front | N/A |
| — rear | N/A |
| Wheelbase | 1590mm (62.6in) |
| Overall length | 2300mm (90.6in) |
| Overall width | 795mm (31.3in) |
| Overall height | 1160mm (45.7in) |
| Seat height | 762mm (30in) |

## CYCLE PARTS

| | |
|---|---|
| Frame | tube steel cradle |
| Rake/trail | 29°/119mm |
| Front suspension | 43mm (1.7in) forks |
| Travel | N/A |
| Adjustment | none |
| Rear suspension | twin shocks |
| Travel | N/A |
| Adjustment | preload |
| Tyres | |
| — make | varies (often Bridgestone Exedra) |
| — front | 110/90 x V18 |
| — rear | 150/90 x V15 |
| Brakes | |
| — make | Sumitomo |
| — front | 2 x 298mm (11.7in) floating discs, 4-piston calipers |
| — rear | 282mm (11.1in) disc, single caliper |

Independent test measurements (above) differ from the manufacturer's claimed maximum power and maximum torque figures.

# YAMAHA   XV1600 WILD STAR

*The twin pipes jutting out the right hand side of the bike look so good they have passers-by doing a double-take.*

**Instruments**
Everything you need is here and mounted on the tank: a slimline single dial incorporates an electronic speedo, odometer, twin tripmeters, clock and fuel, high beam, turn, neutral and engine warning lights.

**Handlebars**
The rubber-mounted bars are 26mm (1in) diameter tubing with a wide and relaxed position.

**Fuel tank:**
The teardrop tank holds a good 20l (5.3gal) which is the least you would expect (and want) from a cruiser.

**Clutch**
The large capacity cable-operated clutch is equipped with seventeen plates and activated by a rack and pinion mechanism for positive feel.

**Pushrods**
Running up the right side of each cylinder, twin 10mm (0.4in) diameter pushrods operated by all-new hydraulic valve lifters activate the inlet and exhaust rocker arms.

**Gearbox**
Five speed and operated by a see-saw type shift pedal.

**Brakes**
At the front, dual 298mm (11.7in) discs with two-pot calipers slow the bike nicely while at the rear sits a massive 320mm (12.6in) disc with four-pot opposed piston caliper.

**Ground clearance**
With a minimum ground clearance of only 145mm (5.7in), this is not the type of bike you want to lean even slightly – and beware big rocks on the road.

**Suspension**
Concealed beneath the rear of the engine is a link-type rear suspension system equipped with a Bilstein-type shock absorber and is adjustable for preload.

*Yamaha's XV1600 Wild Star is equipped with the biggest engine ever built by the company. Although not as popular as Yamaha may have expected, this is not down to a fault of the bike's, more an 'overpopulation' of Yamaha cruisers.*

*In keeping with the styling of the rest of the bike is the huge 221mm (8.7in) diameter chrome headlight, which does the job well and looks fairly stylish.*

*Again, the wheels suit the rest of the bike's styling. The 56-spoke 40.6cm (16in) items with chrome rims are equipped with a 130/90 x 16 tyre at the front and a 150/80 x 16 at the rear.*

**Ignition**
The newly styled ignition switch features a combined handlebar lock and rider's seat lock opener. It is also self-cancelling for ease of use with the turn signal.

*One of Yamaha's proudest claims about the Wild Star's chassis is that it is 'long and low'. It is based around a high rigidity double cradle frame, which is manufactured from large diameter high tensile steel tubing.*

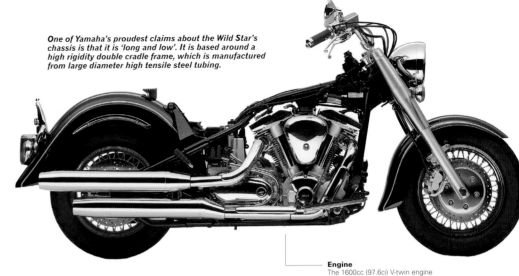

**Engine**
The 1600cc (97.6ci) V-twin engine is mounted rigidly in the frame at five points, which Yamaha claims helps transmit the motor's V-twin pulse through to the rider to 'accentuate the machine's high torque feel' – and it works!

**Seat**
At only 710mm (27.9in), the Wild Star should suit nearly everybody and is comfortable enough with its contoured, leather-look seat and separated well-padded pillion seat. The pillion also has a grab strap.

**Front end**
The forks are large diameter 43mm (1.7in) tubes and the front end is fitted with fat metal shrouds to help protect the forks from stone damage.

**Engine**
This 1600cc four-stroke, air-cooled, four valve, 48°, pushrod-twin the biggest engine ever to be built by Yamaha. It has a bore and stroke of 95 x 113mm (3.7 x 44.5in) and a compression ratio of 8.3:1.

**Final drive**
Something else never seen before on a Yamaha is the belt final drive system on the Wild Star, which Yamaha says is particularly suited to high torque/lowrpm engines like the XV1600.

# **YAMAHA** XV1600 WILD STAR

# Specifications

**The Wild Star is** the largest capacity bike in Yamaha's 'Cruiser' range – a full 1602cc (97.8ci) of it, positioned in a long, low lying chassis. Its **Easy Rider** meets **Titanic** in all respects and is no doubt aimed at the **US** market. Thumpers like this are marvellous testimonies to modern, engineering skills but are, quite frankly, strangely juxtaposed against the average urban skyline. They are okay for Nevada deserts and one-horse towns, but look slightly out of place in your typical town or city.

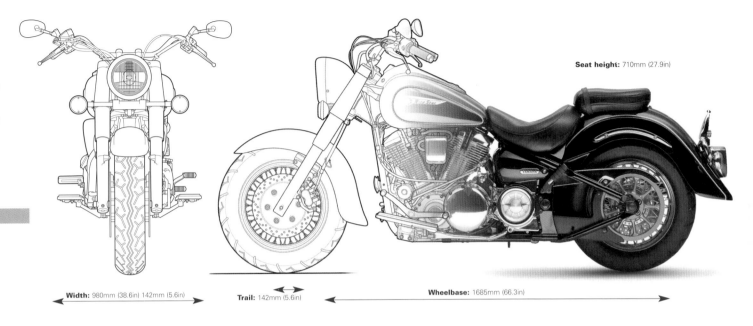

**Seat height:** 710mm (27.9in)

**Width:** 980mm (38.6in) 142mm (5.6in)

**Trail:** 142mm (5.6in)

**Wheelbase:** 1685mm (66.3in)

## ENGINE

| | |
|---|---|
| Type | 4-stroke |
| Layout | OHV V-twin |
| Total displacement | 1602cc (97.8ci) |
| Bore | 95mm (3.7in) |
| Stroke | 113mm (4.4in) |
| Compression ratio | 8.3:1 |
| Valves | 4 per cylinder |
| Fuel system | 40mm constant velocity unit |
| Ignition | Electric |
| Cooling | air |
| Maximum power | 46.7kW (62.6bhp) @ 4000rpm |
| Maximum torque | 13.7kg-m (98.8lb-ft) @ 2250rpm |

## TRANSMISSION

| | |
|---|---|
| Primary drive | gear |
| Clutch | wet multiplate |
| Gearbox | 5-speed |
| Final drive | belt |

## WEIGHTS & CAPACITIES

| | |
|---|---|
| Tank capacity | 20l (5.3gal) |
| Dry weight | 307kg |
| Weight distribution | |
| — front | N/A |
| — rear | N/A |
| Wheelbase | 1685mm (66.3in) |
| Overall length | 2500mm (98.4in) |
| Overall width | 980mm (38.6in) |
| Overall height | 1140mm (44.9in) |
| Seat height | 710mm (27.9in) |

## CYCLE PARTS

| | |
|---|---|
| Frame | double cradle tubular steel |
| Rake/trail | 32°/142mm (5.6in) |
| Front suspension | 43mm (1.7in) telescopic forks |
| Travel | 140mm (5.5in) |
| Adjustment | N/A |
| Rear suspension | Swing arm monocross |
| Travel | 110mm (4.3in) |
| Adjustment | spring preload |
| Tyres | |
| — make | |
| — front | 130/90 x 16 |
| -- rear | 150/80 x 16 |
| Brakes | |
| — make | |
| — front | 2 x 298mm (11.7in) discs, 2-piston calipers |
| — rear | 1 x 320mm (12.6in) disc, 4-piston calipers |

## TORQUE

## POWER

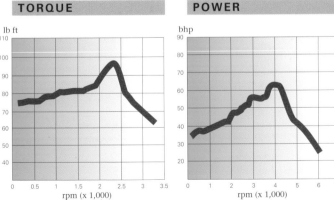

Independent test measurements (above) differ from the manufacturer's claimed maximum power and maximum torque figures.

# Index